The Politics of Religion, Nationalism, and Identity in Asia

Map of Asia. Courtesy of Gregory Veeck and Jason Glatz, WMU.

The Politics of Religion, Nationalism, and Identity in Asia

Jeff Kingston

ROWMAN & LITTLEFIELD
Lanham • Boulder • New York • London

Published by Rowman & Littlefield
An imprint of The Rowman & Littlefield Publishing Group, Inc.
4501 Forbes Boulevard, Suite 200, Lanham, Maryland 20706
https://rowman.com

6 Tinworth Street, London SE11 5AL, United Kingdom

British Library Cataloguing in Publication Information Available

Library of Congress Cataloging-in-Publication Data

Names: Kingston, Jeff, 1957- author.
Title: The politics of religion, nationalism, and identity in Asia / Jeffrey
   Kingston.
Description: Lanham [Maryland] : Rowman & Littlefield, 2019. | Includes
   bibliographical references and index.
Identifiers: LCCN 2019011554 (print) | LCCN 2019012769 (ebook) | ISBN
   9781442276888 (Electronic) | ISBN 9781442276864 | ISBN
   9781442276864¬(cloth) | ISBN 9781442276871¬(pbk.)

Subjects: LCSH: Nationalism--Religious aspects. | Religion and
   politics--Asia. | Nationalism--Asia. | Identity politics--Asia. | Group
   identity--Asia. | Identification (Religion)--Political aspects--Asia.
Classification: LCC BL65.N3 (ebook) | LCC BL65.N3 K56 2019 (print) | DDC
   322/.1095--dc23
LC record available at https://lccn.loc.gov/2019011554

Contents

Chapter One

Introduction

It is impossible to understand contemporary Asia without understanding the politics of nationalism and religion. They are a volatile mix that incites violence and poses a significant risk to secularism, tolerance, civil liberties, democracy, and political stability. This toxic tide has swept the region from Pakistan to the Philippines and Columbo to Kunming with tragic consequences. Recently the nexus of religion and nationalism is featured in headlines about 730,000 Rohingya Muslims being driven out of Myanmar, one million Uighur Muslims being locked up in China, Kashmiris slaughtered in India, and Islamic State affiliates wreaking havoc in Bangladesh, Indonesia, the Philippines and Sri Lanka. Who would have imagined hatemongering Buddhist monks inciting violence and intolerance or setting themselves on fire to protest ethnocide in Tibet? Or pious vigilantes beheading atheist bloggers in Dhaka? This book examines the causes and consequences of these varied phenomena and what they portend for the future of what is often portrayed as the most dynamic region in the world. The twenty-first century may indeed be the Asian century, but the shackles of the past coupled with the anomie of the present cast a shadow over any triumphalism. History is not destiny but does shape and constrain the range of possibilities.

Over the past century, despite premature predictions that modernization would sweep all before it, there has been a flowering of religious sentiments around the world, often blended with nationalism in shaping identities. The spread of secularism and modernization were once viewed as the death knell of religion, but this is manifestly untrue. Religion provides a grid of order and code of proper conduct and remains a powerful anchor of meaning and connectedness while also sanctifying ethnolinguistic nationalism and culture wars in plural societies. Conflicts waged in the name of religion and national

1

identities infused with religious piety complicate the art of compromise crucial to safeguarding harmony and inclusiveness in diverse societies.

This book focuses on the politics of religion and how this intersects with
nationalism and influences identity. As such the emphasis is on how religious
and nationalist sentiments are aroused and manipulated for political ends.
This focus means that I don't explore the beauty of religion or the bounty of
spirituality. I am more concerned with zealots, who in trying to make religion
and/or ethnicity the basis of national identity are promoting an agenda of
intolerance that defies the pluralist realities that prevail across Asia.

Nationalism is often portrayed as a great threat to peaceful relations between nations, but the consequences within nations where identity politics
simmer and flare are arguably more destabilizing and devastating. I argue
that ethnoreligious nationalism in Asia, meaning the conflation of ethnicity,
religion, and national identity, is an acute internal domestic problem that
imperils minorities, a problem exacerbated by the way in which discrimination and violence are justified and legitimized by state authorities in the name
of religion, race, and nation. In Asia's democracies, there is a tendency for
politicians to pander to unelected religious pressure groups in the scramble
for votes. These policies of appeasement respond to the power of religious
conservatives to mobilize followers and intimidate officials into supporting
illiberal agendas. There is a degree of collaboration and cooptation, concessions and compromises that make it difficult to clarify who is using who.
This dynamic involves varying degrees of democratic backsliding that can,
as we see, have adverse consequences for secularists and liberals, along with
ethnic and religious minorities.

One possible check on this sectarianism might be transnational religious
communities that challenge state attacks on their co-adherents, but the inclination within Asia toward strong state authority has made it difficult to build
any sort of transnational movements that target political elites for engaging
in religiously sanctioned violence. The Vatican has done little on behalf of
embattled Christians in the region, while the Organization of Islamic Cooperation has also not been conspicuously effective. To the extent that transnational religious movements are meddling, such as the Saudi-funded wave of
Arabization that has spread a puritan Salafist Islam, they tend to fan the
flames of sectarianism and in some cases are orchestrating violent extremism
by funding and training militants. Transnational organizations such as Islamic State or al-Qaeda are inspiring and sponsoring franchise operations in the
region, but political elites have been mostly insulated from their retributions
and handed a pretext for further crackdowns and extra-judicial killings that
exacerbate sectarian and communal tensions. The targets ranging from Uighurs in China and Rohingya in Myanmar to Muslims in India and the
Philippines and Shi'a and Ahmadi Islamic sects in South and Southeast Asia
remain vulnerable to unchecked majoritarian clout. The state can also rely on

its power over the media and social media to promote preferred narratives, disseminate fake news, and facilitate hatemongering, as is the case with the Rohingya in Myanmar and Islamophobia in China and India.

The rise of religious majoritarianism in twenty-first-century Asia poses a grave threat to diversity and political stability. It is important to differentiate between democracy, the rule by the majority that balances the interests of everyone, and majoritarian rule, a winner-takes-all approach in which the majority advances only its interests and imposes this on everyone else in the polity. In Asia part of the battles over identity are fought over democratic processes versus majoritarian impulses, and these map onto rifts over secularism and religious nationalism. Majoritarian religious nationalism promotes intolerance toward ethnic and religious minorities and hostility toward diversity. In autocratic China this is accomplished without religious sanction.

To assess Asia's future, it is crucial to better understand the causes and consequences of the growing momentum for right-wing illiberalism and the agenda of intolerance promoted under the guise of religious devotion and/or national interest. Secularism is the target of militant religious groups who seek to eradicate the separation of state and religion. In many Asian nations, pro-secular advocates face the threat of violence while secular political parties are making expedient compromises to the dictates of mobocracy that mark a retreat from secular principles and democratic norms in the name of protecting those values. Mobocracy relies on the politics of the streets and is often subject to shadowy influences, including security forces who find them useful to advance institutional interests and predatory elites who seek to maintain advantages and impunity. By pulling strings behind the scenes, these manipulators of mobs channel the passions of religious devotees to achieve their goals. In recent years this political theater has been staged frequently on the streets of major cities in India, Bangladesh, Myanmar (Burma), and Indonesia. Democratically elected governments also rely on arms-length hardline groups to counter their opponents, making a show of force in favor of government policies by mobilizing hardcore constituencies that favor more extreme agendas. Demonstrations can also be a weapon of the weak such as those by independence movements in Kashmir and West Papua or by religious and ethnic minorities throughout Asia who are subject to majoritarian excesses. China is something of an exception here because there are no democratic constraints on authoritarian repression, thus it can lock down whole regions and lock up a million Muslim Uighurs to safeguard Han majoritarianism.

The pro-independence nationalists who led the struggle for freedom from the colonial powers embraced the inherited secular ideals. Over time, this secular commitment has been challenged and reassessed as reactionary forces have wielded religion to shape national identity and force significant concessions from governments that are increasingly resorting to repressive policies such as curbing civil liberties or extra-judicial killings to quell agitation but in doing so betraying liberal democratic principles.

KEY CONCEPTS

I am not here to impose some trending theoretical paradigm or cutting-edge conceptual framework on the messy confluence of politics, religion, nationalism, and identity in contemporary Asia. Reviewing the vast literature and vibrant debate about the nature of nationalism and its variants would involve a lengthy exegesis that I don't believe would significantly contribute to my endeavor here. Rather, I try to make sense of the complexities by providing an accessible analytical narrative about the consequences of this confluence that draws on observations, fieldwork, encounters, and extensive reading over the past four decades. My subjective approach is interdisciplinary, eclectic, and qualitative, distilling what insights I have gained as a curious, open-minded, but skeptical scholar who sometimes unapologetically crosses the line of objective detachment. I do enjoin readers to draw their own conclusions, but in order to make sense of what follows it is important to clarify very briefly some concepts that are at the core of this book.

NATIONALISM

Key for our purposes is debate over the relationship between religion and nationalism. I agree with Smith (2003) that nationalism is a kind of religion in terms of a binding collective identity, shared intensity, and the repetition of rituals of belonging. Moreover, ethnicity, nationalism, and religion are mutually reinforcing markers of social and cultural identification and are ways of identifying oneself to others, of elaborating differences and similarities, and situating oneself in relation to others (Brubaker 2012). The emergence of ethnoreligious nationalism is part of a wider phenomenon of what Brubaker terms "the politicisation of culture and the culturalisation of politics" (Brubaker 2012, 5). Prominent religious and cultural symbols and concocted traditions carry an emotional or spiritual appeal, and herein lies the power of religion in the nationalist toolbox because it sanctifies the cause and also acts as a protective amulet for those who wield it. The banner of religion both empowers and insulates political actors vying with rivals over national agendas, acting as a sacred shield.

As Juergensmeyer concludes,

> The global rise of religious politics is found in every religious tradition, spurred on by the widespread perception that secular nationalism is an ineffective and insufficient expression of public values and moral community in a

global era in which traditional forms of social identity and political account-ability are radically transformed. Religious violence is an expression of this anti-secular protest and the symptom of a longing for a renewed sense of morality and values in public life. (Juergensmeyer 2010, 262)

There is a welter of contending theories of nationalism, but in his seminal *National Identity* Anthony Smith provides a useful starting point, defining the nation as "a named human population sharing an historic territory, com-mon myths and historical memories, a mass, public culture, a common econ-omy and common legal rights and duties for all members" (Smith 1991a, 14). According to Smith, the nurturing of national identity draws on myths of origin, cultural symbols, memories of grandeur, and heroic sagas plus the idea of a homeland (Smith 2000b). The nation-state is based on groups of people who share the common constructs of culture, genesis, memories, and homeland. Nationalism is an ideology that nurtures solidarity and a group identity in this shared homeland emphasizing loyalty to the nation above all else. It draws on a selected past to conjure up a sense of reassuring continuity and solidarity in the present. A history of shared sacrifices—imagined, real, or exaggerated—fosters and sustains that solidarity (Renan 1994).

Anderson defines the nation as an "imagined political community" in which members develop strong bonds based on consuming the same print media in a shared vernacular language without actually knowing most of whom they share such sentiments with (Anderson 1983). Hobsbawm and Ranger (1983) argue that precisely because nationalism is so important it is not left to chance. In their view, nationalism is artfully constructed by elites who conjure up invented traditions to inculcate certain values, create a sense of solidarity, and thereby construct a useful national consciousness. This deliberate social engineering is intrinsic to national building and why battles over history are fought so intensely because control over narratives of the past can be leveraged to bolster contemporary political power. Thus, a se-lected history is projected to suggest continuities and shared grievances that bestow political legitimacy and consolidate social unity. Venerable old tradi-tions are retrofitted for new situations and new ones are invented to bestow an aura of grandeur that offers reassurance in societies experiencing socioec-onomic upheaval.

Breuilly (2001) is sensibly skeptical about sweeping theories of national-ism, arguing that it is principally about gaining, consolidating, and perpetuat-ing political power. It is an ideology that facilitates 1) coordination among elites with divergent interests; 2) mass mobilization of those that don't have a strong stake in the system; and 3) political legitimacy and the authority that confers.

This elite-centric view of nationalism confronts laptop empowerment of ordinary citizens that enables them to challenge elite discourse on national identity and values by reaching wide audiences in their virtual communities (Gurevitch, Coleman, and Blumer 2009). These "imagined communities" of Internet activists and sympathizers are also part of Asia's mobocracy of the unelected, generating their own narratives that feed on palpable grievances in the globalist echo chamber of shared news and sacrifice that transcend national boundaries but resonate powerfully in nations. The hyper-interaction between members, the rapid sharing of fake news, the tendency for hyperbole, and the common vernacular of outrage amplified in a feedback loop of viral postings is quite different from the passive participation in Anderson's imagined communities centered on vernacular print media. But even if keyboard trolls are a potentially subversive force contesting establishment narratives of nationalism and identity, they are also subject to manipulation by interest groups who find in the Internet the perfect means of connecting with the masses, sparking outrage and mobilizing the angry and disaffected in service to elite agendas. Revelations about how Facebook has been used artfully by the military in Myanmar to whip up anti-Rohingya sentiments and downplay allegations of atrocities is a perfect example of this. All across Asia, ethnoreligious nationalism is propagated on social media for arousing shared indignation, identifying targets, and mobilizing both the committed and unwitting.

RELIGION

Asia is home to many religions, but our focus is on world religions in the region: Hinduism, Buddhism, Islam, and Christianity. Most of the world's Muslims (1 billion +), Hindus (1 billion +), and Buddhists (480 million) live in Asia, which is also home to nearly 300 million Christians (Pew 2015a).

Religions are systems of faith and worship that address the timeless questions of who we are, how we should live, why we are here, and what lies ahead. They attend to people's spiritual needs and provide solace and a sense of community, offering a bridge to the past and the future while imparting ways of living and rituals that guide people through the milestones and tribulations of life. They are about how to be good, offering codes of conduct, but are only as good as the believers who don't always live according to them. Much evil is done in the name of religion, and too often politics trumps faith, but this is because human beings often fall short of what their religion asks of them.

Religion plays a crucial role in sanctifying violent responses. The sanctifying power of religion to justify, absolve, and arouse sanctimonious passions to avenge, honor, and desecrate confers an intoxicating appeal and enormous influence. As such religions are also subject to contestation by those who seek to tap their moral authority and mobilize believers for temporal agendas.

IDENTITY

Religion interacts with ethnonationalism and identity in the culture wars that are evident across Asia. Identity refers to how people perceive themselves—who we are and what defines us. This is contextual, meaning that people have various overlapping identities, and what aspects of their identity are invoked as identifiers depends on the context. What are the prime determinants? Identity oscillates between, inter alia, ethnicity, language, religion, nationality, gender, territory, birthplace, workplace, profession, caste, or party membership. Identity is contingent on surroundings—where, when, with who, and what one is doing. It is the basis of defining the in-group and in Othering, determining who does and doesn't belong. In terms of nationalism, ethnolinguistic bonds and religious affiliation play key roles in defining the community of solidarity and the requisite basis of commonality.

As Appiah astutely argues, it is crucial to bear in mind that nobody has but one identity and that an individual's multiple identities are not hermetically sealed off from one another; each is refracted through the prism of other identities (Appiah 2018). Identities are thus porous and not as settled and unyielding as often assumed or implied. This uncertainty and fluidity also mean that identity is not embedded in DNA and doesn't necessarily dictate behavior, thought, or destiny.

Samuel Huntington made some sweeping and misleading assumptions about identity in his controversial "clash of civilizations" thesis about conflict between the Islamic world and the West (Huntington 1996). The terrible events on September 11, 2001, in the United States are taken as vindication of his argument as if the deranged acts of a small band of crazed fanatics represented an entire civilization. The monolithic labels of Islam and the West are misleading because the diversity of societies that are subsumed make a mockery of this monochromatic misrepresentation. As Edward Said pointed out in his trenchant essay "The Clash of Ignorance," "Huntington is an ideologist who wants to make 'civilizations' and 'identities' into what they are not: shut-down, sealed-off entities that have been purged of the myriad currents and countercurrents that animate human history" (Said 2001). In the following pages readers should bear this in mind in considering the notion of identity and how people are shaped by and respond to the various influences that they navigate in their lifetimes. As Said added in the febrile aftermath of 9/11 when cartoonish caricatures became confused with insight, it is essential to understand "the internal dynamics and plurality of every civilization . . . [and] . . . that the major contest in most modern cultures

concerns the definition or interpretations of each culture." These ongoing
contests are about identity and are never won or finished. Sweeping stereotypes applied to over a billion Muslims or Christians spread across the world,
or a billion Hindus in the vastness of the Indian subcontinent, or almost half a
billion Buddhists make the ludicrous ahistorical assumption that these are
discrete and cohesive entities in which collective identities are settled and
unchallenged. Such ill-informed assumptions are the basis for an unedifying
Othering, taking for granted what is patently absurd. They do serve the
purpose, however, of arousing nationalist passions.

Contemporary Asian nations are navigating the familiar challenges of
modernization related to nation building, economic development, and democratization and in this project often deploy nationalism to bolster solidarity and promote social cohesion. The catalyst for Asian nationalism was the
struggle for self-rule against imperialism and colonial subjugation (Chatterjee 1986). As such, Asian nationalism has been indelibly shaped by European and Japanese colonization, while the legacies of this subjugation loom
large in twenty-first-century nationalist identity discourses. The concept of
the secular nation-state in Asia is one of the legacies of colonial rule, but
despite this awkward genesis the state and nationalism remain crucial to
securing political legitimacy and defining personal identity. Yet other collective traumas are invoked that add layers to identity discourse, ranging from
the massacres of Partition in India, Gestapu in Indonesia, and genocide in
Cambodia to the paroxysms of democratization in Indonesia and civil war in
Sri Lanka and Pakistan/Bangladesh along with sustained ethnic conflicts
across the region. The scar tissue from these trauma mask lingering wounds
that are crucial to understanding competing national identities and the unresolved grievances that animate them.

SECULARISM, MAJORITARIANISM, AND GLOBALIZATION

The irresistible urge to mix politics and religion usually comes at the expense
of secularism, tolerance, and vulnerable minorities. Power politics and hatemongering in the name of religion sow seeds of instability and violence. As a
foundation of government, secularism implies that there should be no discrimination against anyone based on their religious affiliation or beliefs and
that the state should not favor any religion over others, enact balanced policies toward religious minorities, and serve as a counterweight to majoritarianism. In Asia we see that secularism is embattled and receding due to an
onslaught of majoritarian chauvinism, notably in China and India, the
world's most populous nations. Majoritarianism is the assertion of rule by the
majority in the exclusive interest of the majority without concern for minor-

ities. It is distinct from democracy, which is based on majority rule but is committed to respecting the rights and needs of minorities. India is a vibrant democracy and has an elaborate system of affirmative action policies for assisting the disadvantaged, but as we discuss shortly, the consensus supporting that system has eroded in recent years due to increasingly assertive Hindutva (Hindu chauvinism). China has long embraced assimilation to promote the interests of minorities, but a relentless wave of majoritarian Han-ification has provoked a sharp backlash in Tibet and Xinjiang due to fears of ethnocide.

Asia's diversity encompasses a resilient ethnonationalism in which identity is rooted in language, ethnicity, and religion. This is a wounded identity, one that finds meaning and menace in carefully nurtured grievances. Colonial legacies and the depredations of globalization stir up a nationalism that exhumes past glories to honor and humiliations to avenge in order to strengthen solidarity. This ethnonationalism draws on narratives about the great civilizations of India and China, the magnificent sway of Mughal India and Indonesia's Majapahit, and the sacred splendors of Angkor, Bagan, Ayutthaya, Borobodur, and Anuradhapura that testify to an Asian grandeur to be reclaimed. These resplendent visions are all the more powerful when refracted through the sacralizing prism of religion. Yet China's state-sponsored brooding over its "century of humiliation" demonstrates that religion is not necessary to ethnonationalism and the theater of political distraction.

In the following chapters we examine the politics of religion, nationalism, and identity in East Asia, South Asia, and Southeast Asia. These regions encompass complex societies of overlapping and contested identities oscillating between religion, ethnicity, language, nation, class, gender, work, sexuality, and family. Labels tend to be misleading because for many people navigating everyday life their identity fluidly shifts and blends depending on context. Identity does not exist in a vacuum and the politics of identity in any society evolves according to external and internal dynamics that may entail a reordering of what seems important.

Globalization spreads norms and values usually associated with some imagined monolith called the West and as such is seen to be a process of Westernization or Americanization. The Internet and the emergence of global mass media have greatly intensified what has been a longstanding interaction that was once intermittent but has now become incessant and ubiquitous. For some, these norms and values are something to actively emulate. Youth in particular are drawn to the lifestyles of globalization, seeing them as cooler than what prevails around them, thus subverting local cultures. More insidious is the unwelcome seepage of values and norms that erode the traditions that provide social cohesion, sparking an inevitable backlash against an aping of alien ways. Arabization and the spread of puritanical

Islam has tapped into such discontents but is itself a rival variant of globalization, propagating alien values and norms that are also inciting a backlash.

There is a search for authenticity as people resist or navigate globalization, finding in religion, ethnicity, and nationalism powerful talismans and
anchors of identity. Authenticity is about purification and purging, about
Othering and blaming in which identity seeks refuge in a potent blend of
ethnoreligious nationalism. Majoritarian sentiments have gained momentum
in twenty-first-century Asia in which plural societies subsume multiple identities under an imagined collective identity; to be Indian is to be Hindu, to be
Sri Lankan or Myanmarese is to be Sinhalese Buddhist or Bamar (ethnic
Burmese) Buddhist, and to be Indonesian is to be Muslim, while to be Filipino is to be Christian. In these majoritarian identities, societies and governments find strength, inspiration, and solace. Solace because globalization and
global hierarchies have gnawed at collective self-esteem and inflicted the
wounds of envy and trauma of deracination.

For ethnic and religious minorities in Asia, the rhetoric honoring diversity
has given way to this ominous reality of majoritarianism. Asia's ethnically
and religiously complex societies are riven by intensified communalism and
sectarian identity politics because the rights of the few are receding due to
the demands and prejudices of the many. There has been a sundering of
arrangements crucial to stability in plural societies that promote a balancing
of interests. The political space for diversity has receded under the onslaught
of an intensified, unapologetic, intentional, and unconstrained majoritarian
chauvinism, bigotry, and discrimination. These sentiments are not new but
are now sanctioned by state-sponsored nationalism infused with religious
devotion and purpose that is igniting the dry kindling of discontent with
baleful consequences for minorities.

The secular and democratic state has protected the rights of minorities
and promoted tolerance. But across Asia there has been democratic backsliding and an erosion of secularism as the demands of electioneering have
heightened pandering to pressure groups that demand concessions antithetical to secularism. Unelected fundamentalist agitators from Dhaka to Jakarta
are pressing their illiberal demands, winning some concessions, and also
provoking illiberal responses from democratic governments that embrace
authoritarian measures to stifle dissent and civil liberties in the name of
stability.

SURFING COMMUNITIES OF
HATE AND EXTREMISM

Extremism knows no religion, but religion is a powerful combustible because
it endows the believer with a sense of sacral dispensation to transgress or

ignore laws and customs in defense of one's beliefs and the community that shares them. One searches the sutras in vain to find anything that would remotely justify the treatment of the Rohingya, or indeed the massacres of Tamils or attacks on Muslims in Sri Lanka, but militant monks feel justified in advocating violence and assert that they are merely defending their religious community. Islamic clerics declare jihad in defense of the ummah and brandish the threat of blasphemy charges to intimidate opponents. Similarly, Hindu extremists swathe their violence and discrimination against Muslims in a "saffronized" (saffron is the color associated with right-wing Hindu nationalism) history of prolonged victimization while the Moros of Mindanao know all too well the menace of Christianity.

Pankaj Mishra exposes the charlatans and opportunists of hatemongering, noting that "the sayings and beliefs of religious fundamentalists are often taken at face value. As fervent believers, they seem not to have any truck with rational politics. But it is important to realise how pathetically little they know about the religious and spiritual traditions that supposedly inform their political beliefs; and how the superior morality they noisily lay claim to is important to them only so far as it can give legitimacy to resolutely unspiritual ambitions to capture state power in their native countries" (Mishra 2002, 15). Extremism's connection to religious doctrine may be tangential, but religion facilitates extremism, lending it a veneer of legitimacy. Opportunists lay claim to religious inspiration because it enables them to forge powerful bonds with other adherents and arouse an indignant religiosity. Like Benedict Anderson's imagined community, believers feel a solidarity with others based on shared rituals, devotion, doctrine, and resentment.

A glowering ethnonationalism, turbo-charged on the steroids of anger and envy, finds in religion a sanctified legitimacy and on the Internet a viral vibrancy (Saunders 2008). This cyberworld is the tabernacle of extremists in which the malicious mendacity of prejudice reverberates with galvanizing menace. These messages are indelible and outlast the extremists who spread them. These men and their groups can be quashed, but the grievances that mobilize support among the faithful and the disaffected remain resilient, lingering in the collective memory. Groups can realign, regroup, and nurture networks of solidarity based on these messages and ideologies. The ideas that propel religious extremism sustain such groups and help them proliferate. State repression serves as validation, providing useful martyrs and traumas to avenge.

Religious communities are real at the local level of prayer, worship, and interaction, but the supra-local bonds to other believers in far-flung places are imagined, making one feel part of something that is spiritually transcendent. These imagined communities are especially powerful in that they are transnational and project a common worldview shared instantly and incessantly online. Perhaps with the exception of China where the Internet is

tightly policed, virtual communities enable fellow believers to instantaneously reach one another over great distances and inhospitable terrain within
sprawling nations and across oceans at little cost to spread grievances, share
anger, and egg each other on is an escalating dialogue of hatemongering that
has little to do with religion. They can also do so closer to home when
mobilizing local denizens for mob action in the mobocracies that are spreading in Asia. For keyboard militants and angry trolls with nothing better to do,
religion serves as the veil for toxic impieties. The diaspora of Muslims,
Christians, Buddhists, and Hindus also forge virtual bonds that can be the
basis for something more as perceptions, grievances, and funding flow more
seamlessly than ever before. The Internet is to these imagined communities
what the printing press was to Anderson's, but in hyper mode. Social media
lends itself to extremism because it spawns imagined communities of fellow
believers who lurk in the shadows where they feel unencumbered by the
usual social conventions and constraints that guide daily behavior. It is a
perfect milieu for hatemongering and frenzied scapegoating where Othering
is the default option. It is a realm where half-truths and falsehoods go unchecked, enabling opportunists to disseminate their quasi-religious agenda in
service to primordial sentiments. Religious creeds about proper ways of living get hijacked by those who feign the sacred while advocating the profane.

Myanmar is a good case to illustrate the power of the Internet to polarize
and incite. Internet penetration only became common with the spread of
mobile phone technology since 2012. Certainly, there were ethnic tensions
and clashes before, and the military has waged war against several ethnic
insurgencies for half a century, but the outbreak of religious-inspired violence maps the spread of mobile networks and the adoption of Facebook, the
social media of choice. Various actors had different agendas and reasons for
stirring violence, but in the absence of social media, translating those dark
desires into grim reality would have been difficult. Facebook has owned up
to being lax in monitoring and removing incendiary postings but until 2018
had just three staff with Burmese language skills. They were charged with
the impossible task of monitoring the postings of tens of millions of users. It
has since beefed up staffing and made bold promises to do better, but in
August 2018, as the world lamented the one-year anniversary of the start of
the military's Rohingya ethnic clearance operations facilitated by hatemongering on Facebook, the media reported that it still was unable to cope with
the deluge. Facebook did, however, block the accounts of the nation's top
general and other high-ranking officers for their role in whipping up Islamophobia and orchestrating national denial about the forced exodus of Rohingya. Facebook's investigation found that they brazenly disseminated fake
news to stoke support for the anti-Rohingya pogrom and to discredit credible
reports of atrocities.

The social media ecosystem is exceptionally susceptible to disinformation, lies, and distortions—the more sensational the more popular. In the echo chambers of chat rooms and forums, and in the cascading "shares" of unfiltered fake news, unwitting and willful arsonists ignite populist wildfires that rage out of control. The need to outrage and shock comes at the expense of responsible fact checking and vetting. Going viral is the goal and that is rarely achieved by a sober assessment of reality when there are so many vile insinuations and odious allegations that people are prepared to believe or at least not scrutinize too carefully, especially in the context of a seething ethnonationalist religiosity. It is a network for spreading propaganda in which validation is judged by eyeballs, shares, and likes. It is a reality-disconnected universe in which vilification of the Other and validation of the "home team" is paramount. There are no self-correcting mechanisms for snowballing shares of untruths and fabrications; the act of sharing confers legitimacy and promotes acceptance. It is an arena in which illiberal views drown out secular tolerance and portray it as capitulation and appeasement, a conspiracy to silence the voices of truth. It is a feedback loop of self-validation and mutually reinforcing prejudices in which confirmation bias reigns supreme and dissenting voices are squelched. The lure of sanctimonious outrage and invented grievance far exceeds any curiosity about what is true or false because perceptions are filtered through the prism of anger. The collective snarling of Internet trolls is a sign of the times, self-appointed vigilantes of a debauched political correctness in which might is right and the vulnerable are sacrificed to the angry.

As Pankaj Mishra argues in *The Age of Anger* (2017), the Internet is a force multiplier for ressentiment, the feeling of envy and rage that has spread around the world of the alienated and disappointed. The broken promises of globalization and denial of entry into what is projected as the good life underscore how much of the world is beholden to the few. This inchoate anger is easily transformed into a nationalist hammer looking for a nail on which to vent accumulated frustrations and humiliations. In majoritarian societies, ethnic and religious minorities are the handy nail for hateful hammering.

History is a powerful weapon in identity politics as rival groups invoke different incidents and lessons to assume the mantle of victimization and seek to sanctify this by drawing on insults to religion. The search for umbrage and outrage is relentless as political leaders appropriate the past for agendas of the present. Gestures and acts of autonomy are perceived as a threat to a national identity rooted in unity and conformity. In responding to these perceived threats, the state tends to rely on the brute power of security forces while intensifying processes of integration and assimilation. Such efforts are intrinsic to the state's nationalism project, one aimed at strengthening a sense of "we" and establishing the figurative and literal boundaries of a nation. In this context, identity politics carry a high risk of sectarian or communal violence. State abuses of authority and impunity therefore transform grievances into a collective identity, generating defiance, militancy, and cycles of violence.

ROADMAP

This book investigates ethnoreligious nationalism in Asia in the hope that readers will come to better understand the complexities of these diverse societies in which secularism, civil liberties, and tolerance are in retreat and religious extremism has gained pernicious momentum. Chapter 2 focuses on the orchestrated surge of Hindutva (Hindu chauvinism) and its consequences in the subcontinent. Chapter 3 examines Christianity in the region, from liberation theology in the Philippines and Timor Leste (East Timor) to the wave of Pentecostalism sweeping through China, South Korea, and Southeast Asia. Chapter 4 focuses on the agenda of militant monks in Sri Lanka and Myanmar and the portents of this activism. Chapter 5 examines Arabization and the shift toward militant religious fundamentalism in Indonesia and Bangladesh, while chapter 6 probes the problems confronting Islamic minorities in Asia including the Uighurs in China and those in India, Thailand, and the Philippines. Chapter 7 scrutinizes the origins and consequences of the Rohingya crisis in Myanmar. Chapter 8 provides comparative analysis of the politics of blasphemy and how accusations are used to hound minorities and silence opponents. Chapter 9 appraises the interplay of traditions, colonial legacies, politics, and religion and the ramifications for contemporary sexualities. Last, chapter 10 provides some conclusions regarding the themes and issues explored here and what they portend.

Chapter Two

Hinduism and Hindutva

Hindutva (Hindu chauvinism) can be translated as "Hinduness," but this is misleadingly innocuous for a concept that is predicated on chauvinism and embraces a malevolent majoritarianism and glowering nationalism. It sanctifies and perpetuates the politics of hate and Othering in the name of religion, asserting that India is a monolithically Hindu nation, one divorced from the reality of considerable diversity. Defining Indian culture in terms of Hindu values, Hindutva is the rallying banner of the Bharatiya Janata Party (BJP). The BJP contests the secularism of the Congress Party that has dominated postindependence Indian politics despite some significant setbacks, notably the emergence of Prime Minister Narendra Modi in 2014. This notion of a Hindustan unsullied by religious minorities is not a new concept. One prominent proponent in the late nineteenth century was Vivekananda, the patron saint of an assertive Indian race-based nationalism. He is known for introducing yoga and Indian philosophy to the West, encouraging interfaith dialogue, and putting Hinduism on the map at the Parliament of World's Religions held in Chicago in 1893. Lionized in the West, he gained stature at home as someone who did the country proud on the international stage by awakening the world to India's rich cultural and philosophical heritage. He also awakened Indians to patriotism, boosting pride in nation and religion while inspiring the anti-British independence movement. Given his advocacy for religious tolerance and interfaith dialogue and concern for the poor and lower castes, he seems an awkward progenitor of contemporary Hindutva because it shares none of those traits. He also embarrasses those who harass and kill Muslims for eating beef in their mistaken belief that it is banned by their religion. Vivekananda wrote, "You will be surprised to know that according to ancient Hindu rites and rituals, a man cannot be a good Hindu who does not eat beef" (Vivekanda 1947, vol. 3, 536). Indeed, the Rashtriya

Swayamsevak Sangh (RSS, National Patriotic Organization), the main hard-core Hindutva organization in contemporary India, once propagated slogans such as "Beef, Biceps, and the Bhagavad Gita" to boost national vigor.

Hindutva embraces nationalism, bigotry, exclusion, and sectarian violence. This darker side of Hinduism is manifest in the BJP currently led by Prime Minister Narendra Modi. Modi and the BJP are linked to the paramilitary RSS that was founded in 1925. It started as a national volunteer organization to inculcate discipline and toughen up members with calisthenics and martial drills, instilling passion for Hindutva while propagating a robust Hindu race spirit. Ironically, for an organization advocating national pride and the unique virtues of Hinduism, the founders explicitly embraced European fascist philosophy and racial theories (Jaffrelot 1996, 2007).

Early leaders such as Gowalkar praised Hitler and Germany's purge of Jews (after Kristallnacht in 1938, but before the Holocaust), enjoining followers to embrace a similar "race spirit" (Ghosh 2012). For him, the key was conflating nation with race and making the management of race a state priority. With independence in 1947, the animosities of race and religion spiraled out of control in the massacres of Partition; Gandhi's assassin was a former RSS member who thought him too conciliatory toward Muslims and Pakistan.

Despite being a self-proclaimed atheist, Veer Savarkar, a prominent pro-independence activist and political prisoner of the British Raj, urged a more muscular national identity based on Hinduism and reconversion of Hindus who had been converted to other faiths. In his book *Hindutva* (1923), he argued that India should be run by Hindus, advocating an ideology of Hindu cultural and political nationalism in order to unify Hindus, raise their social consciousness, and build pride among them in support of his political project. In his view, patriotic unity was essential and proclaimed that Hinduism was one with Buddhism, Jainism, and Sikhism. Savarkar urged a tougher Hindu spirit, dismissing Gandhi as weak for embracing the Buddhist concept of ahimsa (rejection of violence). The current RSS and other Hindutva devotees honor that ambition but ignore his rejection of cow worship and caste discrimination. Indeed, expressing such views now would make one a target of harassment and violence.

More popular are Savarkar's discriminatory views about Muslims, portraying them as savage and immoral, determined to destroy the Hindu way of life. This is the core of what Hindutva is about, vilifying Muslims, conjuring a nonexistent threat to nurture solidarity and justify malevolent posturing and worse. RSS feeds on a potent mix of paranoia and a sense of victimization to legitimize its violent agenda of vigilantism and riots. RSS members have long been active in anti-Muslim rioting and were involved in the gory excesses of Partition in 1947, so much so that they were briefly banned. It has kept a polite distance from mainstream politics, presenting itself as a social organization, but the overlap with the BJP leadership is a more accurate barometer of its political influence. Modi and most of his cabinet have strong links with the RSS; he joined when he was eight years old.

In 1949 Savarkar published *Hindu Rashtra Darshan* in which he argues that Hitler was Germany's savior and compared Jews to India's Muslims, condemning both for failing to assimilate. He also argued that India should be reserved for Hindus alone and suggested purging Muslims from the police, army, and bureaucracy. While Congress launched the Quit India movement in 1942 and withheld support for Great Britain in World War II, Savarkar advocated support as a way to get military training for Hindus and later opposed Partition. He favored the establishment of Israel to create a religious-based state and saw it as a bulwark in the Middle East against Islamic Arab nations.

PARTITION

The Partition in 1947 casts a long shadow into the twenty-first century (Khan 2007). The division of the subcontinent is a collective trauma for contemporary Hindu nationalists. They see this parting indignity imposed by the British Raj as a betrayal of their dream and the creation of an Islamic Pakistan on their soil as a perfidious stain on independence. There has been little to celebrate given the horrors that preceded and escalated following the handover of power. Preparations for this act of decolonization were both inadequate and incompetent, ensuring that the abrupt rupture of empire and homeland left a legacy of troubling problems that remain unresolved, especially the border issues that have flared into wars between India and Pakistan.

Some one million people were killed in the tumult of Partition, an unforgotten orgy of sectarian brutality, rioting, and rape that still poisons communal relations and bilateral ties. Amid the murderous excesses, some fifteen million refugees crossed the hastily drawn borders, displaced from ancestral homes and relatively harmonious communities where peaceful coexistence between those of different religions had been the norm. Once people became defined solely by their religion, however, communalism spread like wildfire, opening space for political opportunists and thuggish paramilitary groups who claimed religious sanction for the carnage they wrought. Partition thus was the deadly opening act of Independence and has resonated powerfully and divisively ever since. Contemporary sectarian politics feeds on the saga of martyrs and misdeeds, leaving the Muslims who remained in India, nearly 15 percent of the population, as a target for repeated acts of revenge.

In the awful aftermath, it was Nehru who steered the nation away from a descent into full bore Hindu communalism against considerable opposition from within his Congress Party and various Hindu nationalist parties and groups. Mistreatment of Hindus in post-Partition Pakistan inflamed the Hindutva movement and gave impetus to its agenda of transforming Indian democracy into a nation run according to the dictates of Hindutva. Nehru, however, would not allow this seething identity politics to derail his plans to modernize India and establish a firm foundation for secular democracy. He saw Hindu bigotry as the main enemy of the plural, inclusive idea of Indian democracy he espoused and acted accordingly. His success in doing so in a nation in which 80 percent of the population is Hindu is a testament to his powers of persuasion, steely political will, and a wily sense of brinksmanship. Nehru's secular idea of India prevailed, but Hindutva religious hardliners never conceded as communalism simmered and flared over the ensuing decades, gaining momentum from the 1990s. The idea of India propagated by Hindutva zealots has no room for pluralism or tolerance of diversity. They cling to their grievances and see no reason to forgive or forget.

Partition baptized Independence in blood and is the basis for contemporary scaremongering and vilification. The BJP and associated Hindutva organizations under the umbrella of the Sangh Parivar tap into the angry passions associated with this touchstone of national identity. This grisly mayhem suffered by Muslims, Hindus, and Sikhs bequeathed a legacy of distrust and animosity that is the wellspring of contemporary sectarian tensions and violence.

The festering wounds of hastily drawn borders remain geopolitical flashpoints that have sparked wars and terrorism. State identities in India and Pakistan draw on this trauma, infusing nationalism with the primordial passions of religion, victimization, and revenge. Pakistan, although united by Islam, seemed designed to fail as predominantly Bengali East Pakistan was divided by 2,000 kilometers, language, and culture from the seat of government in West Pakistan. In 1971, Pakistani armed forces committed widespread atrocities in East Pakistan in rejecting the national election victory won by Sheikh Mujibur Rahman, the candidate from the Bengali-dominated east (Bass 2013). This violent maelstrom, an aftershock of London's bungled Partition, precipitated an exodus of millions of Hindus from East Pakistan into India and a third war between India and Pakistan in the post-Independence era, the others being fought over disputed territory in Kashmir. Bangladesh was born from the ashes of this war, a conflict that claimed as many as three million lives. It is a collective trauma that reverberates in identity politics throughout the subcontinent.

The British have much to answer for. According to Ananya Vajpeyi, author of *Righteous Republic* (2012), "most of the conflicts ongoing in South Asia, whether within India, Pakistan or Bangladesh, or between them, are directly or indirectly products of the unfinished business of Partition, staggered from 1947 to 1971" (interview July 2017). Partition also transformed Kashmir into a warzone between Pakistan and India in what remains one of the world's most dangerous flashpoints. The Indian army's massive and ruthless occupation of a resentful population in Kashmir continues as these nuclear-armed states periodically skirmish, stoking the flames of antagonism. Basharat Peer, author of *Curfewed Night* (2008) an account about the conflict in his Kashmir homeland, says, "The hurried Partition of India was one of the greatest imperial crimes of the British Empire. The massive displacements and the fratricide that accompanied it affected the subcontinent deeply and its legacy has shaped and twisted South Asian societies immensely" (interview July 2017). Divided between India and Pakistan, "Kashmir carries the curse of being the unfinished business of the Partition. The dispute has lingered and exacted a terrible cost for the past seven decades and the hopes of a just peace and solution are very little" (interview July 2017).

Nisid Hajari, author of *Midnight Furies: The Deadly Legacy of India's Partition* (2015), believes that Partition could have been averted but talks to prevent this collapsed due to an absence of trust between the British, Congress, and Muslim League. In Hajari's view, "avoiding Partition wouldn't necessarily have avoided bloodshed. The August 1947 riots may have been prevented, and thus hundreds of thousands of lives saved. But no one knows if the country would have held together or broken apart in ensuing years in multiple, equally bloody Partitions" (interview July 2017). The repercussions of Partition in contemporary India "are playing out in a couple ways. Most obviously, the easy demonization of Pakistan and resort to belligerence and threats—albeit in the face of provocations by Pakistani-backed militants—is a legacy of the enmity created at Partition. It's simply far too easy to cast Pakistan as an enemy and far too difficult politically to make real concessions in the interests of peace" (interview July 2017).

Oxford historian Faisal Devji, author of *Muslim Zion: Pakistan as a Political Idea* (2013), asserts that "unlike what conventional wisdom says, Partition did not illustrate the dominance of religious identities but rather the opposite. For it resulted in the wholesale betrayal by Hindus and Muslims of their co-religionists who remained in Pakistan and India respectively" (interview July 2017). He adds, "One reason why Islam remains so touchy a subject in Pakistan is because it serves to cover over this initial betrayal, but only at the cost of repeating it with the violent subjugation of East Pakistan and eventual independence of Bangladesh" (interview July 2017).

In Hajari's view, "The anti-Muslim current that's taken hold in parts of the country—as expressed in these beef-related lynchings, warnings about 'love jihad' and so on—theoretically have nothing to do with Pakistan. But it blends far too easily into accusations that Muslims—especially those in Kashmir—are 'anti-national' and Pakistani sympathizers if they express any criticism of the government. This sense that Muslims are a potential fifth column has grown out of the deep sense of betrayal forged at Partition, and is easy to revive in times, like now, when majoritarian sentiment is on the rise" (interview July 2017).

Pankaj Mishra, author of *The Age of Anger* (2017), regards the recent cow vigilante attacks by Hindus on Muslims as representing "the unfinished business of partition—its crude logic which was disguised by the rhetoric of secularism for a long time." He rues that in contemporary India, "the nation-state cannot allow equal citizenship to its citizens, so that majoritarianism has to prevail" (interview July 2017).

Siddartha Deb, whose novel *The Point of Return* (2004) examines the consequences of displacement caused by Partition, observes that "the Partition has showed an uncanny ability to replicate itself through the decades, in mini partitions, mini massacres, and the marginalization and brutal treatment of minorities that has become the governing spirit of nationalism in South Asia" (interview August 2017). He laments that "one can see that original genocidal rage burning on, in the violence against Muslims in Gujarat in 2002 that completed the rise to power of the prime minister Narendra Modi as well as in the lynch mob mentality asserted by the right-wing groups to which he belongs, that killed and plundered with glee in 1947 and that continue to do so today."

CONTEMPORARY HINDU EXTREMISM

The Sangh Parivar is an umbrella organization of dozens of Hindu nationalist groups affiliated with or inspired by RSS. The BJP represents the Sangh Parivar in politics and this influence is evident in the party's embrace of Hindutva and the symbols of Hinduism. The BJP sanctifies its political agenda through religious appeals that conflate nation, state, and Hinduism. It represents Hindu nationalism although the various member groups remain autonomous and express different views on a range of religious, social, and political issues. While drawing on the ethos of Hinduism, Sangh Parivar is generally associated with patriotism, bigotry, and chauvinist ideology. However, given the diversity of groups represented by the organization, sweeping generalizations don't do justice to significant differences. Some groups have been involved in social reforms regarding untouchability and caste discrimination, arguing that such discrimination has no basis in Hindu scripture or texts. Other groups have engaged in social services and educational programs serving tribal communities, while some have campaigned against sex-selective abortions. This diversity also means that Sangh Parivar struggles to promote a clear agenda beyond the common vision of a Hindu state.

The Hindutva movement wields powerful symbols and harps on various historical grievances, mounting public spectacles that arouse frenzied support among the masses. Nothing better illustrates this confluence of religious symbolism and grievance with political ambition than L. K. Advani's "chariot procession" (Rath Yatra) to Ayodhya in 1990, making the BJP the driving force, and principal beneficiary, of the temple construction/mosque destruction movement (Jaffrelot 1996). Advani was a co-founder of the BJP and member of RSS since 1942. The BJP had been a small party until the Sangh Parivar orchestrated destruction of the Babri Mosque in 1992 on the disputed site in Ayodhya where Hindu zealots wanted to build a temple in honor of the Hindu deity Rama. The archaeological evidence is fragmentary, and it remains uncertain that contemporary Ayodhya corresponds to Ram's birthplace mentioned in the Ramayana, the legendary Hindu epic. Ram is considered one of the most important and popular deities in Hinduism, a symbol of unwavering devotion to religious values. For purposes of ethnoreligious mobilization, reclaiming Ram's ostensible birth site from Muslims resonates powerfully among many devout Hindus. The sanctified site symbolizes Hindu victimization at the hands of Muslims, invoking past wrongs to justify contemporary reprisals. Rapturous press coverage of Advani's chariot spectacle generated a "Hindu wave" that polarized the nation while his 1990 arrest caused widespread outbreaks of communal rioting. Subsequently, crowds of Hindu fanatics destroyed the Babri Mosque in 1992, sparking communal riots and killings across the nation. In the aftermath, religious chauvinism has become a destructive and divisive staple of Indian democracy.

The BJP's ardent embrace of Hindu chauvinism has been the calling card of the party and the basis of its electoral appeal ever since. Modimania, the effusive, bordering on hysterical reverence for Prime Minister Modi, is a byproduct of this surge in Hindu identity politics that impugns without quite overturning India's secular national identity.

Culture Wars

The battles over identity are waged with particular fervor in the arena of culture. What is authentic, what is ours, what is theirs, what offends, and what arouses outrage or stings wounds of humiliations recalled secondhand represents a contested and cluttered space. For Hindu nationalists, the shuddhi (reconversion) of Muslims and Christians and their *ghar wapsi* (homecoming) to the Hindu community Savarkar advocated are key aspects of the larger cultural war they are waging to reclaim India as their own. This means cutting back on subsidies for the haj pilgrimage for Muslims, passing legislation banning talaq, the Islamic practice of initiating divorce, banning cattle slaughter, slaughtering butchers who defy the bans, pushing claims to disputed sacred sites, and desecrating them by demolishing the mosque on that site. It means electing Narendra Modi as prime minister, a politician who did nothing to prevent or rein in the massacre of at least one thousand Muslims in

2002 and the displacement of tens of thousands more (Nussbaum 2008). Modi is a lifelong member of RSS, and that hardline affiliation led the BJP to appoint him state minister in Gujarat not long before the slaughter. He claims that the Supreme Court gave him a "clean chit" regarding the allegations that he was complicit in the pogrom, but he was never tried or prosecuted. The Supreme Court appointed an investigative body that gathered a large dossier of damning evidence implicating Modi but concluded in defiance of the submissions that it was not sufficient to pursue a case, prompting allegations of political intervention (Deb 2016). In the court of public opinion, Modi has never been able to shrug off his responsibility for the massacre, but this is of little consequence for his loyal constituents. Unrepentant, Modi refers to the displacement centers for those burned out of their homes as Muslim breeding grounds. Regarding the carnage, in 2013 while campaigning he said he was saddened by the loss of life, as any onlooker would be, drawing this troubling analogy: "If someone else is driving, and we are sitting in the back seat, and even then if a small *kutte ka bacha* comes under the wheel, do we feel pain or not? We do." As Siddarha Deb explains, "this translation misses the derogatory implication of the expression *kutte ka bacha* or 'progeny of a dog,'" suggesting unknown lineage, amplifying the insult of comparing Muslims to dogs (Deb 2016).

Shuddhi (reconversion) of Muslims and Christians has become a battle cry for Hindu zealots. Mohan Bhagwat, the RSS chief, laid down the gauntlet in Kolkata in 2014 where he said, "We will bring back our brothers who have lost their way. They did not go on their own. They were robbed, tempted into leaving. Now the thief has been caught and the world knows my belongings are with the thief. I will retrieve my belongings, so why is this such a big issue?" (Das 2014). Reconversion taps into the ideological foundations of Hindutva in which India is both motherland and holy land and under attack from Islam and Christianity, proselytizing religions unlike India's small communities of Jews and Parsis. Just as China's leaders now incessantly invoke the 150 years of humiliation when their nation was weak and prey to imperial powers, Hindu nationalists refer to servitude under Muslim and then British rule when state power was allegedly used to forcibly convert Hindus to Islam and Christianity. Reconversion as payback taps into this collective "humiliation," reminding everyone who the enemy is and urging them to exact revenge. This image of Muslims converting Hindus by sword is not wholly inaccurate, but the focus on coercion elides other reasons why people converted. As Gandhi noted, Islam offered an escape for lower-caste Hindus and a chance to become equals in the ummah and in the realm of Allah. The spread of Islam in India, moreover, owes much to charismatic Sufi saints whose blend of religion and mysticism proved attractive to local communities. The British Raj certainly has much to answer for, but forced conversions is not one of its sins. Colonial administrators were ambivalent about missionaries and secular in governance. There is more to allegations that the British favored Muslims, but that is separate from the conversion issue.

Gandhi was an outspoken opponent of institutionally driven reconversion and thought that it was something best left for people to decide on their own. In his view, proselytization was foreign to Hinduism, only copying other religions. The RSS disagrees and see it as essential to its agenda. Why not? It reminds people of past wrongs that need righting, stirs up angry passions, and provides handy targets that motivate and mobilize. Cloaking prejudice and violence in the saffron colors of the BJP and RSS is as essential to Hindutva as oxygen for fire.

Zealots remain unpersuaded by investigations such as that conducted by the police in Kerala in association with the central Home Ministry that found no evidence of any forced conversions or "love jihad" in examining 7,299 cases of conversion to Islam between 2011 and 2016: 82 percent converted from Hinduism and 18 percent from Christianity (TNN 2018). This suggests that it is the idea rather than the reality that matters as activists invent an incendiary problem knowing that it fuels a patriarchal righteousness that allows hatemongers to feign doing good (see chapter 9). When "they" are going after "our" women, the gloves come off and it is war, in which truth is the first casualty quickly followed by innocents.

Subnationalisms Defy Hindutva

Permit me to digress in order to illustrate why sweeping generalizations about a country as large and diverse as India are misleading. Subnationalisms are rife in the sprawling continent of India, challenging the conceit of the Hindutva movement that Hinduism binds everyone together. Yes, people engage in similar rituals, pray to the same gods, and act according to the same creed and precepts as they know them, but there is significance in the degrees of difference. The monolithic solidarity imagined by Hindutva advocates breaks down even between the groups belonging to the Sangh Parivar, so even with considerable ideological common ground advocates of Hindu nationalism struggle to make common cause on various issues. Given India's geographical breadth and ethnic and linguistic variety, it is not surprising that dreams of a monolithic Hindustan are far fetched.

In Kalimpong, a breathtaking hill station in West Bengal, my innkeeper told me that local Hinduism is a far cry from that practiced in the hot plains below. He said that the town has a large ethnic Nepalese presence and suggested that they practice a more authentic Hinduism than in India proper. Indian Hinduism has been altered by more cosmopolitan and modern influences, a regrettable state of affairs in his view. Another local Hindu I met shared that perspective, explaining that Hinduism should not be about hating and violence, assuring me that locals shun RSS and their ilk. With no Muslims in town, this borderland embraces other grievances that take precedence, especially the movement to establish Ghorkaland that is based in nearby Darjeeling. Locals want to establish a state apart from West Bengal and resent what they see as Bengali cultural imperialism, most recently manifest in the state government's 2017 decree making Bengali language mandatory in local schools. This ignited angry demonstrations and a general strike because many locals prefer Nepali culture.

Thousands of kilometers away in Kerala, a relatively prosperous state along the western seaboard of India's south, one also encounters widespread skepticism toward Modi, the BJP, and Hindutva. This intensified dramatically in the wake of massive flooding in August 2018. A combination of the government's bungled disaster relief response and comments by a BJP politician suggesting that the floods were divine retribution reinforced local views about the BJP. Kerala leads all Indian states in human development indicators, has large Christian (18 percent) and Muslim communities (27 percent), and in some areas the housing is overwhelmingly of Arabic design, reflecting remittances from Indian Muslim migrant workers in the Mideast. There is a high rate of literacy (94 percent versus the national average of 74 percent) among the thirty-four million residents, a strong cooperative movement, and an atmosphere of tolerance. I met a school teacher who, despite being Hindu, lamented the saffronization of school textbooks under the BJP that downplayed Islamic influences and promoted pride in Hinduism. In his view, this politicization of history inculcates intolerance and makes minorities feel marginalized and targeted.

I met the teacher at a theyyam dance held in a remote village, a spectacular celebration that villages host to promote a good harvest and propitiate the gods. It is not a Hindu rite but one of the local customs that has blended in with the religious rituals that animate local communities. In the predawn hours I rode in a car past fluttering red banners emblazoned with the hammer and sickle and a silhouette of Che Guevera, signs of the communists' political dominance in the state. As the event got underway at the village square, I watched as two whirling dancers, straw skirts aflame, shimmied under elaborate, four-meter-high headdresses while circling the central shrine to the beat of drummers amid a buzzing throng. I did not expect a nudge from the local standing next to me, saying, "Watch . . . now it becomes interesting."

A large number of women carrying earthenware jars with flaming wicks then joined the smoky procession of the theyyam dancers as the drumming grew more feverish, the crowds became noisier, and attendants doused the flaming skirts with water to prevent immolation. The dancers began gyrating more spectacularly, entering another trance zone, summoning strength from their sinewy bodies as they boogied and spun under some forty kilograms of costume, sweat pouring down their flame-licked bodies. They busted some awesome moves, egging each other on, headdresses bobbing, drummers grooving, followed by the ladies bedecked in their colorful saris, jars held aloft as they circled the shrine and its flickering camphor oil lamps on wrought iron racks. As dawn faded away and the day grew brighter and hotter, it all wound down rather quickly as a few men from the village, well into their toddy, offered refreshments to the dancers, easing them from their divine trances.

It starts with the makeup. At another theyyam I arrived early and wandered over to a tent where the dancers were being prepped and painted. They were sprawled out on tarps and pillows while assistants began the arduous process of transforming these mortals into gods, taking their heads into their laps and painstakingly applying paints and makeup—dabbing here, brushing there, frowning as they concentrated on the task, while the gods to be extended hand mirrors to watch the progress. It's a family business handed from generation to generation as itinerant troupes of dancers, drummers, and attendants, perhaps a dozen or so, rotated through the same villages every year for nearly four months from December through March.

One god in the making said in the off season he was a manual laborer, but during the theyyam season he devoted himself full time to the business of being a deity. Indelicately, I inquired how much they are paid for their performance—apparently about Rs 3,500 ($50) split between the dozen members, but he added that the fees varied according to the size and affluence of the village. As the daubing continued, his demeanor changed. Asked what it felt like to be in a trance and to become a god, he explained that once he fell into a trance he forgot everything until he awoke, totally drained. He said he recalled none of the dancing nor what it was like to achieve divinity. His body was merely a vessel for the spirits, he explained. I watched in silence as he became his part. Then I was ushered out of the makeshift tent as he prepared to go into his other realm and donned his mask and bangles, body slathered in oil. When he emerged, he stood on a box as attendants helped him with the headdress and arranged his grass skirt over its wooden hoop from which torches protruded. For his dance he also donned a breastplate that made him into Badrakali, a goddess.

According to one informant, there is a passing of the baton, so to speak, as the local priest from the Brahmin caste relinquishes spiritual powers to these holy counterparts, keepers of local traditions. William Dalrymple, in his exquisite book *Nine Lives: In Search of the Sacred in Modern India* (2010), focuses on people practicing traditional religions and customs in modern India. According to the acclaimed Scottish-born writer, the theyyam dancers are from the Dalit caste, otherwise known as untouchables. The theyyam suddenly transforms these lowly men into gods and goddesses, revered by those who are ordinarily above them in station. Even the holy Brahmin pay homage to them when they go into a trance and become deities.

I saw the Brahmins bow deeply and touch the feet of the dancers in an act of homage.

This turning of the social order upside down, at least for a limited period during a specified season, can be seen as a social pressure valve. Or perhaps it is only ritual. But when I asked a young IT engineer who was sponsoring a theyyam in his home village about this, he asked me if I could really think of the dance as mere ritual. He explained that it is not true that the dancers are all Dalits, saying that various castes perform different theyyam dances—although he did acknowledge they were always from lower castes. He did not go into the reversing of the social hierarchy. As for Brahmin ceding spiritual primacy, he suggested (perhaps because he was from a Brahmin family) that might be overstating the situation.

As a Brahmin working in the modern world, he confessed to feeling an emptiness that was somewhat salved by returning to his village and carrying on timeless traditions that made him feel connected to a reassuring taproot of identity. He said that many young professionals like him felt similarly—succeeding in a material sense but still yearning for more. I asked about Modi and Hindutva because urban professionals are said to be supportive of the BJP agenda. Apparently not in Kerala as he heaped scorn on the party for betraying a religion he held sacred, a view he assured me was widely shared among his Hindu colleagues. Some observers suggest that traditional India has a limitless capacity to embarrass modern India, but this young man believes that modern India needs its traditions precisely because continuities help people adjust to the tumult of social convulsions and economic transformations caused by modernization. In the small villages of northern Kerala where theyyam are performed, the farming communities are maintaining this vibrant tradition. It is not just a matter of yuppies looking for their roots but rather people close to the land, subject to the vagaries of weather and pests, propitiating the gods.

In Tamil Nadu, on the eastern seaboard across from Kerala, the prospects for Hindutva anti-Muslim agitation also appear limited. As the eminent intellectual Ashish Nandy wrote in the *Times of India* in 1991, "It cannot penetrate southern India where Hinduism is more resilient, where it is more difficult to project on to the Muslim the feared and unacceptable parts of one's own self." While visiting the ancient Meenakshi (fish-eyed goddess) Temple in Madurai I met a Brahmin priest who told me that he was following his family's unbroken tradition stretching a handful of centuries into the mists of time. The temple and immediate precinct are sacred places where contemporary pilgrims engage in the same rituals as their forebears, wandering a grid of streets and alleys little changed over time where merchants claim similarly long lineages as my Brahmin priest. When asked about Modi, he offered a frown, telling me that Hinduism is not about hating, explaining that Hindutva is new, an invented tradition that manipulates religion to gain political power. He said it is not part of local culture, a reminder that Tamils (Dravidians) see themselves as a people apart with their own language, rich traditions, and distinctive appearance. In Tamil Nadu, one is constantly reminded of the subnationalisms that make a mockery of the monolithic Indian identity that is the conceit of Hindutva. Tamil identity draws from different wellsprings, including but not exclusively Hinduism. Differences with the north and northerners constantly crop up in conversation. Tamils see themselves as relatively laid back and far more tolerant and cultured. The north is portrayed as a cauldron always at risk of boiling over, while communalism is muted in Tamil Nadu, where the presence of Christians and Muslims, each about 6 percent of the state's overall population of seventy-two million, is not used to whip up hatreds. It is striking that the first RSS rally in Madurai was only in 2017 and in the 2016 Assembly elections the BJP gained less than 3 percent of the vote. But the pro-Modi wave has gained momentum in other unlikely spots, gaining a stunning victory in the 2018 Tripura elections in the northeast, a communist stronghold, so local Dravidian parties can't be complacent about the Hindutva challenge. But is not certain that the RSS Islamophobia tactics will work in Tamil Nadu, where invoking the past depredations of the Mughals does not resonate so powerfully given the different historical experience. Moreover, distrust of the central government runs high, and religion is but one of many influences on Tamil identity where language looms large and religious sentiments are different than those advocated by the RSS. Thus, there are good reasons why locals doubt that the saffron lotus, the BJP's iconic symbol, will bloom in Tamil Nadu. Both Kerala and Tamil Nadu have larger Christian populations and longer exposure to Christianity and thus are not as prone to anti-Christian campaigns. And both states have trading and migratory traditions that support tolerance and pluralism.

Textbooks

Textbooks play a powerful role in shaping identities during the formative years that have a lingering influence on adult attitudes and perceptions. In the struggle to figure out who we are, textbooks provide answers that bend to the will of governing powers. They are designed to imbue citizens with knowledge that fosters a collective consciousness and socializes them to hold certain beliefs and embrace norms and values supportive of a particular political order. The politics of textbooks in India illuminate nationalist efforts to control the narrative. The standard storyline about the British Raj and the national independence struggle is not disputed, but that leaves several centuries and other controversies up for grabs. The Hindutva movement of religious fundamentalists seeks to significantly revise selected aspects of Indian history, especially regarding the subcontinent's Muslim heritage and the glories of the Mughal dynasty between the sixteenth and eighteenth centuries. The

Mughal rulers were Muslims but did not impose a theocracy or Islamic identity, instead forging bonds through a Persianized culture. Historians regard the Mughal era as one of religious tolerance and a time of peace, economic growth, and cultural flowering. There was a centralized administration and at its height the Mughals ruled over one-quarter of the world's estimated population. So there are good reasons why this is considered a golden age in Indian history, and that is precisely why Hindu zealots seek to downplay it. Their first opportunity came when the BJP-led coalition government (1999–2004) commissioned a rewriting of national textbooks. Saffron is the party's symbolic color, so this process is dubbed the "saffronization" of history. This Hindu revisionism disingenuously depicted India's Muslim rulers as merely barbarous invaders and the Mughal period as a dark period of Islamic subjugation that extinguished the far greater glories of preceding Hindu empires. The BJP-mandated textbook claimed, for example, that it was actually Hindus who commissioned and designed the Taj Mahal, the Red Fort, and the Qu'tb Minar, all widely recognized as stunning examples of Islamic architecture. The texts also challenged the prevailing mainstream consensus among Indian historians that India developed through mass migrations, trading links with neighboring empires, and is a hybrid civilization based on multicultural borrowings. Hindu zealots prefer to emphasize the uniqueness of Hindu civilization and its resilience to foreign intrusions while marginalizing Islamic and other foreign influences. There were some curious lacunae in the textbook, leaving out the crucial detail that it was a Hindutva activist who assassinated the national icon Mahatma Gandhi in 1948 and providing no explanation of the European fascist influences on the ostensibly nativist ideology of the RSS. With a change of government in 2004, a panel of expert historians commissioned by the Congress Party recommended discontinuing use of the saffronized texts. Congress espouses religious tolerance and sees the Islamic minority as an important constituency, so it backed restoring the mainstream consensus evident in previous textbooks.

After the BJP regained power in 2014, however, Hindutva activists advocated "resaffronizing" school books and syllabi in educational institutions all over the country. The BJP convened a committee to reinstate its revisionist history glorifying Hindu influences, justifying Hindutva grievances, and marginalizing Islamic contributions to Indian culture and civilization. Muslim rulers are again caricatured as villainous plunderers and Hindu rulers are idolized while Hindu myths are invoked to explain natural phenomena. These texts nurture a collective consciousness that encourages bigotry and ill-informed indignation, sacrificing objective and accurate portrayals in service of boosting atavistic sentiments. This politicization of history textbooks is not unique to India but does assert a religious national identity that defies the inclusiveness and secularism enshrined in the nation's constitution.

Modi's Culture Ministry has taken further steps in 2017 to saffronize India's ancient history by charging scholars with finding proof that India's first inhabitants were Hindus, not Central Asians as most scholars contend. The committee is also tasked with proving that ancient Hindu scriptures are facts not myths. These guidelines establish the conclusions that the committee is expected to prove by finding (or bending) evidence to that end. The preordained results will be used to overturn the prevailing view of multiple migrations, invasions, and multicultural blending over the centuries in favor of a purified Hindu-centric view.

The RSS contends that the ancestors of all people of Indian origin were Hindu, even today's 172 million Muslims, and they must all accept their common ancestry as part of Bharat Mata, or Mother India. According to writer Samrat Choudhury, "The RSS functions never have any religious symbols or deities. The only image on display is of Bharat Mata. The Partition is viewed with regret because it dismembered Bharat Mata." In the RSS and across the right-wing spectrum, anger focuses on the millions of Muslims who remained in India despite this loss of so much territory. He adds, "Their frequent jibe towards Muslims of 'go to Pakistan' is based on this" (personal communication October 2018).

This insistence is linked to RSS support for "reconversion," a project that assumes contemporary multicultural India is a corruption of the authentic Hindustan of yore; establishing common ancestry aims at welcoming back those who have lapsed from Hinduism. The goal is to integrate the findings of this "Hindu first" history project into future textbooks. This campaign to reinvent India by saffronizing its history contests the multicultural, secular identity endorsed by Nehru, the nation's founding father. As a result of this campaign, politicians are targeting evident pluralism by hijacking scholarship to assert Hindutva cultural superiority. Researchers have marching orders to find archaeological proof that the epic poem Ramayana is a factual portrayal of ancient India, and they must find a river that corresponds to the sacred Saraswati mentioned in the Vedas, dismissed by critics as akin to funding research on mermaids (Gettlemen et al. 2019). As the Culture Minister Sharma explained, "If the Koran and Bible are considered as part of history, then what is the problem in accepting our Hindu religious texts as the history of India?" (Jain and Lasseter 2018).

SACRED COWS

The nexus of politics and religion is manifest in the agenda of Prime Minister Modi, who in 2014 campaigned mostly on inclusive economic development but also reached out to his Hindutva base with the slogans "Vote for Modi, give life to the cow" and "The cow will be saved, the country will be saved," cashing in on the Hindu belief that cows are holy. The BJP subsequently made good on its promise to ban the selling of cows for slaughter in eighteen states in India and established hostels where cows are cared for in their dotage. In response, feminist activists demonstrated wearing cow masks, expressing envy at how bovines get better treatment than women. And even if India is a pleasant place for cows, what about the poor?

The hypocrisy is jarring given that India is a major exporter of beef, accounting for almost one-quarter of the global market, earning over $4 billion a year. Surely if religious compassion is foremost in politicians' minds, there should not be masses of Indians living in abject poverty or tens of thousands of farmers driven to suicide annually because of debts they can't repay. Moreover, whether Christian, Muslim, or those outside the fold of upper-caste Hinduism, beef is one of the few cheaply available sources of protein. Thus, the slaughter ban disproportionately affects those living on limited means. While the cow was Lord Krishna's favorite animal, making it a symbol of piety serves to accentuate differences among the nation's 80 percent Hindu population and diverse minorities. India is rightly proud of being the largest democracy but failing to uphold the rule of law and allowing self-appointed vigilantes to engage in extra-judicial killings targeting Muslims with impunity betrays the nation's principles. What gets lost in the politics is the fact that most of what is termed beef in India is actually from water buffalo, an animal not considered sacred.

The BJP contends that eating beef is against the idea of India, but is it? Nowhere in Sunil Khilnani's *The Idea of India* (1997) is there any hint that sirloins are subversive. Historian Dwijendra Narayan Jha, author of the *Myth of the Holy Cow* (2002), dismisses claims by Hindu fundamentalists that cow slaughter has always been associated with Muslims, pointing out that eating beef was common among Brahmins long before the spread of Islam to India. According to him, "There is no doubt that beef remained an important part of the Indian haute cuisine and cow was often killed in honor of guests. It is totally baseless to argue that Hindus never ate the flesh of the cow" (Soumya 2014). Hindus only proscribed beef after they lost political power to the Muslims, belatedly embracing cow protection as a symbol of identity and faith. The taboo on eating of beef thus dates to the early medieval era, and then only for upper-caste Hindus.

For exposing the invention of this tradition, one Hindu extremist sentenced Jha to death in a fatwa, ironically a practice exclusively associated with Islam. According to Pankaj Mishra, Hindutva posturing on cows illustrates "how pathetically little they know about the religious and spiritual traditions that supposedly inform their political beliefs; and how the superior morality they noisily lay claim to is important to them only so far as it can give legitimacy to resolutely unspiritual ambitions to capture state power" (Mishra 2002). Jha offended by revealing that ostensibly "immutable" Indian traditions, like all other traditions, are subject to change, revision, and appropriation. Mishra observes that "the cow was far from holy. It is significant that no cow-goddesses, or temples to cows, feature in India's anarchically all-inclusive polytheisms."

Unhappy with these facts, in 2006 the BJP government deleted school textbook references to ancient Hindus eating beef. Food fascism is trending as the RSS in 2017 called for a countrywide ban on the slaughter of cows. One senior judge said the cow should be declared a national animal and people who slaughter cows should be sentenced to life in prison. Curiously, in June 2017 Vaman Acharya, the BJP spokesperson in Karnataka, made televised remarks reminding everyone that cow protection is an invented tradition, an awkward admission for his party that he later retracted.

Protecting cows comes at a high cost to many Hindus as they can be sold for significant sums that represent a safety net for farmers facing drought or crop failure. Moreover, the industry employs many people in procuring, processing, deboning, and packing, in addition to those engaged in production of leather and pet food. Not all Hindus or states support Modi's cow crusade. In April 2017, West Bengal's chief minister Mamata Banerjee declared that the BJP's beef offensive is "maligning Hinduism," adding, "Hinduism is not the BJP's religion. The BJP's religion is swords, murder, killing, riots, all against the Constitution" (Banerjie 2017).

Nowadays in India, butchers risk being jailed or slaughtered by cow protection vigilantes taking advantage of the state's surprising tolerance for such violence. These miscreants feel empowered by a government that sheds crocodile tears for their Muslim victims while fulminating about the need to protect sacred cows in the name of respecting religious sentiments. In Gujarat, the state where Muslims were slaughtered with impunity on Modi's watch, butchers now face life imprisonment, and even transporters of cows can face a ten-year term. "A cow is not an animal. It is a symbol of universal life," Gujarat law minister Pradipsinh Jadeja said in explaining the harsher penalty enacted in 2016. "Anybody who doesn't spare the cow, the government will not spare him" (Global Village Space 2017).

In such a diverse nation, there really is no alternative to tolerance, but in the northern state of Uttar Pradesh, the BJP has other ideas, driven by the calculus of polls rather than religious precepts or human rights. Uttar Pradesh has two hundred million people, including forty million Muslims, many of whom eat beef or are engaged in the beef business. They have even greater reason to be worried because the state's chief of police threatened that anyone trading in beef is now subject to prosecution under the National Security and Gangsters Act.

With butchers now standing alongside terrorists and gangsters, revving up the BJP base apparently means tossing supporters the red meat they crave.

The Supreme Court has other ideas. In a July 2018 ruling the court urged the government to reign in "mobocracy," insisting that "pluralism and tolerance are essential virtues and constitute the building blocks of a truly free and democratic society," adding, "that is the idea and essence of our nation which cannot be, to borrow a line from Rabindranath Tagore, 'broken up into fragments by narrow domestic walls' of caste, creed, race, class or religion" (Indian Express 2018). The court urged Parliament to enact a law to curb the surge in vigilantism. In a barely veiled scolding of the Modi government, the judges fumed, "There has been an unfortunate litany of spiraling mob violence and agonized horror, presenting a grim and gruesome picture that compels us to reflect whether the populace of a great Republic like ours has lost the values of tolerance to sustain a diverse culture. Besides, bystander apathy, numbness of the mute spectators of the scene of the crime, inertia of the law enforcing machinery to prevent such crimes and nip them in the bud and grandstanding of the incident by the perpetrators of the crimes, including in the social media, aggravates the entire problem." There is a method to the madness of mobocracy that illuminates the veneration enjoyed by Prime Minister Modi, who has unleashed this whirlwind of rage and reaped the benefits. The young male vigilantes conjure up stereotypes of the Internet troll, "keyboard jockeys with too much time on their hands, sitting in their childhood bedrooms furiously tweeting about every perceived slight to Hinduism and Modi" (Gowen 2018). They are frustrated because they can't find decent jobs and, due to India's "bachelor bomb" of thirty-seven million more men than women, many are "incels," an unhappy demographic. In Hindu militant groups they can find a sense of purpose and are receptive to the hatemongering and mantra of violence. These alienated men harbor a sense of victimization and find a ready target in Muslims. In social media they find solidarity and the means for propagating communalism and mobilizing the shock troops of sectarian harassment and violence that Modi's mobocracy has mainstreamed.

Modi-Mania

At the peak of his popularity, a Pew Poll found that 87 percent of Indians had a favorable opinion of Modi (Pew 2015b). More than half (56 percent) were satisfied with the nation's direction, more than double the level in 2013, and almost three-quarters thought economic conditions were good. Public support rates for the central government (93 percent) and the BJP (87 percent) were similarly stratospheric. It's an amazing set of results for a leader who has a reputation for being such a polarizing figure. In the theater of "saffronized" politics, he has deftly deployed Hinduism, invoking ancient glories and dog whistling to the firebrands, conveying an image of bold leadership.

In the 2014 elections Modi campaigned as the ultimate outsider with a vision for reform and managed to be all things to all people. Reactionary Hindus saw him as a cultural warrior, industrialists saw him as a supporter of big business, and the middle class saw him as the deus ex machina of their dreams while others hoped he would curb corruption and impose discipline. Policy wonks imagined a bold reformer while disaffected Congress voters abandoned their feckless party in droves, giving up hope that it could tackle India's enormous problems.

Raising so many contradictory expectations risked disappointment. In 2014 the BJP garnered only 32 percent of the national vote, so it was not such a massive mandate, but Team Modi sustained momentum at subsequent polls. Much owes to the fumbling governance of the Congress Party over the preceding decade and the lackluster campaigning by Rahul Gandhi, the designated dynastic heir. Given his reputation and background, Modi raised concerns that he would shred India's secular, inclusive liberal democracy. Not yet, but he has mainstreamed extremist views and averted his eyes from dangerous excesses that undermine secular values. He has also altered the liberal ecosystem that long sustained Congress through patronage and, by coopting the media, was able to expand support outside the BJP's homeland.

Modi manifests the twenty-first-century remaking of the BJP's image from a party capitalizing on and politicizing communal relations to one that champions economic and social development, appeals to aspirations for upward mobility, and crusades against corruption. The BJP realizes that it cannot win elections by relying exclusively on the saffron banner of Hindu nationalism and understands that its militant Hinduism appeals chiefly to a narrow core constituency while scaring away other voters concerned about the consequences of such extremism on the delicate fabric of a pluralist society. The BJP also supports a muscular stance on national security and was the party in power when India exploded five nuclear devices in 1998. It now professes to be a voice of moderation on communalism, and in the 2014 campaign Modi managed to shrug off responsibility for the Gujarat anti-Muslim pogrom in 2002 while he was chief minister, even though "there is by now a broad consensus that the Gujarat violence was a form of ethnic cleansing, that in many ways it was premeditated, and that it was carried out with the complicity of the state government and officers of the law" (Nussbaum 2008, 50–51).

Modi presides over the most right-wing government ever in independent India and his ascendance signals that Hindutva beliefs apparently have widespread appeal that transcends region, caste, and class divides. Moreover, given his reputation, it is extraordinary that Muslims accounted for 9 percent of his aggregate votes in 2014. So what to make of the Modi moment? How can he reconcile the competing expectations of supporters—economic reformers, hardline Hindu ideologues, industrialists seeking red carpet treatment, small-scale retailers seeking protection, and the urban poor with up-wardly mobile aspirations? This is an immense challenge, but the BJP's campaign juggernaut seemed almost unstoppable, leading some to quip that the party could win even if it backed a lamppost to run. There are, however, gathering signs of resistance as allegations of extravagant corruption tarnish Team Modi's reputation while high unemployment, persistent poverty, and a battered farming sector discredit the vikas (development) part of the electoral equation. Thus, the gesture politics of Hindutva, many would say the BJP's true colors, have emerged ascendant with the attendant risks to secularism and tolerance.

DEMOCRACY AND HINDUTVA

The BJP holds power in twenty-one of twenty-nine states as of 2018, including the largest, most populated, and most industrialized states and those mostly richly endowed with mineral resources. It has campaigned on the need for rebooting the way government functions and by harping on religious issues and communalism. Previously Indian governments could hide behind the alibi of lacking a majority to explain away failures to deliver on promised policy reforms, but the BJP victory in 2014 removed that excuse, at least until it lost its simple majority in the lower house of parliament in mid-2018. During the 2019 national elections, deft messaging, news manipulation, and extensive advertising enabled the BJP to divert attention from the gap between its extensive promises and limited achievements. The BJP counters the faltering image of "can-doism" with scaremongering and the politics of hate. A BJP pollster resigned from the party in 2018 partly because of these tactics. He asserted that the "BJP is pushing the national discourse in a dark corner" and that "they've ingrained it into the minds of people that Hindus and Hinduism are in danger, and that Modi is the only option to save ourselves" (Singh 2018). This is precisely the card played in 2019 when the BJP, at a time it looked vulnerable, exploited heightened tensions with Pakistan to gain support and in the end won a landslide victory. This besieged Hindu khatre mein hai narrative is projected on "news channels that are owned by BJP leaders whose sole job is to debate Hindu-Muslim, National-Antinational, India-Pakistan and derail the public discourse from issues and logic into polarising emotions," a campaign strategy that hinged on revving up "pseudo nationalism." As such, Modi's BJP remains the torchbearer of Hindu chauvinism and relies heavily on ethnoreligious mobilization despite its grandstanding on policy. Showering rural Indians with toilets, bank accounts, Modicare, and other political gimmicks still take a backseat to hatemongering. The vote bank of primordial sentiments is a reliable constituency that reproaches India's secular, inclusive, and liberal identity but wins elections.

That is why the BJP signaled its intent prior to the 2019 national elections to build a Ram temple on the controversial Ayodhya site, a sop to the hardcore Hindutva cadre. Promises to build there have been made before, but this doesn't seem to diminish the appeal of fresh pledges.

Rapid economic growth has spawned a nationalistic hubris about prospects for wealth and power that have largely gone unrealized. Campaigns to promote the national brand embraced the slogan Incredible India, but it's impossible to sloganeer away the stark realities of widespread poverty, growing inequalities, and endemic corruption. The ambitious new health care program targeting rural poor dubbed Modicare faces the enormous challenge of an inadequate health care infrastructure to accommodate the sudden enrollment of 40 percent of the nation's population of 1.25 billion, especially given the paltry budget allocation. It is an ambitious undertaking that may deliver improved health care for the needy in coming decades, but for now it is a populist political ploy, offering some hope for India's neglected needy that lends itself to snappy campaign slogans in the politics of mass distraction. Modi has ridden the appetite for greatness and diverted attention from gathering disappointments while pushing liberals into a shrinking political space. On his watch, forced "reconversions" of Muslims and Christians occur with impunity while cow vigilantes run rampant, tapping into what Pankaj Mishra calls the "vengeful nativism" of a wounded civilization's sense of inadequacy, unhinged by dreams of aggrandizement (Mishra 2014). It is an exultant Hindutva that seeks enemies at home—Muslims and Christians—and abroad—Pakistan and China. Modi the statesman has done little to rein in such impulses.

In 2017 Modi appointed Yogi Adityanath, a Hindu monk and ardent nationalist, to be chief minister of Uttar Pradesh. Yogi is a firebrand implicated in rioting and anti-Islamic agitation. The BJP won the Uttar Pradesh elections handily, unseating the incumbent party, and so there was no urgent political need to appoint Yogi to head India's most populous state, one that has been beset by sectarian violence. But this appointment carried implications for national elections and shows to what extent Modi is prepared to play the saffron card of religious mobilization to win reelection, even if it comes at the expense of Modi-nomics and technocratic policy making. Yogi has led the campaign against cattle slaughter and poured fuel on the fires of communal violence, so his appointment appeared risky. He has not disappointed. The belief that power has a moderating influence on hardliners does not seem to apply in Yogi's case. In early 2018 his government changed the color of the Uttar Pradesh Haj Committee office's exterior wall to saffron. This committee is responsible for assisting Muslim pilgrims going on the haj to Mecca. The repainting of the wall from green and white signifying Islam was provocative because the color saffron is associated with the BJP and Hindutva and thus confronts Muslims with the ominous portents of ramped up

Chapter 2

majoritarian agitation. It is a gesture that resonates with political mischief
that extends well beyond the haj office. Saffron is now the color of choice for
curtains, microphones, furniture, and even top officials' clothing, government buildings, and schools.

Adityanath represents Modi's ardent side and religious convictions,
crossing the line between political activism and religious piety. He is a Hindustan zealot, the head priest of a temple, and founder of a militant Hindu
youth organization. Like Modi, he conflates national identity with religion,
asserting that India is a Hindu nation and is unapologetic about a record of
Muslim baiting and mobilizing followers for communal violence. His relations with the BJP old guard have been strained because he thinks their brand
of Hindutva is too tame. He is heir to a more vigorous and militant strain of
Hindutva, tracing his political lineage to those who in 1949 seized the controversial Babri Masjid in Ayodhya, Uttar Pradesh. Adityanath is a charismatic
campaigner and shores up the legitimacy of the BJP leadership among the
party faithful. Modi has toned down his rhetoric and repositioned the BJP as
the party of economic growth and prosperity, so Adityanath is a useful reminder of the BJP's core DNA. Having an independent power base in the
nation's most populous state gives him enormous influence in the party and a
degree of latitude other members don't enjoy. As chief minister he has centralized power and issued edicts that require civil servants to "volunteer" one
hundred hours of service to the Swachh Barat Mission and banned tobacco
and paan in government offices. He intensified the crackdown on slaughter-
houses and ordered the establishment of anti-Romeo squads aimed at curtailing premarital dalliances and so-called love jihad by Muslims seducing Hindu girls (see chapter 9). Back in 2005 he was implicated in the forced conversion of about 1,800 Christians to Hinduism, what he called a purification
drive. A 2011 documentary *Saffron War—Radicalization of
Hinduism* charged that he incited communal violence through hate speech.
His hatemongering and incendiary rhetoric are awkward for the BJP's quest
for respectability but arouse the party's base. When he threatens to kill one
hundred Muslims for every convert from Hinduism, the crowds cheer, and
when he promises, "if they take one Hindu girl, we will take 100 Muslim
girls," the response is rapturous. He desires to place Hindu deities in every
mosque and is a great admirer of President Donald Trump's travel ban targeting Muslims.

Adityanath embodies the BJP's electoral dilemmas and calculations. To
the extent that Modi plays solely the Hindutva identity card based on grievances and aggression, the base becomes more emboldened, causing turmoil
and thereby alienating swing voters. With good reason they question the
BJP's commitment to an inclusive state, communal harmony, and respect for
the rights of minorities and women in society. To the extent that he can
energize the Hindutva base and combine this with vikas, he and the BJP

stand to broaden their appeal. The trouble for the BJP is that by diluting its messaging to win over swing voters, it risks losing the ardent base, and it also needs to contend with caste-based politics that potentially divide the Hindu vote.

Modi has brewed a magic elixir of Hindutva and economic growth, cutting a bold figure on the international stage while trying to unleash the nation's economic potential through various reform measures aimed at lifting the deadening hand of bureaucracy. He projects a brash nationalism that appeals to national pride, but he has also raised hopes and expectations for improved living conditions that he has not met. Moreover, some significant policy miscues, such as the abrupt, poorly managed withdrawal of large-value banknotes in 2017, ostensibly to prevent money laundering and tax evasion, tarnished the brand and harmed the economic interests of many while reinforcing perceptions that he acts in favor of the wealthy and well-connected. It is also evident despite a fawning media that Modi is selling off assets at a discount to those well-connected vested interests. The blatant favoritism did not start with Modi, but under him has flourished while trick-le-down neoliberal economic policies have not benefitted the poor.

Caste-based politics are tricky. To the extent that Modi has unified Hin-dus behind Hindutva and vikas the BJP prospers, but it is vulnerable to caste-oriented politics that divide the Hindu bloc. The secular Congress Party at one time enjoyed success in nurturing vote banks among lower-caste groups and Muslims but fell on hard times due to a perception among voters that it was riven with corruption, nepotism, and incompetence. The BJP has been effective in riling up Hindus to emphasize what they have in common, with an appeal ranging from Bombay financiers to small businessmen and farmers and from Brahmins to Dalits. While Brahmins dominate the upper echelons of government, bureaucracy, and the media, the BJP boasts a Dalit president and OBC (Other Backward Class) prime minister, helping to soften its neo-liberal, pro-business stance and present it as the party of the common people and upward mobility.

In terms of electoral appeal there are no direct socioeconomic benefits associated with Hindutva as is the case with caste-based issues where parties pledge to help specific groups. Political leaders who make caste appeals promise educational opportunities and jobs through reservations, offer justice by promising protection from the powerful, and endow favored groups with power to bully others. The BJP's allure lies in leavening Hindutva with vikas, offering the prospects of an individual becoming rich and realizing personal ambitions through entrepreneurial success. The BJP's messaging is religious but also targets aspirational individuals with a pro-business mantra of deregulation and free markets. It promises to remove the shackles of the license raj, the legal and regulatory legacy of British colonial rule that is shorthand for red tape. The BJP also promises to remove the system of reservations for disadvantaged castes and to create an India based on merit and initiative. But these promises challenge the inclusive and tolerant identity enshrined in the Constitution. The pledges also don't acknowledge that the BJP has favored the vested interests of big business, showering them with bargain deals, subsidies, tax breaks, and loans based on privileged access. Waving the trident (Lord Shiva's weapon of choice) in one hand, Modi woos the hardcore and like a sorcerer uses the other to dish out backhanders and favors to the business elite who back him. The corruption, favoritism, and hatemongering are swaddled in saffron, providing a thin veneer of legitimacy.

Back in 1991, Ashish Nandy predicted a limited future for Hindutva, asserting that there is a fundamental contradiction between Hinduism and Hindutva (Nandy 1991). He observed, "Hindutva is the ideology of a part of the upper-caste, lower-middle class Indians, though it has now spread to large parts of the urban middle classes. The ideology is an attack on Hinduism." He argues that it fans resentments stemming from the broken promises of upward mobility, writing, "The minority consciousness that Hindutva protects survives on anger. It is the anger of Indians who have uprooted themselves from their traditions, seduced by the promises offered by the modernization of India, and who now feel abandoned. The process of seduction has included not only the promise of a good life but also the promise of a special political role for those having modern education and modern professional skills." Nandy concludes that the wellsprings of Hindutva are similar to Islamic fundamentalism and laments "the death of Hinduism in India will be celebrated by all votaries of Hindutva. For they have always been embarrassed and felt humiliated by Hinduism as it is. Hinduism, I repeat, is a faith and a way of life. Hindutva is an ideology for those whose Hinduism has worn off." With savage irony he adds, "Hindutva at this plane is Western imperialism's last frenzied kick at Hinduism. It is an ideology meant for the super-market of global mass culture where all religions are available in their consumable forms, neatly packaged for the buyers." Nandy saw in Hindu nationalism a "psychological defense against the encroaching forces of the market, the national security state, and the urban-industrial vision."

Nandy wrote this about Hindutva before the demolition of the Babri Mosque, before the BJP's ascension to national power in 1997, before the Gujarat pogrom in 2002, and before the Modi-mania that swept the country in 2014. This does not mean Nandy was wrong about Hindutva being an affront to Hinduism and an attack on it, but nobody anticipated how the BJP would evolve and manage to migrate from the religious fringe to the mainstream on the strength of its economic program, campaigning as the champion of good governance and asserting a populist Hindutva that has enabled it to spread power into states long dominated by Congress. In this makeover, it has been enormously helped by the hapless Congress Party, a party run into the ground as the Gandhi/Nehru family enterprise. It has become the discredited champion of secularism and liberalism and has come to represent what many voters feel is wrong with India. This inclusive and tolerant national identity still enjoys strong public support, but that potential has been squandered by an inept elite. Thus, the shift toward the BJP is only partly due to a surge in a Hindutva national identity, combined with populist posturing and a pro-business, pro-development agenda packaged and marketed like a product launch. Branding has been the key to the BJP's rise. Deploying traditional media assets and social media, it has ignited and shaped populist politics. In the marketplace of identity politics, Modi has adroitly tapped into the anger of the dispossessed, convinced business leaders and professionals that he is their man and seduced the masses with his saffron populism and development agenda. Conjuring itself as champion of both the aspirational and the reactionary, the BJP has instigated and won cultural wars on its own terms, promoting a modern, nationalist identity steeped in religion. It has been adept at the politics of outrage, quick to take umbrage, relying on fake news to push its line while overwhelming voices of dissent. It revels in the politics of confrontation and sectarianism, driving wedges through communities for political advantage. It hatemongers with political purpose, tapping into the anti-Muslim prejudices that it continually stokes. Reminders of who is the dangerous Other are omnipresent in BJP campaigning, invoking past wrongs and contemporary anxieties in a potent potion of communalism.

SAFFRON CULTURE

The BJP has triggered a surge of populism seeded with patronage and scaremongering to score remarkable gains in state elections far beyond the BJP's home pitch in northern India while consolidating control in the Hindutva heartland, the so-called saffron belt. Sometimes this is explained in terms of different historical experience. Mughal (Muslim) rule from the sixteenth to the eighteenth century left deeper scars on the collective consciousness in the north where Islamic influences and legacies are more profound, a readymade set of grievances for igniting outrage and tapping into the reservoirs of revenge lingering from this "humiliation." The Mughal influence on what is now called Indian culture is profound, ranging from language, culture, architecture, and art to food, social customs, values, and dress. This extensive influence antagonizes by its ubiquity, threatening an imagined Indian identity free of accretions and impurities. This helps explain the strange decision in 2017 by the Uttar Pradesh state tourist board to remove the Taj Mahal from its tourist brochure, a saffron backlash from the new BJP government because this breathtaking jewel of a mausoleum was commissioned in 1632 by Shah Jahan, the Mughal emperor. Given that it is one of India's best-known attractions, a World Heritage site that welcomes seven million visitors a year, it doesn't need promoting, but its removal does reveal an abiding anxiety and resentment that the glory belongs to India's Muslim heritage. In 2017 the court heard evidence from the Archaeological Survey of India (ASI) urging the judge to reject a petition by Hindu plaintiffs seeking permission to pray at the Taj Mahal. The ASI experts refuted their claims that the mausoleum was actually built on a temple constructed by Hindus dedicated to the deity Shiva before the Mughals repurposed the space. There has been an ongoing series of lawsuits along these lines filed by zealots despite the Supreme Court's precedent setting decision in 2000 against such claims.

The culture wars extend to Bollywood as well. The government deployed riot police around cinemas nationwide in 2018 because Hindutva zealots were offended by the film *Padmaavat*, sight unseen. But rumors about depictions of an interfaith romance involving a mythical thirteenth-century Hindu queen and an invading Muslim sultan were sufficient to get the hatemongers onto the streets. The buzz began during filming when the director was assaulted on the set—his hair was pulled—and reportedly this led to the deletion of some offending scenes. Violent mobs rampaged through several northern cities on the strength of salacious rumors of a love scene to block the release of the film, prompting clashes with security forces. The fairytale queen was immortalized in a sixteenth-century Sufi epic poem and is revered especially by Rajputs, a warrior caste. Karni Sena, a hardline Rajput Hindu organization, lead the protests, stoking a controversy that gained national visibility. Some BJP members of parliament joined the fray, capitalizing on the fury by pandering to this key constituency in the run up to state elections in their Rajastan homeland. A Gujarat state ban on the film was overturned by the Indian Supreme Court, arguing that free expression must be protected from threats and violence. All of this drama ensured a mediocre film enjoyed a decent but not spectacular run while breaking the overseas box office record for a Bollywood film's opening weekend. This manufactured spectacle and media feeding frenzy also revealed the extent of polarization and intolerance that prevails in Modi's India and also how culture wars are key battlegrounds for the manipulated politics of rage. In the end, Bollywood delivered what all the detractors craved, honoring the valor of Rajput warriors and the virtue of Rajput women as the queen committed self-immolation before the sultan could compromise her honor. Serving up hoary stereotypes of Muslims, viewers were treated to "an unhinged, barbaric Sultan, who is consumed with a ravenous libido for power and flesh. He unleashes an animal magnetism on screen with a scarred face, kohl-lined eyes and a greased torso. The scenes between him and Shahid (the Rajput King and husband of Padmaavat) are some of the most engrossing, as both flex their acting muscles at opposite ends of the moral spectrum" (Soans 2018). The caricature of Muslim-Rajput, bad-good disfigures Islam, exposing the political grandstanding as a venomous farce that looks like artful PR and serves as a garish metaphor for Modi-mania. The *New York Times* (Saltz 2018) dismissed the film as "something of a bore: a lavish 3-D pageant with the depth of a children's pop-up book," adding, "The movie's Muslims . . . eat dirty, fight dirty and follow the lead of a marauding brute who dishonors his own wife." Similarly the *Indian Express* (Gupta 2018) lampooned the cartoonish Sultan, "who bites into mounds of meat (serving well the prototype of the Muslim savage)" and mocks the "black-and-white delineation of the good Hindu and the bad Muslim (who could also, gasp, swing both ways)." Perhaps, according to the *Indian Express*, the real controversy raised in this extravaganza is "how do we deal with the fact of a woman being forced to jump into a pyre to save the 'honour' of her husband, and her people?"

IMPLICATIONS

Indeed, such are the awkward contradictions that expose the chicanery of Hindutva and its patriarchal values. In terms of national identity, Modi's majoritarianism has subverted the liberal, tolerant, and secular society he inherited (Mishra 2014; Deb 2016). Despite not delivering on his lavish 2014 campaign promises, voters in 2019 succumbed to what Pankaj Mishra refers to as the "moronic inferno" of Modi's swaggering Hindutva and jingoist saber rattling (Mishra 2019). India's online population has doubled since 2014, creating new opportunities for Team Modi to circulate fake news, "enhanced by India's troll-dominated social media as well as cravenly sycophantic newspapers and television channels" (Mishra 2019). Pratap Bhanu Mehta, one of India's foremost public intellectuals, offers a devastating assessment, describing India under the BJP as the Age of Cretinism, pointing to the debasement of democratic discourse and the glowering assertion of majoritarian privilege backed by goon squads. He asserts that the prevailing morality is defined by the need to seek new enemies and laments that "the danger is not the existence of cretinism; it is its routinisation and elevation: a stunting of our moral imagination and the supplanting of it with an aggressive coarseness" (Mehta 2018b). Sadly so.

Chapter Three

Christianity in Asia

In Asia, Christianity is often associated with the spread of European imperialism from the fifteenth century and played an important role in the ensuing political, socioeconomic, and cultural oppression. Some believers assert that Thomas the Apostle initially introduced Christianity after he landed in Kerala, India, in 52 AD, although scholarly consensus dates the early spread of Christianity from the sixth century AD. Subsequently, the propagation of Christianity sanctified imperial expansion in the name of God, transforming colonized societies while also influencing Europeans in multiple ways. Christianity is also seen as a force of secularization, spreading the principle of the separation of Church and state, a concept at odds with prevailing precepts in Asia in which these roles and institutions were deeply intertwined as they had been in Europe not long before the imperial encounter.

Mistreatment of missionaries was common and sometimes invoked as an excuse to impose colonial rule such as France in Vietnam in the nineteenth century. Elsewhere, the Japanese Tokugawa government (1603–1868) was especially hostile to Christianity, slaughtering and torturing thousands of converts and banning the religion, seeing it as a threat to the shogunate's monopoly of power. Martin Scorcese's film *Silence* (2015), based on the 1966 novel by Endo Shusaku, a Roman Catholic, depicts these grim realities in seventeenth-century Japan. The Portuguese were the first Christians to arrive in Japan, but their aggressive proselytizing provoked a sharp backlash. The authorities were more comfortable with the Calvinist Dutch who were more interested in trade than saving souls and allowed the Dutch East India Company to operate in a small island enclave called Dejima adjacent to Nagasaki.

Despite such early resistance, Christianity has sunk deep roots in Asia, gaining considerable momentum from the sixteenth century due to the intensifying advance of European imperialism and sustained missionary activities. In Asia, it only became a majority religion in the Philippines, a legacy of Spanish colonial rule. Ironically, US president William McKinley, apparently unaware that the Spanish had been converting Filipinos for more than three centuries, justified annexing the islands following victory in the Spanish-American War (1898) based on praying to God for inspiration. Apparently, the answer to his prayers was an American divine mission to "uplift and civilize and Christianize them, and by God's grace do the very best we could by them, as our fellow-men for whom Christ also died."

Missionaries gathered converts while the Christian officials of the colonial state propagated secularization, drawing on prevailing European norms. Confident in their civilizing mission, Europeans did not question the wisdom of promoting secularization, seeing it as the sine qua non of modernization and progress. Something that had happened organically and incrementally over centuries in Europe was abruptly imposed in colonized territories. Across Asia leaders encompassed both spiritual and temporal roles, and this was crucial to symbolic ritual, legitimacy, and the theater of the state. They were a divine presence tasked with the spiritual well-being of those in the realm. Whether the Mughal emperors of India, the rajahs and sultans in the Malay world, the Buddhist monarchies in Burma, Siam, and Vietnam, or Chinese emperors exercising the mandate of heaven, the court was infused and tasked with nurturing the spiritual. Subjugation by Europeans undermined and bisected this encompassing totality. Christianity was seen as a trojan horse by Muslim clerics who believed that there can be no separation of religion and state under Islam. They believed that Islamic law, shariah, must be the foundation of any government and thus religion is intrinsic to the state. The role of indigenous religious authorities, however, was suddenly circumscribed and marginalized from affairs of state. Shariah lost its expansive role as the foundation of governance and was relegated to a minor supporting role in managing family affairs. The colonial idea was based on the state maintaining a neutral role in religious matters and thereby promoting freedom of religion and pluralism, again encroaching on notions of an all-encompassing oneness that prevailed among Muslims, Hindus, and Buddhists.

In the following sections I explore the contemporary politics and impact of Christianity and how it has shaped identities around the region. Since the 1980s, the number of Christians in Asia has expanded enormously, driven mostly by the dynamism of Pentecostalism. Where Christianity has spread most successfully, it has gradually indigenized the clergy and adapted to local cultural norms and practices. Vernacularization, the translation of the Bible and conducting mass in local languages, has also furthered expansion by enhancing accessibility and empowering indigenous interpretations of Christian principles and practices. Christianity has also provided institutional and spiritual support for activist movements promoting socioeconomic and political reform, thus running afoul of authorities and the privileged.

LIBERATION THEOLOGY

The Philippines and Timor Leste (East Timor) are Christian majority nations where religion has played a key political role related to efforts by priests to address problems of poverty and injustice. The Second Vatican Council (Vatican II) convened by Pope John XXIII concluded in 1965 and inter alia gave birth to liberation theology, the concept that the Church should not confine itself to spreading the word and saving souls but also work to alleviate suffering in this world. This avowed commitment to social justice, human rights, and poverty endowed the clergy with a new mission more relevant to the issues they confronted and felt passionate about in the wider context of upheaval and challenges to authority in the 1960s. It was also a belated effort to overcome the Church's lingering Eurocentrism, a significant impediment to making the Church globally and locally relevant.

Overall, liberation theology and political engagement by priests and nuns are associated with developments in Latin America from the 1970s. This engagement often involved messaging and actions sympathetic to, or supportive of, Marxist guerrilla groups active in the region. Activist clergy shared the common cause of battling extensive human rights abuses under right-wing military regimes protecting the economic interests of entrenched oligarchies at the expense of the impoverished and marginalized. This social activism provoked a sharp negative reaction from Pope John Paul II (1978–2005), who drew on his own experience of fighting left-wing oppression under communist rule in Poland. Cardinal Joseph Ratzinger, who later became Pope Benedict XVI (2005–2013), served as Pope John Paul's point man on Church doctrine. He declared that liberation theology was unacceptable and penned a detailed critique in 1984 issued by the Vatican. In that critique, however, he did concede that "the seizure of the vast majority of the wealth by an oligarchy of owners bereft of social consciousness, the practical absence or the shortcomings of a rule of law, military dictators making a mockery of elementary human rights, the corruption of certain powerful officials, the savage practices of some foreign capital interests constitute factors which nourish a passion for revolt among those who thus consider themselves the powerless victims of a new colonialism in the technological, financial, monetary, or economic order" (Ratzinger 1984). He added, however, that "theologies of liberation" erred in conflating "the 'poor' of the Scripture and the 'proletariat' of Marx," arguing that class conflict was not consistent with the Church's creed or a basis of salvation. Cardinal Ratzinger went on to condemn liberation theology and the mixing of politics and religion as a threat to the Church and summoned prominent activist priests to Rome and censured them.

For many priests, however, Vatican II clearly sanctioned their political engagement, and this often meant working with left-wing labor unions and political groups. They believed that the Church had for too long sided with the ruling conservative elite and forces of repression and exploitation and should return to what they believed was the message of Jesus and the Gospels, serving as a voice for the poor and oppressed. Archbishop Oscar Romero in El Salvador was the most prominent Latin American proponent of liberation theology, defying Pope John Paul II. He bravely condemned the right-wing death squads that operated with impunity, leading to his murder in 1980 while celebrating mass, but in the following decades the Vatican blocked recognizing his sacrifice and martyrdom, only beatifying him in 2015 under Pope Francis, the first pontiff from outside Europe and the first Jesuit. Pope Francis hails from Argentina and thus understands the right-wing barbarism that Romero confronted with fearlessness. Finally, in 2018 he was canonized as a saint for giving his life for his faith.

The notion of the Church serving as an instrument of the oligarchy resonated in the Philippines, a country with massive disparities, extensive landlessness, and abject poverty. About 85 percent of Filipinos are Roman Catholic. Inspired by liberation theology, many younger priests committed themselves to the war on poverty, spreading the word of God while also trying to alleviate the prevailing misery. From the 1970s, the communist New People's Army (NPA) was engaged in an active insurgency against the central government and an oligarchic system that favored the wealthy elite. Many priests were sympathetic with the NPA's struggle and supported them in various ways, seeing the revolution as consistent with the duty of priests to protect the poor against injustice. These priests established Christians for National Liberation and played an active role in the National Democratic Front organized by the Philippine Communist Party. Their clandestine activities sparked a rift in the Church and censure by the authoritarian government of President Ferdinand Marcos, who was waging a counterinsurgency and declared a state of emergency in 1972 suspending civil liberties. Marcos complained that these activist priests were using Church-run public health programs to give propaganda lectures favoring the NPA, in effect sanctifying the insurgency. Back in 1986, *New York Times* correspondent Fox Butterfield observed, "The problem has been particularly troublesome for the church because as the Marcos Government became more corrupt and oppressive and the living standard of many Filipinos fell, large numbers of priests, nuns and senior church leaders, including Jaime Cardinal Sin, the Archbishop of Manila, became more active in the opposition" (Butterfield 1986). During this period, priests were arrested and some even executed. Conservative Church authorities were sensitive to government criticism and criticized their colleagues for being naïve, charging that they had been duped and manipulated by the NPA. Perhaps, but given their moral authority in local areas, the clergy had considerable political influence and believed it was imperative to put the Church on the right side of history and end its complicity with the forces of oppression.

Under Marcos, the government shut down suspect programs and media outlets linked to the Church to prevent it disseminating anti-government views. The Church was divided and had to walk a tightrope between what the government would tolerate and what many of its priests saw as their pastoral duty. One priest in Negros asserted, "It used to be the church said killing could only be justified in self-defense. But in our case, where there is what we call structural injustice, we believe you don't have to wait for the other person to kill you first before you kill them" (Butterfield 1986).

Cardinal Jaime Sin, the influential and charismatic Archbishop of Manila, played a key role in the ouster of President Marcos and subsequently President Joseph Estrada, signifying that the Church saw that it had a political role and would act on behalf of the impoverished majority that needed more than spiritual succor. Sin inspired tens of millions of Catholics over three turbulent decades before stepping down in 2003. He shepherded the country through the trials of martial law under a corrupt and brutal dictatorship and later oversaw the transition to the restoration of democracy in the 1980s. He was an unabashed champion of the poor and outspoken in his criticisms of Marcos and others who abused their powers. Bravely, he condemned the imposition of martial law in 1972 and in 1974 denounced torture by the military. When Marcos lifted martial law in 1981, Sin kept up the pressure and his remarks became more pointed in directly condemning Marcos and his family's greed.

In 1983 Marcos's rival Senator Benigno Aquino was gunned down as he deplaned after returning from exile to campaign for the president's ouster. Subsequently, Sin supported his widow's presidential election campaign. Marcos tried to limit Corazon Aquino's access to the media, but Sin gave regular addresses on Catholic radio in which he rallied support for her. Marcos tried to rig the election and ignore the results, but Sin urged the people to thwart the aging strongman, invoking the moral authority of the Church to sanction their efforts to ensure free and fair elections and respect for the outcome. Aquino won election in 1986, but only after the Church weighed in against Marcos's efforts to rig the ballot counting in his favor. Marcos sought to remain in power, but Sin called the people out into the streets to defend rebel military commanders who broke with Marcos by refusing to shoot demonstrators. This demonstration of people power, in which the clergy played a visibly prominent role, toppled Marcos. The Church made protecting human rights its business. Cardinal Sin was aware that Pope John Paul II was opposed to the clergy getting involved in politics but noted that while the pontiff was lecturing others not to get involved, he also played a key role in Poland's political transition. Again in 2001, Sin orchestrated street protests to topple President Estrada, accusing him of betraying the poor who elected him and for being unfaithful to his wife. After Estrada's ouster, however, there was a backlash against the cardinal's political machinations that led to his retirement.

President Rodrigo Duterte has had a confrontational relationship with the Church since his 2016 election, reacting harshly to criticisms about thousands of extra-judicial killings conducted by state security forces in his controversial war on drugs. He has repeatedly denounced Church leaders in earthy language, vaguely threatening to kill critics who invoke God or religion and has even called God stupid. This did not go down well with the nation's nearly eighty-five million Roman Catholics, many of whom express intense devotional fervor. He asserts that there must be a separation of Church and state and that the Church is not respecting that division by actively playing a political role. He has also sought to undermine the moral authority of the Church by drawing attention to corruption and sexual abuse scandals involving priests and longstanding cover-ups. The president maintains he was sexually abused as a child by a priest, so the antagonism is personal and longstanding.

Poverty, according to Duterte, is the Church's fault because it opposes birth control. This opposition, Duterte contends, has undermined government efforts to stem explosive population growth and mitigate poverty. When he was mayor of Davao City, he actively promoted family planning and has long been an outspoken critic of Church policies that he believes saddle poor parents with too many children and contribute to the archipelago's social ills. He has also voiced sympathy for same-sex marriage and legalizing divorce, both red lines for the Church. In 2017 he ignored a Supreme Court temporary restraining order and issued an executive order to implement the controversial Responsible Parenthood and Reproductive Health Act of 2012 designed to promote sex education and contraception.

The Church may have waning influence in politics and daily life, but Duterte's profane broadsides against Church hypocrisy have generated a unifying backlash. No doubt he is mindful of how the Church brought down other leaders it opposed, but he has not shied from confrontation and is unapologetic about his tirades. Although piety overall may be on decline, Duterte's sacrilegious attacks are rousing even those who are less than devout but still honor a Catholic national identity.

The Church has warmed to liberation theology and Pope Francis has "unblocked" the beatification of Bishop Romero and has made it Church policy to oppose the death penalty and promote protection of human rights, suggesting that unlike during the 1980s, the Vatican strongly supports the Church in the Philippines. But unlike in the 1980s under Marcos, Duterte is a populist leader admired for his no-nonsense approach to governing. Polls suggest his war on drugs has considerable public support despite police abuses and summary executions of drug suspects. It remains to be seen what his legacy will be, but it is certain that the Church will remain a powerful institution across the archipelago and that religion will remain a powerful element of national identity.

TIMOR LESTE

In Timor Leste priests were involved in the struggle for independence from Indonesian rule (1975–1999). Following the 1974 military overthrow of the authoritarian government in Lisbon, all of Portugal's colonies gained independence. During the colonial era, the Church was a powerful institutional actor aligned with the state in the island's subjugation. As McGregor notes, "Church and state worked together . . . the Colonial Act of 1930 giving representation to the Church, along with Portuguese plantation owners, the army and colonial administrators, on local legislative councils. This influence was further formalised in 1940 when Portugal signed the Concordat and Missionary Agreements with the Vatican allowing the Church to operate freely and pursue its 'civilising mission'" (McGregor, Skeaff, and Bevan 2012, 1131).

The exodus of priests in February 1942 after the Japanese took control during World War II reinforced local perceptions about the alien nature of the Church. After World War II, however, the Church played a critical role in spreading Lusophone culture and Christianity among the animist communities in the hilly hinterlands. The clergy had more influence than colonial administrators in these rural areas and became closely involved in the communities where they preached. As a result, they served as interlocuters between the state and the local people, trying to soften the burdens imposed by corvée labor and the poll tax. Toward the end of the colonial era, however, some progressive Jesuits had become advocates of limited social and political change. By the 1970s about one-third of the island's population of 660,000 were practicing Catholics and there had been a significant indigenization of the clergy, with Timorese constituting more than half of all priests. Yet the Church was still seen as an alien presence as the language of liturgy remained almost entirely Portuguese or Latin, while adherence to animist rituals remained robust in local communities. However, the Church in Timor Leste belatedly became a critic of the dictatorships of Salazar (1932–1968) and Caetano (1968–1974) using its privileged position to publish a progressive Jesuit weekly despite strict censorship laws. This included regular instruction in Tetum, the local language, and essays by locals who went on to become leaders of the independence movement.

The 1974 pro-democracy "Carnation Revolution" in Portugal ended dictatorship and colonial rule, creating space for the formation of political parties in independent Timor Leste. However, at the end of 1975 the Indonesian military invaded, beginning a brutal occupation that lasted until 1999, one that claimed over 100,000 lives during a prolonged insurgency (Nevins 2005). In terms of identity politics, this was a decisive era with the Church providing institutional support for the independence movement, lobbying overseas, and keeping the struggle on the global radar screen, while also alleviating the baleful effects of Indonesian repression. The Church became the voice of the people against the powers that be, speaking truth to power. However, the Church initially had reservations about the Marxist revolutionaries in Fretelin, the political arm of the insurgency. Dom Joaquim Ribeiro, the last Portuguese Bishop of Dili, was critical of the young leftist activist returnees from Lisbon, warning parishioners not to be taken in by them. But he rapidly changed his mind soon after the Indonesian invasion, condemning widespread atrocities and abuses by soldiers against the local population. The arrival of the Indonesians sparked an exodus of Portuguese from Timor Leste, accelerating an indigenization of the clergy that was an important factor in the Church repositioning itself vis-à-vis state power. It was at this time that the spirit of Vatican II spread on the island as Bishop Ximenes Belo emphasized the concept of the "People's Church." He believed "that 'the Catholic faith of the people is a kind of symbol to unite them, it is a way of expressing the fact that they are Timorese'" (as quoted in Archer 1995, 127).

Since the mid-1970s, the Timorese Catholic Church has reinvented itself as the defender of the people's interests and became intrinsic to their national identity (Carey 1999). The violence and turmoil caused by the Indonesian occupation drove the Church closer to the people. Seeking refuge, priests fled to mountainous areas and shared the suffering felt by everyone. Timor Leste was cut off from the world, forcing the Church to embrace a new mission, one that aligned more closely to Timorese nationalist aspirations. Priests also witnessed firsthand the positive efforts of leftist insurgents in Falinitil, the armed wing of Fretelin, providing social services, education, and agricultural expertise. This experience forged strong bonds between the Church and guerilla leader Xanana Gusmao, who subsequently served as president and prime minister in independent Timor Leste. This solidarity was reinforced by the sense of betrayal felt by priests who waited in vain for their brethren in Indonesia and the Vatican to condemn Indonesian human rights violations. This institutional silence overseas and sense of abandonment made it clear to Timorese priests that they must focus on doing what they could for their followers and the nationalist movement of independence.

Indonesian law requires that everyone choose a religious affiliation among sanctioned faiths, causing the Christian-identified Timorese population to jump from one-third to 95 percent during the occupation. This helped

Christianity become a symbol of unity and solidarity in the struggle for national self-determination. Indonesian efforts to curb religious expression among these new "converts" and soldiers' harassment of priests and desecration of sacred symbols only deepened faith over the twenty-four years of occupation.

The Vatican intervened in 1981, recalling the Timorese apostolic administrator at Jakarta's behest because he had condemned the military's massacre of five hundred Timorese. Archbishop Belo, his replacement, did not prove as compliant as those who appointed him anticipated. He became the voice of the oppressed, condemning widespread atrocities and calling for a peaceful act of self-determination to end the Indonesian occupation. He steadfastly maintained this defiant position, denouncing widespread torture and drawing attention to Indonesian efforts to assimilate the Timorese by eradicating Tetum culture and "Indonesianizing" them, a policy he termed ethnocide. He lobbied the UN for a plebiscite from 1989, drawing the ire of Jakarta, but survived three assassination attempts. By putting his life on the line in taking a principled stand against the Indonesian occupation, Belo strengthened the solidarity between the Church and Timorese nationalism. The Church also won the respect and loyalty of the people by looking after the families of resistance fighters, feeding and housing them while educating their children. By easing its stance on animism, the Church embraced the religiosity manifested in local ancestor worship and other belief systems. As the Indonesians cracked down on Tetum totems as exhibiting support for the outlawed Fretelin resistance, the Church iconography was absorbed by locals into their rituals (Carey 1999, 84). Sacred Tetum sites were consecrated with statues of Christ and crosses, a symbolic syncretism between traditional religions and Christianity. Priests also celebrated masses in Tetum, as the Portuguese language had been banned and Indonesian was problematic, making the liturgy more accessible to the masses. This was also a crucial choice in nurturing a Timorese Christian nationalist identity. Religion evolved from a marker of social status to a symbol of political defiance and cultural expression. As Peter Carey argues, drawing parallels with Ireland and Poland, "individual experience of suffering and oppression in East Timor shaped a deep personal faith . . . [with] a national dimension" (Carey 1999, 86).

The Church became a space for dissent and protest and offered safe haven to the displaced and those at risk, especially women because rape was a widely deployed weapon of war in occupied Timor Leste. Unlike most international NGOs, Catholic organizations were allowed to operate and provide essential food and social services that provided tangible benefits. The Church also carefully documented and publicized human rights abuses, even as the Vatican kept silent. Subsequently, the Vatican was accused of ignoring the pleas for help from Timor Leste because it "was concerned to protect the Catholic Church in Muslim Indonesia, maintained public silence on the matter and discouraged others from promoting the issue" (Kingston 2006a). Belo, however, often invoked Vatican II to justify the Church's overt political role, arguing it obliged him to speak out against injustice. His words were broadly disseminated internationally through Catholic networks, shining a harsh light on Indonesia that mobilized activism and diplomacy against the occupation.

Pope John Paul II visited Timor Leste in 1989, bringing global attention to the plight of the Timorese and providing them moral support. Over the previous fourteen years the island had been sealed off under Indonesian occupation. The papal visit was a reminder that they were not alone and that Indonesia had not gotten away with its illegal seizure. It was a delicate balancing act for the pontiff as he did not want to offend the Indonesian hosts or make life difficult for Indonesia's sizeable Christian minority, but he also could not ignore the widespread suffering. He spoke out vaguely against all abuses without singling out Indonesia while leaving no doubt about who he was condemning to the tens of thousands who attended his open-air mass. With the international media looking on, young Timorese scuffled with security forces, giving the world a glimpse of the grim realities. When Pope John Paul II died in 2005, there were three days of official mourning in Timor Leste, acknowledging a pope who had made a difference by belatedly aligning the Vatican with the island's activist clergy.

The Church thus positioned itself as central to Timorese identity and culture while serving as the only local institution able to provide a global voice advocating for human rights and justice. Bishop Belo won the 1996 Nobel Peace Prize (shared with Jose Ramos Horta, then special representative of the Fretelin resistance movement) in recognition of his steadfast advocacy for human rights and bold criticism of the Indonesian occupation. President Suharto visited in 1996 for the first time in eight years, soon after Bishop Belo was awarded the Nobel Peace Prize. At a press conference following his meeting with Suharto, Bishop Belo remarked how strange it was that the president had not congratulated him on his Nobel Prize because he was the first Indonesian citizen to ever win this distinction.

In secular New Order Indonesia, human rights accolades for an activist Catholic cleric critical of Jakarta's occupation was somewhat awkward in terms of nationalism and identity politics, perhaps because the Roman Catholic Church played a catalytic role in Timor Leste's struggle for independence and eventual attainment of nationhood. The Church opted to take a political stand and not stand above the fray. It inspired the resistance fighters, the older generation of political leaders, and younger student activists at home while supporting diplomatic efforts internationally that bore fruit with the decision by Suharto's successor, B. J. Habibie, to hold a referendum on independence in 1999. In that referendum voter turnout was an astronomical 99 percent with 78 percent voting in favor of independence.

Since then the Church has remained a dynamic force in civil society. For example, after gaining independence there was a widespread yearning for justice. Those who had suffered under Indonesian rule wanted to hold perpetrators accountable. The Church backed such efforts and the holding of hearings around the nation where people could tell their stories and lodge their accusations. This transitional justice process known by the Portuguese acronym CAVR lead to publication of a final report titled *Chega!* (Enough!) in 2005 detailing the findings of the investigation team and suggesting remedies, including prosecution of high-level perpetrators by an international tribunal under the auspices of the United Nations. This never happened. At that time, President Xanana Gusmao and his foreign minister Jose Ramos Horta both told me that the need for reconciliation with Indonesia was essential for Timor Leste and that pursuing justice against high-ranking military officers would derail that process and pose a risk to democratization in Indonesia (Kingston 2006b). They also doubted there was any support in the international community for funding such a tribunal, especially after the 9/11 terrorist attack on the United States. Indonesia suddenly became a valued moderate Islamic ally and the United States was not inclined to back such an undertaking. There was an ad hoc tribunal in Jakarta that led to some convictions of lower-ranking officers, but all were overturned on appeal.

For Gusmao and Horta, the essential task facing the nation was to overcome the past rather than remaining fixated on the miseries endured and to consolidate democratization, good governance, and the rule of law at home. Gusmao was also concerned by the dangers of awakening dormant antagonisms and sparking a descent into renewed chaos if the government prosecuted perpetrators still living in Timor Leste. However, the desire for justice had been awakened by the public hearings, and the continued presence of collaborators and wrongdoers in the communities where they had committed crimes generated significant local tensions.

The local Church sided with victims and civil society organizations in criticizing the government's reluctance to pursue justice. Father Martinho Gusmao, then director of the Justice and Peace Commission in the Catholic diocese of Bacau, told me, "There is no need for reconciliation between Indonesian and Timorese people. We have no problems. The problem is that Indonesian security forces committed crimes here and they need to be held accountable. This is also part of the process of building democracy here. We need to see that nobody is above the law, and the victims in our country need to see that the victimizers—whoever they are—are prosecuted" (interview December 2005).

Now the Church was intervening politically against the independence fighters and activists who were running the government. It did not help that Prime Minister Mari Alkatiri (2002–2006), a committed socialist and Muslim, had a difficult relationship with the Church. He moved to end compulsory religion classes at school and provoked a firestorm of civil unrest that culminated in his resignation. To the extent that the Church exerted its moral authority and criticized government policies, relations soured. In response, President Horta initiated a policy of funneling large sums of money to the Church beginning in 2007, a mending of fences that some critics suggest has undermined the Church's ability to freely act as the social conscience of the nation, especially because of a lack of transparency and accountability regarding the large subsidies earmarked for anti-gang violence programs and building renovation projects.

In 2008 the government also passed legislation granting special recognition of the Church's role as the nation's moral arbiter, enabling it to promote traditional Catholic values consistent with the views of Pope Benedict XVI, the former critic of liberation theology. Instead of social justice and political freedom, the Church now prioritizes traditional gender relations, banning contraception and abortion, criminalizing prostitution, and promoting family values. This retreat from Bishop Belo's progressive political agenda includes curbing the activities of Christian-affiliated development organizations that don't toe the new line. This shift in the Church's stance in favor of the establishment is one of the new realities of postindependence Timor Leste. Despite the sacrifices made during the independence struggle, the Church's influence, and attendance at mass, is receding. Younger Timorese are now focused on the struggle to find jobs. The government subsidies have sustained the organization's institutional capacity while imposing fetters on what it can do. Yet it operates the best schools in the country, giving it a chance to influence the values of rising generations. And unlike many international NGOs that depend on short-term cycles of project funding, Church-based organizations have staying power and unrivaled institutional support reaching the remotest corners of the country where it has a grassroots presence. It is also important to bear in mind that the Church in Timor Leste is not monolithic and not all the clergy are enthusiastic about the conservative turn, and many like Father Gusmao still embrace progressive values.

The Timor Leste case is especially interesting because it is a unique case of a repressive government transforming a minority religious identity into an oppositional majority subnationalist identity that then became a core pillar of national identity after independence. Under Portuguese rule the Church had relatively few converts as most locals practiced animism, but then after being occupied by Indonesia, Timorese were forced to choose an affiliation with a government-sanctioned religion. Most chose Christianity, becoming a majority in the province but still a minority in Muslim Indonesia under a secular government. Religion was not the main driving force of Fretelin's secular nationalist independence movement against Indonesian rule but was a powerful source of solidarity. In the postindependence era Christians became the nation's majority, a legacy of Indonesian rule. The absence of Indonesian repression, however, has led to a decline in piety and religious influence in society. Even so Timorese identity is woven from the crucible of occupation and nationalist resistance with strands of religion and Tetum culture, a striking example of hybrid ethnoreligious nationalism.

INDONESIA

Chega! accused the Vatican of not doing enough to support Catholics in Timor Leste out of fears that this might generate a backlash in Indonesia. Indonesia recognizes six religions (Islam, Christian [Protestant], Catholic, Hinduism, Buddhism, and Confucianism) with a significant Muslim majority (87 percent), but the overall Christian community (10 percent) of Catholics and various Protestant denominations numbers about twenty-five million, making it the fourth largest in Asia after the Philippines, India, and China. There are about seven million Catholics, making it one of Indonesia's largest Christian denominations, and it operates an extensive network of schools, hospitals, and media that confer fairly significant institutional influence. The largest concentrations of Christians are in the eastern islands of Indonesia where in some provinces they constitute the majority. In Java, the most populous island in the archipelago, they are concentrated mostly in cities in Central and Eastern Java; in Jakarta, the capital, about 12 percent of the population is Christian.

The national motto of Indonesia is "Unity in Diversity," a daunting aspiration in this sprawling archipelago of more than fifteen thousand islands, three hundred ethnic groups, and seven hundred languages. The Portuguese first introduced Christianity, but the Dutch Reformed Church dominated during the Dutch colonial era from the seventeenth century until the end of World War II. Since then Christian identity has spread because the Suharto New Order (1967–1998) government required everyone to list a religious affiliation as a means of eradicating communism.

The mass killings in 1965–1966 that claimed several hundred thousand lives are officially blamed on a failed coup by the Indonesian Communist Party (PKI) that allegedly was launched at the behest of Beijing. Scholarly consensus dismisses this narrative and it is clear that most of the killing targeting suspected communists (and unwanted others) was committed by Islamic youth organizations and paramilitary groups acting with the support of the Indonesian military. In the aftermath, conversion to Christianity was common among Indonesia's vulnerable Chinese minority. Because China was blamed for orchestrating the coup, vigilante reprisals took a toll while the government banned the use of the Chinese language. This Othering made it essential for ethnic Chinese to recalibrate their identity, and many sought to avoid persecution and gain protection in joining Christian congregations.

This may not have obscured their perceived identity (Chinese usually have a comparatively fair complexion) but did comply with government demands and connected them with the international community and associated networks of support and influence. They thus have entwined identities as Christian Chinese Indonesians. It is important to add that there are significant numbers of non-Chinese Christians from various other ethnic minorities such as Bataks in Sumatra, Dayaks in Kalimantan, and Papuans in West Papua.

Variations among Chinese and the broad range of Christian denominations caution against monolithic interpretations and illustrate how identity shifts over time and is shaped by context. Although differences are fading, ethnic Chinese identity remains somewhat divided between totok (earlier migrants who have maintained a stronger Chinese identity) and peranakan (more assimilated) and to some extent this difference maps onto Christian congregations. However, anti-Chinese discrimination and periodic violent pogroms targeting them during the New Order pressured all ethnic Chinese to maintain a low profile and blend in. After Suharto's ouster in 1998, various discriminatory measures against ethnic Chinese have been incrementally lifted, but anxieties linger. The military is charged with preserving political stability but has demonstrated great capacity for mayhem as occurred under Special Forces Chief Prabowo Subianto (Suharto's former son-in-law and presidential candidate in 2014 and 2019) when he orchestrated anti-Chinese riots in 1998. This has become part of the ethnic Chinese identity, one that draws on a history of persecution and leaves many concerned about lingering prejudice.

In twenty-first-century Indonesia, as a consequence of Arabization, religious tolerance has declined with radical Islamic groups targeting Christians as a menace to Indonesia's identity as a Muslim nation (see chapter 4). At the turn of the century anti-Christian violence spread to the outer islands in Sulawesi and the Moluccas while several churches in cities across Java were bombed on Christmas Eve in 2000. Subsequently, there have been numerous burnings and bombings targeting Christians. In May 2018, for example, three churches of different denominations in Surabaya, Indonesia's second largest city, were attacked within a short time span by a family of suicide bombers, including a nine-year-old child. These incidents were linked to the Islamic State and an incident in west Java just days beforehand that left five policemen and four terrorist suspects dead. Hundreds of Indonesians fought for IS in Syria and upon returning home a number have been involved in terrorist actions. A local IS-affiliated organization Jamaah Ansharut Daulah was implicated in these 2018 attacks and a previous church bombing in 2016 in Samarinda, East Kalimantan. Earlier that year, a jihadist returnee from Syria attacked a priest in Medan Sumatra while he was celebrating mass. Clearly, Christianity in Indonesia has been thrust into the crosshairs of global jihad and a more extremist Islamic identity among a tiny minority of Indonesians.

Revivalist mega-churches attract mostly middle-class urbanites. Pentecostal-Charismatic denominations are growing fastest as the fervent style, spiritual immediacy, and upbeat messaging about materialism appeal to a younger, upwardly mobile demographic. As Chong notes, "Religious ecstasy and its sensual satisfaction has nudged Pentecostalism more closely to mass consumption and popular culture than any other Christian denomination" (Chong 2018, 3). Moreover, as we see elsewhere in Asia, Pentecostalism's animated spiritualism communicates in local idiom and offers a reassuring resemblance to folk religions. The prosperity gospel also veers away from the usual Christian condemnation of inequality and injustice, making it more palatable to professionals who have embraced the opportunities of capitalism. As Chong explains, "Questions continue about whether the prosperity gospels appeal to the aspiring middle class because it offers hope for upward mobility, or to the wealthy because it serves as divine legitimacy of their social status" (Chong 2018, 8).

Indonesia's Pentecostal-Charismatic congregations are well funded and have circumvented government restrictions on Church building permits by erecting multipurpose convention halls that can accommodate up to twenty thousand attendees. Yet while the rapid rise of China has spurred ethnic pride, pressure on ethnic Chinese to demonstrate their "Indonesianess" persists, making it prudent to cloak Chinese identity with Christianity. (Hoon 2016).

Elaborating on the rise of religious nationalism among Pentecostal mega-churches, Chong argues that "patriotism and nationalism are often fused with theology, not only to lay bare the nation's divine destiny, but also to mobilize for political activism. Indeed, the postcolonial character of many Southeast Asian societies, as well as the acknowledged absence of good governance in these societies, rampant corruption, and high crime rates, draws religion and nationalism into logical conflation" (Chong 2018, 12).

JAPAN AND SOUTH KOREA

The fractious relationship between these frenemies draws on the brutal era of Japanese colonial subjugation and the collective trauma of cultural degradation that ensued. During the colonial era, Christianity in Korea "provided an 'oppositional ideology' for resisting the Japanese government. As a result, many Christians became deeply involved in the independence movement and refused to cooperate with the Japanese government in countless ways. Throughout this difficult period the affirmation of Christianity became a way for Koreans to assert their national identity over and against the culture of their Japanese colonizers" (Mullins 1998, 171). Thus, for Koreans a Christian identity was an anticolonial identity linked to the struggle for dignity and independence. Faith was an act of resistance against the imperial power. Due to this legacy of missionary activity empowering Koreans in their darkest hour, nearly one-third of South Koreans are Christian. Although foreign Protestant missionaries were apolitical, they had an ambivalent relationship with Japanese colonial authorities, having to make institutional concessions to Tokyo's demands, especially during the 1930s era of Japanese militarism and hyper-nationalism. As in Japan, Korean Christians were required to pay obeisance to the emperor at Shinto shrines. At the time, the emperor was the head priest of State Shinto and the expanding war in Asia 1931–1945 was officially proclaimed a holy war waged in his name. Some Christians viewed the acceptance of Japanese demands to pay respects at Shinto shrines tantamount to apostasy, but Church authorities decided that the risks of noncompliance would entail serious consequences and justified the concession as a necessary evil.

Christianity has never been popular in Japan, partly because it was banned for two centuries from the Tokugawa era (1602–1868) until 1873. Moreover, as Mullins points out, "Christianity necessarily encountered a negative reaction in Japan since its interpreters emphasize exclusive belief in one transcendent god" (Mullins 1998, 168). This insistence generated a cultural discontinuity with the pre-1946 deified emperor and Japanese syncretic religiosity, a conflict that limited its appeal as evident in the tiny number of Japanese Christians, just 1 percent of the entire population. Roman Catholics are the largest denomination with about a half million members, about one-third of all Christians in Japan. Unlike in other Asian nations, Evangelicals and Pentecostals have not had much success, perhaps because Japanese are usually less effusive in their conduct. As Mullins argues, "Japanese Christians tend to be less demonstrative about their faith . . . [and] there is still a degree of stigma attached to Christianity. An individual's cultural identity as a 'Japanese' seems to be threatened by membership in a Christian church" (Mullins 1998, 172).

Despite considerable commitments of time and resources, including indigenization of the clergy, Christianity is marginalized because it is seen as too deviant from local traditions even if adherents are disproportionately represented in the elite. The US occupation (1945–1952) disestablished State Shinto and rescinded the wartime Religious Bodies Control Law, but this did not redound to the advantage of Christianity. Unlike in Korea under the Japanese, Christianity was associated with the occupying, alien power and thus represented the antithesis of an oppositional ideology. Christianity went from being the religion of the enemy in wartime Japan to the religion of the subjugating power. Even if most Japanese were happy about the end of a military-dominated government that had recklessly led them into a war that devastated Japan, welcomed US initiated demilitarization and democratization, and were keen about many aspects of American culture, this allure did not extend to Christianity because it remained alien to Japanese spiritual norms and needs and incompatible with Japanese cultural integrity. Where Christianity has boomed is in wedding ceremonies, as couples seek to tie the knot in pseudo-Christian style in which "priests" and celebrants are hired for the occasion, for them a job rather than a vocation. There is an adage in Japan that one is born Shinto, marries Christian, and dies Buddhist, associating religion with life stages as opposed to unadulterated votive commitment.

In recent decades the general problem of an aging and shrinking population has hit Japan's diminutive Christian congregations hard. In this context, the post-1990 surge of migration from Brazil has been a lifeline. To address labor shortages the government eased working visa restrictions for overseas migrants of Japanese ancestry, and in the early 2000s nearly 350,000 resided in Japan, mostly from Brazil. Many of these nikkeijin were Christian as were most Filipinos, tens of thousands of whom worked as entertainers in bars and nightclubs. Japanese churches responded by offering social services, counseling, vernacular masses, and a community open to outsiders in a relatively closed society. As Japan further opens the door to limited migration on a temporary basis, various denominations may benefit from an infusion of new blood, but Christianity will remain on the margins of Japanese society and identity.

In contrast, since the colonial era ended in 1945, Christianity has boomed in South Korea, and as of 2010, 29 percent of citizens are Christian, exceeding the 23 percent who identify as Buddhist; 46 percent have no religious affiliation (Pew 2014). There are over sixty thousand churches of various denominations nationwide, and despite a strong Buddhist tradition, South Korea is perhaps the most Christianized non-Western developed nation in the world. As we see in other nations, Christianity has had a positive influence on education and health care. The Korean War (1950–1953) left the peninsula devastated and, in this context, churches played an important relief role, tapping into international networks to raise funding to provide a range of social services.

The mainline Catholic and Christian Churches shaped national identity and political outcomes by aiming their oppositional ideology at a succession of authoritarian Cold War–era governments. They provided moral support for the pro-democracy movement just as they did for the pro-independence movement in the colonial era, contesting the arc of repression that spanned eight decades under successive Japanese and Korean authoritarian governments. Four of South Korea's six presidents since the blossoming of democracy in the 1990s have been Christian: Kim Young Sam (Presbyterian), Nobel Peace laureate Kim Dae Jung (Catholic), Lee Myung Bak (Presbyterian), and currently President Moon Jae-in (Catholic). Both Kims drew on their Christian principles to rally the public in support of democracy and human rights. Clearly, Christianity is embedded in South Korea's culture of dissent and protest, most recently playing a prominent role in the Candlelight Revolution that toppled President Park Geun-hye and led to her impeachment in 2017.

One of the most striking developments in Korean Christianity is the flowering of evangelical and Pentecostalist denominations. As in China, India, and Indonesia, they have their Billy Grahams who have popularized Christianity through revivalist preaching and made for media mass spectacles. For example, Paul Yonggi Cho established the Full Gospel Central Church in 1958, a humble Pentecostal tent church that has grown into an empire. Now renamed the Yoido Full Gospel Church, it boasts over eight hundred thousand members, one of the largest congregations in the world. As elsewhere in Asia, the Pentecostal Three-Fold Blessing proclaiming that health and wealth are as important as spiritual salvation has proven immensely appealing. So too are the promises of healing and shamanistic miracles that have seen the Church fully engage with local spiritual and mystical traditions.

The "shaman-ization" of South Korean Pentecostal denominations has been a key to its indigenization, an embrace emulated by its rivals. Mullins observes, "The point here is that Pentecostal churches tend to 'empower' members through instruction and gifts of the spirit. Whereas established religions and churches tend to monopolize spiritual power in the hands of an elite clergy, Pentecostal churches and New Religions provide opportunities for rapid upward spiritual mobility" (Mullins 1998, 180). Although charismatic or shamanistic powers are not always restricted to the founder or pastor, there are limits to this "democratization of magic"; dynamic preachers own the magic wand in the spectacle of collective ritual and draw the crowds.

Yoido island in central Seoul is ground zero for a weekly Sunday spiritual extravaganza that plays to a packed house of twelve thousand parishioners for each of the seven services, not to mention three masses every weekday morning. It proclaims that Jesus wants to make you rich and illnesses can be cured if one has sufficient faith. The healing is taken care of by the Holy Spirit, notably including the curing of Pastor Cho's tuberculosis. The charismatic preaching by Pastor Cho and his designated successor Lee Younghoon fires up the ecstatic crowds. As one observer put it, "He sings and he prays, and the crowd loses their shit. They break out in tongues, they sing Hallelujah, they raise their arms, they cry, they collapse. And then Lee delivers his gentle sermon, of wayward homosexuals returning to God's fold, of the Lord curing cancer, of the importance of giving thanks and salvation, in this world and the next. He literally thumps the Bible" (Hazzan 2016). And then they pass around red velvet bags to collect offerings from the assembled believers. The Church is unapologetic about promises of prosperity through the grace of Jesus Christ, offering hope to many who have none and redemption for all believers. The focus "on individual prosperity is similar to the shamans of old that Koreans have believed in for millennia. Shamans heal the sick by driving out evil spirits and pray for material reward and prosperity" (Hazzan 2016). The conviction of Pastor Cho and his son for embezzling some $12 million in 2002 has not diminished his influence, although he is officially retired.

As Hazzan notes, "Mega-churches are popular with Koreans, who live in a very group-centered, organization-heavy culture. You are defined by what you are a part of, and it's good to be part of something big. Of the 20 biggest churches in the world, Korea has five of them" (Hazzan 2016). Unlike Japan, a demonstrative religiosity is in the Korean comfort zone.

INDIA

Christianity faces different challenges in contemporary India due to the rise of Hindutva (Hindu chauvinism) since the late 1980s and the current political dominance of the Bharatiya Janata Party (BJP) and its toxic agenda of Hindu nationalism that has seriously undermined the tolerant secularism enshrined in the Constitution (see chapter 2). In a massive subcontinent with over a billion people from various ethnic groups, practicing different religions and speaking an array of languages, pluralism has been a necessity. However, this pragmatism has faded under the onslaught of communalism across the board. As the writer V. S. Naipaul observed in *India: A Million Mutinies*, "When I was there last year India was full of this rage. There had been a general awakening. But everyone awakened first to his own group or community; every group thought itself unique in its awakening; and every group sought to separate its rage from the rage of other groups" (1990, 490).

There is considerable debate as to why this happened but far less disagreement about the negative consequences for India's minorities. The secular principles that once guided intercommunal relations have ebbed due to recurrent violence (Varshney 2002). A menacing and aggrieved Hindutva has propelled the BJP into power and like any political party it panders to its core constituencies. This development has mainstreamed the saffron fringe of bigots, chauvinists, and nativists who are now empowered to pursue their prejudices with impunity, denigrating and lashing out against the Other. Mostly the narrative of Othering targets the 15 percent of the population that is Muslim, but Christians are also fair game. They represent some 6 percent of the population and number some eighty million believers. Due to their relatively small numbers, however, they are not important enough in terms of electoral politics to merit the institutionalized riot system that targets Muslims (Brass 2003b). Yet in twenty-first-century India there has been an intensification of violence directed toward Christian communities (Sahoo 2018).

The various Hindu nationalist organizations collectively referred to as the Sangh Parivar oppose the intensification of Christian missionary activity because it is seen to subvert their idealized Hindu nation. In 1999 Pope John Paul II visited India and spoke of "a great harvest of faith," tantamount to a declaration of war for the Sangh Parivar, heralding more aggressive policies of conversion and a plot to reimpose Western supremacy. As "Christiano-phobia" gained momentum in twenty-first-century India, it sparked intensified persecution of missionaries and converts (Shortt 2012). The number and scale of attacks has risen considerably since the late 1990s. Between 1964 and 1996 there were only thirty-eight minor incidents while in 2015 alone there were 365 major attacks on Christians involving eight thousand people (Sahoo 2018, 5). Identity politics has heated up in India, partly driven by competing conversion efforts by Hindus and Christians, while in this "age of anger" (Mishra 2017) those inclined to resort to violence feel empowered by the BJP government's support for the hatemongering that permeates public discourse.

Conversion to Christianity is also perceived as an assault on the Hindu caste system. Missionaries have long targeted the iniquities and inequalities of caste to promote conversion. As Sahoo argues, "Conversion thus acted as a form of protest against the hegemonic caste system and provided freedom and opportunity to low-caste and tribal communities" (Sahoo 2018, 8). Ironically, however, "instead of eradicating caste, Christianity has incorporated/accommodated caste into its social structure, which continues to persist and govern the life world of Indian Christians" (Sahoo 2018, 8). This has nullified what some believe is the main "sales point" of Christianity because converts remain acutely aware of caste distinctions and maintain them in their religious observance. Sangh Parivar activists, however, find little solace in this failing and accuse missionaries of duping and coercing Dalits (untouchable caste) and Adivasis (tribals) to convert, taking advantage of their poverty and marginalization while undermining the unity of the Hindu nation. Hindutva advocates insist that conversion is a Christian conspiracy that exploits their susceptibility and demands reconversion of what they view as lapsed Hindus. In this context, Hindu xenophobes and those intent on orchestrating these constructed grievances for political benefit often portray converts as subversive agents of foreign interests. However, some Hindu organizations with state support have been engaged in development efforts and improving education and health care for these disadvantaged communities in a bid to reduce the appeal of Pentecostalism and curb conversion (Sahoo 2018, 163). For Hindus this rivalry is driven by vote bank politics, the notion that "saffronizing" Adivasis will nurture a loyal electoral constituency for the BJP. These efforts provide context for understanding the politics of Pentecostal conversion and what Sahoo calls "the production of anti-Christian violence in India" (2018, 163).

For many of these Dalits and Adivasis, however, conversion makes sense as a way to escape the most onerous aspects of their caste-driven fates. The fact that caste hierarchies of power and privilege are transferred to their new churches is nothing compared to the grueling indignities of their lives as practicing Hindus. For someone born into the shit-carrying Bhangi caste, for example, lingering petty discrimination pales in significance to a nasty task enforced and sanctified by the Hindu community. Frykenberg observes, "for ages beyond memory, each of their women, whether a small girl or an aged widow, is obliged to go into latrines and to scrape up by hand all defecations or faeces of the previous night and, after depositing this into a handmade reed basket, carry this load away on her head" (Frykenberg 2008, 469). For them, conversion opens the doors to education and upward mobility that the caste system firmly denies them (Frykenberg 2008, 469). It is striking that more than a million Bhangis out of twenty million Dalits among the more than 160 million Indians living in Uttar Pradesh have converted to Christianity in what is called the "cow belt" stretching across northern India where the politics of Hindutva are most menacing as vigilantes attack Muslims for slaughtering cows and other invented offenses.

Hindutva proponents are profoundly skeptical about an individual's capacity for the inner transformation necessary for religious conversion. They attribute conversion to baser motives or coercion rather than a spiritual awakening. Hinduism posits that people are born to be what they are and thus conversion interferes with the natural "cosmic order" of society (Frykenberg 2008, 478). Perhaps, but in common practice people make all sorts of compromises and concessions that seem to subvert rigid dogmas in their ritual observance and everyday spiritual practice. Conversion does not necessarily entail a complete discontinuity in a convert's lived experience and spiritual sensibilities. While scholars and priests may be confounded or exasperated, the converted appear untroubled by what others may view as inconsistencies and sacrilege.

Relatedly, Henn (2014) draws on fieldwork in Goa where he observed that a strong Hindu identity does not impede syncretism, a concept that encompasses the mélange of rituals, traditions, cultures, and religions that is evident in religious observance everywhere. But he also warns against misinterpreting what syncretism signifies. Although a fluid syncretic practice blends identities and blurs boundaries between religions and communities through shared practice, ritual, and sacred sites, it does not necessarily connote tolerance or indeed a weakening of identity (Henn 2014, 180).

India is not the only society in which there is an "oscillating identity," meaning that people don different identities depending on the situation. In the Indian context, this means there are many "secret" converts who officially maintain their Dalit or Adivasi status in order to maintain the advantages pertaining thereto such as reserved jobs or welfare benefits (Sahoo 2018, 9).

Apparently, these crypto-Christians are numerous because converts are concentrated in the communities that stand to lose status linked state-provided perquisites by making their conversion public (Frykenberg 2008, 458). Because Dalit and Adivasi converts constitute 50 percent and 20 percent, respectively, of all Christians in India, the disincentives for declaring suggest the Christian demographic may be greatly underestimated (Sahoo 2018, 6).

Pentecostals have been at the forefront of conversion efforts, earning the enmity of Hindutva activists and mainline Christian denominations. Hindu nationalists do not distinguish between Christian denominations and thus all are tarred with the same brush. Pentecostalists are thus blamed by mainline denominations for irresponsibly inciting anti-Christian violence and prejudice by their aggressive actions. This is probably true, but for Pentecostals such arguments are the language of appeasement and capitulation. As Sahoo observes, "Pentecostals equate Catholicism with Hinduism and do not see much difference between the two. For them, Catholics have distorted the basic tenets of Christianity and moved away from the theological doctrine of the end of the world. They are no longer working for saving souls" (2018, 161). Preaching the gospel and making converts is a calling, they argue, not something that can be abandoned because it makes others unhappy.

Based on extensive fieldwork in Rajastan among Adivasis, Sahoo concludes that "Pentecostalism has helped Adivasis to convert to 'modernities'" (2018, 158). In concentrating on the poor and marginalized, Pentecostal missionaries are providing "a new identity to tribal men and women, making them feel empowered and self-assured. The tribal converts consider this newly acquired identity superior to that of their Hindu counterparts" (158). He adds, "conversion has made them free of bondage, ignorance and discrimination. For the converts, the Pentecostal church has provided an egalitarian space" (158). In addition, "the concept of miracle healing has immensely helped the Pentecostals in a context where the indigenous shamanic system as well as city-based modern healthcare systems have been exploitative and the state has failed to provide basic health care services in the villages" (159). The Pentecostals' strict moral code has also improved family life as the "inner worldly ascetisim" has lessened domestic violence and brought economic improvements.

In terms of identity politics, Christian conversions serve to reinforce a swaggering and vengeful Hindutva identity. Concerns over conversion appear overwrought and exaggerated, translating into a fractious political issue that the BJP is exploiting to energize their base. For these Hindutva activists, conversion is a call to arms, adding credence to conspiracy theories and justifying violent retribution. In a nod to this passionate base, in 2017 the BJP passed the controversial and ironically named Religious Freedom Bill banning religious conversion.

CHINA

The Chinese Communist Party (CCP) assumed power in 1949 and since then has provided very limited space for religion. Before that Christian missionaries had been active in proselytizing and Pentecostalism was relatively popular due its hostility to hierarchy and "rationalistic" Christianity and perhaps more importantly its "emphasis on the supernatural was in sync with Chinese folk religion . . . [offering] spiritual power to everyone regardless of status or achievements" (Anderson 2017, 346). Owing to the powerful tide of anti-Western sentiments that prevailed at the time, many churches cut overseas ties and offered what they presented as "true biblical teachings based upon apostolic principles" (346). Subsequently, missionaries were expelled from Mao's China, but the pre-1949 proselytization efforts help contextualize the phenomenal growth in the past two decades. Christianity has never been formally banned but maintained a low profile with small congregations until the 1990s.

Even before 1949, reformers across the political spectrum assailed the "backwardness" of Chinese folk religions, asserting that they were a significant barrier to modernization. There was a consensus that "Chinese religion was a social ill that needed to be radically reformed or destroyed in order to save China" (Johnson 2017, 25). This antipathy toward deeply engrained traditions and customs was ubiquitous among the intelligentsia and political activists and extended toward all religions, foreshadowing the anti-Christian hostility during the Mao era from 1949 to 1976.

During the Cultural Revolution (1966–1976) zealots engaged in a rampage of destruction, targeting all places of worship and humiliating priests and nuns. From 1950, an estimated five hundred thousand Christians were killed, about half during the Cultural Revolution, while countless more were imprisoned, especially members of underground churches (Anderson 2017, 349). Following Mao's death, the CCP acknowledged some errors in dealing with the "religious question" and in 1982 "rehabilitated" religion and issued a directive known as Document 19 barring coercive measures. This directive, Johnson argues, is "the foundation of China's religious revival" (Johnson 2017, 28).

In contrast to the ongoing Protestant boom, Catholicism plays a minor role in China. It's estimated ten to fifteen million followers constitute less than 1 percent of the population. The main reasons for the Church's relative weakness are its ties to the Vatican and the failure to indigenize the clergy before 1949. Beijing severed ties with the Vatican, seeing it as a rival for people's loyalty, and expelled foreign missionaries. This meant that the Catholic community was decapitated and came under the sway of government functionaries. The Chinese government established the Patriotic Catholic Association in 1957 to manage the Church but has also tolerated an underground Church that remains loyal to the Vatican.

The Vatican and China have engaged in sustained negotiations, but the main sticking point is whether the former will relinquish the power of appointing bishops and cardinals. China is seen as important to the future of Catholicism and Beijing is pressing its advantage. Under Pope Francis, the Holy See recognized seven government-appointed bishops, something that has been anathema to Rome, and has signaled it is prepared to withdraw recognition of Taiwan. It also appears that the Vatican will bow to Beijing's wishes to retire loyal bishops that it had approved and replace them with government appointees. It is unclear what these concessions will beget and what impact they will have on Chinese Catholics, but some may take a dim view of such kowtowing. It appears that the CCP trumps God in setting the rules, and the Vatican is prepared to sacrifice quite a bit in order to build its market share. For those who have risked practicing their faith underground, these significant policy shifts might smack of betrayal. In terms of Catholic identity politics, some may draw the conclusion that religion is being run more like a business than a sacred calling, although others might be more forgiving about pragmatic concessions that might help strengthen the Church presence and give it more room to maneuver. Certainly, the faithful have endured worse.

There are an estimated fifty to eighty million Protestants of various stripes in China, including some twenty million in government-run churches, and it is the most rapidly expanding religion there. It is not altogether surprising that China's rapid growth and transformed lifestyles have generated widespread anomie and spurred individuals to seek something beyond the prevailing creed of Mammon. This surge in religiosity is also propelled by urbanization and upward mobility as converts search for meaning in their uprooted lives and an ethical way of living in a moral vacuum. In a materialistic society riven with corruption they seek something scrupulously incorruptible. For Chinese seeking an upright and high-minded life, ersatz versions of global religions recognized by the state won't do as they want the real thing, and thus the young and well educated are gravitating toward Evangelical and Pentecostal revivalist congregations. These are not officially recognized by the state and thus all the more appealing even if they operate in a gray zone of vulnerability at the sufferance of authorities.

Until the twenty-first century the two main centers of Chinese Christianity were the city of Wenzhou and Henan, an inland rural province. Ian Johnson notes that "they were uniquely Chinese forms of Christianity: Wenzhou was home to family-run businesses whose employees often belonged to a Church sponsored by the company boss, while in Henan charismatic leaders ran rural churches that often opposed the government and sometimes violently clashed with it" (2017, 364). According to Johnson, these two models are ebbing in influence. The Wenzhou paternalistic family-run business model is fading in favor of modern-style firms while urbanization is sapping the population of Henan. Moreover, growing awareness of global Christian norms has reduced the appeal of China's statist versions. Johnson observes, "people seek global norms, not local forms of their faith" (364). They seek to tap into modern trends and thus flock to the new dynamic Churches that have sprung up in cities where the economy and population has grown considerably in a short time. Many are deracinated from supportive communities from whence they migrated and find reassurance in their faith and congregations. In a society navigating profound upheaval, people are seeking the grid of rules and the bonds of group that religion can provide. In a time of mass deception, they need trustworthy fellow seekers and believers who share their anxieties and aspirations. The quest for spirituality is also a search for something people can believe in. Moreover, in Christianity they can find repertoires of contention and sanctified concepts for a critique of the current political order. Cultivating oneself doesn't mean ignoring the grim realities that abound but can also be a springboard for hope and a vision of change; proper conduct in the Confucian tradition is something that emanates from the individual and family to the collective sphere. Although China's Christianity is not a call to arms, it does offer salient messages about the social ills Chinese are confronting and offers a code of conduct that nurtures civic virtue. It is striking that many of China's now incarcerated activist human rights lawyers are Christian while Taiwan's post-1987 democratization also drew on religious precepts and faith-based organizations (Madsen 2007). Such examples suggest that the religious perspective influences not only how people should act but also expectations about how governments should govern.

Repression is the Chinese state's default response as it circumscribes what faith-based organizations are allowed to do. In the case of the Falun Gong spiritual movement, in 1999 the state banned it, incarcerated followers, and systematically eradicated it. This seeming overreaction to what was an apolitical group dedicated to promoting meditation, breathing, and stretching exercises drawing on Chinese tradition reflects a collective paranoia in the ruling elite about how independent movements could undermine their grip on power by subverting from within. Perhaps a moral philosophy centered on the tenets of truthfulness, compassion, and forbearance was awkward for the Party.

Paradoxically, the crackdown on Falun Gong may have helped create space for other religious movements as the state appears to now think it is better to accommodate religious sentiments and carefully monitor them rather than cope with the unpredictable consequences of driving them underground (Johnson 2017, 32). Currently faith-based organizations are pegged as auxiliary service providers allowed to assist where they are needed, such as disaster relief and poverty alleviation, but barred from anything smacking of political or social reform. Repression and harassment, however, feed a sense of persecution that reinforces Christian identity because it is a narrative that has long defined the lives of the faithful. But to understand the contemporary boom in Chinese Christianity it is important to look beyond such narratives because they are but one aspect of the appeal.

In the context of repression and relentless monitoring, accommodation of state needs is a strategic response to create political space for religious practice (Koesel 2017). Thus, fulsome patriotic displays are common in religious life involving gestures that reassure the state of members' loyalty. These gestures are calculated to address suspicions that Christian Churches are subversive forces acting at the behest of foreign powers. In contemporary China there is no overstating the insistence on displaying patriotism in all walks of life even if the words and gestures are perfunctory. State policy regarding the patriotic duty of religion is laid out in Document 19 issued in 1982. This directive titled *The Basic Viewpoint and Policy on the Religious Affairs during the Socialist Period of Our Country* encourages religious leaders to "love their motherland" and "support the socialist path." The authorities insist that religion must "play a positive role in social harmony" and for "believers to walk the road of patriotism." In practice this means socializing religious groups to be loyal citizens. Religious actors understand that espousing patriotism is essential for gaining a degree of tolerance, especially for nonregistered denominations. In China, all religions operate "in a restrictive political context where the Chinese state sets the parameters on religious freedom, and religious life is tolerated so long as it aligns with the interests of those in power" (Koesel 2017, 242).

Unrecognized Evangelical and Pentecostal churches operate under close scrutiny in a hostile environment and are subject to raids and destruction of their churches. Pastors and preachers are often placed under house arrest and sometimes sent to political reeducation camps. Thus, emphasizing nationalist identities and patriotic loyalty is a necessary survival strategy for these church leaders and a means to secure a fragile legitimacy in a climate of pressure and uncertainty. Often referred to as "unregistered house churches," some of these congregations have over one million members and extensive networks. About 75 percent of these house churches are Pentecostal (Koesel 2017, 245). It is hard to come by reliable statistics, but there may be as many as eighty million Pentecostals and Charismatics and they are the fastest expanding segment of the Christian faith, representing "some of the largest and most robust forms of associational life operating outside of the state and its institutions" (245). This is precisely what makes them a threat to the state and why they must prominently display their patriotic devotion and embrace Chinese nationalism. They also must contend with other mainstream Protestants denouncing them as religious cults of fanatics.

The prosperity doctrine of Pentecostalism sanctifying and encouraging the accumulation of wealth has a strong appeal. This creed resonates with contemporary China's materialistic zeal and confers a purifying redemption on such endeavors. Paradoxically, the greed and acquisitiveness that underpin corruption and moral decay are also propelling a religiosity that seeks absolution for getting rich (Koesel 2017, 249). And these marginalized and harassed Churches, facing one of the most hostile operating environments for religion on the globe, embrace and pray for their oppressors and pledge fealty to an antagonistic state. This nationalistic identity layered with religious devotion is also projected on pastors' social media as they seek to counter assertions that they are subversive cultists. In disaster relief and poverty alleviation activities they seek to convince the state they are reliable contributors to social harmony, downplaying religious identity in favor of a positive civic-minded identity. As Christian outsiders, community outreach activities are a means of embedding in society and as Koesel argues, "Patriotism is a language that resonates with those in power and sends the message that these churches are not threats, but valuable and contributing members of society" (253). Patriotic displays serve various tactical functions simultaneously, enabling their congregations to project a socially acceptable identity while reducing vulnerability to state repression by crafting a politically more palatable identity. They are illegal organizations so to reassure followers they need to project an identity they can live with that doesn't put them in harm's way. Thus churches, in navigating this hostile operating environment, are mindful of the needs and concerns of parishioners and authorities and message accordingly. While at one level patriotism may appear to be just empty slogans to placate the state, by conflating patriotic duty with religious observance, pastors can energize their followers and strengthen internal loyalty.

Faith, values, and the search for answers to universal questions and doubts "are returning to the center of a national discussion over how to organize life" (Johnson 2017, 16). China's growing prosperity has raised living standards remarkably in a generation, but having "made it," many of these beneficiaries yearn for more and seek meaning and spirituality in a deeply secular society awash in materialism. Many feel lost and are desperate for a moral compass to order and organize their lives. The "religion" of communist ideology has been replaced by a triumphalist and sanctimonious nationalism that dwells on China's century of humiliation and the need to settle scores. While this narrative clearly has a strong appeal, resolutely reinforced by government propaganda, it does not have spiritual or redemptive dimensions that address some of the basic transcendent questions in modern society: Why are we here? What is the purpose of life? How should I live? How can I make sense of the injustice and suffering that prevails? The Ten Commandments offer a guide on how to live and what to do and not do if one wants to be saved and lead an exemplary life. It is a moral code that resonates in a society infused with Confucianism, an elaborate code of conduct for many who are reinventing themselves and want to know how one should live and what one should do. Mass also provides elaborate ritual in a culture that values performative acts, especially by charismatic preachers who understand the anxieties and hopes that draw the congregation. Moreover, the Pentecostal messages of forgiveness for past transgressions, sanctifying wealth and promising salvation offer much that is desired by acquisitive urban migrants navigating a precarious world of inconstancy who find little allure in the dogma of Party ideology.

Pentecostalism emphasizes the power of the Holy Spirit to radically transform and rehabilitate lives of believers. This promise of renewal and rebirth resonates with patriotic practice, as devotion and duty become mutually reinforcing. In terms of identity this spiritual nationalism is "part of a redemptive process to overcome victimization and suffering inflicted by a secularized modernity" (Johnson 2017, 254). Members are not challenging authority or insisting on democratization, instead cultivating an image of productive and virtuous patriots. In that sense it represents a prudent risk management strategy in the context of a nation cracking down on religion. It is unclear, however, whether these concessions to power politics may undermine the moral authority of these Churches and if they will suffice should the Party face challenges in maintaining its grip on power and look for scapegoats. But for now, wrapping religion in the flag of Chinese nationalism has been an enormously successful strategy for spreading the word, building networks, and expanding congregations, perhaps with unanticipated consequences. For now, this layering and blending of identities seems eminently sensible to pastors, their congregations, and the authorities. Looking beyond this pragmatic accommodation, however, can the state also be awakened and reborn? Not if the Party can help it.

Chapter Four

Arabization and Islam in Asia

Over the past few decades, a process of Arabization has influenced the practice of Islam in Asia, spreading a more devout and less tolerant creed that nurtures fundamentalism and militancy. The suicide bombings by Islamic extremists in churches and hotels in Sri Lanka on Easter 2019 are a tragic example of the consequences. Saudi Arabian financing for mosque building and educational programs has promoted a profound shift in the role of Islam in society and national identities across the region. Five times every day Muslims pray in the direction of Mecca and see it as their duty to perform the pilgrimage to Mecca; thus, many Sunnis view Saudi-style Islam as the gold standard of religious practice because it is the homeland of Islam.

Saudi financial power based on the surge in oil prices since the mid-1970s has promoted a resurgence of reformist Islam often referred to as Wahhabism or Salafism, spreading a puritan piety among Muslims in societies in which pious religious observance has not been the norm. There are marked affinities between Salafism and Wahhabism, sects demanding a return to the uncontaminated practices of early Islam, austere discipline, renunciation of Western ways, and striving for personal purity. Followers are often young and disillusioned, "lost souls" searching for discipline and commitment in their lives who want to make a difference and value sacrifice. They also enjoy a sense of community based on a common creed, outlook, lifestyle, and appearance. Through ascetic discipline followers nurture their spiritual purity and in some cases resort to violence as a purifying act to demonstrate their faith and commitment.

Over the centuries Islamic religious practice in Asia has incorporated local customs, superstitions, and other faiths and philosophies. This syncretism has long been a source of tension and inspiration for religious renewal and reform but is condemned as an adulteration of the true faith by reformists. Contesting faith and practice fuels identity wars that carry religious and political implications that shape national identities. The battle between traditionalists and reformers focuses on Islamic practice and proper conduct that refracts fundamental nationalist concerns about "who we are" and, more importantly perhaps, "who we are not." Clashes over the "true" Islam and the role of Islam in society and government tap into existing political divisions over national identity in Muslim majority nations.

In the transitions from colonial rule to independence in Asia, nationalist leaders established independent states that drew on established secular modes in the West, emulating in this crucial respect the political system that once subjugated them. This lingering legacy of secularism has been contested in nations with Muslim majority populations because Islam does not recognize a firm boundary between the sacred and matters of the state. For many Muslims it is an article of faith that shariah (Islamic law) should be the law of the land and achieving that a sacrosanct mission. Moderate Muslims who accept the secular state and non-Muslims are both viewed as opponents by fundamentalist Muslims. Some even view democracy as antithetical to an Islamic state. Arabization has put wind into the sails of these fundamentalists as they challenge secularism. Some advocates work through dakwah (preaching and outreach), while for those who are less patient and more militant, jihad (holy war) beckons, sanctifying violent extremism as a force for purification. For the angry and disenfranchised, for those suffering from the envy and frustrated longings of ressentiment, the catharsis of violence and destruction in the name of Allah consecrates barbarous actions with sanctimonious motives (Mishra 2017). Terrorist actions are thus rationalized, the elusive end justifying the gory means.

Arabization has polarized the Islamic word in Asia, fanning the flames of sectarianism, bigotry, hate, intolerance, and terrorism. The contemporary Salafist wave has strongly influenced religious practice and mainstreamed Islamic reformism, but in threatening national unity and peace it has also generated a backlash by secular nationalists and the institutions of the state they have nurtured since independence. Thus, the battles over religion are also political battles over temporal power and national identity.

Oxford historian Faisal Devji believes that the pivot of Islam will shift inevitably toward Asia, where most Muslims live and where wealth is expanding. He also believes that Saudi Arabia is compromising its role as the religion's homeland due to a more aggressive foreign policy under a new leader, Crown Prince Mohammed bin Salman. Prince Mohammed is also seeking to promote secularism at home at the expense of clerics and clans while retaining a tight authoritarian grip. Devji believes that "the project to make Saudi Arabia a politically rather than religiously defined state is likely to demolish the century old vision of an Islamic geography, which has always been premised upon Arabia constituting its depoliticized center" (Devji

2018). Perhaps over time, but in the meantime Arabization in Asia has considerable momentum due to Saudi financing. In 2009, Wikileaks released a memo by former US secretary of state Hillary Clinton stating, "Donors in Saudi Arabia constitute the most significant source of funding to Sunni terrorist groups worldwide . . . a critical financial support base for al-Qaeda, and other terrorist groups" (Wikileaks 2009). This funding has sowed the seeds of political extremism in Europe, the Middle East, and Asia.

Islamic fundamentalism is a global movement but not monolithic. It is an umbrella term that encompasses a range of beliefs and practices that seek to reinstate Islam as central to believers' identity and actions. For reformers it involves a return to the unadulterated origins of the religion and eradication of corrupting non-Islamic practices, customs, and interpretations. For traditionalists it means more devout observance and gestures of piety. This return to fundamentals aims to revive Islam and heighten religious observance by focusing on literal interpretations of the primary sources: the Quran and the Sunnah. At the same time, for at least some adherents, contemporary fundamentalism reopens the window of ijtihad (independent reasoning) in interpreting what that original intent was; the hadiths (interpretative commentaries) have long been the source for understanding Islam, Muhammad, and the Quran. This awakening aims to reinvigorate the ummah (community of believers) by reintroducing a purified Islam closer to what it is thought the prophet Muhammad intended. The term "fundamentalism" is controversial for Muslims committed to this agenda of purification and revival because nonbelievers use it in a sweeping manner that is alarmist, condescending, pejorative, and misleading. Alternative designations of this purifying, more assertive trend include radical Islam, puritanical Islam, or Islamic revivalism.

The terminology issue may seem excessive, but there are important political connotations in public discourse, especially after the 9/11 terrorist destruction of the World Trade Center in New York City. Since then Islamic fundamentalism has been conflated with extremism, fanaticism, terrorism, and anti-Americanism. Militant Muslims are frequently referred to as Islamists, those who focus on asserting the political role of Islam. In terms of contemporary Islam, there are frequent references to Saudi-linked Wahhabism and Salafism (adherents are known as Wahhabists or Salafists), indicating Muslims who favor stricter observance of religious tenets and implementation of shariah law and reject religious innovation and tolerance for other religions and rebuke Muslims who are less devout and passionate about Islam. It's worth noting that some Salafists bristle at being conflated with Wahhabists and there are differences over legal matters, while others maintain that Salafism is essentially a rebranding of Wahhabism. This discourse highlights the danger of applying labels monolithically and the importance of recognizing that such shorthand references can be misleading by masking critical differences.

Asia is depicted as a battleground between the forces of Arabization and globalization (Westernization). The term "Arabization" is as problematic as "globalization" in that both terms assume a misleading homogeneity in the Arab and Western worlds. Both concepts also err in downplaying agency on the part of those being exposed to such cultural flows that are subject to selective appropriation, adaptation, and indigenization as they blend with prior appropriations and foreign influences. Societies and cultures are organic and as such are in constant flux, absorbing influences from various sources that are refracted through local traditions and mores. What may appear to be distinctive cultures are, in reality, not the product of isolation but rather the nuanced amalgam of accretions resulting from sustained interactions that facilitate transregional cultural flows. As Martin van Bruinessen argues, "Cultural borrowing was a creative process, in which the 'foreign' elements were soon incorporated into a distinctively local synthesis" (van Bruinessen 2015, 62). Various cultural brokers from the Arab world in addition to locals who returned from pilgrimages there (haji) transmitted a panoply of evolving practices and norms. It is also problematic that these terms essentialize complex civilizations and varied societies by asserting monolithic images. Many Muslims around the world see globalization as the equivalent of a crusade threatening to overwhelm their values and norms through an onslaught of popular Western culture, liberal values, secular attitudes, religious pluralism, and promiscuous lifestyles. Anxieties have intensified due to the communications revolution over the past few decades beaming and streaming Western music, films, fashion, and images of the "good life" throughout the ummah. This ubiquitous exposure to Western ways, penetrating Muslim minds and reinforcing a sense of weakness and subordination, provokes a backlash mobilized by conservative religious groups who try to assert a reinvigorated Islam as an authentic indigenous response. Yet what is authentic? There have been successive waves of Arabization of Islamic practice over the centuries as traders, clerics, and hajis have spread their religious practices and interpretations. These waves involved promoting renewed visions of a purified and true Islam but are subject to contestation.

In the two case studies examined shortly—Indonesia and Bangladesh—battles between moderates and fundamentalists are fiercely fought. Moderates argue in favor of local syncretic practices as reflecting an authentic indigenous religious culture. They distinguish between religion and Arab culture, maintaining that one can be a genuine Muslim without embracing Arab culture. In contrast, zealous reformers seek to impose a more ostensibly authentic Arab-centric Islam and denigrate any deviations from what they determine is correct.

In some respects, Arabization represents a cultural invasion mirroring globalization, both welcome and resented. For many Asian Muslims, an Arab-centric Islam is part of their identity, one that is cosmopolitan and gives them entry into an imagined community of global believers. They are influenced by the intellectual ferment and Islamic experiences around the world, adapting and responding to what they see and learn. Often this imagined community is an Internet echo chamber of the like-minded, demonstrating the common tendency toward confirmation bias. It is a low-cost, low-commitment participation that entices through instantaneous access to developments in the Islamic world that encourages sympathy toward Muslim struggles ranging from Palestine and Kashmir to Afghanistan and Syria. There is an immediacy and sense of empowerment of feeling solidarity with unknown people in distant places and having empathy for their suffering.

Arabization enables Saudi Arabia to shape this experience and nurture a discourse that promotes its agenda. Educational programs and scholarships help it sway opinion by credentializing capable people who can exert influence over others. The networks established from this interaction provide access and contacts, meaning that Indonesians or Bangladeshis can seek immediate advice on religious matters and request fatwa from Saudi ulama that carry added weight. These transnational connections and resonances confer legitimacy and generate conformist tendencies.

There are 1.2 billion Muslims in the world, including several hundred million in Asia, and thus it is hard to make sweeping generalizations that can withstand careful scrutiny. The media estimates without offering convincing evidence that just 1 percent of Muslims are jihadi, meaning some ten million people worldwide. It is alleged that Salafists/Wahhabists condone violence and provide funding and arms to extremist groups who carry out terrorist attacks. The estimated fifty million Salafists, including some twenty to thirty million in India alone, are not united under a single banner nor belong to a single organization but instead are believed to be the fastest growing Islamic sectarian movement. They promote a literal understanding of the sacred texts of Islam and repudiate liberal reformist movements. They have also been implicated in violent attacks on Sufis and other moderate Muslims who are seen to be lax in their observance and overly tolerant of local cultural accretions that dilute and diminish Islam. Saudi charities are linked with funding of such operations, along with educational and mosque-building initiatives across Asia.

Fundamentalism encompasses a range of beliefs and practices that are generally more exclusivist and intolerant. As globalization has intensified, often used interchangeably with Westernization, there has been a fundamentalist backlash that addresses issues of a religious identity seen to be under assault. Going back to basics is a way of reaffirming faith and identity for those who feel threatened by the secularizing influences of globalization. Globalization carries implicit assumptions that religion is incompatible with modernization and progress and that those goals should be prioritized at the expense of spiritual aspirations. In common usage, Islamic fundamentalism/

fundamentalists and Islamism/Islamicists have become synonymous and are associated with militancy, activism, extremism, and intolerance. This revivalism is often associated with jihadism, holy war sanctioned by religious belief, and terrorism. It is seen as a global revolutionary movement, an ideological backlash against secularizing forces that encompasses social, political, and religious goals.

The influence of Wahhabism spread in Asia during the nineteenth century due to the increased number of Muslims who went on the haj, stayed a few years for religious study, and then returned to their homelands as respected holy men who came to influence local religious practice based on their experiences as hajjis. They contributed to Islamic revivalism or puritanism, exhorting Muslims to deepen their devotion and abandon non-Islamic practices. In Indonesia, Malaysia, and the Philippines, Islamic fundamentalism sparked nineteenth-century anticolonial uprisings and resistance movements, especially against the Dutch in Sumatra and western Java where the pepper trade had generated enough wealth for more people to undertake the costly and arduous haj. Suppressing Islamic fundamentalism thus became part of the colonial project of pacification. During World War II, the Japanese tried to mobilize Islamic groups in Indonesia and provided military training, but overall the holy war waged in the name of Emperor Showa (Hirohito) did not resonate with the devout.

During the Cold War the United States and its allies countered Soviet influence by covertly supporting fundamentalist groups in the Middle East and South Asia. At that time, leftist nationalist movements deemed sympathetic to the Soviet Union were viewed as a threat to Western nations and their interests, so support for fundamentalists was seen as useful in terms of the US containment doctrine. In 1953 the CIA orchestrated the ouster of democratically elected prime minister Mossadegh, who was threatening Western oil interests with nationalization, and installed the Shah as Iran's autocratic leader. He ruled ruthlessly while providing the United States listening posts on Iran's border with the Soviet Union, making large purchases of US military hardware, and serving as a loyal ally in the volatile Mideast. However, in 1979 the Ayatollah Khomeini overthrew the Shah in an Islamic revolution in this Shi'a majority nation, establishing an Islamic republic in which religious officials still exercise supreme political power and the United States is routinely vilified as the Great Satan. This was the delayed but sustained blowback from the 1953 US intervention. Around the world, Muslims drew inspiration from the 1979 Iranian revolution, an event that captured the imagination of the oppressed and provided a welcome spectacle of American humiliation during the hostage crisis. Islamic leaders witnessed the power they could gain and wield, with subsequent repercussions in Asia.

From the 1970s, Middle East oil-producing nations were suddenly awash with petrodollars due to the spike in oil prices. The United States made common cause with Islamic nations (excluding Iran) to fight godless communism and counter leftist nationalist leaders and movements. Increasingly, Saudi Arabia funded such initiatives, winning goodwill in Washington while spreading its political influence and advancing its religious agenda. The US-Saudi-Pakistan effort to destabilize Soviet-occupied Afghanistan from 1979 by funding, training, and arming fundamentalist groups in the Afghanistan-Pakistan border region proved successful, but here too there was considerable blowback. This covert intervention included support for Osama bin Laden's militants and also paved the way for the Taliban to take control of Afghanistan. It is there that al-Qaeda established training camps from where strikes were orchestrated by bin Laden against US targets in the Mideast, Africa, and New York. This transformed the fundamentalists from strategic ally to enemy, as President George W. Bush unleashed a "war on terror" and in public comments suggested this was a crusade, invoking a history of invasion, occupation, and resistance that pitted Christianity against Islam. The Muslim faithful, fundamentalists, terrorists, and Islam became the undifferentiated enemy.

The war on terror provoked radicalism among many Muslims globally because they felt besieged by the United States, the new post–Cold War target of America's military industrial complex. In this escalating polarization of perceptions, brilliantly depicted in Mohsin Hamid's *The Reluctant Fundamentalist* (2007), attitudes hardened, and for many Muslims, a stronger religious identity was thrust upon them by the attendant vilification. They became suspect and were hassled, detained, and killed merely for their religious affiliation, a degrading and alienating experience that led some to seek dignity and liberation in a more strident Islamic identity. Afghanistan is where the United States has waged its longest war since 2001, serving to recruit and provide training and inspiration for jihadists from around the world. Similarly, the 2003 toppling of the secularist Saddam Hussein regime in Iraq created opportunities for al-Qaeda and facilitated the rise of ISIS, arguably the most profound blowback of this ill-considered intervention.

Asia has felt the ripples of these distant conflicts and clashes, finding in Islam a source of identity, an ethos of dignity, and an ideology of resistance against the forces of secularism and state oppression. In this chapter we examine the antecedents and evolution of political Islam in Indonesia and Bangladesh to better understand the appeal of Salafism and the proliferation of violent extremist groups dedicated to asserting an Islamic national identity in secular nations. These nations have, respectively, the largest (225 million) and third largest (155 million) Muslim populations in the world and provide interesting parallels and contrasts. In both countries radical Islam is not new, and following independence in each there have been ongoing disputes over the role of Islam in society. Internal political dynamics, inequality, and poor governance have left both nations with a vast reservoir of discontented youth

open to extremist ideology. This potential pool of recruits has been aroused
by various historical grievances, Arabization, jihad in Afghanistan and Syria/
Iraq, the perceived failures of secular nationalism, capitalism and socialism,
and, most dramatically, the explosion of social media.

The sorrows of globalization have been packaged and relentlessly propagated, igniting the combustible mix of despair and envy that afflicts both the
marginalized and the comparatively privileged. The Internet has given potent
momentum to political Islam and has lowered the barriers to disseminating
information, analysis, and agendas. It is a powerful tool of persuasion and
mobilization, creating what Benedict Anderson called an "imagined community" (1983). The gap between the virtual world of extremism and actual
jihad and terrorist action is not narrow but being a part of such an imagined
community nurtures solidarity, shared ideas, and common cause. The sense
of exclusivity, danger, dedication, and ostensible potential for making a difference forges strong bonds. Extremists with limited resources can reach
wide audiences and exert a disproportionate influence by having a deft web
strategy and astute understanding of the psychology of who they are trying to
cultivate. The powerless can find meaning, dignity, status, and power in
these imagined communities of hardcore Muslims they can't find elsewhere.
With few other options, why wouldn't they at least dabble in cyberspace and
from there perhaps take the plunge?

INDONESIA

I recall in late 1984 walking around Jakarta's Tanjung Priok port area not
long after massive riots by Muslim activists demonstrating against the Suharto regime. Indonesian security forces crushed the protests, but a few months
on I saw a poster in this slum depicting Suharto with his head held back by a
local Chinese tycoon who was pouring a cascade of US dollars down his
throat. Around that time there was also an Islamic uprising in Lampung,
southern Sumatra, targeting the Suharto family's business interests, suggesting that Islam had become a vehicle of social protest in authoritarian Indonesia.

During the Suharto era the authoritarian government ruthlessly repressed
all threats to political stability and tried to depoliticize Islam. In the massacres of hundreds of thousands in 1965 and 1966, the military mobilized
Islamic youth paramilitary organizations in its campaign to exterminate communist influence in the archipelago. It was not until 1999 that Nahdlatul
Ulama (NU) leader Gus Dur acknowledged his organization's complicity in
this pogrom. For much of the Suharto era the government carefully monitored religious groups to ensure they didn't engage in activities that might
destabilize society. With communism eliminated, Islam was the only poten-

tial institutionalized threat to military rule and thus it operated under strict constraints. There were some violent riots, quickly and ruthlessly quashed, but it was only in Aceh that fundamentalism was involved in a prolonged insurgency under the Gerakan Aceh Merdeka (Struggle for a Free Aceh [GAM]). It took the 2004 tsunami to end that conflict.

In 1998, the end of President Suharto's New Order regime sparked euphoric hopes and explosions of brutal violence around the archipelago. Under his authoritarian government conflicts were suppressed through a reign of terror, creating a fragile and volatile situation. Long suppressed memories of the 1965–1966 massacres generated apprehensions as Indonesia coped with the insecure legacy Suharto left behind. It was a time of shadowy organizations, provocateurs, settling of scores, and mysterious masterminds. Hope focused on the return of the military to the barracks, asserting civilian control over government and security and establishing the rule of law. But all around the periphery of the archipelago these hopes confronted a cycle of violence that spun out of control in Aceh, Irian Jaya, Papua, Sulawesi, and Ambon (Lloyd-Parry 2005). Armed separatist rebels and sectarian clashes threatened Indonesia's political transition. The nightmare of an unraveling state beset with spiraling violence, often invoked during the Suharto era to justify repressive measures, had metamorphosed into reality.

Indonesia enjoys a reputation for a moderate and tolerant Islam. An Islamic renewal movement in the 1970s and 1980s supported liberal, secular, and pluralist ideas while NU leader Abdurahman Wahid opposed an Islamic state and instead supported a more robust civil society by establishing liberal NGOs (Menchik and Trost 2018). Muhammadiyah, the second largest Islamic organization, also promoted pluralism and tolerance. But those most disaffected from the New Order were those who embraced more austere Wahhabi/ Salafist tenets propagating their version of a true Islam that rejected cosmopolitanism and the middle-class modernist renewal movement that sought to embrace an Indonesian Islamic identity anathema to these puritans. They represented the same forces that supported the Masyumi political party, banned in 1960, and its agenda of establishing an Islamic state. Thus, fundamentalist Islam has deep roots in Indonesian political culture and is not just a consequence of the more recent waves of Arabization emanating from Riyadh but has been significantly reinforced thereby.

From the 1990s, this more fundamentalist Islam gained momentum in Indonesia partly due to government meddling and social grievances, in addition to global developments in the Islamic world. Intensified globalization in the 1990s, fueled by the Internet and global media, produced a backlash, and many found in Islam a comfortable redoubt for preserving local identities. It is essential, however, to recognize that reform Islam has a long history dating back to the nineteenth century, playing a key role in Indonesian nationalism throughout the colonial era and also during the 1945 revolution (Menchik and Trost 2018, 391). Menchik and Trost note that Indonesia espouses a "Godly nationalism" demanding citizens affiliate with one of the official religions, a pluralist stance favoring orthodox theism. In this historical context, it is therefore not altogether surprising that for some Indonesians national identity is powerfully shaped by a pious Islam that seeks to arouse and rectify.

In the 1990s Suharto, for reasons that are not entirely clear, pivoted toward his scripturalist critics, establishing the Association of Muslim Intellectuals (ICMI), dominated by reformists under B. J. Habibie, his vice president and successor, and brought them into the government while also sponsoring an Islamic bank and newspaper. With the connivance of the regime, Muslim street politics also became more prominent in the 1990s, a radical shift in the New Order's previous emphasis on depoliticizing Islam and crushing all protests. Following Suharto's resignation, there was a realignment in political Islam as different factions, groups, and leaders sought to take advantage of the power vacuum and mood of reformasi. The 1999 elections saw a proliferation of parties, and none of those that embraced an explicitly Islamic agenda did well while those linked to NU and Muhammadiyah appealed to a broader constituency by espousing pluralism and diversity.

Muslims constitute some 88 percent of Indonesia's population of 225 million and almost all adhere to the Sunni sect, but about 2 million are Shia and 500,000 belong to Ahmadiyya. In general, Indonesians have practiced a moderate form of Islam and have an affinity for tolerant Sufi traditions, but stricter observance has long been the norm in western Sumatra and in Aceh. In Aceh since 2001 the government has authorized shariah courts and ordinances on proper dress and proper gender relations as part of its "special autonomy" agreement to end the separatist war waged in the province. These laws are enforced by a shariah police force known for harassment, arbitrary arrests, and detention for dating. Vice vigilantes try to promote religious virtue by enforcing bans on drinking, gambling, and what is termed "seclusion"—couples of the opposite sex being alone together, even if in public places. There have been public canings in Aceh since 2005 to punish transgressors, while the fashion police ensure that women don't wear clinging or revealing clothing. It is the only province where such courts are authorized, although in Java some communities have passed ordinances requiring residents' behavior conform to conservative principles, that is, alcohol should not be served at business establishments, women should dress modestly, not meet men alone, and remain at home at night, etc. In 2013 the Aceh government moved to apply shariah law to everyone whether Islamic or not, although dropping demands for death by stoning for adulterers. Non-Muslims who are charged with offenses not criminalized by national laws are now subject to these shariah courts.

While Arabization is not the only reason for the wave of puritanical Islam in Indonesia, where the genealogy of fundamentalism is long and complex, it is clear that "transnational networks—along which people, money, and ideas move—have become extremely important but they are not the sole determining factor. Saudi money has undeniably played a role in shaping debates in Indonesian Islam and in promoting certain interpretations and attitudes rather than others" (van Bruinessen 2002, 149). Van Bruinessen adds, "The remarkable prominence of Indonesian Arabs in the leadership of the more militant groups is probably related to the increasing importance of transnational communications too (besides the religious prestige commonly attributed to Arabs in Indonesia). Arabs have played a prominent part in the transmission of neo-fundamentalist and *jihadist* discourse from the Middle East to Indonesia" (149). Yet he explains, "This has not been universally welcomed; there are now the first signs of an anti-Arab backlash among indigenous Indonesian Muslims, who consider this radicalism as alien" (150).

Since the end of the New Order authoritarian regime in 1998, the highly centralized administrative structure has given way to greater regional autonomy. This shift was a pragmatic adjustment to simmering anti-Jakarta resentments, the realities of diversity in the Indonesian archipelago, and the difficulties of micromanaging affairs remote from the center. Greater autonomy has also heightened identity politics in the regions and in the fray of electoral politics, touting candidates' Islamic credentials and backing from local clerics has assumed much greater importance. In the competition for votes in local elections, candidates are under considerable pressure to stake out more Islamic positions than rivals, generating conditions favorable to fundamentalism. What starts as pandering to demonstrate legitimizing "green" (Islamic) credentials generates momentum as fundamentalist views seep into political discourse and campaigning.

Political parties assert ethnic-based claims to political power and seek to reinvigorate local ethnicity, customs, and practices to that end. In some regions this means elevating one local identity over others. Regionalism thus has had countervailing consequences, enabling assertion of identities that highlight autonomy and separateness from the mainstream while suppressing local diversity by crafting new orthodoxies that leave minorities vulnerable. In some regions such as Aceh, the government encourages moral policing that regulates proper dress and comportment, while establishment of shariah law has reinforced an already strong Islamic identity, putting everyone at the mercy of conservative sentiments.

Muhammadiyah and Nahdlatul Islam, large moderate Muslim organizations with vast networks and a deep institutional presence, have long dominated Indonesia's Islamic political culture. They are not sympathetic to fundamentalist Islam and have considerable influence because they contribute tangibly through education and social welfare programs to communities where they operate. But since the 1990s, public discourse about the role of Islam in Indonesian society has shifted toward more fundamentalist views in line with global trends, as discussed earlier, due to changing political dynamics in the post–New Order transition that have facilitated a reemergence of a puritan political Islam. What is striking, however, about Indonesian politics is Islamic parties' lack of success in national elections. The hardline message has not resonated at the national level, and prominent Islamic parties remain committed to the pluralist founding principles of Indonesia and don't support a blanket imposition of Islamic law.

Yet undeniably there has been growing support for purifying Islam and encouraging stricter observance in society, especially on the island of Java, which has the largest population in Indonesia and where attitudes have long been more relaxed and tolerant. Clifford Geertz (1960) once noted that there are two prominent strands in Indonesian Islam that have been a source of dynamic tension: the majority of syncretic abangan, who are nominally Muslim and less devout, and the far fewer but more pious santri. Following the 1965–1966 massacres and anticommunist witch hunt, many abangan inclined worried about being seen as atheist and potentially sympathetic to communism and thus became more pious in their public devotions. Yet the "live and let live" mentality in Javanese culture remained resilient. This more accommodating ethos survived as religion was viewed as one important aspect of life shaping social norms and values but refracted through local customs and traditions. Since the 1950s' Darul Islam rebellion in West Java, fundamentalists promoting a dominant political role for Islam and Islamic nationalism have contended with this more moderate religiosity. In the post-Suharto era, however, they have gained considerable momentum in an evolving landscape of religiosity far from what Geertz observed in the 1950s (Ricklefs 2012).

Religious practice around the world exhibits syncretic tendencies as customs, common law, and the lingering influences of other religions are assimilated. Indonesia is thus not unusual in this respect, but such moderate tolerance doesn't sit well with others who call on believers to purify their faith and practice. The santri are more devout and less inclined to tolerate the syncretic nature of Indonesian Islam that dominates. Santri-oriented organizations advocate a cleansing of local customs and superstitions from Islam, unaware perhaps that some of what they view as local accretions were spread in previous waves of Islamization and are actually Arabic in origins. In seeking to promote an Islamic national identity based on stricter moral codes and the centrality of Islam in life and society, they challenge the pluralist foundations of the secular state.

Back in the mid-1980s when I lived in Indonesia and traveled widely, relatively few women wore head coverings and even fewer men wore Arabic-style robes or long beards, sexes intermingled relatively freely, flirting was common, some would openly drink alcohol, nightclubs were packed, prostitution including wariya (transvestites) was widespread and tolerated, and overall the atmosphere was unimaginably different from the contemporary scene in which hardliner vigilantes campaign to close bars, massage parlors, and saunas and harass the LGBT community and women who are out in the evening or wearing outfits deemed too provocative.

Fundamentalist orthodoxy has gained traction due to a variety of factors beyond the opening provided by Suharto's ouster and historical antecedents. This agenda has ridden a wave of 1) increased levels of pilgrimage to Mecca by Indonesians; 2) massive funding for mosque building and educational programs from Saudi Arabia that has boosted Salafist influence throughout the Muslim world; 3) globally heightened Islamic identity politics; and 4) the spread of social media. Over the past two decades more Indonesians are making the haj to Mecca, something obligatory for Muslims who can do so. Rising incomes and a growing middle class are boosting demand for the annual haj and there are long waiting lists for aspiring pilgrims. Hajis bring back with them attitudes and practices from Saudi Arabia that they believe more authentically represent Islam. This means head coverings for women, stricter segregation of the sexes, stricter moral codes, and targeting of practices considered inconsistent with how Islam is practiced in its Saudi homeland. Hajis return with aroused religious passion, and many feel it is their mission to promote purification and awaken fellow believers to the error of their ways. Due to their elevated status, hajis often exercise considerable influence in their communities, and as their numbers have increased so too has their impact.

The cascade of funding from Saudi Arabia, estimated at $200 billion worldwide since the 1980s, for the building of mosques (more than 150 in Indonesia alone as of 2017), hospitals, orphanages, and over a hundred boarding schools there has reinforced this Salafist trend (Weiss 2017). The Institute for the Study of Islam and the Arabic Language (LIPIA), a university program in Jakarta since 1980, is another example of Saudi funding for spreading Arabization. Classes are sex segregated, there are strict rules governing behavior (i.e., no music, TV, or loud laughter), women are fully veiled, and classes are taught in Arabic. Tuition is free and students also receive a stipend. Promising graduates are offered scholarships to continue their studies at the home campus in Saudi Arabia, and when they return, they have enhanced status that enables them to promote fundamentalism. LIPIA alumni also play a prominent public role as preachers and teachers. It is indicative that a 2013 Pew poll found that 72 percent of Indonesians supported making shariah the law of the land (Pew 2013b). Although only 2 percent of Indonesians are sympathetic to IS versus 95 percent who are not (Weiss 2017), some 20 percent of high school and university students support establishment of a caliphate and proclaim themselves ready to wage jihad in order to do so (Reuters 2017).

In 2017 the Saudi king Salman bin Abdulaziz Al Saud visited Indonesia and announced plans to fund the opening of three additional branches of LIPIA and renovations of the Jakarta campus as part of a $6 billion investment package. Clerics at such Saudi-sponsored institutions depict Indonesia's moderate Islam as backward and deviant while disseminating Salafist principles. These resonate powerfully in the post-9/11 world of the US war on terror, campaigns against the Taliban in Afghanistan and ISIS in Iraq and Syria, the killing of Osama bin Laden, and longstanding support for Israel's repression of Palestinians. These developments all stoke the fires of hardline Islamic identity politics in Indonesia.

Alumni of LIPIA include Laskar Jihad founder Jafar Umar Thalib. Laskar Jihad recruited Muslims to fight Christians in Ambon, where some five thousand people were killed and more than seven hundred thousand displaced in communal violence between 1999 and 2002 when it was disbanded. Another prominent graduate is Habib Rizieq, exiled head of the Islamic Defenders Front (IDF; also known as FPI, the Indonesian acronym for Front Pembela Islam) that ousted the ethnic Chinese governor of Jakarta in 2017 on trumped-up blasphemy charges (see chapter 8). Similar campaigns have been launched against other minority governors in the archipelago and in 2017, the local Chinese Confucian temple in Surabaya had to place a white sheet over a large statue of Guan Yu, a Chinese warrior-god. Local Islamic groups protested this idolatry as blasphemy, tapping into anti-Chinese sentiments. The threats to Indonesia's multicultural identity, symbolized in the national motto "Unity in Diversity," are thus manifest and expanding, including proposals to ban alcohol and impose shariah. Moreover, as many as two thousand Indonesians joined the IS jihad in Syria. Those that survive will return as battle-hardened jihadists; it does not take many militants to cause mayhem.

NU, founded a century ago, has more than forty million members, espouses a more tolerant Islam, and repudiates extremism, but the rise of more militant groups in recent years such as the IDF continues unabated. NU is doctrinally opposed to Salafism and supports religious pluralism, and remains very influential despite growing competition. For example, Indonesia has a new mass religious organization, Wahdah Islamiyah, which follows Salafi practices and has branches in every province and more than 174 schools. It was founded in 1988 by students in Makassar who severed links with Muhammadiyah because of its adoption of Pancasila, Indonesia's foundational principles emphasizing national unity and religious pluralism.

Social media is a ubiquitous conduit for spreading fundamentalist tenets and disseminating the teaching of Salafist preachers to large and impressionable audiences. It is useful to mobilize against targets ranging from minorities, deviants, blasphemers to anyone who defies fundamentalist exhortations. For opportunists eager to push agendas in the name of Islam, this is an ideal platform for projecting their views and gathering followers. Social media enforces conformity with the growing fundamentalist consensus as users fear being ostracized or criticized in their virtual communities. In this way, fundamentalist norms and values are mainstreamed as "friends" go along with what others are doing and saying. As one of my Indonesian research assistants explained, if everyone else is wearing a veil, why not? If everyone else thinks something is blasphemous, maybe it is and disputing this only makes one a target.

Noorhaidi Hasan argues, however, that the pendulum is swinging back and that Salafism is receding at the local level (Hasan 2018). Van Bruinessen also found that local kiais in the town of Cirebon on the north coast of Java have worked to preserve local Islamic traditions, resisting the homogenizing and puritanical tendencies of Salafism (van Bruinessen 2015, 79). He wryly notes "that the efforts to strengthen local culture to resist the influx of 'Arabian' puritan Islam in Cirebon involved cultural traditions reflecting an earlier synthesis of Arab and Javanese cultures" (80), featuring Egyptian-style pop music and typically Arab percussion! Thus, this campaign invoking the virtues of Indonesian authenticity draws on traditions infused with influences from prior waves of Arabization.

Salafism is associated with jihadist activism such as the Laskar Jihad in Maluku at the turn of the century and the Jemaah Islamiyah (JI) terrorist group in Southeast Asia held responsible for several bombings in Bali and Jakarta in the 2000s. Yet according to Hasan, some Salafi authorities "actively engage in countering violent jihadism" (2018, 251). In terms of propagating Salafist doctrine, Hasan also finds that Salafi madrasa only attract small numbers and thus exert limited influence on the wider Muslim community. Within central Javanese communities where Hasan conducted fieldwork, Salafists rose to positions of authority but are now facing a backlash against their censorious ways because they impinge on the conviviality and harmony of village life (252–54). In a society in which there has long been an "accommodating" ethos, Hasan argues that Salafist rigidity has triggered cultural resistance and its influence appears to be ebbing (255). However, even if the Salafist wave faces resistance, it probably elicits varied responses, so it is potentially misleading to project from the apparent backlash in Java to the rest of this diverse archipelago.

Hasan's and van Bruinessen's fieldwork does provide, however, a useful reminder that narratives of an unabated rise of Salafism ignore the evident grassroots identity politics and cultural mechanisms of resistance at the village level. This backlash raises important questions about identity contestation as transnational Islam confronts local politics and resilient customs, norms, and traditions that reject what appears alien and unappealing to villagers. This is a cautionary reminder that an Arabization stemming from geopolitical machinations, massive funding, and political instrumentalism is not inexorable because mobilizing people depends on winning them over.

Salafism may indeed be spreading piety and influencing many Indonesians, but its top-down agenda confronts a large community of grassroots moderates and backsliders who find it excessive. Saudi Arabia's global campaign may not be receding elsewhere, but in the nation with the world's largest Islamic population, it may well have peaked.

Hadiz (2018) explains that Islam has not become a potent populist political force in Indonesia because of organizational and doctrinal incoherence and sharp divisions within the ummah that inhibit solidarity. Unlike in Turkey, where Islamic populism has become mainstreamed by the ruling Justice and Development Party (AKP is the common Turkish acronym by which it is known) under President Tayyip Erdogan, there has been no successful political party in Indonesia articulating such an agenda. In contrast to Turkey, Indonesia lacks a powerful middle class engaging in charitable activities that nurture support among the poor and thus has been unable to forge a powerful cross-class coalition with a shared agenda. Instead Islamic organizations have been compromised by direct and indirect involvement in money politics, losing credibility. Under the New Order, the United Development Party (PPP as it is known in Indonesia) was the official Islamic party but played a largely ornamental role (Hadiz 2018, 300). The two main mass Islamic organizations, Muhammadiyah and NU, also failed to act as dissenting voices against New Order repression and were incorporated into patronage networks. More recently, reformist Islamic organizations have been active in street politics, but because they eschew participation in elections and view democracy as anathema to a cohesive Islamic state led by the pious, they are self-marginalizing. However, such fringe Islamic groups, in competing to show they are the most devout by embracing rigid dogmas and values associated with orthodox Islam, are contributing to politically illiberal tendencies in mainstream parties that pander to their conservative social agenda (Vatikiotis 2018).

Populism can gain momentum by addressing socioeconomic grievances stemming from the broken promises of development and neoliberal globalization. For Indonesians, inequality, penury, and employment are combustible issues as youth's aspirations are thwarted in a world in which the "good life" beamed around the globe remains well out of reach. The AKP has embraced neoliberalism and convinced enough Turks that this is in their interests, but in the Indonesian context, reformist and radical Islamic groups view this as apostasy.

Islamic Militancy

Human rights problems affecting minorities remain serious in Indonesia. Religious minorities are subject to violence and discrimination while the government and police have been tolerant of such abuses. Public opinion does not support Islamic religious extremism and the concomitant targeting of religious minority groups, but the government has encouraged and accommodated religious intolerance through discriminatory laws and decrees at the national and local level that undermine the civil rights of minority groups. Moreover, security officials inadequately protect those who are threatened or attacked by Islamic militants. They represent a small percentage of Indonesians, but their penchant for violence endows them with disproportionate leverage in Indonesia's twenty-first-century identity politics.

Radical Islam retains a visible and loud presence on the streets, as various domestic political actors sponsor groups to exert pressure or serve as vigilante gangs. In the post–New Order era, as authoritarian pressures ebbed, some groups found an opening for their puritanical reformist agenda, most notably Laskar Jihad. Its embrace of radical activism and violence was prompted by communal clashes in the Moluccas, where it sent holy warriors to defend the ummah against Christian infidels.

In this febrile atmosphere the IDF emerged, ostensibly driven by an Islamic agenda despite a dubious reputation as little more than a gang for hire. Its founder and leader Habib Rizieq Syihab, a Jakarta-born sayyid (Arab descent), studied in Saudi Arabia and played a prominent role in ousting the popular governor of Jakarta for blasphemous remarks. Subsequently the tables were turned and he was accused of blasphemy, leading him to seek refuge in Saudi Arabia to avoid prosecution.

State security monitoring of Islamic groups has become much more extensive after the Bali bombings in 2002 that killed over two hundred people. JI, a terrorist organization in Southeast Asia, was implicated in the bombings, prompting strong antiterrorist countermeasures by Jakarta that succeeded in rolling up JI networks. Many of the recruits were traced to pesantren (Islamic schools) near the ancient capital of Solo in central Java where observance of Islamic tenets had been more casual and syncretic. The teachers were santri and sought to spread more devout religious observance and a "purer" form of Islam shorn of indigenous influences.

Incidents of violence by Islamic militants targeting religious minorities have become frequent in contemporary Indonesia. They act with impunity and thus are emboldened. Even when prosecuted they get light sentences, signaling an official tolerance if not complicity. In 2012 the religious affairs minister declared that the minority Shia and Ahmadiyya Islamic sects are heretical and suggested they convert to the dominant Sunni faith. There have also been prosecutions for blasphemy on the basis of "improper" teaching of the Quran and atheistic postings to Facebook. While the rise of intolerance and branding certain beliefs heretical or blasphemous is alarming, such extreme cases are not representative of mainstream Indonesia. But they are signs that Islamic hardliners are shaping national identity and political discourse.

Jemaah Islamiya

JI is a radical Islamic group based in Southeast Asia since the early 1990s that at times was quite active operating and recruiting in Indonesia. JI, launched in Malaysia in 1993, traces its ideological roots to the Darul Islam insurgency in the 1950s and 1960s that fought the Indonesian secular state in three different regions. It was vanquished as an insurgency, but the embers of an aggrieved religious identity and fundamentalist agenda lingered. Darul Islam militants and contemporary Islamicists in Indonesia maintain that the government is failing to uphold the 1945 Jakarta Charter, a declaration of the national independence movement's principles that required Muslims to abide by Islamic law. This charter became the basis for the preamble to the Consti- tution, but crucial wording regarding obligatory adherence to shariah for Muslims was omitted, leaving many feeling betrayed. There has been a series of efforts in Parliament to restore the wording but none have succeeded, generating considerable discontent because the nation's Islamic identity has been denied.

JI has been affiliated with al-Qaeda and Abu Sayyaf (an Islamic terrorist group based in the southern Philippines) and seeks to establish an Islamic state, enact shariah in Indonesia, and through jihad establish a caliphate in the region encompassing Indonesia, Malaysia, Mindanao, and subsequently Brunei, southern Thailand, and Singapore. JI gained world attention with the 2002 and 2005 Bali bombings. Previously, on Christmas Eve in 2000, JI mounted its first terrorist operation in Indonesia, bombing twenty-eight churches in Java, Sumatra, and Sulawesi. Subsequently, public opinion turned against JI, smoothing the way for the government to embrace ruthless counterterrorism measures. JI was also implicated in a series of attacks in Mindanao in the 2000s, but between 2005 and 2009 there was a lull that was ended by the simultaneous bombings of two luxury hotels in Jakarta. Then in 2010 security forces raided a JI training camp in Aceh, arresting 120 mili- tants. By 2013, much of the top leadership had been killed and over three hundred members arrested by the police. Problematically, prisons have been hothouses for recruitment as JI inmates spread their jihadist doctrine to a "captive" audience who on release tend to get little rehabilitation support from the government but are welcomed with open arms by JI operatives who provide economic, spiritual, and emotional support.

The doctrine of jihad invokes Islam to justify violent attacks targeting non-Muslims. Assuming non-Muslims will never allow Muslims to live in peace according to their precepts, it is necessary to conduct perpetual war against these enemies of Islam. Those who die in jihad are consecrated as martyrs and revered for their sacrifice, posthumously gaining a holy status that reflects well on their surviving relatives. The infidels are viewed as legitimate targets because they oppose Islam and jihadists are defending it.

This defensive strategy, however, carries the seeds of mission creep so that extremists wage jihad not only to defend the ummah but also to extend it. Muslim scholars assert that only defensive war in the strictest sense, that is, unprovoked attacks, is justified.

Abu Bakar Bashir, a co-founder of JI, joined jihadists in Afghanistan and Pakistan where he developed his extremist ideology, operational skills, and transnational links. He and co-founder Hambali drew inspiration from al-Qaeda ideology and jihadi terrorist doctrine. When President Suharto stepped down in 1998, Bashir and Hambali returned to Indonesia, calculating that the end of the authoritarian regime might open up possibilities to realize their dreams of a caliphate. Hambali is associated with a more militant strategy to establish an Islamic caliphate, while Bashir favored a gradual approach through preaching and education. Hambali was the advocate for the attacks on soft targets and suicide bombings that became signature JI tactics and was implicated in the failed 1993 attack on the World Trade Center in New York City. In 2003 he was arrested, but given JI's decentralized structure of autonomous cells it continued to operate. He is held by the United States in extrajudicial detention at Guantanamo Bay.

JI was nearly destroyed in 2007 when a shootout in Sulawesi led to the capture or death of key leaders. The base in Poso (central Sulawesi), a site of sectarian violence at the turn of the century, was crucial to JI's efforts to regroup and thus its destruction was a key blow to an organization that was already on the ropes financially and in terms of militant capacity. At that time, JI was even unable to support the families of incarcerated members, a key to ensuring loyalty. A further blow to JI came from Bashir's establishment of Jamaah Anshorut Tauhid in July 2008, as the high-profile cleric drew away potential recruits, senior commanders, charismatic preachers, and rank-and-file members.

After 2009, JI went dormant, devastated by a ruthless crackdown by an Indonesian special police unit Detachment 88 that involved extra-judicial killings. Funding also appeared to dry up. JI has relied on al-Qaeda and other extremist organizations and individuals in the Middle East while also raising funds through extortion, arms smuggling, and other criminal activities in Southeast Asia. The depletion of its cadre of militants and the global crackdown on terrorist financing and organizations reduced the available funding to recruit, train, and carry out operations. The results can be seen in the less sophisticated and lower-impact operations that it has conducted since 2009. Bashir's severing of all links with JI followed by a 2014 pledge of loyalty to IS from his prison cell reinforced perceptions of JI's demise.

In 2011 Bashir was convicted of inciting terrorism in connection to a jihadi training camp in Aceh for which he raised money and was sentenced to fifteen years in prison. He is viewed as the spiritual leader of the terrorists who carried out the 2002 Bali bombings, but two previous prosecutions to link him to terrorist activities were unsuccessful, including a conviction that was overturned in the Bali attacks. Although not operationally involved, Bashir has provided vital religious and ideological sanction for violent extremism, explaining a frustrated government's persistent efforts to put him behind bars. At the conclusion of his trial he rejected the proceedings and commented that "this verdict ignores shariah law and is based on the infidel law, so it's forbidden for me to accept it" (Wright 2018). In 2019 the government announced that it was preparing to reduce his jail term on humanitarian grounds, igniting a firestorm of criticism that forced reconsideration of that plan amid accusations of political pandering to Islamicists.

Over the past two decades a number of key members have been killed or jailed, but JI's militant Islamic doctrine and jihadist ideology sanctifies and sustains its mission. Counterterrorism eliminates actors but not the ideas, goals, and grievances that generate new recruits and keep the threat alive. JI recruiting relies on charismatic preachers and a network of a few dozen pesantren (Islamic boarding schools) that inculcate students with jihadist doctrine. Training for recruits was conducted in Pakistan by Lashkar-e-Taiba and in camps in Mindanao while jihadists returning from Afghanistan and Iraq have trained on the battlefield jihad. In 2017 the Institute for Policy Analysis of Conflict (IPAC) issued a report warning that JI has rebounded from a series of setbacks and is reemerging although not as a significant terrorist threat (IPAC 2017).

Despite Bashir's defection, JI has slowly regrouped and reorganized and now ostensibly prioritizes dakwah over jihad. The role of the military wing, according to IPAC, is not to conduct terrorist operations but to prepare for some eventual conflict, and to that end militants have been dispatched to Syria and Iraq for training and combat experience. This repositioning of JI aims at gaining greater political influence as the jihadi strategy nearly destroyed the organization, imperiling its goal of establishing an Islamic state. Whereas the old JI rejected mainstream politics, the new JI permitted participation in the 2017 street rallies targeting Basuki Tjahaja Purnama, known as Ahok, and seems inclined to cooperate with other Muslim organizations. But the IDF and Forum Umat Islam have become mass Muslim fundamentalist organizations that JI is unable to compete with. Because this niche is already filled, JI faces an identity crisis. Militancy and terrorism have been its calling and undoing, but Islamic politics has evolved in ways that leave it marginalized and overtaken by events. Some members castigated the leadership for renouncing violence, condemning moderation as a betrayal of JI's principles. For this hardcore following, playing it safe and embracing nonviolent methods lack sufficient religious zeal. Under the circumstances, there is a risk JI might attempt to reestablish itself by resuming jihadist violence or that trained militants in JI's military wing will grow impatient and splinter off to form a group that will.

In other parts of Asia, such as the devastating 2019 Easter Sunday coordinated suicide bombings in Sri Lanka, we see how Salafist movements are gaining ground and exploiting the possibilities of what Juergensmeyer portrays as the theater of terrorism, staging gory incidents aimed at maximizing media exposure, impressing those who share similar grievances and jolting targeted groups out of their complacency and disregard (Juergensmeyer 2014). In Sri Lanka, Christians were targeted, ostensibly as revenge for the mosque shootings in New Zealand the previous month. In many other cases, extremists target secularism on behalf of the marginalized, justifying their acts as religiously sanctified redemptive revenge for the accumulating humiliations of the weak and oppressed.

BANGLADESH

On July 1, 2016, the world suddenly discovered with a vengeance the threat of Islamic extremism in Bangladesh, a predominantly Muslim nation that has been fighting to retain a secular and tolerant national identity since its bloody birth in 1971. Five militants took control of the Holy Artisan Bakery and held several dozen hostages, later releasing Muslim staff and customers. The terrorist attack claimed the lives of twenty-nine people altogether, including twenty hostages, of which nine were Italians and seven were Japanese engaged with development projects under the auspices of the Japan International Cooperation Agency. The militants executed the hostages during the siege as security forces launched a counterattack. Subsequently they killed the alleged mastermind of the attack and many more Islamic militants in numerous extra-judicial killings.

The execution of so many foreigners, clearly for the attention this would draw, was a grisly incident that shocked Dhaka society because it occurred in an upscale neighborhood where the wealthy and expats gather. Moreover, three of the five youthful terrorists were from comparatively privileged backgrounds. This discovery sent shudders up the collective spine of the nation's elite because "they" were suddenly and undeniably "us." A local counterterrorist expert explained to me that recruiters target troubled sons of the elite precisely because they have a much higher PR value. The media pays more attention to them than they would to a suicide bomber hailing from one of the thousands of madrasa (Islamic schools) where the less privileged and destitute study. Knowing that most militants are actually from deprived backgrounds is not especially reassuring when that constitutes the vast majority of this nation's nearly 170 million people packed into a land area smaller than Florida, but it is more alarming somehow when even the scions of the upper crust are joining the fray.

In the wee hours following the bakery attack my Bangladeshi research assistant informed me what happened. At the time, I had her researching Islamic extremism in Bangladesh. She later confided, "The shock we all suffered from the attack is still following us like a shadow and it has become impossible to resume normal life let alone enjoy this Eid," adding," The most surprising aspect of this attack is that it was done by people who are pretty much like us. They are the average young people who are believed to lead the society; they come from affluent, educated families, went to elite private schools at home and abroad but the only key difference is that somewhere down the line, they changed into monsters." In her view, social media is implicated in the popularization of jihadist extremism, asserting that "the sickest aftermath of the attack is the opening of Facebook fan pages for the terrorists. While many of us have still not recovered from the horror of our own people taking part in this brutal killing, a group of nonsensical girls started 'having a crush' on these young attackers making more and more people interested in their cause" (personal communication July 2016).

Opinion is divided over whether the Holy Artisan Bakery attack was the work of domestic terrorist organizations or the handiwork of Islamic State (IS), al-Qaeda, or a combination of both. IS claimed credit for the Holy Artisan Bakery attack, but the government asserts this was homegrown extremism, fingering a splinter organization from the local Islamic extremist group Jamaat-ul-Mujahideen (JMB). Local informants wonder whether this group actually exists other than as a fig leaf for government denials of international connections. Counterterrorist expert Asheque Haque attributes the government's reluctance to acknowledge transnational terrorist links to the loss of face this would entail for Prime Minister Sheikh Hasina, who has committed to eradicating Islamic extremism, and government concerns about the potential fallout with donors and investors (personal communication September 2018).

One of the privileged bakery attackers was a twitter follower of a Bangalore (India)-based IS propagandist, and experts believe that social media is one of the most prevalent means of radicalization. Some argue that Bangladesh terrorists might be inspired by IS and may receive limited external assistance and training, but it is essentially a domestic movement that manifests wider trends in the Islamic world. Returnee jihadists who fought in Afghanistan, Iraq, and Syria provide expertise to extremist groups while the influx of donations from the Middle East funds mosque building and supports clerics who tout a Salafist hardline. There are some 2.8 million Bangladeshi overseas workers in the Middle East with half in Saudi Arabia alone, often living and working in dreadful conditions. Some propagate the Salafist doctrine they are exposed to and their remittances ($16 billion worldwide) sway relatives' attitudes and provide relief in a nation suffering widespread destitution.

My research assistant, born in the early 1990s, observed that "Islam has taken a turn in Bangladesh. I remember seeing very few men with beards and very few women clad in burkhas when I was little. Nowadays, hijab has become a fashion and the beard a trend." In her view, the greater outward displays of piety are indicative of changing norms and social pressures to conform.

Contesting Identity, Seeking Justice

Those trends are sketched with searing skepticism by novelist Tahmima Anam in *The Good Muslim* (2011). She examines the rise of Islamic fundamentalism in Bangladesh and the jarring transformation of the secular protagonist's brother into a charismatic religious leader and popular preacher. He carried the scars of Bangladesh's war of independence from Pakistan in 1971, a horrific civil war that devastated the country in a paroxysm of genocide carried out by Pakistan's military, claiming an estimated three million lives. That war to secede from Pakistan casts a long shadow over contemporary Bangladesh. It resulted from the hasty and poorly planned Partition of India in 1947 by the departing British colonial government (see chapter 2). Pakistan was established as an Islamic homeland for India's Muslims and when the British brought down the curtain on empire in August of 1947 there was a mass migration of over ten million Hindus and Muslims in both directions, an exodus marred by violent clashes and the death of some one million people. Thus, the creation of independent India and Pakistan was baptized with blood while the latter was sabotaged by geography.

Bangladesh was East Pakistan and culturally and linguistically Bengali while West Pakistan's population was dominated by Urdu-speaking Punjabis. This split state was an administrative nightmare, with the central government located in the west and the majority population located in the east. The results of the 1970 presidential elections won by Sheikh Mujibur Rahman, the Bengali candidate from Dhaka, were ignored by the government in Islamabad, West Pakistan. This sparked demonstrations in East Pakistan that the military used as a pretext to ruthlessly crackdown on protestors, sparking civil war. This brutal conflict displaced many Bengalis and Hindus; ten million sought refuge in India, prompting Indira Gandhi to dispatch Indian troops against the Pakistan military, inflicting a decisive defeat. These were the birthing pains of a new nation, one left devastated by the nine-month-long Liberation War and divided internally between the victorious independence fighters seeking a secular state founded on principles of tolerance and democracy and those who had sided with the Islamic Republic of Pakistan.

The Pakistan army and its local paramilitary and militia committed widespread atrocities (Bass 2013). The paramilitary and militia were associated with prominent Islamic groups, especially JI, that actively collaborated with

Pakistani forces. From 2000 calls for prosecuting war crimes carried out by these collaborating groups gained momentum. This gaping national wound became a political battleground between the relatively secular Awami League and the comparatively more Islamic-oriented Bangladesh National Party (BNP) and JI. JI's leadership was deeply implicated in the war crimes for which many Bangladeshis wanted to hold them accountable.

In 2008 the Awami League returned to power, partly due to its electoral platform promising accountability for Pakistan's collaborators in 1971, and quickly passed a resolution in 2009 to prosecute war criminals. In 2010 it established a tribunal to do so and in 2013 the leader of JI was found guilty of crimes against humanity and sentenced to life in prison while confederates guilty of various atrocities ranging from murder to rape were given lighter sentences. The JI launched a nationwide one-day general strike to protest the verdict against its leader. But most Bangladeshis were outraged that the convicted war criminals got off lightly, expecting that they would be executed given the horrors they had inflicted. There had been intense media coverage of this gruesome past, and the older generation shared their experiences and loss with their children, awakening a thirst for retribution and justice that spread like wildfire over social media. A mass, peaceful movement erupted in 2013 at Shahbagh Square in Dhaka calling for the execution of the war criminals, a ban on JI from politics, and a boycott of all institutions, media, and businesses associated with the party and the paramilitary organizations that had fought against independence. Hundreds of thousands of protestors mounted a series of mass demonstrations to pressure the Awami League government of Prime Minister Sheikh Hasina to carry out the "will of the people." It was an assertion of a secular identity consecrated by the blood of civil war that highlighted the treachery and brutality of the JI and its affiliates.

Perhaps influenced by the turn of events, later in 2013 the tribunal sentenced a vice president of JI to death for crimes of genocide, rape, and religious persecution against the Bangladeshi people, sparking violent clashes nationwide instigated by JI supporters. Khaleda Zia, leader of the opposition BNP, upped the ante, urging her followers to protest against the Awami League's corruption and repression. The rioting and violence escalated as JI members attacked police and also targeted Hindus, destroying their houses, temples, and statues just as in 1971. The government amended laws so that it could appeal the sentence for the JI leader, and he was subsequently sentenced to death and executed at the end of 2013. The JI has also been banned from politics, so the Shahbag movement of secular liberals demanding justice for four-decade-old war crimes succeeded in securing retribution and portraying the Islamic end of the political spectrum as traitors to the nation. But in doing so they sparked a violent backlash from Islamic parties and people that had been pushed into the corner who were fighting for their honor and survival.

JI at one time was the largest Islamist party in Bangladesh but was banned for the second time in 2013. It was previously banned in 1971 after independence due to its collaboration with the Pakistani military in committing atrocities, forcing its leaders to go into exile in Pakistan. While in exile, JI leaders raised money from Saudi Arabia, claiming that Hindus were persecuting Muslims in Bangladesh. In 1975 they returned and reestablished JI following the assassination of President Sheikh Mujibur Rahman (father of Sheikh Hasina) during a military coup. The Saudi government quickly recognized the new military government, paving the way for JI's return. Its goal is to impose shariah and to ban un-Islamic practices, laws, and organizations. Military rule ended in 1990 and since then JI has participated in BNP-led coalition governments. In 2008, however, it won only two seats in the three-hundred-seat Parliament, suggesting a significant drop in popularity, partly due to corruption convictions against top leaders.

Following the 1975 military coup, the government declared Bangladesh an Islamic Republic, and following another military coup in 1982, the Constitution was amended in 1989 to make Islam the national religion despite secularism being one of the four founding principles of the nation. However, in 2010 the Supreme Court ruled the amendment unconstitutional and void, thus reinstating secularism. Islamists have ignited contemporary identity wars in Bangladesh because they can't abide secularism with hardline clerics inciting violence to overturn constitutional principles and the rule of law. It is also clear that since 1975 the military has aligned with such fundamentalist Islamic groups and tried to use Islam as a political tool to revamp the national identity with an Islamic essence. Arabization has influenced the evolution of this identity, flooding the country with funding for mosques and madrasa throughout the country and building institutional networks of influence that propagate a Salafist Islam that challenges secularism and tolerance. As Khan argues, "the country's powerful military began to use Islam as a countermeasure to Awami League's secular, ambiguously socialist policies and Bengali nationalism. In fact, the military-backed government attempted to change the identity of Bangladesh from a liberal Muslim country to an Islamic country" (Khan 2017, 192). This military-endorsed and Saudi-financed project has come at the expense of religious and ethnic minorities by promoting fanaticism and extremism (Lintner 2002). The appeal became evident in the mid-1980s when some three thousand Bangladeshis joined the jihad in Afghanistan, returning with fighting skills and a radical Islamic ethos (Hasan 2011).

In addressing the threat of religious extremism, the avowedly secularist Awami League government relies on a carrot-and-stick approach of symbolic concessions and harsher measures. Overall, despite the banning of five militant groups between 2006 and 2013, the Shahbagh Movement, the execution of five JI leaders for war crimes, and a security crackdown rife with extra-judicial killings (crossfire and encounter are the euphemisms of choice), Islamists are gaining ground while secularists are on the defensive. Ironically, the successes of the Shahbagh Movement lit a fire among Islamists, creating martyrs and a sense of being besieged. Domestic developments are also shaped by external influences as regional terrorist organizations see great potential in Bangladesh.

Extremism

Transnational terrorist groups have long had links with homegrown terrorist organizations, providing ideological support and in some cases training and funds (Khan 2017). While domestic militant groups are banned and leaders arrested, they regroup and rebrand, tapping into "anxieties over perceived threats to their identity, values and ways of life" that are amplified by a perfect storm of "disparities, mis-governance, alienation, distortions of religious doctrine and 'global narratives of oppression'" (Kahn 2017, 200). IS and al-Qaeda Indian Subcontinent (AQIS) have exploited the opportunities of state dysfunction. Khan adds that "IS has outsourced its activities, using the franchise model used by food chains such as McDonald's, to JMB (Jamaat-ul-Mujahideen) in Bangladesh" (209). IS-linked JMB provides the organization and foot soldiers for establishing an Islamic state through armed struggle, while AQIS relies on its digital presence to engage in targeted recruiting among the angry and disaffected. This strategy appeals to "the Internet-enabled generation that is able to carry out online propaganda and cyber radicalization by promulgating jihadist ideology and training manuals to guide terror attacks" (203).

Both outfits and several other militant groups promote intolerance and violence in terms of an Islamic identity that draws on an aggrieved sense of persecution. They also see Bangladesh as ripe for extremism and their engagement is helping domestic terrorist groups thrive, aided immeasurably by the state's considerable failings. This involves not only what the government is not doing to improve public welfare but also what it is inflicting on them in terms of extra-judicial killings and the overall erosion of the rule law.

Failures of the state have no doubt put wind in the sails of the militants, but for secularists such flaws are comparatively minor compared to what might ensue under the Islamist opposition. While secularists show episodic resolve, their Islamist opponents are well organized and able to sustain large-scale protests and force the government into empowering concessions. Bangladesh is a deeply conservative and religious society and ambivalent about a secular national identity imposed by the liberal elite. Addressing such concerns, Sheikh Hasina has repeatedly clarified that secularism is not devoid of

Islam, advocating what she calls Islamic secularism. She references the seventh-century Medina Charter to back her hybrid concept. Following the hijra when the prophet Muhammad fled Mecca for Medina, where many Jews lived, he issued a charter that protected the rights of minorities and protected freedom of religion, thereby embracing the essence of secularism and pluralism. Prime Minister Hasina invokes this charter to delegitimize Islamic militants' violence and hatemongering against nonbelievers and minorities while reaffirming her Muslim identity. She has to tread carefully in these identity politics as a 2013 Pew Survey found that 82 percent of Bangladeshi Muslims support making shariah the national law and 71 percent said they supported having religious judges settle family and property disputes.

Dr. Mohammed Anwar Hossen, a Dhaka University sociologist, links climate change–induced droughts coupled with water diversion by Indian dams affecting the Ganges River basin to the rise in religious extremism; the lack of water has hammered the livelihoods of over forty million Bangladeshis in this basin who depend on farming (interview April 2017). The state doesn't provide much support for affected households, leaving the already destitute even more desperate. In his view, the environmental crisis feeding extremism will intensify as there are plans afoot in China and India that will divert water from the Brahmaputra River, the other main water supply affecting 70 percent of the nation's population.

In these rural areas, Allah is the only help on offer as Islamic groups provide food, medicine, and education in addition to spiritual support and guidance. Hossen believes that the resulting sense of obligation inspires blind devotion to local clerics and their fundamentalist message of purification and egalitarianism, one that targets the secular state. He confides that fieldwork there is hazardous as outsiders like him are distrusted and closely monitored in a region where militants administer frontier-style justice. This is the fundamentalist heartland where extremist groups have considerable leeway and operate with impunity.

Some argue that it is not secularism that is under attack but Islam itself. Violent extremism and a rigid version of Islam is a threat to the tolerant, pluralist Islam that has prevailed in Bangladesh prior to the wave of Arabization. There are a number of factors specific to Bangladesh that fuel this trend. Chief among these is the bulging angry demographic of those aged fifteen to twenty-four, about thirty million people, who find stiff competition for educational and job opportunities. About twelve million in this cohort are not in education, employment, or training, a large pool of disaffected youth who have nothing to lose. The job market is so tough that even half of university graduates don't have a job, meaning a frustrated and educated group that is susceptible to militant recruiting because they have no stake in the current system and resent those who are making their way in careers and lives. It is this "locked out," comparatively privileged group that suddenly appeared on the radar screen with the Holy Artisan Bakery attack.

Clerics' attacks on secularism and liberal conceits about freedoms and rights resonate with disaffected youth from across the social spectrum seeking meaning in life. For some, death offers more than life. K. Anis Ahmed, writer and entrepreneur, rhetorically asked, "What's more appealing than self-sacrifice for a glorious cause? This is what keeps counter-terrorist experts awake at night, trying to separate the purifying glories of religion from the purifying glory of death" (interview April 2017).

Another factor boosting extremism is the swift upsurge in social media as Internet users jumped from less than one hundred thousand in 2000 to over twenty-one million in 2016. This development has made it much easier for militants to spread their message, stoke anger, arouse religious passions, and reach out to the disaffected and recruit them. One counselor said that very little is done for the growing number of students who develop drug or alcohol problems or are depressed due to poor grades, isolation, or romantic setbacks, and thus they are easily drawn to those who show compassion and offer help and spiritual guidance (interview April 2017). Militant clerics are said to prey on these vulnerable youth, showing empathy to those who have lost their way.

Intolerance and Appeasement

The blogger killings in Bangladesh that began in 2013 and escalated in 2015 and 2016 are a troubling sign of the times. These attacks by Islamists targeted atheists, liberals, and advocates of LGBT rights. The victims were hacked to death by machete-wielding militants because their blogs were deemed objectionable, allegedly for defaming Islam. Four were killed in 2015 and a further fifteen in 2016, demonstrating the inroads of radicalism and sending a chill that extended beyond the progressive blogger community. One was an advocate for gay rights who launched Bangladesh's first LGBT magazine. Some of the militants were arrested, but the grisly executions cast a shadow over public discourse and in some cases led to emigration to safe havens overseas. The uproar that ensued was precisely what Juergensmeyer (2014) terms the "theater of terrorism," maximizing attention through the sheer barbarism. Hacking off heads was a made-for-media display designed to attract attention and provoke an overreaction by the state, one that aimed to challenge a smug global insouciance by targeting liberals espousing the shared values of that imagined community. In that sense, the machetes made a powerful statement that rallied supporters while also exposing the bloody potential of Islamic intolerance.

These attempts to silence secularists were preceded in 2013 by bloody protests demanding the state institute a blasphemy law with provision for capital punishment, a tool often used by Islamists in other Muslim majority nations to persecute political opponents and critics. Prime Minister Sheikh Hasina rejected this demand, arguing that there are already laws in place that enable the government to prosecute anyone harming religious sentiments.

Hefazat-e-Islam (Guardians of Islam), the Islamic group that orchestrated the blasphemy demonstrations, has extracted some concessions from a government eager to burnish its Islamic credentials. It organized a mass protest in front of Dhaka's Supreme Court in April 2017 demanding the removal of a statue known as Lady Justice. The statue was visible from the mosque across the street and was seen as an affront to Islamic values because it is female and thus distracting and because it allegedly represents Western jurisprudence (although the sculptor denied he modeled it on the Greek goddess Themis), anathema to Islamists who advocate adoption of shariah. This was a divisive political issue that pits secularists against religious fundamentalists in a nation where it is open season on free thinkers. The outcome of the antistatue movement was curious, involving its brief removal from the prominent site visible from the mosque and then its reinstallation in a less visible spot nearby soon thereafter. It is indicative that Prime Minister Sheikh Hasina probably agreed to both the removal and reinstallation, walking the tightrope of Bangladesh politics while appeasing divergent critics. This compromise solution is emblematic of numerous accommodations that are denounced by her secularist supporters as the slippery slope of appeasement. They may be right, but the priority for Prime Minister Sheikh Hasina and her Awami League party was to retain power by all means necessary. With the main opposition party leader sidelined on corruption charges, victory in the 2018 elections seemed a predetermined outcome, but paranoia is not reserved for the weak. In the event, the Awami League and its allies won a controversial landslide victory, securing 288 out of 299 seats amid allegations of vote rigging.

Liberal secularists condemn appeasing hardline Islamic groups as a counterproductive dead end. These enemies of secularism are emboldened despite being marginalized in mainstream politics because they have been able to force the ruling Awami League to make symbolic gestures to counter claims that it threatens the nation's Islamic identity. Rather than quelling such demands, clerics portray these concessions to followers as vindicating victories and gain momentum. These unelected religious hardliners are pressuring Bangladesh's elected government to embrace Islamic values as they define them, resorting to street protests and inciting violence to achieve their aims.

In 2017, the banned religious-based party JI along with other Islamic groups condemned a key part of the nation's traditional April New Year celebrations known as Pohela Boishakh as haram or forbidden in Islam. These celebrations, recently awarded UNESCO World Heritage status, include the raucous and colorful procession known as the Mongol Shobhajata-ra, which features dancing and large carnival floats depicting animals, serpents, and other motifs careening through the crowds. This is what JI leaders object to, in addition to intermingling of the sexes, alleging that the parade includes "anti-national cultural elements" because it celebrates Hinduism and Krishna's birth. Religious hardliners believe this is yet another manifestation of what they view as a conspiracy to destroy Bangladesh's Islamic heritage and culture. The government maintains that the event has nothing to do with religion or promoting alien culture. Dhaka University's contingent denounced the rise of Islamic militancy and called for fellow citizens to shun religious demagogues while displaying a large sun. A university administrator explained that "the sun stands for our call to come to the light shunning the darkness. Militancy wants to drag us into the darkness. This time, we are calling for people to ignore the call of darkness and look towards light" (Mahmud 2017).

In contrast to the university, the ruling Awami League caved in by canceling the party's participation in the procession. It also backed down by issuing revised school textbooks that cut seventeen poems and stories that the radical Hefazat-e-Islam deemed atheistic. Moreover, in 2017 the government moved to grant official recognition to previously unauthorized Islamic schools known as qawmi madrasa. The curriculum focuses on religion so that graduates are poorly prepared for the job market. Now that the government recognizes the madrasa degrees as equivalent to a university master's degree in Islamic or Arabic studies, graduates are eligible to take civil service examinations. However, they appear poorly prepared to excel in these exams, geared as they are toward those with standard educations, sowing the seeds of another grievance. Moreover, unappeased by such concessions, Hefazat is demanding more reforms, such as a blasphemy law, capital punishment for atheists, and cancellation of government programs promoting gender equality.

The divide between Islamist and secular Bangladeshis appears to be widening with vigilante radicals hacking bloggers to death because of liberal values deemed antithetical to Islamic precepts. Target lists with names of prominent secularists are also circulating in efforts to shrink the public space for intellectuals and pundits by intimidation. By not disavowing Hefazat and similar groups, the Awami League government is demonstrating tolerance toward those who are intolerant of the nation's secular ideology and betraying those who embrace that identity. Hefzat may not directly engage in terrorism but does support the puritanical Salafist Islam that inspires those who do.

In this context, the government's accommodating approach to radical Islam troubles champions of secularism like K. Anis Ahmed. He helped found the University of Liberal Arts Bangladesh, organizes the annual Dhaka

Literary Festival, and has provided space for the reopening of the Holy Artisan Bakery, site of the nation's worst terrorist attack in 2016. It is a powerful symbol of a defiant secular Bangladesh identity that militant clerics target, but this boldness comes at a cost as he is accompanied by an armed bodyguard. In his view, the main trauma defining Bangladesh identity is the 1971 war for liberation from Pakistan. Problematically, leaders of Islamic groups that collaborated with the Pakistani army in this genocide enjoyed impunity for four decades. Contemporary Islamists seek to portray these leaders as martyrs and victims of a political witch hunt, but Ahmed maintains they were traitors, belatedly and deservedly subject to justice.

hmed worries that Bangladesh is sliding in the wrong direction. He is disappointed about how the government has gifted one concession after another to religious hardliners in order to broaden support without getting anything in return. The politicization of Islam, he argues, is contributing to a decline in democratic institutions, reducing their capacity to curb extremists and preserve what's left of the dwindling space for tolerance. Despite deep reservations about the current government's tactics, he believes that the Awami League "is infinitely better than the alternative" (interview April 2017). The alternative in his view are the dark forces of Islamists who seek to eradicate secularism and establish an Islamic state.

While the battle to remove the goddess of justice statue from the front of the Supreme Court may seem trivial, Ahmed argues that it is about the larger issue of the rule of law being sacrificed to mob pressure; who is sovereign— the elected government or militant clerics? Thus, whether it is the statue, the parade, or textbook poetry, comparatively minor issues considered on their own, they represent the thin edge of the wedge that is fracturing society and its secular identity. He thinks the government's short-term electoral tactics carry the seeds of long-term catastrophe and worries that by allowing militants to position themselves as aggrieved victims, it is unwittingly bequeathing validation to them and their claims.

Democratic Deficit

Aside from intolerance, the other big problem for secularism is the nation's democratic deficit, where there is a shrinking space for democracy, dissent, and opposition parties while human rights are under assault. The military has mounted coups and taken over government for various reasons, meaning that democracy is exercised at the forbearance of the security forces and civilian control is fragile.

Undemocratic practices have also taken root. For example, in 2013 the Awami League banned the JI from participating in elections and the main opposition BNP boycotted the 2014 elections out of concern they would not be conducted in a free and fair manner. The Awami League had refused to abide by the existing practice to cede power to a nonpartisan caretaker government during the election campaign to ensure a level playing field. As a result, Awami candidates ran unopposed for half of Parliament's seats. Due to widespread violence, intimidation, and the BNP's call for a boycott, voter turnout was only 22 percent, way down from 87 percent in the previous election. This meant that the Awami mandate was minimal and that voters favoring a more Islamic identity and polity were disenfranchised. The democratic system for debate over the issues that divide failed to function, leaving the public increasingly polarized. Because democracy is the foundation of the nation's secular identity, this backsliding carries important implications. An illiberal democracy is amplifying the divide between secularists and Islamic hardliners and not providing a pressure valve, thus enhancing the legitimacy and influence of street politics as an expression of popular will denied at the ballot box.

The deficit is widening as in 2018 the government sidelined the leader of the BNP, Khaleda Zia, on corruption charges. Zia is a former prime minister who led the government from 1991 to 1996 and again from 2001 to 2006. She and current prime minister Sheikh Hasina have a longstanding political feud. They are both scions of assassinated former presidents who cooperated back in the late 1980s to oust the military government and restore democracy. Since then the "battling begums" (a term for high-ranking Muslim lady), as the Hasina-Zia feud is known, have rotated the premiership between them in fractious elections marred by vendettas of violence spurred by the personal animus of the rivalry. Back in 2006 Hasina was jailed by the military caretaker government for various corruption scandals and in 2018 the high court convicted Zia of embezzlement.

This dynastic feud is the context for the uninspiring 2018 election results that saw the Awami League take virtually all the seats. Parliament without credible opposition might seem farcical, but in the context of Bangladeshi politics and ferocious battles over national identity, there is a logic to the overkill. Essentially, the Awami League represents the secular forces that fought Pakistan in the 1971 war of liberation, whereas the BNP is linked with the antiliberation forces that sided with Pakistan, diametrically opposed positions that leave little room for compromise (Ahmed 2019). The BNP took power in a 1975 military coup and joined forces with Islamic radicals and revived the JI that had been banned as Pakistani collaborators and traitors to the nation. The clash of visions, 1971 versus 1975, still divides the political world and is referred to as the "unfinished revolution." An assassination attempt in 2004 on Awami League leader Sheik Hassina and senior leadership that killed dozens and injured more than two hundred left a poisonous legacy of deadly enmity between the Awami League and BNP. For the Awami League, survival depends on victory, and this translates into decimating political rivals. The mortal blow delivered to its ideological enemies in

2018 makes sense from this perspective, but such dramatic democratic backsliding bodes ill for political stability and the nation's future.

The gutting of the BNP generates concerns about the collapse of the two-party system and what this portends. Zia's son and other party members were also convicted on embezzlement charges. If the BNP remains frozen out of mainstream politics, hardliner politics of the street will intensify and some of the disaffected and disenfranchised will join militant groups. Either way political risk is increasing in Bangladesh. Excluding enemies from the political mainstream to safeguard secularism does not appear to be a sustainable solution, betrays secular principles, and sow seeds of further radicalization under the banner of Islam and its legions of besieged, angry, and desperate devotees.

Saudi Funding

In 2017 Prime Minister Hasina announced $1 billion in Saudi financing to build 560 mosques across the nation in the name of spreading Islamic culture, extending the potential reach of Salafism. The Saudi government has denied reaching a formal agreement but since the 1980s has poured vast sums into religious projects in Bangladesh. Locals worry that this Arabization through Salafist education and outreach programs will overwhelm the local Sufist traditions. Sufism emphasizes individuals establishing a direct spiritual connection with Allah, one infused with ecstasy rather than the Salafist rigid dogma of living "by the book" that dismisses other strains of Islam as blasphemy. Given that almost 90 percent of Bangladesh's population of nearly 170 million is Muslim, there seems little need to spread an Islamic culture that is already ubiquitous, but the governing Awami League is eager to enhance its Islamic credentials and ride Saudi-funded Arabization to electoral success. The nation already has 250,000 mosques in various states of disrepair, while Dhaka alone has 6,000 mosques, but the new mosques are touted as facilities that will double up as disaster evacuation sites.

IMPLICATIONS AND PARALLELS

Arabization and the intolerant creed of Salafism is gaining momentum in Muslim majority Asia due to lavish Saudi funding and socioeconomic grievances that anger and frustrate youth in these nations. For them, the status quo and moderate Islam offers inadequate solace and little hope of change or a brighter future. Globalization, tarnished as it is by failures and broken promises, gives impetus to Arabization. These unmet expectations reinforce a sense of neoimperial subjugation and powerlessness, as remote and unresponsive forces discriminate, dictate terms, and determine destinies.

Militancy feeds on this discontent and alienation while fundamentalist Islam calls on believers to purify society, rendering this a sacred mission. The religious community empowers and endows those who join the struggle with sacral dignity, status they would not otherwise enjoy, and a sense that they matter, that they are making a difference, and that they are needed. To the extent that democratic space for dissent and reform shrinks, fundamentalists are drawn to militant methods. The forces of secularism remain resilient but appear to be on the defensive and losing the battle for youth in societies in which too many feel acute despair due to scant chances of advancement for themselves or their religious identity. It doesn't matter that Arabization or fundamentalism don't offer any sustainable solution or that extremism is a dead end. The righteous message is a tonic for the bypassed and deracinated dupes and prey of globalization. The legions of the aggrieved have a sense of being under assault, spawning a greater commitment and willingness to sacrifice in the name of Allah. It may seem hard in Muslim majority nations to conjure up credible threats to the primacy of Islam, but fearmongering clerics and state provocations stoke the necessary siege atmosphere.

The ideas and ideology fueled by Arabization are gaining adherents, creating momentum to continue challenging their country's religious identity and national character. These advocates are skilled at manufacturing threats to the ummah, even in nations with some of the world's largest Muslim populations. Bangladesh and Indonesia are targets of Saudi-funded Arabization that is shifting Asian Islam toward a Salafist intolerance and reformist zeal that threatens minorities, the differently devout, and political stability. Manufacturing or exaggerating threats, quick to take umbrage over minor or imagined insults and slights, showing little inclination to forgive and overcome differences, sanctimoniously denouncing and threatening Muslims or nonbelievers who disagree with or diverge from their austere religious vision, the growing influence of Salafists in Asia has been bad news for moderate Muslims, secularists, non-Muslim minorities, and social cohesion.

There are interesting parallels between Indonesia and Bangladesh as they navigate the cross-currents of globalization and Arabization. Both nations embrace a secular identity in their respective constitutions, but this has been challenged ever since they achieved independence by Islamic groups who seek to impose shariah and establish an Islamic state. A secular national identity has been maintained, but this has involved significant concessions to Islamic hardliners. Unelected pressure groups in both nations have exploited democracy and electoral politics to force secular leaders to grant concessions. Indeed, President Joko Widodo selected an Islamic hardliner as his running mate for the 2019 elections in order to fend off the prospects of an Islamic attack campaign like the one that unseated his close ally in the 2017 Jakarta gubernatorial campaign. Choosing a vice presidential running mate who supported that campaign may have disappointed some Jokowi supporters but represented a sensible risk management strategy. Prime Minister Sheik Hasina has also made a series of concessions to Islamic groups and undercut secularists, revealing her anxiety about being portrayed as insufficiently Islamic. This pandering has gained momentum despite facing no significant opposition party. Unlike Indonesia, Islamic parties have held power in Bangladesh, but with the sidelining of the BNP, political Islam has been marginalized from mainstream politics and thereby radicalized. Not having a stake in the parliamentary system, Islamic groups are not subject to the constraints of party politics and appear to have little trouble shrugging off bans on their activities. Moreover, discontent with the Awami government helps discredit secularism and reinforces fundamentalist rejection of democracy as antithetical to Islamic precepts.

In both nations the military has connived with Islamic groups against political forces on the left. In the case of Indonesia, the CIA supported regional rebellions in the Cold War 1950s to destabilize President Sukarno's left-leaning government. In 1965 and 1966 the Indonesian military, with tacit US support, slaughtered many while also helping Islamic youth groups carry out widespread massacres against suspected communists, an orgy of orchestrated violence that claimed several hundred thousand lives. Since 1975 in Bangladesh the military has resorted to coups and manipulated militant Islam to neutralize the leftist leaning, secular Awami League. Remarkably, it even sponsored the rehabilitation of JI, the Islamic group that fought with Pakistan's military to quash Bangladesh's independence, engaging in brutal atrocities. Another military leader revised the Constitution in 1988 to make Islam the national religion, attempting to assert the primacy of religion in national identity and thus overturn the language-based secular national identity that was at the core of the civil war and embraced by the Awami League since independence in 1971. Militants in Indonesia remain bitter that the state has not fulfilled the promises of the Jakarta Charter of 1945 requiring all Muslims to abide by shariah, an agenda shared by their counterparts in Bangladesh. Islamic extremism and terrorism have also led to extra-judicial killings by the security forces in both nations, thereby undermining the rule of law that is essential to democracy and human rights.

Both nations have experienced significant backsliding in their secular and tolerant pluralist national identities. Although Saudi Arabia has devoted considerable resources to promote a more rigid Islam, in Indonesia there seems to be a more widespread pushback against a Salafist identity at the local level, whereas in rural Bangladesh too often the only effective educational, health, or spiritual support on offer emanates from Saudi-financed initiatives that limit the scope for defiance. In both nations, Saudi promotion of intolerance toward Islamic minorities such as the Shi'a or Ahmadiyya has gained momentum, and in both blasphemy has become a powerful political weapon. Finally, in both nations Islamic militant groups maintain important transnational ties, owing a degree of allegiance while gaining enhanced legitimacy and in some cases training and funds. These are run on both a franchise model relying on existing outfits or through targeted recruiting. The Muslim Brotherhood, AQIS, and IS provide varying degrees of external inspiration and promote radicalization that is riding in on the latest wave of Arabization, making the most of shambolic governance and vast inequalities.

Aside from educational scholarships, an important conduit of Salafism is the annual haj. The greatest number of hajis come from Indonesia, 221,000 in 2017, while Bangladesh is number four (127,000) after Pakistan (179,000) and India (170,000). These Asian countries account for 700,000 out of the worldwide annual total of two million haji. Usually pilgrims spend forty days touring religious sites in Saudi Arabia, and this is often a transformative experience that exposes hajis to religious practice in the home of Islam, boosting their religiosity and stature back home. Moreover, overseas workers in the Middle East encounter discrimination and harsh treatment but have prolonged exposure to Salafist practice and thus are an additional source of transmission. With over a million workers in Saudi Arabia alone, half of all those Bangladeshis working in the Mideast, this constitutes a significant potential influence especially given prolonged periods of residence. Indonesia completely banned the dispatch of Indonesia workers to the Middle East since 2015 due to widespread abuses, but this doesn't affect most of the 1.5 million Indonesians already working in Saudi Arabia.

Compared to previous waves, Arabization since the 1980s has been a tsunami involving sustained multidimensional interactions, hyper-connectedness, and lavishly funded institutionalization that marks it as vastly more powerful than anything that has come before, sweeping up far more people in even the remotest hamlets. It is an Arab-centric strand of globalization, carrying similar implications as both are viewed as external homogenizing influences that provoke local backlash and unanticipated consequences. Conservative, authoritarian, and intolerant, contemporary Arabization is infusing national identities and polities with religious zealotry.

In pushing an illiberal agenda, hardline clerics have elicited illiberal responses from Jokowi and Hasina, thus sacrificing the tolerance and democratic values they are putatively trying to save. Marcus Meitzner calls this backsliding "democratic deconsolidation" (Meitzner 2018), a retreat from the values that contribute to political stability, heralding an escalation of religious-centered identity politics. The defense of democracy is best served, he argues, by deploying democratic means and the rule of law, not by criminalizing groups or adopting accommodationist policies. Banning only strengthens and further radicalizes targeted organizations, gifting them an incendiary issue to rally around, while appeasement encourages incessant demands by those who insist on an Islamic national identity and nothing less.

Chapter Five

Militant Monks, Abiding Anxieties

The notion of militant monks seems like an oxymoron, challenging prevailing views that monks are ethereal beings, nonviolent and detached from the petty concerns of the world in which we live. But the appealing image of sutra-chanting monks serenely contemplating the universe while developing their inner spirituality and renouncing power and political engagement is, like all stereotypes, misleading. It is essential to distinguish between the philosophical precepts of Buddhism and Buddhist actions in a specific cultural, temporal, and political context. The way of living espoused by Buddhism is an ideal that guides adherents, whereas how life is lived will necessarily vary due to the imperfect circumstances we confront as imperfect beings; identity is not created in a vacuum and is layered and oscillating (Jerryson 2018). Moreover, people have multiple situational identities, and each is refracted through the prisms of other identities (Appiah 2018). From their quiver of shifting and overlapping identities, people adopt what seems appropriate and fitting depending on who they are with, where they are, and when. People are complicated, so someone who is a devout Buddhist can also be a violent activist or bigoted zealot without one identity canceling out the other.

The piety and devotion of the devout can be subject to broader social and political currents including nationalism and its exponents. It is precisely the legitimacy that religion confers that makes it so appealing to those with such agendas. Buddhism endows monks with a moral authority that some of them feel they should invoke to mitigate pain and suffering, to challenge injustice, and to engage in activism to protect the sangha (Buddhist community of monks, nuns, novices, and laity). In some situations, this rationalization of activism is manipulated for political purposes, wrapping glowering nationalist purpose in the saffron robes of religious piety. This is an empowering identity that provides more immediate release and results than the karmic cycle of becoming, and therein lies its appeal for the engaged or impatient.

Before examining the cases of militant monks in contemporary Myanmar and Sri Lanka, first we briefly explore the rich tradition of their engagement in Asia challenging, or collaborating with, political authority and defending what they believe is important to the sangha.

TRADITION OF ENGAGEMENT

In fifteenth-century Japan the ikko ikki monks of the Jodo-Shinshu (Pure Land sect) were also warriors who believed that death in battle earns one passage to heaven while cowardice is the path to hell. They controlled a fairly large territory and rebuffed efforts to tax them or locals. But after attacking the imperial capital of Kyoto in 1528 and laying waste to some of it, they antagonized powerful warlords who saw them as a threat to their own aspirations for political power. Oda Nobunaga, a samurai warlord who emerged as primus inter pares in the late sixteenth century, spent a decade battling them and eventually prevailed in 1580, slaughtering an estimated twenty thousand monks. Thereafter, under Tokugawa rule (1603–1858), the shogunal authorities cracked down on religious communities, torturing and executing thousands of Christians in the western end of the archipelago near Nagasaki while also making sure monks never again became a military threat.

In contemporary Japan, Soka Gakkai (value creation society) is a lay religious organization that carries on this tradition of Buddhists engaging in politics minus the swords. It boasts some eight million members, exaggerated no doubt, but is known for its formidable voter mobilization operations in support of its affiliated political party Komeito and its coalition partner the Liberal Democratic Party (LDP) (McLaughlin 2018). It is a stalwart defender of Japan's pacifist identity as enshrined in Article 9 of the Constitution, but Komeito's participation in the ruling coalition led by the LDP has been problematic for some members given the Abe Doctrine of easing constitutional curbs on Japan's armed forces and boosting military cooperation with the United States (McLaughlin 2015). Komeito is also a powerful advocate for environmental issues and support for low-income households, while Soka Gakkai operates educational institutions and media outlets. About 3 percent of Japanese self-identity as members, a rarity of religious devotion in a nation where more than 70 percent acknowledge having no religious faith. The military fanaticism associated with wartime state Shinto casts a shadow over Japan's post-World War II religious landscape even as the traditional rituals remain widely practiced and woven into Japanese life and identity (Hardacre 2017).

During the escalating American involvement in the Vietnam War, Washington's handpicked president, Ngo Dinh Diem, adopted increasingly repressive tactics to sustain political power and neutralize enemies. Diem was from the Catholic minority in South Vietnam and so it was never going to be easy for him to gain popular support in the Buddhist majority nation. He presided over a corrupt government in which relatives held key positions and abused their power. While favoring Catholics and promoting public displays supportive of their faith, security forces cracked down on Buddhist groups, pulling down their banners and disrupting their celebrations and rallies while arresting supporters. This triggered nationwide anti-Diem demonstrations that were met with draconian measures. This crackdown offended popular sensibilities and provoked more protests in a cycle of escalating repression. Security forces, by entering Buddhist temples without removing their boots, trampled on religious taboos, a breach of etiquette that antagonized and unified the Buddhist community. The haunting 1963 image of a monk committing self-immolation in downtown Saigon in protest against Diem was the beginning of the end for his government. The gruesome photograph of the flames consuming the monk as he sat in the lotus position thrust Vietnam into the American conscience. The media explained why the American puppet was loathed and feared by a nation supported by the United States. And so Diem became expendable, especially after his sister-in-law publicly sneered at the display on television, caustically referring to monk BBQs. The Diem family's arrogance, brutality, and isolation precipitated their downfall, a political liability eliminated with a wink and a nod from Washington as top South Vietnamese generals assassinated Diem and his brother and seized power.

Self-immolation is the ultimate sacrifice in what must be one of the most agonizingly painful ways to ends one's life. Imagine planning such a public act of defiance, allowing the gasoline to be poured on yourself, knowing that a fiery, excruciating death is your final act. It is a weapon of the weak against the powerful, a shaming political statement by those who have no other means to convey their anguish, as with Tibetan monks in China (Ramsay 2016). Monks feel responsible for their community, and when they see it defiled, oppressed, or otherwise abused, there is a compulsion to act. While state security forces enjoy massive advantages when it comes to violence, monks rely on their moral authority to reproach those in power.

In Tibet, the seeds of resistance were sown in the 1950s and 1960s when China took over, suppressing rebellions and insurgency while dismantling the existing feudal social order. The widespread desecration of sacred Buddhist temples by Red Guards during the Cultural Revolution (1965–1972) and abiding communist antipathy to the theocracy and religious practices that are the heart of Tibetan culture have sparked a clash of civilizations in the Tibetan plateau. The Chinese government may have abandoned communism, but the brash nouveau riche materialism that has emerged equally threatens to overwhelm Tibet as Beijing mobilizes its natural resources to bolster economic growth with scant concern for the environmental or social consequences. The ongoing "gold rush" at the roof of the world involves massive mining operations for gold, copper, lithium, silver, and chromium while civil engineers divert watersheds and threaten regional river systems in South and Southeast Asia. Along with spiritual desecration, this resource plundering and consequent environmental despoilment represents a further affront to Tibetans. They shoulder the attendant costs while Han Chinese reap the rewards. Similarly, China seeks to hollow out Tibetan culture and commodify it for mass tourism, but this conceit of transforming Tibet into a theme park also rankles.

Bloody riots erupted in Lhasa in 2008, spreading throughout the plateau. This widespread unrest exposed the emptiness of Beijing's claims about "harmonious ethnic relations." Local Tibetans targeted ethnic Han businesses, venting their frustrations about the social, cultural, and economic harm caused by the increasing presence of strangers in their homeland. There was a harsh security crackdown and widespread human rights violations that triggered a wave of self-immolations. The Chinese government has tried to limit domestic media coverage of these ongoing tragedies precisely because they underscore the failures of Chinese attempts at multiculturalism. The state insists on redoubled efforts to preserve China's national unity based on intensified assimilation and blames external interference for simmering ethnic tensions. The Chinese Communist Party (CCP) has not coped well with the legacy of marginalization and repression that has created huge impediments to its assimilationist policies. Paradoxically, the CCP's prioritization of maintaining stability militates against bold reforms but doing so is generating instability. Calls for ending regional autonomy and minority preferences confront vested interests that support continuation of such policies even if they have been a failure. Problematically, ethnic policies are a relatively low-level priority for China's leadership and ethnic issues only crop up when there is violence. Threats to public order are dealt with by intensified security measures that exacerbate grievances and perpetuate the cycle of violence.

Between 2009 and 2017 at least 148 Tibetans have protested against Chinese rule by resorting to self-immolation. The immolations embarrass the Chinese government because they make a tragic counterpoint to government claims about Tibet and the benefits of Chinese development. Aside from the media crackdown, the government has also convicted monks and supporters of inciting and coercing people to self-immolate. The Dalai Lama in exile is cautious about provoking China and refrains from commenting about the suicides. It is unlikely that Tibetans will regain independence or a measure of justice, but that does not keep them from hoping. Tibetan leaders seek common ground with the over three hundred million Han Chinese Buddhists who also strive for greater cultural and religious freedom, but there are no signs yet of such solidarity.

The Dalai Lama has long been a nettlesome presence for Beijing because he has been an articulate spokesman for his people and nurtures global sympathy for their plight. Based in northern India, where about one hundred thousand Tibetans live in exile, he is lionized around the world. A tireless traveler, he has been an influential ambassador for his people and Buddhism, meeting many heads of state. Perhaps more importantly, he continues to attract massive and positive media attention, giving him a platform to shape international perceptions.

When the Olympic torch toured Europe prior to the 2008 Beijing Olympics, at several points along the procession pro–Free Tibet protestors disrupted the procession, a tangible sign of the Dalai Lama's effective diplomacy in shaping global perceptions that leaves Beijing seething. China also underestimates the power of the sacred to animate an identity that cannot be erased by repression, try as it might. More effective may be the ongoing drowning of Tibetan culture by mass tourism and an influx of Han migrants for whom Buddhism is a curiosity rather than a way of life.

SAFFRON REVOLUTION

In September 2007 soldiers fired on unarmed monks demonstrating on the streets of Yangon, Myanmar, in protest against the ruling junta's economic mismanagement and the prevalence of poverty. The monks were bravely using their unquestioned moral authority to draw attention to the grave problems faced by a public driven to despair by a repressive government that thwarted its democratic aspirations. In 1990 the military government gambled on multiparty elections to gain legitimacy, just two years after the bloody repression of the 1988 student-led pro-democracy demonstrations. The people had not forgotten and delivered their verdict, handing a landslide victory to Aung San Suu Kyi's National League for Democracy (NLD). The military refused to accept this outcome and retained power in defiance of the popular will. This derailing of democracy prompted international condemnation and sanctions that worsened already grim economic conditions. Development assistance and financing from international financial institutions dried up as the international community pressured the government to make a transition toward democracy. But the military government hid behind sanctions, blaming them for the economic problems that their policies had caused. It was a corrupt system of cronyism and nepotism, but proponents and apologists maintained that without the firm hand of the military the nation would explode, pointing to the numerous ongoing, armed rebellions on the nation's periphery.

Dire conditions undermined the regime's blood-spattered legitimacy. The UN estimated that as of 2007 that more than 90 percent of the nation's fifty-six million people lived on less than $1 a day, 75 percent subsisted below the poverty line, and 10 percent of children died before the age of five (Petrie 2007). The despair of Myanmar's people stemming from this humanitarian crisis was vented in protests led by monks that erupted all over the country in September 2007. It took great courage to march against the government at that time knowing as marchers did what the regime was capable of. The collective memory of the brutal crackdown in 1988, when at least three thousand protestors were killed and thousands more imprisoned and tortured, loomed menacingly over the Saffron protestors.

The government's decision on August 15, 2007, to cut fuel subsidies caused a sudden surge in fuel prices and the doubling of commuting costs. This was the spark that ignited the dry kindling of desperation as monks in their thousands staged peaceful protests all over the nation. Monks I interviewed toward the end of 2007 in various parts of Myanmar all said that they marched out of concern for the worsening plight of the people; they wanted the government to lower commodity prices and address the needs of the people (Kingston 2008). Dependent as they are on daily alms, monks understand well the living conditions of ordinary Burmese. Every morning long lines of shaven-headed monks wearing maroon robes carry alms bowls and stop in front of devout Buddhist women who spoon out portions of rice and in some cases offer canisters of condiments. As economic conditions worsened, more families sent their young sons to become novices, leaving them in the monasteries for longer periods of time, an informal social welfare system that was bursting at the seams. In the absence of initiatives by the State Peace and Development Council (SPDC), the military junta's official name, to help alleviate the suffering of the poor, the sangha became the safety net of last resort. However, as the ranks of the monks swelled and the alms offered by an increasingly hard-pressed citizenry declined, the monks felt they had to act. They were encouraged by radio broadcasts from the '88 Generation of student exiles in Thailand who urged monks to take to the streets, never imagining that the monks would be treated so brutally.

Chanting sutras and carrying placards urging the government to reduce commodity prices, legions of peaceful monks put the SPDC on the spot for its woeful inability to alleviate the people's misery and provide basic needs. Desperate and angry people risked joining the monks because they wanted political change and viewed the military as an impediment to a better life. Threatened by this spontaneous groundswell of protest, the government attacked as soldiers shot into the crowds, beat and rounded up demonstrators, including monks, and carted many off to jail. A UN investigator documented thirty-one deaths among protestors and implicated the government in the disappearance of many monks (Pinheiro 2007). He noted arbitrary arrests and the taking of family "hostages" to pressure dissidents to surrender and drew attention to "appalling detention conditions which fail to meet international standards on the treatment of prisoners and in fact constitute cruel, inhuman and degrading treatment prohibited under international law." Moreover, he alleges that "a ruthless campaign of reprisals took place, targeting monks, nuns, political activists, human right defenders and other individuals who organized or participated in the peaceful demonstrations, as well as their family members."

Several weeks after the military had mowed down monks on the streets of Yangon, one monk observed, "The soldiers had a choice between going to jail now [for refusing orders] or hell later [for killing monks] and they made the wrong choice" (interview December 2007). Another monk in Sittwe told me that generals do not fear going to hell, but rank-and-file soldiers may not be so unconcerned about their karma. No one can relish rebirth as a "mangy, shit-eating mutt," as a few angry monks put it. I was also taken aback when they asked why the United States did not send F16s to bomb Naypidaw, the dystopian capital the junta built for itself, saying that's where the "bad men" are. Such was the depth of resentment that even monks were calling for airstrikes! This is not what I expected, but in scenic Mrauk U, a few hours' riverboat ride away, I met other monks with the same question. In both places, antigovernment invective was laced with vitriol about Rohingya and Muslims.

It was my first inkling that my assumptions about Buddhism needed rethinking. Jerryson argues that there is a lot of violence in Buddhism and attributes the disconnect between our perceptions and reality to "a tendency in modern Western discourses to distinguish religion from power and politics" (Jerryson 2018, 2). He explains how this taxonomy is not evident in the more holistic view of Buddhism that regards religion as inseparable from the context in which it is practiced. Moreover, he explains, violence is not necessarily negative and can have positive connotations, especially if accompanied by compassion. Monks are endowed with cultural and moral authority in the sangha that at times can require them to engage in conduct that appears to be at odds with Buddhist precepts but is acceptable in terms of promoting the greater good as they see it. Religion is not abstract or something distant from everyday lives but rather woven inextricably into them, and thus it organically evolves and adapts to the needs and circumstances of adherents. Involvement in political and economic matters may seem the antithesis of religiosity, but again this view overlooks local perceptions about Buddhism as an encompassing way of life that must be nurtured, respected, and protected. Perceived threats may be manipulated or invented by actors with other agendas, but anxieties sowed can render such actions into moral imperatives for the righteous.

Asked if the rupture between the military and the sangha could be repaired, a nun in Sagaing noted ruefully that, as with a shattered clay pot that has been mended, cracks remain visible. Across the river, in December 2007, Mandalay monks made a stir by refusing to accept alms offered by a top general who was also a government minister, and around the nation there were reports that monks refused donations from anyone related with the military, turning their alms bowls upside down. This very public rebuke prevented military personnel and their families from earning merit or participating in lifecycle rituals that are deemed crucial in Myanmar. Excommunicating the military earned public respect and reflected the seething anger in the monasteries over the killing, beatings, and humiliation of monks.

Desperate attempts by the government to brand the protesting monks as convicts and hooligans or assert that foreign governments orchestrated the protests were widely dismissed as propaganda, a precursor of the military-orchestrated fake news that now inundates social media. But not everyone in the wake of the Saffron Revolution was convinced that democratization was the magic wand for healing the deep wounds and divisions that have bedeviled Myanmar since independence in 1948. The monks had rallied the people in defiance of the government, triggering a crackdown that shredded the regime's remaining legitimacy, but ousting the tyrants in a nation that had been run by the military for half a century carried significant risks. As Morten Pedersen pointed out quite prophetically, "it could also open up the way for demagoguery and agitation based on ethnic and religious identity that would fuel latent conflicts" (Pedersen 2008, 264). At the time nobody imagined that some ultranationalist monks would soon be the ones pouring oil onto these embers of communal strife.

ULTRANATIONALIST, HATEMONGERING BUDDHISM

Ashin Wirathu is the heavy metal rockstar monk of Buddhism in Myanmar. He is a controversial member of the Ma Ba Tha (Association for the Protection of Race and Religion [MBT]) who graced the cover of *Time* magazine on July 1, 2013, with the caption "The Face of Buddhist Terrorism: How Monks Are Fueling Anti-Muslim Violence in Asia." In response to the *Time* article, President Thein Sein defended Wirathu while the latter tried to blame Islamic extremists for the article and alleged it was part of their plans for jihad against Myanmar. Demonstrations condemned *Time* and displayed a banner proclaiming Wirathu was "Not the Terrorist, but the Protector of Race, Language and the Religion," the nationalist trifecta.

MBT was established in mid-2013 and rocketed to prominence in 2014 after the state banned the Buddhist 969 movement for suspected complicity in communal rioting. Wirathu was involved in promoting the 969 movement that advocated boycotts of Islamic shops. This movement drew on the symbolism of the numbers that refer to the virtuous three Jewells of the Buddha, the number 9 representing his nine great attributes and 6 representing the six great attributes of the Dhamma (or Buddhist law), while the third number 9 represents the nine great attributes of the Sangha. The 969 movement issued stickers emblazoned with the numbers for shop owners to display so that Buddhist shoppers knew where to shop and where not to.

The core message of 969 was that Myanmar was for ethnic Bamar (Burmese) Buddhists and represented an attempt by activist monks to strengthen the Burmese business community by dissuading Buddhist customers from patronizing Muslim shops. This anti-Islamic economic boycott started in the southern town of Mawlamyine and quickly spread throughout the central Burmese heartland due to the support and influence of likeminded monks eager to empower the sangha. It is not a big leap from a boycott to some incident igniting riots, deaths, and looting. By inflaming communal tensions and wreaking havoc, these Buddhist militants have much to answer for, but they enjoyed impunity because security forces were supportive.

The 2013 Mektila riots in central Myanmar were sparked by a commercial dispute between a Muslim merchant and Buddhist customers and quickly escalated, claiming the lives of forty people, including one monk, and displacing thousands more from their torched neighborhoods. Police stood by and watched violent mobs running amok, in one instance attacking an Islamic boarding school and killing thirty-two teenage students and four teachers. Buddhist monks were among the rampaging rioters who were armed with machetes, pipes, and chains and caught on video killing two Muslims by setting fire to them. Perpetrators and instigators on both sides were prosecuted, but in the wake of the Mektila incident communal rioting erupted in several other towns.

These majoritarian impulses that animated 969 found an even more powerful and menacing expression in MBT. In early 2014, MBT established a branch in Mandalay where Wirathu is based, and he became the most prominent member. He had been involved in the 969 movement and built on its efforts to promote race and religion laws while championing Buddhist nationalism and hyping the Islamic threat. MBT penetrated into remote parts of the country and became the most prominent Buddhist group advocating a religious-nationalist majoritarian identity.

Wirathu, the poster child for hate speech in Myanmar, was also dubbed the Osama bin Laden of Buddhism and the subject of a full-length documentary *The Venerable W.* In a review for the *Guardian*, Peter Bradshaw (2017) wrote of Wirathu's "pure irrational malevolence, something that does not have a political or ideological explanation. Maybe it's a clinical pathology. Nationalist fever could simply be a pretext for a bacchanal of violence." This malevolence, he adds, feeds on "paranoia over territory and the same self-pitying overdog victimhood—beating up a smaller minority, and claiming that they are in fact the larger force, backed by foreigners. Wirathu even deploys an outrageous 'false flag' claim: that Rohingyas are setting fire to their own villagers to get international support." The documentary exposes Wirathu's intense Islamophobia, expressed in sermons and displayed on a wall of his monastery that is covered in gruesome images of maimed bodies attributed to Muslim violence, reminders of what the fight is about; "they are comings after us, so we must get rid of them first."

Such notoriety doesn't come easy, but Wirathu has made a name for himself through high-profile hatemongering on social media and cultivation of mainstream domestic and international media. He has declared war on "love jihad," targeting the unproven runaway population growth of Muslims due to polygamy and conversion of women to Islam though marriage. His shrilly racist and unspiritual sermons are reproduced in bestselling CDs and DVDs. Security forces did little to interfere with his street demonstrations, lending credence to rumors that MBT was linked to state security forces.

As Myanmar was making the difficult transition toward democracy, it appears that Wirathu and the MBT stoked communal violence aimed at boosting voter support for the military's political arm, the Union Solidarity and Development Association (USDA), in the run up to the 2015 elections. The logic was that fueling communal clashes would enable President Thein Sein of the USDA to portray Myanmar as a powder keg ready to explode, requiring a robust security approach and thereby undermine the appeal of Aung San Suu Kyi's untested NLD. A more devious aspect of this campaign sought to maneuver Aung San Suu Kyi into the position of appearing overly solicitous toward Muslims and the vilified Rohingya, thus "betraying" the Buddhist majority. This proved a colossal miscalculation and the NLD won in a landslide, suggesting that MBT was not as influential as many believed at the time. Or perhaps the public hated the military more than they feared Muslims. At any rate, the generals and militant monks could not dissuade the people from voting for change as the USDA was decimated at the polls, winning just 41 seats overall versus the 390 won by the NLD.

It seems that this overwhelming repudiation of the USDA had more to do with the military's record of brutality, corruption, and suppression of democ-racy than a rejection of the MBT's signature agenda. The four bills known as "Laws for the Protection of Race and Religion" that the MBT helped draft and persuaded the USDA to pass in 2015 before the election appear to enjoy widespread public support. Huge rallies gathered to celebrate passage of the legislation that regulates Buddhist women's marriage, religious conversion, population control, and monogamy, tapping into widespread anxieties and resentment toward Muslims, whipped up by the MBT. A Buddhist woman under the age of twenty now must get her parents' permission or that of a legal guardian to marry a man of a different faith. The local township officials can only approve the marriage two weeks after the announcement of the pending nuptials, when objections by any citizen to the interfaith marriage may be registered and a court case lodged to prevent the union. Those who don't comply face the possibility of imprisonment and/or confiscation of assets. Not only does this deny Muslim men freedom of religion, it also infringes on the rights of Buddhist women. These new laws weaken women's rights and grants parents (or guardians) control over the most intimate and important decision many people will make in their lives. The conversion bill forbids conversion to another religion for anyone under the age of eighteen. Adult converts must also apply for permission from the authorities, who are obliged to interview the aspiring convert several times over several weeks to ascertain whether the decision is voluntary and their belief is genuine, checking familiarity with the religious tenets, before any conversion can take place. The population control measure can be implemented at authorities' discretion if certain groups have a "considerably higher" population growth than others. This gives the state power to require a space of three years between the births of children, although no penalties are specified. At the time of passage, Muslims were the apparent target of this provision. The monogamy bill bans the Islamic practice of polygamy and also criminalizes living with a partner who is not one's spouse. Taken together they represent a significant step toward an intolerant majoritarianism that stokes prejudices toward, and fears about, the Muslim menace.

The MBT ultranationalists wrap an angry ethnic Bamar nationalism targeting minorities in the soothing saffron robes of religion. Bestowing religious sanction on the pogroms and harassment confers a veneer of legitimacy on this exclusive and intolerant nationalism. The MBT dominates the political space regarding Buddhism's role in society, even after the State Sangha Council tried banning it. MBT is certainly more than its anti-Islamic activism, but this is a significant aspect of the organization's exploits, giving it wide exposure and influence over public discourse as "defenders of the faith." Not everyone felt comfortable with the racist vitriol, but dissenters were intimidated by the brutishness on display and deferred to the star power of Wirathu. In January 2015, for example, he led a rally in Yangon, and in unusually coarse language denounced Yanghee Lee, the UN Human Rights envoy to Myanmar, declaring, "Don't assume you are a respectable person, just because you have a position in the UN. In our country, you are just a whore" (Pilgrim 2015). He added, "If you are so willing, you may offer your arse to the *kalar* [racist slur commonly used to denigrate South Asians and Muslims in Myanmar]. But you will never sell off our Arakan State!"

So why was Wirathu lashing out at the UN Special Rapporteur? Lee had criticized the discriminatory 2015 Protection of Race and Religion legislation and called on Myanmar to grant citizenship to Rohingya born in the country (see chapter 6). She ignored his vile tirade while commenting, "Fundamental rights are not hierarchical—they aren't conditional upon one another. They're inalienable" (Pilgrim 2015). Perhaps so, but not if the mad monk and his legions of supporters have a say in the matter. Wirathu isn't someone who anyone wanted as an enemy with his masses of devoted followers. His checkered history of inciting violence against Myanmar's Muslim minority and reputation as a bigoted rabble-rouser with ties to "dark forces" made him a scary presence in the monastic community. Unlike almost all other monks, he has been jailed for various offenses related to his political activism. On the day of his UN vitriol, he marched through Yangon with about five hundred supporters, in a nation where such large demonstrations require a police permit, except if one is well connected.

So what is with these militant monks? Certainly they are forcing us to reconsider the stereotype of monks as sutra-chanting lotus eaters dedicated to mindfulness and detachment through quiet meditation. These firebrand extremists are wolves in saffron vestments, defaming their faith and urging others to engage in acts of violence. Wirathu's incendiary rhetoric whips crowds into a frenzy, promoting a Buddhist nationalism that taps into the miseries of endemic poverty and offers a handy scapegoat.

The 2015 landslide victory by the NLD left the MBT looking weakened as a political force because it had publicly backed the USDA and urged members to vote for it. Given that the USDA had delivered on its side of the quid pro quo—passing the Protection of Race and Religion legislation the MBT had lobbied for—it appeared that the MBT was unable to reciprocate by leveraging its national network to mobilize voters. But the NLD and everyone knew that the USDA's rout was not an accurate barometer of the MBT's still massive influence in a nation where 88 percent of the population is Buddhist and where any attempts to counter the legislation or denounce the rampant bigotry could trigger a powerful backlash. The MBT retained legitimacy among not only nationalists but also those who were anxious about the profound socioeconomic upheaval and influx of foreign influences accompanying Myanmar's opening up to the world that threatened the way of life they were familiar with. The post-2011 transition toward democracy and embrace of social media, along with a surge of foreign investments and tourism, left people rattled and uncertain, seeing no hope in the USDA but worried that the NLD was too liberal and tolerant and thus incapable of fulfilling the state's traditional role as protector of the faith. Buddhism was the anchor people relied on in the maelstrom of sweeping changes and the MBT tapped into those anxieties and offered support not just in terms of legal reforms but also in various educational, welfare and disaster relief activities. In Myanmar/Burma historically Buddhism and the state were inseparable, and the government is expected to promote and defend the faith. Buddhist nationalists, however, wanted more than just a defense of religion, also demanding protection of the nation's ethnic Bamar cultural identity amid fears of inundation by Muslims, other ethnic groups in Myanmar, and the forces of globalization. This meant a blending of political and nonpolitical activism in support of the majority's national identity in which religion played a key role as intrinsic to that identity and the nation's culture. The MBT's strident vilification of Islam also resonated with the nation's Buddhists because they shared the organization's alarmist views of Islam as a religion prone to violence, aggressive conversions, intolerance of other faiths, mistreatment of women, high fertility, and ultimate goal of imposing shariah law. Muslims are seen to be opposed to reciprocating the religious freedom on which they insist. Even though they represent less than 5 percent of Myanmar's population, fears of a demographic explosion abound, whipped up by social media, fake news, and militant monks. This was one of many deep-seated grievances unleashed by the relaxation of authoritarian restrictions post-2011 when the military transferred responsibility to a civilian government while retaining authority. The sudden and rapid dissemination of social media on newly established mobile phone networks provided a platform for airing and amplifying such grievances and Burmese Buddhist chauvinism.

It was not until July 2016 that the NLD government moved against MBT, getting the government's Sangha State Council or Ma Ha Na (MHN) to declare the MBT an unlawful monk's association because it was not operating according to monastic rules. MBT countered that it was not bound by these rules because it was not just a monk's association and involved lay people. In May 2017 MHN called on MBT to disband and cease all activities, warning members would face sanction and legal penalties if it did not comply. Although the government ban on MBT called for removal of all signage around the nation, local affiliates have defied this order and still engage in a variety of social welfare services, while some affiliates have rebranded as Buddha Dharma Philanthropy. MBT in whatever guise remains resilient because it has more legitimacy than the government or the state-linked MHN on religious issues and has a cadre of charismatic monks, not just Wirathu, who broaden its appeal. MBT supporters might not back the involvement in politics or the hatemongering, but at the community level MBT is associated with educational, legal aid, disaster relief, and welfare initiatives that provide tangible benefits while its Buddhist Sunday classes are enormously popular. It is a powerful voice on moral and spiritual issues and attends to the sense of crisis swirling through villages caught up in the larger whirlpool of rapid transformation. This is something the state has been unable to do.

The NLD's hope is to separate the ultranationalist hatemongering agenda from the community services efforts, but tensions over the proper role of Buddhism and monks in modernizing Myanmar will persist because the government is seen as too solicitous of minorities. Aung San Suu Kyi has invested much in trying to advance ethnic reconciliation, but prioritizing this agenda heightens concern that she is inclined to make concessions that undermine the paramount role of Buddhism and an ethnic Burmese-dominated national polity by accepting federalism. MBT thus finds her efforts on ethnic reconciliation useful in rallying and broadening its base, hyping the threats and fearmongering about the state betraying the sangha and thus abnegating its traditional duty to promote and protect the faith. The government, however, is bound to uphold the secular 2008 Constitution that recognizes the "special position of Buddhism as the faith professed by the great majority of the citizens" while also acknowledging that Christianity, Islam, Hinduism, and Animism have adherents in the country. Moreover, given that one-third of the population is not ethnic Burmese, there are practical reasons for tolerance toward diversity.

The International Crisis Group (ICG) noted that efforts to rein in the MBT "have been largely ineffective at weakening the appeal of nationalist narratives and organisations and have probably even enhanced them" (ICG 2017). Following political liberalization in 2011, there has been an upsurge in extreme Buddhist nationalism, anti-Muslim hate speech, and deadly communal violence, involving not only the Rohingya in Rakhine State but also across the country. Certainly, MBT is involved in channeling the angry resentments of Myanmar's impoverished majority but banning it will not tame the wave of majoritarian prejudice and intolerance it has unleashed.

Religious nationalism is rising along with concerns about identity and culture in a world of intensified globalization. Social media helps disseminate this trend but is also a powerful tool to challenge it and reassert religious values. The process of democratization in nations with weak state institutions like Myanmar leaves the public especially open to religious chauvinism. In such situations, the state has strong incentives to embrace religious nationalism and position itself as defender of the faith to bolster legitimacy and enhance authority. Acting to discredit monks and MBT for engagement in politics is risky because even if most Buddhists don't think that such participation or hatemongering is proper for monks, they understand that the monks and MBT are compensating for the state's perceived shortcomings. They are acting because the state is failing to both properly carry out its religious duties and attend to the needs of the destitute. Moreover, MBT is working to counter the erosion of Buddhist culture, stem the surge in secularism, especially among youth, and propagate shared Buddhist values. So even if MBT has been partially suppressed, the movement has not been derailed because it remains relevant to the lives of the faithful, retains moral authority, and is viewed as an authentic voice for Burmese Buddhist culture. As Schonthal and Walton point out, "many Burmese Buddhists see religious, ethnic, and racial identities as essential components of national identity" (Schonthal and Walton 2016, 84).

The government decision to disband MBT in May 2017 came soon after it banned Wirathu from delivering sermons for one year. In trying to turn down the heat of communal tensions and to remove Wirathu from the limelight, the government ordered him to refrain from giving his ultranationalist, Islamophobic sermons in public, arguing that he was inflaming tensions and inciting violence. Subsequently, Wirathu made several public appearances with his mouth taped shut to mock this ban and protest his silencing by authorities. He mostly complied, but in December 2017 he gave a typically combative interview with the Irrawaddy, justifying the military's ethnic cleansing campaign targeting Rohingya Muslims in Rakhine State and faced no legal sanctions for doing so (Wirathu 2017).

Wirathu also was very active on social media with a large Facebook following in the hundreds of thousands in Burmese and English. In 2017 Wirathu complained that Facebook was impeding access and removing some posts, but much of his vitriol kept appearing, largely unimpeded, on a daily basis. Often he posted graphic images of dead and dismembered bodies he blamed on Muslim violence and his updates were brimming with false information vilifying Muslims and insisting that all Rohingya are outsiders, Bengali migrants from neighboring Bangladesh who have no right to be in Myanmar (see chapter 6). In Myanmar, Facebook is the Internet as there are some thirty million users, about half the nation's entire population. Until 2018 it was a largely unregulated soapbox for fake news and misinformation about the Rohingya. During the ethnic cleansing campaign waged by the armed forces against the Rohingya from late August 2017, MBT and Wirathu were watching their handiwork bear grotesque fruit. Since then Facebook has closed the accounts of prominent hatemongers and disseminators of fake news.

U Dhammapiya, a Yangon-based senior monk in MBT, made it clear he thinks Wirathu has been bad news for the organization and it would be better off without him (interview December 2017). In his opinion, Wirathu is too emotional and speaks without considering his words and their impact, sacrificing the mindfulness required of monks for the limelight of media attention. He explained that MBT is only known for Islamophobia due to Wirathu's actions and invective, overshadowing the important social welfare and educational work of the organization. MBT advocates free compulsory education through the end of high school, but because the government lacks the will and/or wherewithal to do so, MBT tries to do what it can because, Dhammapiya says, education is the key to poverty alleviation. He holds a doctorate in philosophy and is a well read, thoughtful, and exceptionally articulate monk who exudes serenity, the antithesis of Wirathu's bombast and hyperbole. In his view, Wirathu's rants and outbursts are counterproductive and provoke censure and unwelcome notoriety. However, he does not oppose the campaign against Muslims and the Rohingya, agreeing with Wirathu that the latter are Bengalis who should return to Bangladesh. Thus, it's more a matter of style and nuance as opposed to objectives.

Dhammapiya helped draft the controversial interfaith marriage law that was part of the Protection of Race and Religion legislation, saying it encourages peace among different faiths and protects Buddhist women from being forced to convert to Islam when they marry Muslim men. He argues that the four laws are necessary to protect women from impoverished backgrounds who are vulnerable to trafficking and being married off to rich and higher-ranking older men, not only Muslims. He also says it is important to protect younger women from polygamy because younger wives are often subject to abuse by the other wives and tend to be treated like household servants. Poor families are often induced into accepting such marriages for their daughters and have few options, so the legislation provides necessary safeguards to protect young women from such disadvantageous arrangements and promotes moral values in a society in which materialism runs rampant. Dhammapiya is also unapologetic about banning child marriage by raising the age of consent to fourteen, saying it is important to encourage young women's education to help them escape the cycle of poverty. He rhetorically asks, "What chances does a child bride of 16 with three children have in life, and what can she do to help them secure a better future?" (interview December 2017). Thus, MBT views the marriage and family legislation as an important contribution to promoting human rights and dignity but has been attacked by liberal elites and Muslims who resent the safeguards. Regarding criticisms of the legislation for reinforcing patriarchy and limiting women's right to choose her partner without interference, he points out that the legislation enjoyed widespread support from nuns and laywomen who petitioned and rallied in favor of it.

In his view, the 969 movement that preceded MBT has also been totally misrepresented. He says that it emulates the Islamic 786 initiative—meaning "In the Name of Allah, the Compassionate and Merciful"—a campaign designed to appeal to Muslim shoppers by displaying this number on storefronts. In Myanmar and elsewhere in Asia, Islamic business associations pool resources to support community initiatives, so they recycle some of their profits for the benefit of fellow Muslims. Monks behind 969 wanted to do the same to address the crushing poverty that affects their communities by channeling spending to Buddhist businesses just as 786 does for Muslim shops. So, he argued, it was never a boycott but more a self-help effort to divert some of the profits made from Buddhist consumers to endeavors beneficial to Buddhists, akin to "Be Buddhist, Buy Buddhist." In this light, 969 was focused on alleviating poverty, providing social services, and responding to the needs of the desperate. However, supporters of 969 have been less measured in their assessments of 786, arguing that it is a ploy to boost jihadist Islam and conquer Myanmar. After all, $7 + 8 + 6 = 21$, so suspicious minds believe this indicates a Muslim plan to take over Myanmar in the twenty-first century.

Dhammapiya rejects allegations that MBT secured USDP support for the Protection of Race and Religion legislation in exchange for electoral support, pointing out that the USDP lost in a landslide so that it obviously was not getting much MBT support. He estimates that only 10 percent of monks got involved in the campaign. MBT is a national network of monks that extends down to the village level and, he argues, is extremely influential because it focuses on providing education and social services to underserved communities. He argues that the media failed to appreciate that MBT monks were just as sick of military rule as everyone else and happy to see the USDA ousted from power.

The media, in Dhammapiya's view, has exaggerated the role of Wirathu in MBT, pointing out he was not a founder and is not the leader despite his fame. He argues that MBT is responding to the very urgent threats to the sangha from globalization, the emergence of market forces, and social media. There has been a dramatic decline in the number of novices because they have other options in a developing economy. Donations of food have also declined as farmers now want to maximize their harvest income. In some cases, farmers have been victims of land grabs for development projects and, especially in the north around Mandalay, Chinese commercial interests have bought up their land. Thus, with a shrinking influx of novices and donations, many monasteries are facing difficult times. The rapid spread of social media since 2011 has been a double-edged sword, providing a platform for monks to disseminate their sermons and views to a rapidly expanding niche of smartphone users but also undermining faith and devotion among the young. Social media exposes them to various influences that distract them from Buddhism, and thus religiosity is not the default mode that it once was.

MBT, Dhammapiya maintains, is a reformist organization trying to make Buddhism more relevant and helpful, drawing a contrast with the remote State Sangha Council. He is sympathetic toward Aung San Suu Kyi but disappointed by the lack of progress on ethnic reconciliation and economic development and thinks the NLD is not politically skillful or effective. The longer she is in power, he adds, the more she appears to understand what she should be doing, offering praise for the way she has handled the Rohingya problem despite intense international pressure for her to condemn the military and defend the citizenship rights of the Rohingya.

Notwithstanding government efforts to disband and marginalize MBT, Dhammapiya asserts that it continues its social and educational efforts and has not pulled down the banners and signs as instructed. In his view, MBT has deep roots in local communities and is appreciated by them, forcing the government to refrain from enforcing the crackdown. This positive perception of MBT playing a valued role as protector and propagator of Buddhism finds scholarly agreement that "this is likely the lens through which many Buddhists in Myanmar encounter and evaluate MaBaTha activities, especially the organizing of Buddhist *dhamma* schools in towns around the country" (Schonthal and Walton 2016, 6). Citing MBT programs in a number of destitute ghettoes on the outskirts of Yangon that have no access to social services, Dhammapiya thinks that MBT is more a valuable partner of the state than a threat to law and order as its critics allege.

As discussed in the following section, MBT has also forged international ties. In September 2014 Ashin Wirathu attended a "Great Sangha Conference" in Columbo, establishing ties with BBS and another charismatic monk with a flair for vitriolic invective.

SRI LANKA'S FIREBRAND MONK

"Trump is a good man and I pray for him every day," Galagoda Atte Gnanasara Thero told me in April 2017, later bragging that he is even better than US president Donald Trump. Gnanasara is Sri Lanka's notorious rabble-rousing monk and leader of the Bodu Bala Sena (BBS), Buddhist Power Force, a radical nationalist religious organization. He draws crowds of tens of thousands and is infamous for inciting violence targeting Muslims with his inflammatory rhetoric. Gnanasara's praise for Trump came when I asked him about the president's Muslim travel ban.

Gnanasara whips crowds into a frenzy, passionately exhorting Buddhists to rise up and protect what is being threatened—their Sinhalese Buddhist identity. At a mass rally in 2013, he proclaimed, "This is a government created by Sinhala Buddhists and it must remain Sinhala Buddhist. This is a Sinhala country, Sinhala government. Democratic and pluralistic values are killing the Sinhala race" (Al Maenna 2013). He insists he is not anti-Islam but only anti-Islamic extremism. In person, he is mild mannered and thoughtful, a man living with minimal security despite making many enemies. In his monastery in central Columbo, there is a bank of security monitors, but aside from a few acolytes the compound is only watched over by a large statue of Kannon, the goddess of mercy. Gnanasara confided, "I think I have the most amazing ability compared with many other Sri Lankans because around 400 Christian Evangelical organizations here are all against me. And you know Muslims meet every Friday in their mosque, they all denounce me. Because they cannot physically kill me, they try to kill my character" (interview April 2017). He is unrepentant about agitating in areas where holy sites are disputed with Muslims, saying that they are asserting claims to Buddhist sites without any basis. There are dozens of such contested sites where he has been arousing local Sinhalese against Muslim communities, part of his self-proclaimed mission to awaken and incite.

The BBS was established in 2012, following Sri Lanka's long civil war from 1983 to 2009 that pitted the nation's Buddhist ethnic Sinhalese majority against the Hindu ethnic Tamils in the northeast of the island who were fighting for an independent homeland. The nation remains deeply scarred by this conflict, one driven initially by linguistic issues and socioeconomic disparities and amplified by communalism (Holt 2016). BBS Chief Executive Officer Dilanthe Withanage, who once served as an adviser to the Ministry of Education on social integration and is a lay person, says that BBS emerged from efforts to promote reconciliation between Sinhalese and Tamils and was also influenced by some Muslims who expressed their concerns about the spread of fundamentalist Islam by migrant workers returning from the Mideast and funding by Saudi Arabia (interview April 2017). Prior to BBS, Gnanasara belonged to Jathika Hela Urumaya, a small political party led by Buddhist monks, but apparently it was too moderate. Initially one of the main BBS issues was the controversy over migrant workers from Sri Lanka who were barred from practicing Buddhism in the Mideast and punished if they did so. Early on, BBS also advocated a single legal system applicable to all Sri Lankans regardless of religion, preferential treatment for applicants to university who had taken classes in Buddhism, hiring of monks by schools to teach about history, culture, and religion, and banning certain birth control methods. Withanage maintains that BBS was a response to the obvious problems facing people and the need to boost the island's social capital and level of economic development while fending off forces that threatened the nation's Buddhist identity.

Farzana Haniffa, a sociologist at the University of Columbo, told me BBS was launched to mobilize militant monks and the public against Muslims because the state was looking for a new enemy to help unify the Sinhalese community (interview April 2017). Gotabhaya Rajapaksa, at that time defense minister and brother of then-president Mahinda Rajapaksa, openly supported BBS, enabling it to operate with impunity even as its gangs roamed the country attacking Muslim targets (Haniffa 2016). Withanage acknowledges having met with Gotabhaya and discussed the problem of Islamic extremism and believes that based on the BBS representations the Ministry of Defense then set up a special unit to gather intelligence about fundamentalist activities. Other sources assert that BBS-affiliated thugs are hired by Sinhalese merchants to intimidate Muslim rivals to move or shut down operations, a lucrative racket that often involves violence and seems to have little to do with Buddhist precepts.

Apparently state sponsorship endowed BBS with impunity, power, and funding, but when the Rajapaksa government was ousted in the 2015 elections, this meant that the BBS lost its patron and protector. Since then Rajapaksa has blamed his defeat on the BBS for alienating Muslim voters who overwhelmingly backed his rival, Maithripala Sirisena. Gnanasara acknowledges that this may be true, even if it was not his intention. Muslim voters believed that the BBS orchestrated the attacks on their community, including the 2014 burning of Muslim shops and homes just south of Columbo following incendiary BBS rallies. Disingenuously Gnanasara denies any responsibility for these incidents, accusing the media of sensationalism for blaming his hatemongering speeches for subsequent mob actions.

When I asked ex-president Mahinda Rajapaksa about his support for Buddhist extremism, he downplayed allegations linking his family to BBS but defended the violence, saying that monks "are only human," adding, "I have never seen a Buddhist monk advocating killing" (interview June 2016). Gnanasara believes that Rajapaksa has had to distance himself but actually supports BBS: "My feeling is that he knows that what we discuss is correct, but he cannot openly say this to the public" (interview April 2017). The Rajapaksa family is also associated with the Lion's Blood campaign of Sinhalese Buddhist nationalism that suddenly became ubiquitous following his shocking defeat in the 2015 elections. Again, a smiling Rajapaksa denied involvement, saying it emerged from the people's will. The name *Sinhale* refers to what many consider the proper traditional name for the island nation. The posters and ubiquitous stickers depict a lion, an iconic symbol of bravery, on the national flag holding a kastane sword, and below it the name is written in Sinhalese. The Lion and the script for *Sinha* (lion) are in yellow while *le* (blood) is written in red. Many taxis, buses, motorcycles, and other vehicles around the nation sported the stickers, as did shops, while graffiti depicting the image was seen in Muslim neighborhoods. The Sinhale campaign is similar to the 969 campaign in Myanmar, enabling consumers and clients to know who they are dealing with, but is equally menacing. The campaign asserting a resurgent Sinhalese nationalism serves as a threatening reminder of a willingness to sacrifice blood to preserve the nation's Buddhist character. It is also something of a riposte to President Sirisena's improbable victory, possible only because the two main minority groups, Tamils and Muslims, voted en masse (84 percent) for him, while the Sinhalese vote was split.

Even if there is no immediate threat of an Islamic tsunami, some alarmist demographic projections anticipate one. Indeed, BBS is credited with distributing posters that exaggerate the decline in the Sinhalese Buddhist proportion of the population. The erroneous propaganda poster raises the question, "Will a proud nation disappear from earth? In 1971 Sinhalese were 74% of the population. In 2013 reduced to 61%" (Gao 2014). In fact, according to the

2012 national census, Sinhalese constitute 74.9 percent of the island's population of twenty million while Sri Lankan Tamil were 11.1 percent, Moors (Muslims) were 9.3 percent, and Indian Tamils were 4.1 percent. Be that as it may, Withanage believes that by 2050, based on current reproduction rates, the Muslim population will be in the majority and that will be an existential disaster for Buddhism and Sri Lankan identity because Islam is intolerant of other faiths.

Gnanasara complains that "a Sinhalese man can only marry one woman. Muslims can marry four or five" (interview April 2017). This law, he argues, is why the Muslim population is rapidly expanding, posing a gathering demographic threat to the Sinhalese Buddhist character of the nation, something he seeks to defend by imposing a limit on the number of children per family. "We have a problem with inter-race marriage and are against Sinhalese men marrying a Muslim woman," Gnanasara says, adding, "We do not ask her to change her name, nothing. But when a Muslim man marries a Sinhalese woman, immediately she has to change her name, religion and everything. So that's what we do not like, and we will lobby for a maximum number of children for each family" (interview April 2017). He envies Ma Ba Tha's legislative success in Myanmar on these issues and advocates similar reforms in Sri Lanka.

Special legal dispensations for Muslims push tolerance too far according to the BBS because they are discriminatory toward Buddhists. Regarding unifying the law for all communities, Gnanasara lamented that President Rajapaksa "lost his opportunity. Soon after the war he could have, but he missed it. He could have been not only Sri Lanka's Buddhist leader, but the Buddhist leader of the entire religion." Why did he miss this chance? Gnanasara attributes this to "corruption and the personality of his relatives."

Gnanasara bristles at the suggestion that BBS monks are militants, asserting their activism is justified because it defends Sinhalese culture. "So when they [Christians and Muslims] come to disturb us, we are fighting, but that does not mean we are militants" (interview April 2017). He adds, "Buddhism does not mean that you should allow anything to happen." Sri Lanka, he warns, is overly tolerant, asserting that such tolerance doesn't exist in any Muslim majority nation. If nothing is done to stop the creeping Islamization of Sri Lanka, he believes that intolerance will prevail. "They are a minority in number but if you look at their economic power and their international network, they are not a minority," he warned (interview April 2017). He seems to argue that it is necessary to fight extremism with extremism.

So does BBS represent preemptive intolerance? Gnanasara contends that twenty-first-century Islam is quite different from the Islam that previously prevailed on the island and the government has been remiss in not understanding what is at stake. The Easter Sunday bombings in 2019 by Islamic extremists exemplify his concerns. This radicalization is a result of Arabization funded by Saudi Arabia and spread by the Internet, an Islamic wave of globalization (see chapter 4). To some extent, this campaign is a Cold War legacy as the United States sought to counter Soviet influence in the Mideast and Afghanistan through proxy organizations funded by Saudi Arabia, wielding religion to battle communism. In the post–Cold War era the flow of such funds in support of a more fundamentalist Islam has continued unabated. The impact in relatively poor and less developed nations like Sri Lanka has been enormous, providing resources that plug gaps in local government services and thus endow recipients with enormous influence.

Combatting this wave of Arabization animates the BBS. The threat is seen to come from the Middle East as Saudi money promotes mosque building and religious education centers (madrasa) where students are taught what Gnanasara terms "jihadist" Islam. He contends that the number of Muslim women wearing the veil has dramatically increased over the past two decades and that contemporary Islam is very different from what had prevailed in the island's moderate Muslim communities before the influx of Saudi funding. And younger Muslim migrant workers who return from the Mideast are bringing back more fundamentalist Islamic beliefs that are sharpening communal divisions by undermining the basis of coexistence. In his view, the problem is not Islam per se but rather "jihadist Islam" and the cultural wars it instigates by challenging established patterns. The BBS views the Easter suicide bombings by Islamic militants as validation for its longstanding agenda and has been active on social media asserting this and lamenting that its warnings had been ignored.

This jihadism represents what Gnanasara identifies as the fourth wave threatening the island's Sinhalese Buddhist identity (Holt 2016). The earlier waves were British colonialism (1815–1948), communism in the 1970s, and Tamil nationalism in the civil war (1983–2009). In these previous crises, he points out that monks played a key role in resisting these profound threats to the island's ethnoreligious identity. This record of resistance underscores his point that being a monk doesn't necessarily mean political disengagement or passivity. As community leaders enjoying the respect of the people, he believes that monks have a duty to preserve national culture and are justified in resorting to violence. Highlighting the successive and unending threats underscores the importance of constant vigilance and the need to be proactive, tapping into the millenarian current of Theravada Buddhism that anticipates an apocalyptic end.

Referring to nineteenth-century militant monks in Kandy fighting British colonialism, Gnanasara confided, "I think I live in reincarnation," adding, "once I complete my task here, I will go back to my religious activity." How will he know when his goal is achieved? When Sri Lanka is "one country, one nation, one law. That is one of my tasks, to have common law for everybody. I will fight until such time that a leader can say that this is a country of Sinhalese Buddhists" (interview April 2017). That goal doesn't seem to entertain the diversity that now prevails in an island where one-quarter of the population is not Sinhalese Buddhist. This fusion of ethnic and religious identities endows Sinhalese nationalism with enormous power that is used to target minorities and nurture an angry solidarity at odds with Buddhist precepts. It is hatemongering under the guise of protecting the sangha. But in a solidly Buddhist majority country in which the state is committed by the Constitution "to give to Buddhism the foremost place" and to protect and foster the Buddha Sasana (teachings of Buddha), it is hard to see any urgent threat. Freedom of religion is guaranteed, but the constitutional bias favoring Buddhism is a basis for marginalizing minorities. Withanage disagrees, arguing that the ostensible constitutional privileges accorded Buddhism are ornamental and not actually evident in policies that he argues are overly tolerant of religious minorities. The BBS, inter alia, stands for banning Sri Lankan women going to the Middle East for work, overseas financing of mosque building, wearing burkas, and halal certification.

What's in a label? According to BBS, halal labeling has become prevalent in Sri Lanka and was a large source of revenue for the disbanded All Ceylon Jamiyyathul Ulama (ACJU), the Islamic association that administered the vetting and endorsement process (Haniffa 2017). Gnanasara charges that there is no monitoring of the revenue and that it could be used to support terrorist activities or fund programs that boost the jihadist agenda. In 2013 the ACJU offered to transfer responsibility for halal certification to the government, but the BBS demanded complete eradication of the program. ACJU then proposed only certifying products destined for exports to Islamic countries, but again the BBS rejected this compromise. The government then withdrew the ACJU's authority to issue halal certificates in 2013, showing that the BBS had significant influence in government circles in which it had raised the specter of terrorist funding from certification fees. However, in 2014, continuing on a purely voluntary basis, the Halal Accreditation Council took over responsibility for auditing and certifying compliance with halal standards in Sri Lanka.

This furor over halal labels is a symptom of greater disquiet about policies regarding proper place for minorities and cultural concessions. BBS questions why halal labeling has become so ubiquitous given that only 10 percent of the population is Muslim. To them it is yet further proof of special treatment and a government that is overly solicitous to a group that takes advantage of such tolerance. Muslims counter that there is similarly no monitoring or taxation of the vastly greater sums donated to the sangha. The BBS position is inconsistent in that it supports economic development initiatives, but in opposing halal certification, which is completely voluntary, it threatens to lock Sri Lankan businesses out of the booming export market for halal products and the jobs that would sustain. Halal is related not just to food and beverages but also to products ranging from medicines to cosmetics. Due to the BBS campaign, many firms have suspended plans to seek certification, not wanting to risk running afoul of an anti-Muslim populist backlash.

Looking back over the first five years of BBS, in 2017 Gnanasara proclaimed himself satisfied that his message about "cultural destruction and the threat of Islamization" has become mainstreamed, claiming this a major success. Professor Haniffa, who is Muslim, laments that he is essentially correct because in her view anti-Muslim sentiments have become widespread largely due to his efforts and have become far too accepted in society (interview April 2017).

The BBS leadership advocates shifting focus away from hatemongering in what it calls its second phase over 2017–2022 to focus on social welfare issues like education, family planning, and health care while working to eliminate corruption and ignorance in the Parliament. According to Gnanasara, this is an uphill battle because "50 percent of parliamentarians are without basic education" (interview April 2017). Asked about his commitment to the new BBS shift toward social welfare policies, Gnanasara was evasive. He craves the limelight, enjoys stirring controversy and rousing crowds into a feverish pitch of venomous delirium. He is like a fire-and-brimstone revivalist preacher and acknowledges that his charisma and strident oratory are his strengths, not the prosaic work of promoting social welfare programs; he is an agitator not an administrator. Yet he has faced significant legal problems from a state less tolerant of his hatemongering and vilification by a state-controlled media more inclined to probe into his personal life and finances. His mainstream media profile declined after the ouster of Rajapaksa and is generally unflattering. Nonetheless, he has a vast following on social media, makes regular radio broadcasts, and does online video interviews that attract over a million views. So he has been adept in keeping in the public eye on his own terms despite state efforts, and his message of an assertive Sinhalese Buddhist nationalism resonates powerfully in society. Educated liberals may regard him as little more than a thug in saffron, but he has a broad appeal despite conviction for contempt of court and threatening the widow of a disappeared journalist who had been critical of the Rajapaksa government. In 2018 he was sentenced to a six-year prison term, but in May 2019 the president pardoned him soon after the BBS threatened protests. President Maithripala Sirisena's decision drew flak for pandering to hardcore Sinhalese Buddhists in the wake of the Easter bombings. Critics also assert the president undermined the rule of law, human rights, and accountability.

Asked about the situation in Myanmar (prior to the massive exodus of 730,000 Rohingya later in 2017), Gnanasara expressed a low opinion of Aung San Suu Kyi, saying she could not deliver on what she promised because she is weak like the Dalai Lama. He denounced the Dalai Lama for calling on Buddhist monks in Myanmar and Sri Lanka to end violence toward Muslims. In his view, the Dalai Lama was misinformed, relying on false information supplied by Muslim extremists. Conversely, he expressed strong admiration for the world's most notorious monk, U Wirathu, whose agenda and tactics inspire BBS. In particular he was envious of Wirathu's success in promoting legal changes that restrict interfaith marriage, the conversion of Buddhists to Islam, and family size. The two monks have exchanged visits, are periodically in contact, and provide reciprocal moral support. Letting his ego get the better of his humility, Gnanasara told me of Wirathu's praise for his efforts to make Sri Lanka the true home of Buddhism, acknowledging this as his goal.

Apparently, the politics of hate remain unquenched and the BBS's stated intention to transform itself into a social welfare–oriented organization remains elusive because that is not really what it is about. In May 2017, shortly after we met, Gnanasara was implicated in several incidents and attacks against Muslim targets that sparked riots, in one case resisting arrest when a phalanx of monks surrounded him and prevented police from taking him into custody. During the subsequent manhunt, he went into hiding, reportedly enjoying the protection of an advisor to President Sirisena. This is a delicate matter for the government because it doesn't want to alienate the Sinhalese majority and knows that Gnanasara and his bigotry are popular. In June 2017 he turned himself in and in September the government dropped charges. On top of countenancing impunity for violating the law, President Sirisena, echoing Gnanasara, voiced his concerns about the "Arabization" of Sri Lankan Muslims, especially in the Eastern Province where there are Muslim majority districts. Such is the influence of Buddhist nationalism in Sri Lankan politics where BBS has shifted the frame of reference and mainstreamed Islamophobia.

The Easter suicide bombings of churches and hotels across Sri Lanka, claiming over 250 lives, were taken as vindication by BBS that its warnings about the threat of Arabization and Islamic jihadists should have been taken more seriously. Indeed, in 2016 Gnanasara publicly criticized Thowheed Jamath, the militant organization that carried out the attacks. There is an intriguing report that both BBS and Thowheed Jamath, along with other various Sinhalese and Muslim extremist organizations, were funded from a secret account of the Defense Ministry under Gotabhaya Rajapaksa that was coordinated by his close ally (Jeyaraj 2013; *Sri Lanka Mirror* 2016; Senaratne 2019). The *Sri Lanka Mirror* article also alleges that "Thowheed Jamath's secretary Abdul Rasik Rafiquedeen was an Army intelligence member." These revelations raise awkward questions about why the accurate intelligence about the impending attack was not shared with the nation's political leaders, or acted on, and whether there was any intention to influence the 2019 presidential elections.

PARALLELS

There are interesting parallels between the two charismatic monks. Gnanasa-ra and Wirathu espouse similar xenophobic claims about Muslims converting Buddhist women and luring them into immoral polygamous marriages and penchant for swindling Buddhists and taking advantage of their tolerance and passivity. Both conjure up a Muslim demographic explosion that does not exist. Both Sri Lanka and Myanmar have large, state-backed Theravada Buddhist majorities with small Muslim communities, and both nations have experienced prolonged ethnic conflicts that have left deep scars, undermined trust and civility, and lowered barriers to violence. They now have powerful and popular extremist Buddhist nationalist organizations featuring hatemongering monks who leverage social media to amplify their chauvinism.

In terms of identity politics, both movements promote a virulent ethnoreligious nationalism that stokes Islamophobia, undermining tolerance and pluralism. In both nations, religion has become an essential source of political legitimacy and is central to national identity, creating opportunities for militant monks. Both movements emerged in the wake of traumatic eras: a twenty-six-year civil war against ethnic Tamils in Sri Lanka and prolonged authoritarian repression in Myanmar under military rule and numerous ethnic insurgencies. Emerging from these cauldrons of violence, there was a need for an enemy to nurture cohesion. In Sri Lanka the government found the Muslim community a handy target to maintain solidarity within the Sinhalese Buddhist majority. The BBS enjoyed state sponsorship, allegedly from President Rajapaksa's cabinet and family as Defense Minister Gotabhaya Rajapaksa served as its informal "godfather" (Jeyaraj 2013; *Sri Lankan Mirror* 2016; Senaratne 2019). In Myanmar, there are no "smoking gun" links between state security and the 969 or MBT movements, but there are unsubstantiated rumors suggesting that Wirathu might have such shadowy ties. More importantly, the Rohingya crisis has been useful to the still military-dominated state, promoting solidarity among the Buddhist majority and transforming Aung Suu Kyi from an icon of human rights and democracy into an international pariah. Even though she remains popular inside Myanmar, she is weakened because her international standing was a tremendous source of power that threatened the military.

There are, however, some important differences. The two groups have contrasting origins as the MBT developed as a grassroots organization while BBS enjoyed political patronage and "is a creature and product of elite Colombo politics" (Schonthal and Walton 2016, 96). Moreover, Sri Lanka's democratic traditions have remained resilient under duress, endowing activists with skills and experience that are in short supply in Myanmar, a nation that is just emerging from extended military repression that greatly restricted the political space for activism. The main difference, however, is that MBT has actually delivered a range of social services and engaged in educational initiatives whereas these remain aspirations for BBS. MBT is much more than hatemongering bigotry whereas the BBS hasn't done much else and appears to have limited capacity to escape from Gnanasara's glowering shadow.

Chapter Six

Rohingya

Race, Religion,
and Ethnonationalism

The nightmarish saga of the Rohingya, a Muslim ethnic minority in Buddhist majority Myanmar, captured the world's attention in 2017 when some 730,000 were driven out of Rakhine State to seek refuge in neighboring Bangladesh. Médecins sans Frontières (Doctors without Borders) estimated that eleven thousand died in the military's clearance operations (MSF 2017). This profound humanitarian crisis brought into sharp focus the riptide of race, religion, and identity and the tragic consequences this has unleashed. It has also intensified the divide between Buddhists and Muslims within Myanmar, fanning ethnonationalist sentiments and enmities.

Back in 2007 when I visited Sittwe and Mrauk U in Rakhine (western Myanmar) in the aftermath of the Saffron Revolution, I interviewed monks about the reasons for their peaceful uprising and the consequences of the military's brutal crackdown. I was passing a road maintenance project and noticed that the manual laborers, including many colorfully dressed women wearing headscarves, had extremely dark skin and asked about them. A local ethnic Rakhine Buddhist monk told me they were "like your gypsies, nobody wants them." He said they didn't belong in Myanmar, calling them dirty and dishonest, again drawing a parallel with gypsies. Subsequently I spoke with another local monk who explained they were only temporary migrants. He called them kalar, a vulgar slur for South Asians that is widely used to refer to the swarthy Rohingya. I had not expected a monk to voice such prejudice, but further encounters in Rakhine showed it to be ubiquitous. It seemed that these discriminatory attitudes were more about ethnicity than religion, although it is difficult to disentangle such influences and probably being Mus-

lim reinforced the sense of Other that informs prejudices. In visits to Rohingya villages near Mrauk U, the level of destitution was dreadful as I saw
children with distended bellies and reddish hair, symptoms of malnutrition.
Rakhine is one of Myanmar's poorest states, but the Rohingya enclaves are
even more badly off. The roofing was tattered, compounds unkempt, fencing
broken, and the adult residents appeared listless even as children noisily
scampered about. Another day I saw a line of Rohingya workers walking
ahead of me on a road that passed by a monastery, but before approaching the
cluster of young rowdy monks performing ablutions, they left the road and
detoured across the rocky fields in the way one does to avoid trouble.

Rohingya have no political representation in Parliament or networks of
influence and their presence is deeply resented by the Buddhist majority of
Rakhine (formerly known as Arakan). They were the unwelcome majority in
the Muslim enclave located in northern Rakhine. The total Rohingya population in Myanmar is uncertain but was estimated at about 1.2 million (out of a
national population of 52 million) before the ethnic cleansing campaign in
2017. They were not counted in the last census in 2014 because the government denies Rohingya as a legitimate ethnic identity. The numbers have also
been affected by previous "clearances" in 1978, the early 1990s (about
250,000), 2012, and 2016. South (2008, 81–82) estimates that by 2007 there
were 28,000 Rohingya in refugee camps near Cox's Bazaar in Bangladesh,
while a further 100,000 to 200,000 Rohingya refugees were living illegally in
Bangladesh.

In the first two purges under military rule in the 1970s and 1990s, most of
the refugees were repatriated under the auspices of the UNHCR. The prospects for repatriating the post-2012 successive waves of refugees are not
good because many fear returning due to memories of the military atrocities
targeting them (ICG 2018). Furthermore, the military has bulldozed many
villages previously inhabited by Rohingya and built bases and guard posts on
the land. This leveling of abandoned villages feeds speculation that the military sought to eliminate potential evidence of atrocities. There are no signs
that ethnonationalism in Myanmar overall, or in Rakhine in particular, is
abating, and this creates an unfavorable context for repatriation. Aid agencies
counsel caution on repatriation given prevailing concerns about the security
and well-being of Rohingya should they return. Moreover, Myanmar's
government has slow walked the repatriation process in negotiations with
Bangladesh and has insisted on a cumbersome verification process for reent-
ry that requires documentation that few refugees are likely to possess or have
access to. This extreme vetting aims to establish whether refugees actually
have a right to return while limiting their ability to prove that and making
sure repatriates won't constitute a security threat. This red tape barrier has
come under heavy criticism, especially in Bangladesh, because it seems designed to limit repatriation to little more than a trickle. The military justifies

its "clearing operation" and careful vetting as an antiterrorism campaign, driving out the masses to isolate remaining cells of Islamic separatists like the Arakan Rohingya Salvation Army (ARSA) and rid the country of terrorists and their sympathizers. The historical background to this crisis is illuminating, contested, and complex.

CITIZENSHIP DENIED

The 1947 Constitution, the first in independent Burma, did not exclude the Rohingya, and Article 11 (iv) seemed to offer a basis for citizenship, although Article 12 acknowledged Parliament's right to determine who had such rights. Parliament detailed criteria for citizenship and naturalization in the Union Citizenship Act of 1948 that again established a basis for Rohingya inclusion but also established the basis for denying eligibility. The Rohingya were not specifically mentioned in either document, and this identifying term denoting a collective ethnicity was not in use at that time.

During the 1950s, as an Islamic separatist insurgency simmered in northern Rakhine, the government flirted with the idea of offering citizenship for Rohingyas. Instead they were given National Registration identity cards that were used as de facto proof of citizenship until the 1982 Citizenship Law revoked any such claims. The census of 1961 actually recognized "Rohingya" as an ethnic designation, but the 1962 military coup derailed hopes for official recognition as General Ne Win embraced a Burmese-centric ethnonationalism. This resulted in the 1982 Citizenship Law that specified three categories of citizenship: citizen, associate citizen, and naturalized citizen. According to the 1982 Citizenship Law, people in Burma (now Myanmar) are divided into "citizens," those belonging to the recognized 135 ethnicities living in Burma prior to 1823, "associate citizens," who acquired nationality based on the first nationality law that was enforced in 1948 when Burma became independent (mainly Indian, Chinese, and Anglo-Burmese people), and "naturalized citizens," namely foreign people who have been legally naturalized. Although "associate citizens" and "naturalized citizens" are eligible to become "citizens" after three generations, until then they are subject to discriminatory treatment. For example, associate citizens or naturalized citizens are not allowed to serve in managerial positions in the civil service.

The Rohingya are not included in the list of 135 recognized ethnic groups in Myanmar and thus are denied citizenship because the government selected 1823 as the cut-off date for belonging. The law's anti-Rohingya Muslim bias was unmistakable and linked to borderland unrest in the late 1970s (Seth 2003). Leider concludes that "the ethnocultural tensions between the Arakanese and the Rohingya on the one hand, and state policies of exclusion on the other, have been drivers of a lasting and violent conflict that reaches back to the late colonial period" (Leider 2018).

CONTEXTUALIZING CONTESTED IDENTITIES

As Kei Nemoto argues, "Most Burmese today appear to entertain no doubts concerning the '1823' criterion for inclusion as posited in the nationality law. Nevertheless, when considered from a historical perspective this stipulation appears to be no more than an illusion conjured up by Burmese nationalists, for since the beginning of the Burmese empire in the late 18th century (Konbaung Dynasty, 1752–1885), Muslims, Hindus and Christians, and Chinese, Indians, Afghans, Persians, Armenians, and Portuguese, have been co-existing with Theravada Buddhists, even in the royal city of Mandalay" (2016, 220). He adds, "It should also be noted here that they were not mere transients, but residents who had been living in Burma over several generations. They were duly approved and protected by the then royal authority, since they contributed to the kingdom through a variety of commercial roles. The royal authority at the time did not divide its subjects on the basis of 'ethnicity' or 'religion.'"

The majority Buddhist ethnic Rakhine subnationalism draws on accumulated resentments toward Bamar (ethnic Burmese) nationalism, beginning with the invasion and subjugation of their Arakan Kingdom, also known as the Mrauk U dynasty, back in the late eighteenth century. Situated on the border between Buddhist and Muslim Asia, the kingdom had strong economic, trade, and other relations with the Sultanate of Bengal. For some 350 years prior to British colonialism the region was subject to extensive Indian and Muslim influence and there was a high degree of cultural syncretism and the Arakan kings held Islamic titles (Sultans), had Indian and Muslim advisors, and styled themselves after Mughal potentates.

Aye Chan (2005), a Japanese-trained and -based scholar originally from Myanmar, argues that the archival evidence does not support the Rohingya claims to be an indigenous group, while Nemoto (2016), Crouch (2016), Ibrahim (2017), and others disagree, often citing Buchanan (1799) and Luce (1985) in support of their arguments. Luce rejects Rohingya claims to one thousand years' presence in the region but believes they established themselves there following a thirteenth-century Muslim invasion that destroyed the Buddhist kingdom of Patikkara. He thus rejects the government argument that they are colonial-era coolies brought over from Bengal. Leider (2013) demurs, noting that many were, and asserts that Rohingya as an ethnicity is a modern construct. In his view, "The Rohingya are best defined as a political and militant movement as its foremost aim was the creation of an autonomous Muslim state" (Leider 2013, 208). He refers to an imagined Muslim community of varied backgrounds that have become "unified" based on a misleading narrative reflecting "the dynamics of ethnification." He argues, "The term Rohingya embodies an ongoing process of identity formation that has unified Muslim communities in the North Arakan region with a similar cultural profile, but a diverse historical background" (Leider 2018). This Muslim group identity formation, he asserts, gained momentum in response to repressive military rule post-1962.

During the British colonial era there was an influx of so-called Bengali Muslims. Arakan (modern day Rakhine) was one of the first parts of modern Myanmar to fall under British sway when it was absorbed into British India's Bengal Presidency following the First Anglo-Burmese War (1823–1826). Over the ensuing decades there was a large migration of Muslims from the Chittagong region of what is now Bangladesh into northern Rakhine, where many Muslims had previously settled and lived for generations. Most of the new migrants were looking for land to cultivate. In 1937 the British administratively separated what became Burma from India, and Arakan was incorporated into this new crown colony. Herein lie the seeds of discord as there are some Muslim residents with longstanding roots in the territory that became Burma spanning several generations and more recent migrants, providing a pretext to sow doubts about the bona fides of all Muslims and thereby deny citizenship rights and protections to the Rohingya community.

It is important to consider the fluidity and porousness of borders and the frequency of population migrations during much of the time when Arakan's population was in flux. When the Burmese invaded the Arakan Kingdom and overthrew the Mrauk U dynasty in 1784, many locals fled to the west seeking refuge from the marauding soldiers. Undoubtedly, after the violence receded, some returned to an area they regarded as home, not only Muslims but also local Rakhine Buddhists who both regarded the Burmese invaders with hostility and suspicion. Subsequently, under British colonial rule, those who regarded Arakan as their ancestral homeland might have returned because they felt they had a right to do so and might fare better under the British than the Burmese, perhaps imagining that colonial rule would bring law and order and end endemic dacoity.

Thus, the 1982 Citizenship Law that only accords recognition to indigenous groups resident on the eve of the Anglo-Burma War might seriously distort the Arakan region's demographic history, locking it into an 1823 moment. This is relevant to the point that Nemoto (2016) makes in arguing that arbitrarily choosing 1823 as the cut-off date resonates with political purpose. This chosen date appeals to Burmese ethnonationalism because it negates what occurred under subsequent British colonial rule. Nemoto connects this to the Dobama Asiayoun (Our Burma Association), an ethnonationalist independence movement in the 1930s dominated by ethnic Burmese (Bamar) who resented what they perceived as British favoritism toward minorities. Since January 1948, heirs of this movement have dominated the political scene, advocating the importance of Theravada Buddhism and the Burmese language as the foundations of a Burmese-centric national identity despite religious, ethnic, and linguistic diversity; about one-third of modern Myanmar's population is from non-Burmese ethnic groups that embrace quite distinctive identities.

During World War II, when British colonial administrators and armed forces abruptly fled to India as the Japanese advanced on Burma, the ensuing power vacuum provided an opportunity for a settling of scores. Communal tensions had been simmering before the Japanese invasion due to disputes arising from the British administrators awarding long-term leases to Muslim migrant farmers on land claimed by Rakhine Buddhists, but these tensions were largely kept in check by the British. When they hastily departed, however, lawlessness and violence erupted. The British established "V-force" (volunteer guerilla units) by arming Rohingyas in northern Arakan to harry Japanese forces and impede their advance, but instead they focused their attacks on Buddhist villages. Pro-Japanese Rakhine Buddhists targeted pro-British Muslims, largely Rohingya, and vice versa, with unconfirmed reports of more than twenty thousand dead and tens of thousands more displaced.

Intercommunal violence and escalating retaliations led to an exodus of Muslims from Buddhist-dominated southern Arakan and Buddhists from the Muslim enclave in the north around Maungdaw as British influence evaporated and a counter-offensive was abandoned. This process of internal displacement baptized in blood sharpened enmities that have smoldered since with periodic outbursts of violence (Yegar 2002).

According to Chan the anarchy of communal violence during the Japanese occupation left a legacy of mutual distrust between Muslims and Buddhists and reinforced religious identities; "in the wake of independence most of the educated Muslims felt an overwhelming sense of collective identity based on Islam as their religion and the cultural and ethnic difference of their community from the Burmese and Arakanese Buddhists. At the same time the Arakanese became more and more concerned with their racial security and ethnic survival in view of the increasingly predominant Muslim population in their frontier" (2005, 410). From this perspective, the conflict in Rakhine is primarily religious based, but in twenty-first-century Myanmar the mainstream consensus is that the turmoil is primarily ethnic in origin and that the so-called Bengalis (Rohingya) must go. Islam is certainly salient but not deemed the critical factor that "disqualifies" them from citizenship. Prior to the post–August 2017 expulsions of Rohingya there were more than one million Muslims scattered across Myanmar. In Yangon, there is a vibrant Muslim business community and mosques that have not been affected by the anti-Rohingya hostility. And in Rakhine, there are some Muslims who eschew the Rohingya label. The Kaman, for example, are Muslims in Rakhine that are officially recognized as one of the 135 ethnic groups based on their role as mercenaries fighting for the Mrauk U dynasty. Privately some Muslims express sympathy for the Rohingya, previously the largest Muslim group in Myanmar, while others agree with the government that they are economic migrants from Bangladesh who are making things difficult for all of Myanmar's Muslims.

When the British decided to leave India and partition it in 1947, Rakhine Muslims petitioned to have their enclave in northern Rakhine in western Burma be included in the new Muslim homeland of Pakistan to no avail. Islamabad had irredentist concerns about Kashmiri Muslims but had no such sympathies for the Rakhine Muslims on the other side of the subcontinent. During Bangladesh's war of independence from Pakistan in 1971, Rakhine Muslims supported West Pakistan rather than neighboring East Pakistan (Bangladesh). Given that Rohingya are dismissed in Myanmar as Bengalis, and Bangladesh is culturally Bengali while Pakistan is dominated by Urdu speaking Punjabis, their support of Islamabad rather than Dhaka undermines assumptions implicit in contemporary narratives. After the war, Dhaka disowned what it termed the "Chittagonian Bengalis of Rakhine" for having supported Pakistan. Chan (2005) argues this is the reason why they embraced a Rohingya identity and reject the Chittagonian label. (Chittagong is an administrative district of Bangladesh adjacent to Rakhine.)

The term "Rohingya" as the name of an ethnic group emerged only after 1950 (Nemoto 1991). In this sense Rohingyas can be viewed as a "new" ethnic group, but as Francis Wade sensibly points out, all ethnic groups are modern constructs based on state needs to classify and tidy up messier realities (Wade 2017). The 135 ethnic groups are imposed identities based on shared language, culture, and historical experiences that conform to the dictates of governance rather than primordial communities, imposing a rigidity where there had been fluidity, but over time such designations have become the lived realities of those groups. Ironically, classifying people based on ethnicity is one of the legacies of British colonial rule that otherwise Burmese nationalists are eager to overcome. The anticolonial struggle for independence forged solidarity based on Theravada Buddhism and Burmese language as the cultural core of national identity, ramping up an ethnoreligious nationalism that has not abated.

POLITICS OF STATELESSNESS

Burma gained independence in 1948, but an Islamic insurgency persisted in Rakhine and there were demands in 1960 for a Rohingya state. The U Nu government instead established a special frontier administration that ostensibly conferred a degree of autonomy and appeared to recognize Rohingya ethnic claims but in practice extended the military's sway. Rohingya aspirations were derailed when General Ne Win staged a coup and seized power in 1962, embracing ethnonationalism, taking a hardline stance on ethnic minorities, while ignoring his predecessors' constitutional amendment making Buddhism the official state religion.

The 1982 legislation only recognized as citizens those residents from 135 ethnic groups that had been in Burma prior to the First Anglo-Burmese War (1823–1826) and it was determined that this did not include the Rohingya. Thus, many who had resided for generations inside the Union of Burma's borders were abruptly declared stateless. According to the 1983 census, Muslims constituted 24.3 percent of Arakan's population and most were suddenly designated as Bengali, not Rohingya, an ethnic group not recognized by successive governments since then. Various Rohingya political groups have agitated for recognition as an officially recognized ethnic group while more extreme activists have called for establishing an independent Islamic state, but neither effort has gained traction.

The government and public don't accept the Rohingyas as an indigenous ethnic group. On the contrary, they view them as "illegals," some of who migrated to Burma from Bengal under British rule and others who are post-World War II arrivals. Some Rohingyas were forced into becoming "asylum seekers" in Burma due to Ne Win's 1978 operation called "Naga Min" (Dragon King) aimed at registering and classifying all residents and determining whether they were legal citizens. Myanmar's citizens tend to regard this discrimination with indifference, and many do not accept use of the term "Rohingya'" and often call them "Bengalis" (or worse) instead. In particular, many of the Buddhist Rakhine (Arakanese) people reject the term "Rohingya" because it suggests some legitimacy to their claims of being a dispossessed indigenous ethnic group. Moreover, Rakhine not only view them as "illegal immigrants" but also resent the presence of large numbers of Muslims in their land of Buddhism and are prejudiced against them because they have notably darker complexions. Thus, it is a case of religious and racial discrimination. What underlines such attitudes is the Burmese majority's historical understanding that the Rohingya people were not residents of Burma prior to 1823 and uncritical acceptance of the discriminatory provisions of the Nationality Law of 1982 that distort historical realities.

The battles over nomenclature are revealing. There are officially no Rohingya in Myanmar because such an ethnic group is, according to the government, an invention. The government maintains that the self-identified people known as Rohingya are in fact Bengalis from Bangladesh with no rightful legal claim to citizenship. By asserting this name, it is argued, they are trying to deceive the international community as there is no historical basis for either the name or the claim to citizenship. This point is hotly contested as some scholars are skeptical about Rohingya claims (Leider 2013, 2018), while others conclude that they do constitute an ethnic group and that their claims have a solid basis in history (Nemoto 2016; Crouch 2016; Ibrahim 2017). Clearly, the increasingly harsh treatment since Burma's post-1962 surge in Burmese Buddhist nationalism strengthened this collective identity over the ensuing five decades and more recently in the diaspora communities in Bangladesh, the Middle East, and Southeast Asia.

Following widespread rioting in 2012 that displaced some 140,000 Rohingya internally, the government bowed to international pressure and offered associate citizenship provided they would identify as Bengali. This was unacceptable to most Rohingya because their preferred name had become a symbol of their rightful claims and the state's insistence on Bengali was taken as an affront to their self-respect and struggle for justice. As Derek Mitchell, former US ambassador to Myanmar (2012–2016), explains, "Activists and leaders in the [Rohingya] community are very protective of that name. They see it as protective of their identity and dignity after so many basic rights have been taken from them in recent years. The name has also been essential to their international campaign for attention" (Calamur 2017).

Problematically, extending recognition to the Rohingya would, under the terms of the 1982 Citizenship Law, confer the right to an autonomous zone in the Wild West of northern Rakhine, which has long been a hotbed of drug smuggling, separatism, and now terrorism. This would be unacceptable to the military, which fears that autonomy would worsen the security situation and spark problems in neighboring states where an escalating insurgency might flourish. There are also concerns about safeguarding projects such as China's oil and gas pipelines that run through Rakhine into southeastern China. It is also not forgotten that prior to independence in 1948 Rohingya leaders sought annexation by Pakistan and when this didn't happen subsequently fought a sporadic separatist insurgency until the 1960s. These distant and implausible ghosts of separatism still haunt the Rohingya in the twenty-first century and make any Myanmar government concessions on citizenship unlikely.

In a 2013 speech in Tokyo, reacting to the large-scale persecution of the Rohingyas in August 2012, Aung San Suu Kyi proposed reexamination of the Nationality Law of 1982 to ensure it was fair and met international standards (Aung San Suu Kyi 2013). This proposal, however, sparked vitriolic domestic criticism, including from some of her loyal supporters, and Burmese communities overseas also began to censure her. This was because in their view she was taking the side of the Rohingya. She maintained that it was necessary to reconsider the irrationality inherent in the definition of "citizens" as stated in the Nationality Law of 1982 (i.e., the 1823 divide) and the manner of classifying "citizens" into three categories but has since retreated from this position following a chauvinist backlash. A peaceful and inclusive future for a multiethnic and religiously diverse Myanmar depends

on the extent to which the exclusivism of the ascendant ethnoreligious nationalism can be reined in; positive signs are scarce. A revision of the nationality law constitutes the first step toward doing so, but the politicization of
the citizenship question by religious and political leaders makes this unlikely.
Ironically the democratic transition from military rule has not helped vulnerable minorities and the ruling National League for Democracy (NLD) did not
field even one Muslim candidate in the 2015 elections.

Rohingya seek recognition as an ethnic group because full citizenship is
contingent on taingyintha, being one of the officially recognized national
races. Generations of residence thus don't matter because Rohingya are excluded from the taingyintha and thus denied citizenship (Cheesman 2017).
Aung San Suu Kyi now refers to them as the "Muslim Community in Rakhine State," and her government requests that international stakeholders, including Pope Francis on his 2017 visit, not use the term "Rohingya." When
the Pope didn't use Rohingya in public comments during his Yangon visit he
was criticized in the international media for failing to stand up for them, but
then when he did so on the subsequent leg of his tour to Dhaka, the Myanmar
media slammed him. In Rakhine there is particular antipathy toward use of
the term "Rohingya" as it is seen to help "illegals" trying to scam their way
into citizenship.

The 2014 census did not include an estimated one-third of Rakhine's
population because the Rohingya refused to identify as Bengali Muslims, the
official nomenclature for them. This refusal was motivated by concerns that
accepting such a designation might support the government's position insisting they are aliens, not citizens. In consequence, the unenumerated Rohingya
were left off the 2015 election voter rolls, disenfranchising them, although
that story is a bit more complicated. Until 2015 Rohingya had temporary
identity cards providing access to health and educational services. In February 2015 the Assembly of the Union, Myanmar's bicameral legislature,
passed a bill granting the two million "white card" holders, including many
Rohingya, the right to vote by an overwhelming majority, 328 lawmakers
approving the measure, 79 voting against it, and 19 abstaining. But the Constitutional Court rejected this bill and the government decreed that these
"temporary identity cards" had to be surrendered by May 31, 2015. This
decision deprived the Rohingya of proof of their residence and identity.

The rationale for rendering the Rohingya stateless as a matter of state
policy is attributed to various factors that boil down to a consensus that the
Rohingya are uninvited guests who have overstayed their welcome. The
military, Rakhine Buddhists, extremist monks, and politicians across the political spectrum share this prejudice and nobody in a position of power advocates otherwise. In the end, the new Parliament elected in 2015 did not have a
single Muslim member for the first time since the nation gained independence.

ETHNIC CLEANSING

The UN initially called the 2017 exodus of 730,000 Rohingya to neighboring Bangladesh "a textbook example of ethnic cleansing," and some suggested it was tantamount to genocide (Ibrahim 2017). By August 2018, the UN was also invoking genocide (UNHRC 2018). Comparisons to the horrors of Rwanda and even the Holocaust became commonplace as the world tried to digest this latest gruesome case of inhumanity. The "never again" refrain rang hollow, however, as the flight continued despite an outpouring of righteous indignation, condemnation, and collective handwringing. The global community looked on with growing outrage as week by week in the autumn of 2017 and into 2018 the flood of refugees into Bangladesh continued. It was powerless in the face of the military's determination, denials, and claims it was fighting terrorism, an excuse that has elsewhere provided political and diplomatic cover for war crimes and atrocities committed by the United States and other nations.

The military's narrative focuses on a cluster of attacks at thirty border guard posts in northern Rakhine State where there is a Muslim majority population of mostly Rohingya. The ARSA claimed responsibility for these coordinated attacks on August 25, 2017, that killed a dozen security personnel. ARSA is a small band of lightly armed insurgents numbering in the hundreds who press gang local villagers to aid them, and it has also been implicated in the targeted assassinations of moderate Muslims who cooperate with the government. The military alleges that this group is linked to IS and is funded by diaspora Rohingya in Saudi Arabia and the Gulf States. It is also reported that ARSA's leader hails from Pakistan and was a jihadi in Afghanistan and that there are training camps for the insurgents along the border with Bangladesh (Lintner 2017).

International criticism of this ethnic cleansing is widely dismissed in Myanmar as ill informed and exaggerated. Much blame is heaped on the diaspora Rohingya community's media campaign that has spread "disinformation" and whipped up a frenzied condemnation of Myanmar. Similar arguments were made in the 1990s and 2000s when the international community condemned military excesses and authoritarian rule. Apologists claimed then that critics failed to appreciate that the military was the only institution capable of governing and that its alleged excesses were overstated or offset by the relative political stability it ensured. The military's actions are again in the cross-hairs of international opprobrium, although now it co-governs with the NLD (while maintaining a firm grip on power) and finds useful political cover by maintaining a low profile and letting Foreign Minister Aung San Suu Kyi take the flak.

The government established a nine-member Advisory Commission on Rakhine State led by former UN secretary-general Kofi Annan to examine the anti-Rohingya violence in 2016 (Annan 2017). This 2016 operation was so similar to the events of 2017 that it appears to have been a dry run for the subsequent far more extensive pogrom. Like in 2017, the clearance operation by the military against the Rohingya was precipitated by an attack on border outposts followed by the razing of villages and the displacement of 92,000 Rohingya; 65,000 of them fled to Bangladesh where they joined 230,000 Rohingya refugees already in the country, the beleaguered flotsam of endemic harassment and violence targeting them. The October 2016 border guard post attack is attributed to Harakat al-Yaqin (later renamed ARSA), a Muslim armed group allegedly funded by Rohingya émigrés residing in Saudi Arabia.

The August 2017 Annan Report about the events in 2016 addresses the narrative of Buddhist victimization not by downplaying the suffering of Rakhine's Buddhists but by pointing out that the violence and destruction was lopsided, with far greater loss of Muslim homes and lives. It also questions the discriminatory criteria for determining citizenship, saying that the 1982 law falls short of international norms, violates the principle of equal treatment and thus the government's international commitments, and is inconsistent with the nation's 2008 Constitution. The most controversial recommendation involves revising the 1982 Citizenship Law, a reform that would facilitate Rohingya gaining citizenship.

On August 25, the day the report was released and endorsed by Aung San Suu Kyi, ARSA launched its coordinated assault on thirty border posts, providing a pretext for the military's brutal rampage in the region under the cover of conducting an antiterrorist operation. Some local skeptics, invoking the concept of cui bono, speculate that this 2017 attack might have been a false flag operation or otherwise involved military complicity to justify resumption of the similar 2016 anti-Rohingya operations. From the military's perspective the attacks provided three main benefits: 1) the ARSA attack marginalized the Annan Report and its unwelcome recommendations; 2) the military gained a free hand to respond without constraints; and 3) Aung San Suu Kyi bore the brunt of international condemnation, just as in 2016.

The Annan Report suggests that Rakhine is suffering from an interlocking development, human rights, and security crisis stemming from poverty, discrimination, and communal violence. It found that "protracted statelessness and profound discrimination have made the Muslim community particularly vulnerable to human rights violations. Some ten percent of the world's stateless people live in Myanmar, and the Muslims in Rakhine constitute the single biggest stateless community in the world" (Annan 2017). The commission advised against a security first militarization of the communal violence and stated that "reintegration, not segregation, is the best path to long-term stability and development in Rakhine State." That is not what is happening.

There is little doubt that Rohingya have endured rampant violation of their human rights. The reports of military atrocities in 2016 and 2017 are consistent with its counter-insurgency efforts all around the nation where the military has waged war on various ethnic groups seeking greater autonomy since independence. State-sponsored statelessness has facilitated enduring human rights abuses, including what amounts to incarceration in IDP camps, forced labor, arbitrary arrest, limitations on access to jobs and social services, and travel restrictions. The year 2012 is often cited as a watershed, not because the situation was so good beforehand but because it suddenly grew so much worse afterward. In 2012, intercommunal rioting erupted in June, with an alleged rape case igniting mutual animosities. President Thein Sein's request that year for UNHCR assistance in resettling a million Rohingya in Bangladesh or some other country was rebuffed. The tit for tat violence escalated and some 140,000 Rohingya were displaced. After the rioting, security forces relocated the Muslim residents of the capital Sittwe to IDP camps. As of 2018, 120,000 Muslims still remain in these grim camps where their movement is restricted by security forces. Ostensibly, compelling them to remain in the camps is for their protection, but segregating them in this way impedes any progress toward restoring any semblance of normalcy.

MILITARY MACHINATIONS

In the wake of the 2017 clearance operations the military denied access to the media, aid groups, and international rights monitors. It appears that these security campaigns against the Rohingya involved extra-judicial killings, rape, torture, and arbitrary arrests. In many cases the security forces acted systematically, according to refugees, by surrounding villages, separating men of fighting age from everyone else, and razing all the houses. The women were often subject to sexual abuse and rape.

In early 2018, UK Foreign Secretary Boris Johnson visited the Rohingya refugee camps in Bangladesh and then toured Rakhine before holding meetings with Aung San Suu Kyi and other officials. Johnston suggested that there should be accountability and prosecution of the evident crimes against humanity at the International Criminal Court. The Myanmar military investigated the allegations of massacres and rapes and, unsurprisingly, exonerated itself of all wrongdoing. As of 2019 no high-ranking officers have faced criminal proceedings. Evidence from satellite photos of the burning and bulldozing of villages in 2017–2018 where there may have been mass graves indicates a possible cover up. The government has refused to allow access to UN investigators or journalists, claiming the area remains unsafe. Efforts to justify the crimes as part of an antiterrorist sweep failed to convince as the military's disproportionate response in Rakhine looked well planned and premeditated.

Even though the military carried out the pogrom and everyone understands that Aung San Suu Kyi does not exercise effective authority over the military, she has become a lightning rod for international condemnation. Various organizations have rescinded awards, removed portraits, and lambasted her for not standing up for the Rohingya and justifying the military's actions. The military believes that as long as it can concoct a scenario of plausible deniability, invoke terrorism, play up IS links, and conceal the evidence of crimes against humanity, it can avoid accountability. Why not? The military has a track record of acting with impunity for much of the independence era, derailing democracy, plundering the economy while running it into the ground, and slaughtering students in 1988 and monks in 2007 to cow critics. It is still wreaking havoc in the name of preserving the nation, embracing brutal scorched earth tactics against several ethnic insurgencies, and manifesting a virulent ethnonationalism that threatens minorities and critics.

In 2017 a guide at the Shwedagon Temple in Yangon vigorously defended Ma Ba Tha (Association for the Protection of Race and Religion, a Buddhist nationalist group) and the military campaign against the "Bengali," asserting that the term "Rohingya" is invented to gain international sympathy (see chapter 5). She expressed the talking points of the pro-military media. In her view, Muslims can't be real Myanmarese because it is a nation of Buddhism and ethnic Burmese. She condemned their presence as a lamentable legacy of British colonial rule, claiming, "They are not part of our country, they are migrants and don't share our values. In no nation dominated by Muslims do they have human rights because they don't respect human rights." She was incensed by international criticisms and dismissed reports that soldiers were raping Rohingya women. She said that no self-respecting Burmese would touch let alone rape a Rohingya because they are considered so dirty, dark, and repulsive. It would be an affront to their dignity, she added, to have sex with such women, something she called unimaginable. She expressed utter disdain for the Rohingya, blaming them for spreading malicious lies to defame Myanmar to gullible foreigners. She argued that the military is only acting to protect Buddhism, so its actions are justified. Her respect for the military was in contrast to her condemnation of Aung San Suu Kyi, who she said was really a Baptist (a reference to her mother's religion). She insisted that when the Lady visits Shwedagon she never prays and her marriage to a foreigner (Michael Aris a British academic who died in 1999) reveals her true colors.

Another guide I met there had a totally different view. He described himself as one of the '88 Generation of students and said reports about the military's ethnic cleansing campaign and atrocities are credible because it's how they have always operated. He also thinks that the Rohingya have a legitimate claim to citizenship and was critical of Ma Ba Tha for stirring up anti-Islamic sentiments, condemning the hatemongering as something that has no place in Buddhism. He also opposed the 969 boycott of Muslim businesses and believes that the military has orchestrated these movements from behind the scenes. This, he argued, was an effort to sow chaos and turmoil to discredit the NLD and undermine the democratic transition and thus benefit the military. He further asserted that the military deliberately destroyed education in Myanmar to make it easier to control and mislead the public. But he believes the people see through the military's fog of lies and deception and know that it is sabotaging Aung San Suu Kyi and thus stand with her.

A prominent Burmese lawyer also believes that the Rohingya crisis was manufactured deliberately by the military to discredit democracy. Such military machinations have a long history in Myanmar. While the military may not explicitly collaborate with Ma Ba Tha he believes there is an implicit understanding of shared interests. The monks and military both want the Muslims out of the nation and the Rohingya crisis serves to generate support for the sangha while unifying the people under the banner of Buddhist Burmese ethnonationalism. These sources of solidarity present a dilemma for Aung San Suu Kyi because electoral competition makes it difficult to stand up for the reviled Rohingya. There is no incentive to publicly moderate views toward the Rohingya and thus democratic competition has further marginalized them. The lawyer also explained how it is far easier for outsiders to gain a clear understanding of what is happening to the Rohingya precisely because they are not constantly subjected to the monks' hatemongering and military-sponsored propaganda. In his view, the military has been enormously successful in managing the media and using it to convey their propaganda and promote their agenda of ethnoreligious nationalism. The people and even intellectuals, he said, "have fallen for their lies hook, line and sinker" (interview December 2017), encouraging a patriotic circling of the wagons in the face of international criticism. He believes that Aung San Suu Kyi has not pushed hard for international access to northern Rakhine because she believes that it would intensify the international condemnation that stokes patriotic sentiments and bolsters support for the military. He noted that at the time (before his account was closed down in 2018) the military chief had 1.2 million Facebook followers, enabling him to disseminate military views without any filtering or fact checking, creating a landscape skewed against rational discourse and objective assessments.

Frontier is an edgy English-language magazine published in Myanmar that often criticizes the government and military. Sonny Shwe, its editor, was jailed for eight and a half years by the previous military government on trumped-up charges, a victim of a high-level military purge that enveloped his father, a high-ranking military officer. Shwe acknowledges that "whatever happened to the Rohingya was such an ugly thing" but believes ARSA deliberately provoked the military, putting so many innocent lives in jeopardy for political gain (interview December 2017). In his view, the Muslim and Buddhist communities had been living harmoniously when suddenly they were caught between the extremists and the military, forcing them to flee to Bangladesh where they knew they could at least receive food and shelter. In the camps they no longer need to fear the Myanmar military, but Shwe contends they are subject to pressures from ARSA militants who have infiltrated and are recruiting supporters and harassing leaders who won't cooperate. For Rohingyas that remain in Rakhine, the dangers from the military and extremists push them to support both sides because "they have no choice but to say yes" and then face reprisals for doing so.

Shwe doesn't support Rohingyas' claim to citizenship and views ARSA as an IS-linked terrorist group seeking to establish an Islamic state in the region, bankrolled by diaspora Rohingya. The new dynamic in Rakhine is not Muslim-Buddhist conflict but rather the spread of a more extremist Islam by outside forces taking advantage of the poverty and remoteness of the region where the presence of the government is weak. In his view, Wirathu is trying to destabilize the government and using Ma Ba Tha to gain fame and brainwash followers by vilifying Muslims. Shwe also believes that Wirathu crosses the line of what is acceptable behavior for a monk and opposes the "blind nationalism" he promotes, calling it very dangerous, especially given the power of social media. "There's lots he should not be doing if he is serious about the robe he is wearing," Shwe says, adding, "Religion should teach people to do good and not do bad," but instead Wirathu incites his rabble of followers (interview December 2017). As far as the Rohingya are concerned, he considers Wirathu a facilitator, not an instigator, and agrees that the marriage law Ma Ba Tha helped push through Parliament was necessary to stop so-called love jihad whereby Muslim men marry Buddhist women with the purpose of converting them.

Shwe argued that extremist Muslims are responsible for undermining peace in Rakhine by calling for jihad and that the military's response to the terrorists was reasonable. He dismissed rumors that the military might have somehow orchestrated the attack or allowed it to happen to gain a pretext to resume ethnic cleansing operations. Ethnic cleansing, he thinks, misrepresents what the military has done in Rakhine and he doesn't think it used excessive force. Comparing the situation to the US war in Vietnam, he said it is hard to determine who are friends and foes and thus the clearance operations are a "drain the pond" tactic to locate and destroy the terrorists.

Blaming Aung San Suu Kyi is also unfair, Shwe said, because she "has no influence whatsoever on the military," but "it's too late to salvage her legacy" (interview December 2017). Criticizing the military, he thinks, is pointless because "they are brutal and have done the same to Karen, Kachin and Shan. If they feel they have to attack they will do so regardless of international pressures." He thinks that ongoing efforts by the United States, European Union, and Australia to nurture better ties with the military, upgrade security cooperation, and fight terrorism suggest a cynical pragmatism on the part of these governments regarding accountability for any atrocities.

PRESS FREEDOM BESIEGED

In December 2017 two Reuters reporters were jailed for doing their job. Their "crime" was investigating the military's crimes in Rakhine and finding credible evidence of mass executions of Rohingya by state security forces. In January 2019 the appeal of these reporters—sentenced in 2018 to seven years in jail—was rejected, a decision with far-reaching consequences for Myanmar's reputation and freedom of expression. The ruling is further evidence of the state's determination to bury the truth about the 2017 atrocities in Rakhine. In May 2019 the reporters were pardoned and released from prison, but their conviction stands and there was no apology for the gross miscarriage of justice or for the year and a half of separation from their families.

In December 2017 I was struck by how many liberals I met in Myanmar exhibited a collective blind spot over the Rohingya issue. One young Myanmar intellectual told me that her sources in the Muslim community said that the refugees were returning to Bangladesh because they were homesick! It's easy to dismiss such nonsense, and indeed many other Yangon residents including Muslims scoffed at the "plague of homesickness," but empathy seemed in short supply.

Activists and intellectuals who had been ardent critics of the military rallied in support of Aung San Suu Kyi and bought the military's line that what happened in Rakhine was purely retaliation for a terrorist attack on state security forces by ARSA. No matter that ARSA was a lightly armed, poorly organized rag-tag band posing little real threat to the government and the military's operations were vastly disproportionate. I was told that Myanmar was doing what any other state would do when faced with a similar situation. The alleged atrocities were brushed off as anti-Myanmar propaganda while the bad press and stripping of awards only seemed to enhance the embattled Lady's stature.

Inside Myanmar it doesn't appear many people are losing much sleep over the plight of the Rohingya and there is little enthusiasm for their repatriation. But as of late 2018, many NLD supporters of activists, intellectuals, journalists, lawyers, and politicians have become deeply disillusioned (interviews November 2018). The Wizard of Oz moment was the trial of the two Reuters reporters in 2018. They were arrested for possessing allegedly secret documents, but during the 2018 court proceedings the reporters' lawyer proved that the documents were not secret. Then a police captain testified that he was ordered to plant the documents on the reporters and frame them. In the court of public opinion, the military narrative depicting these reporters as traitors blackening the name of the nation collapsed. How could the judge arrive at a guilty verdict given the damning testimony exonerating the reporters? The lawyer complained that the Lady influenced the verdict by thrice publicly stating that the reporters had violated the Official Secrets Act and insisting the case was not about press freedom. This made it very difficult for the judge to absolve the reporters.

The real problem was that the reporters had been investigating military and police atrocities in Rakhine against the Rohingya, gathering testimony and photographic evidence. So essentially state security was hoping to intimidate other journalists from doing their jobs by going after the Reuters reporters. Their lawyer Than Zaw Aung explained that during the trial, the military court martialed seven soldiers for the execution of ten Rohingya based on the evidence produced by the Reuters reporters, inadvertently lending credibility to their case. The murderous soldiers were sentenced to ten years in prison, only a few years longer than the Reuters journalists.

Maung Saungkha, a young democracy activist, maintains that press freedom is receding dramatically under Aung San Suu Kyi. He asserts that the previous military-linked government was far more media friendly precisely because it knew it lacked credibility, whereas the Lady has been very aggressive in going after critics. He was the first person prosecuted under Article 66d of the 2013 Telecommunications Law for defamation. He posted a poem on Facebook suggesting he had a tattoo of President Thein Sein's image on his penis and that on his wedding night his wife was inconsolable. Apparently prosecutors didn't have a sense of humor or understand poetic license. And nobody bought the defense that if such a tattoo existed it would be a vivid gesture of patriotic loyalty.

While on trial, the Penis Poet spent seven months in the notorious Insein prison before the judge set him free. Although not required to present evidence in court, I was assured that he has no tattoos and is unmarried. He has gone on to establish Athan (Voice) to monitor press freedom in Myanmar and found that the previous government only prosecuted eleven reporters under Article 66d while the NLD has gone after more than 160 as of November 2018. This explains his painful decision to relinquish membership in the NLD. He was incredulous in October 2018 when the Lady gave an interview in Tokyo dismissing allegations of a press crackdown. Ironically, on the night she returned from Japan three reporters were jailed for "defaming" the head of the Yangon regional government, her protégé, over a shady bus contract implicating him.

The NLD and the Lady seem to have forgotten how freedom of expression was once a core value. Critics assert that she has become increasingly authoritarian, isolated, and intolerant of criticism. Why doesn't she criticize the military for its outrages? Although it sounds like a callous calculation, a diplomat believes Aung San Suu Kyi is unwilling to call the military out on its atrocities against the Rohingya because the fate of that one million people with uncertain claims to citizenship may not be worth risking the fate of the democratic transition affecting more than fifty million others. The worry, he explained, is that the NLD government and democratization remains vulnerable to the military's considerable influence and strength. From this perspective, the Rohingya are expendable, regarded as collateral damage of the ongoing democratic transition.

Her dwindling number of defenders among the local intelligentsia speculate that she hopes to get the military's agreement to amend the constitution to remove the proviso that bans her from becoming president. Others assert that she fears a military coup. Critics scoff at the prospects of either scenario and grumble that she even vets what issues NLD members can raise in Parliament, rarely delegates, and relies on a small inner circle of advisors mostly with military ties.

CONTESTED OTHERING

Ko Ko Gyi is a leader of the '88 Generation Students, a movement founded in 2005 that draws inspiration, and its name, from the military's bloody suppression of student pro-democracy demonstrations in 1988. Despite spending eighteen years in solitary confinement, he is philosophical about his detention and torture, noting that people identify with him and his colleagues because of all they endured to end military rule. Thus, he is someone who would not naturally support the military's actions. When we met in 2012 soon after waves of anti-Rohingya/Muslim rioting, he emphatically dismissed their right to citizenship and was fine with the 1982 law and their exclusion. At the time he expressed ambivalence about joining mainstream politics, but in 2018 he launched the People's Party. In 2017, in an NHK World interview, he positioned himself as an aspiring politician who could resolve the Rohingya problem (NHK 2017). He proclaimed himself in favor of repatriation and a vetting based on the 1982 Citizenship Law, a policy that few viewers would have realized was a dead end for most refugees. All aspiring returnees face a catch-22 situation because in order to pass the vetting based on the 1982 Citizenship Law, they must produce national identity cards that they don't have anymore because the government confiscated them, creating a stateless people as a matter of state policy. And even those who might have held on to these crucial identity documents may not have had the presence of mind to bring them as they fled marauding security forces torching their villages, raping women, and killing randomly. Like Aung San Suu Kyi, he refrained from criticizing the military's clearance operations.

In contrast, a Burmese veteran of international NGOs confided she was appalled at the mistreatment of the Rohingya but did not feel comfortable voicing such concerns in public given simmering anger among local colleagues and friends about international criticism. She worried about being out of step with public sentiment and the risk of confrontation or ostracism because the battle lines are drawn rather sharply. Speaking out in favor of the Rohingya or defending their human rights takes courage when the media message is relentlessly hammered home that they have no right to be in Myanmar because they are Bangladeshi migrants and terrorists who got what they deserved. Indeed, it is hard to find anyone willing to go on record who contests that narrative.

I met "VJ Joshua," however, the Burmese video journalist who provided visceral footage of the Saffron Revolution, capturing scenes of beatings, shootings, and arrests that made the Danish documentary *Burma VJ: Reporting from a Closed Country* (2009) so powerful. The chance encounter happened while Joshua Min Htut was helping out on a new Danish documentary project about Myanmar's democratic transition. What began as a paean to Aung San Suu Kyi and the teething problems of democratization became more complicated and interesting because of the Rohingya problem, one that starkly illustrates the limits of her power and the fragile state of democratization. He emphasized that the Constitution bars her from the presidency while the military remains in control of security and is not subject to civilian control in any meaningful way. While she has moral authority in Myanmar, this has eroded considerably overseas due to her failure to exercise it in condemning the military's actions, but at home this has boosted her support. The world is puzzled why the Nobel Peace Laureate who boldly spoke truth to power at considerable cost to her freedom and family cannot now find her voice. Joshua suggests it may be that the burdens of power and managing the democratic transition have made her more cautious, but there is also the double risk of condemning without any substantive impact on the military's actions, thereby exposing her powerlessness while provoking a military backlash injurious to democratization (interview December 2017). In Joshua's view, the public in Myanmar has been brainwashed by the government and media on the Rohingya issue. The key, he argued, is to educate people and to guide them away from ethnonationalism toward civic nationalism, but this is a long-term process that offers no immediate relief.

Clear and consistent messaging by the state and media outlets vilifying and marginalizing the Rohingya has nurtured a collective hostility. They have become the designated target, but Joshua still thinks Aung San Suu Kyi should speak out, and if she backs repatriation and/or calls the military out, he thinks the public would side with her. He dismissed the pro-military rallies held in late 2017 as rent-a-crowd efforts and said that popular suspicions of the military and its ongoing threat to the democratic transition remain powerful.

The recommendation of the Annan Commission in August 2017 to revise the controversial 1982 Citizenship Law is, as Joshua notes, "political dynamite for politicians because the worst thing to be accused of these days is being pro-Rohingya" (interview December 2017). There are many urgent challenges facing the government that imperil the democratic transition but perhaps managing this polarizing "blood and race" issue is the most crucial test facing Aung San Suu Kyi. In Joshua's view, religion complicates the Rohingya problem, but the basis is ethnic, drawing on the deep antipathies of the Rakhine people toward these "strangers" in their midst. He adds, however, that if they were Buddhists, they would never be so mistreated.

U Dhammapiya, a senior monk in Ma Ba Tha, the Buddhist nationalist organization that helped instigate anti-Muslim rioting across Myanmar, is adamantly opposed to revising the 1982 Citizenship Law (interview December 2017). He participated in the Annan Commission but doesn't agree with the recommendations, believing them to be misguided and counterproductive. Since there are already 135 ethnic groups recognized officially, why not one more? He argued that this might open the floodgates as many other groups would also want to claim citizenship. When pressed to name which groups, he suggested that Myanmar might suddenly have a large population of unwelcome ethnic Chinese demanding citizenship. He likened the situation with illegal Mexican immigrants in the United States, drawing on his experience studying for a doctorate in California where he saw firsthand the prejudice against them. There have been amnesties for such illegal migrants in past decades, granting them full citizenship rights in the United States, but this is not something Dhammapiya thinks is appropriate in Myanmar. In his view, many are simply economic migrants fleeing poverty in Bangladesh where land is scarce. While he agrees that Buddhists should show compassion for fellow human beings; this is a case in which the law is clear and has been violated and thus the military's clearing operations targeting illegal migrants is acceptable. He also said that the allegations that Rakhine Buddhists were attacking Rohingya were far fetched because they are the minority in the northern area of Rakhine and it would be rash to do so. Downplaying reports of atrocities, he asserted that these have been exaggerated by pro-Rohingya groups to elicit international sympathy. So why not allow journalists and independent investigators access to the zones of violence to confirm the situation? He said (as of December 2017) that it was still too dangerous to travel in Rakhine and thinks the ban on travel sensible to avoid further incidents.

Since the 1990s, Saudi Arabia has vigorously promoted Wahhabism in Asia, with significant repercussions on identity politics in Myanmar (see chapter 4). According to Dhammapiya, the spread of Islamic fundamentalism has led to more mosque building, more devout religious observance, and wearing of clothing that signifies a distinct Muslim identity, fueling Buddhists' anxieties and hostility toward Muslims. He disagreed with the view that anti-Muslim agitation and rioting by the Buddhist majority and hatemongering by monks might be reinforcing Islamic religiosity, thus sharpening the divide.

REGIONAL REPERCUSSIONS

There has been saber rattling over the Myanmar military's clearance operations that drove so many refugees to seek refuge in Bangladesh, causing some Bangladeshi's to view this as an act of war. At the November 2017 Dhaka Literary Festival, many participants harshly condemned the ethnic cleansing and some even spoke of going to war and advocated boosting the military's capabilities in order to do so. There were poignant reports by participants who had just returned from the squalid refugee camps near Cox's Bazaar, relaying some of the horrific stories they heard about the atrocities committed by Myanmar's military.

Frustrations with Myanmar's government were building due to the slow progress on arranging repatriation, leading the finance minister to say in March 2018, "They are evil, a rogue government," adding, "Burmese are not trustworthy" (Ellis-Petersen 2018). Although Bangladesh insists the Rohingya will be repatriated, the finance minister said this is unlikely: "I do not believe the Rohingya can be sent back . . . very few will return to Burma. The first reason is that Burma will only take a few and secondly is that the refugees will never return if they fear persecution."

A repatriation agreement was signed by the two countries in November 2017 to repatriate any Rohingya willing to return to Rakhine, stipulating that they should be returned within two years. The generosity of Prime Minister Sheik Hassina has earned kudos abroad, but the refugee exodus is a heavy burden for an impoverished nation. Patience has given way to frustration and anger as efforts to repatriate the refugees have stalled. Progress stalled because Rakhine remains unsafe for the Rohingya, especially because most NGOs and international organizations faced a ban on operating there. Meanwhile, in 2018 Rohingya continued to stream into Bangladesh to escape ongoing persecution. In March 2018, Andrew Gilmour, UN Assistant Secretary-General for Human Rights, asserted that "the ethnic cleansing of Rohingya from Myanmar continues. The nature of the violence has changed from the frenzied bloodletting and mass rape of last year to a lower-intensity campaign of terror and forced starvation that seems to be designed to drive the remaining Rohingya from their homes and into Bangladesh" (UN 2018). Given what has happened it is hard to imagine the Rohingya regaining trust in Myanmar's security forces to safeguard them.

Following two waves of violence in 2012 an estimated 120,000 Rohingya fled the country by boat, seeking a better life in Malaysia, Indonesia, or Thailand, but many died trying, either drowned or killed by unscrupulous traffickers. Jakarta and Kuala Lumpur have tried to goad ASEAN into collective action, as they have domestic Muslim constituencies demanding more forthright action. ASEAN's policies of noninterference in each other's domestic affairs and unanimous consensus have hampered its effectiveness in tackling controversial issues. Senior government officials in Malaysia and Indonesia have not been quite as outspoken as counterparts in Bangladesh but are quite critical of Myanmar. Muslim majorities in both nations share Bangladeshi perspectives about the Rohingya being persecuted for their religion. In Jakarta petrol bombs were hurled at the Myanmar Embassy in 2017 and police arrested a man who threatened a suicide bomb attack on Buddhists in Jakarta in retaliation for the mistreatment of Rohingya. The Myanmar Embassy has also been subject to large protests staged by the Islamic Defender's Front. Its chairman Rizieq Shihab told protestors, "Our brothers in Rohingya have been tortured by Myanmar military, Buddhist monks and Buddhist people in Myanmar. There is no other way for our Muslim brothers in Rohingya, we have to wage jihad" (Langlois 2013). He has also criticized President Joko Widodo, known as Jokowi, for not doing more on behalf of fellow Muslims.

In response Jokowi has waged an aggressive diplomatic campaign, visiting the refugee camps, providing aid, and raising the issue at a summit of the ten ASEAN leaders held in Sydney, Australia, in March 2018. Given the sensitivity about human rights issues among member states eager to avoid scrutiny of their own records and the ASEAN tradition of trying to maintain group harmony and consensus, Jokowi's criticisms of Myanmar and Aung San Suu Kyi at the summit suggest just how much impact the Rohingya issue has had on identity (and electoral) politics in Indonesia. Similarly, Malaysian Prime Minister Najib Razak (since ousted in the 2018 elections) sent aid and condemned the mistreatment of fellow Muslims by the Myanmar government, a contrast to the reticence of both governments when the military was shooting monks on the streets in 2007 and keeping Aung San Suu Kyi under house arrest. This humanitarian crisis, however, is on a much larger scale, and they believe that the Rohingya are being targeted because they are Muslim.

The Rohingya issue has thus exposed a religious divide in ASEAN that has never been a significant source of tension among members beforehand. In order to get around the domestic meddling constraint, Malaysian Prime

Minister Razak argued at the 2018 ASEAN summit in Sydney that the Rohingya refugee crisis was not solely a domestic issue for Myanmar, warning
of the potential for terrorist radicalization that could threaten the entire region. Although Razak was accused of grandstanding on this issue for political gain by shoring up his Muslim credentials and deflecting attention away
from his financial scandals, a more serious criticism involves the Rohingya
refugees in Malaysia. Unlike the high-profile campaign to send aid to overseas Rohingya, those in Malaysia have not gotten much government support.
Malaysia closed its borders to Rohingya refugees in 2015, but about 150,000
settled there and registered with the UNHCR, living in a legal limbo because
they don't have proper documentation. Malaysia bars them from working or
attending government-run schools, partly to deter more from coming. While
neglecting these Rohingya at home, Prime Minister Razak dispatched aid
convoys to the camps in Bangladesh and Myanmar.

Thailand has long been a hub for human trafficking networks involving
Rohingya refugees. In 2015, the "discovery" of trafficking camps and mass
graves in southern Thailand—Thai officials knew of the existence of the
camps for years and were complicit in the operations of traffickers—precipitated a crackdown by Thai and Malaysian authorities. As a result, traffickers
abandoned boats of refugees and migrants at sea, often without adequate
water, food, or fuel. Thailand's military government responded to the 2015
boat crisis by enforcing a "push-back" policy, towing boats filled with hun-
gry and malnourished refugees into international waters, preferring they land
in Malaysia or Indonesia. ASEAN brokered an agreement involving these
member states that allowed boat people to stay for one year but provided no
support or follow up. Apparently, Australia paid the people smugglers to turn
around and bring their Rohingya passengers back into Indonesian waters.

From 2012 to 2015 ASEAN held just two meetings to address the Rohingya crisis but did very little. In contrast, the Organization of Islamic States
has taken a leadership role in rallying support for the Rohingya and sponsoring a UN General Assembly resolution condemning the Myanmar military's
clearance operations. ASEAN member states divided over the resolution that
was adopted by a vote of 122 to 10 with 24 abstentions. ASEAN members
accounted for half of the nays; Cambodia, Laos, the Philippines, and Vietnam joined Myanmar in voting against the resolution. The resolution calls on
Myanmar to allow access for aid workers, ensure the return of all refugees,
and grant full citizenship rights to the Rohingya to no avail.

The scale of this ethnic cleansing represents the most extreme triumph of
majoritarian politics in Asia (Kesavan 2018). The persecution of the Rohingya has made Myanmar something of an inspiration to majoritarian parties in
neighboring states. The Indian government, led by the Hindu nationalist
Bharatiya Janata Party, announced in August 2017 that the forty thousand
Rohingyas in India (refugees from an earlier exodus) would be deported

because they were illegal immigrants. In Sri Lanka the BBS extremist Buddhist organization verbally and physically attacked the tiny Rohingya community, making it clear they are also not welcome there.

GUILTY

In late August 2018 the United Nations' Human Rights Council released the results of an investigation into the clearance operations conducted by Myanmar's military (Tatmadaw), concluding that "criminal investigation and prosecution is warranted, focusing on the top Tatmadaw generals, in relation to the three categories of crimes under international law; genocide, crimes against humanity and war crimes" (UNHRC 2018). The report provides detailed accounts of coordinated atrocities, including rapes, mass killings, and arson, suggesting that criminal liability extends up the chain of command. The UN recommended that General Min Aung Hlaing, the commander in chief, along with five other senior military officials, be investigated for genocide at the International Criminal Court. It is a damning recommendation drawing on significant and credible evidence. While an International Criminal Court prosecution may well occur, it will take a long time if indeed it is ever pursued.

Facebook moved more expeditiously, banning twenty senior military figures from its platform in 2018, including Min Aung Hlaing. The general had two pages with about four million followers on the nation's social media platform of choice. He frequently posted on his pages, brazenly denigrating the Rohingya and denying international accusations about atrocities. He asserted all the accusations were "fake news" and that there is no religious discrimination in Myanmar. The impact of his postings and those by other officers and soldiers was huge in a nation where three-quarters of Facebook users say that getting the news is their main reason for using the site. This provided the military with an effective tool for shaping the domestic narrative about the Rohingya, rallying support, and whipping up an ethnoreligious nationalist backlash to international accusations. Based on an in-house investigation of the postings, Facebook concluded that its platform had been conscripted into the anti-Rohingya campaign and hired more staff with Burmese language skills to weed out hate speech. The company was trying to counter severe international condemnation for complicity in the ethnic cleansing by not being more proactive in removing such postings. But there is little to celebrate as the hatemongerers, Islamophobics, and deniers still find ways to evade the inadequate monitoring, while the Rohingya languish in Bangladesh and their plight recedes from the international limelight.

Chapter Seven

Islamic Minorities in Asia

In this chapter we further examine cross-currents of Islamic fundamentalism, national identity, and extremism in contemporary Asia. As we discussed regarding the Rohingya in the preceding chapter, the state's tendency to overreact to exaggerated threats and inflict unimaginable suffering on vulnerable minorities is an inescapable reality. In China, India, the Philippines, Thailand, and Sri Lanka, Muslim communities are in the minority and have suffered the usual discrimination, injustices, and repression that majority populations typically inflict, provoking a subnationalist backlash of resistance that elicits further repression. For the dispossessed and marginalized, religion provides a redoubt for strengthening solidarity and defending identity. As we explore shortly, central governments find it hard to resist counterproductive policies involving majoritarian repression, intrusion, and assimilation that alienate Muslim minorities, sometimes pushing them to an extremism that draws on shared grievance. Even though minorities are not monolithic and extremism is rejected by most believers, they tend to be tarred with the same brush and thus pay the same price for their faith.

CHINA'S UIGHURS

China is home to numerous small ethnic minorities, but multicultural rhetoric notwithstanding, under the Chinese Communist Party (CCP) ethnic Han culture dominates in a pervasive and frequently discriminatory manner. Balancing the dictates of national integration, China's overriding priority, with the need for managing ethnocultural diversity has been an ongoing struggle and in Xinjiang an abject failure. This failure was underscored by reports in 2018 that hundreds of thousands of Uighurs are being detained in "vocational training" camps across the troubled region (HRW 2018; Wong 2018).

As Georgetown's James Milward observes, "The CCP's mass internment and coercive indoctrination of Muslim minorities is intended to forcibly remake their identity. The party now increasingly finds Islamic faith and even non-Han ethnic culture to be inimical to the goal of homogeneous Chinese identity" (Milward 2019). Mass incarceration just for being Uighur is a desperate measure that suggests the government has run out of ideas on how to restore law and order or accommodate diversity. Well not entirely as "during a campaign named Ethnicity Unity Becoming Family Week in December 2017, a million CCP cadres moved in to live, eat, and work with Uighurs. In these repeated stays, the Han officials are meant to teach Chinese to Uighur 'little brothers' and 'little sisters,' instruct them in Xi Jinping Thought, and sing the Chinese national anthem, while helping out around the house" (Milward 2019). These home visits it turns out were more about gathering intelligence than ethnic amity, helping the state identify who should be sent to the reeducation camps for "vocational training" in China's gulag archipelago.

Over the past fifty years, there have been several uprisings and violent outbursts in Xinjiang, and all have been resolutely quashed. Beijing has amplified ethnic tensions that undermine its goal of strengthening national unity by embracing draconian security measures. Ethnic polarization in the remote and thinly populated western region of Xinjiang has risen in recent years due to expanding restrictions on religion and cultural expression aimed at curtailing the ostensible menace of "separatism." This has sparked attacks by Uighur militants targeting the security presence and reprisals involving disproportionate use of force by state security.

In strategically sensitive frontier border areas like Xinjiang, Beijing emphasizes security and consolidation of its control. The CCP came to power in 1949 and has aggressively promoted assimilation, tightly circumscribing space for religion. The only faith embraced in secular China is communism, but this is a discredited ideology that has been progressively abandoned since economic reforms were initiated in 1979. Since then, materialism has become the de facto creed of China. The expanding economic and political brawn of Han Chinese weigh heavily on the Uighurs and they find little to celebrate in the rising China story. Despite statistical claims of improved well-being and social services, Uighurs overwhelmingly resent the Han dominance in their homeland and are understandably not grateful for the claimed improvements that leave them feeling disempowered and downtrodden.

It's worth emphasizing that Chinese nationalism is all about Han nationalism. In a country that has lost its moorings while experiencing tremendous socioeconomic convulsions, nationalism is a reassuring and expedient ideology that creates a sense of unity among a people riven by yawning disparities, injustice, and corruption. The Party has discovered a lifeline in nationalism, appealing to Han chauvinism to assert a dubious legitimacy. In such a context, non-Han Chinese face an accelerating threat to their way of life and identity. The Han have inadvertently reinforced subnationalisms, stoking antagonism and cycles of violence through acts of cultural arrogance and harsh oppression.

The expansion of transport and communication networks has brought the fringes of China under ever-increasing Han sway, generating frictions and uncomfortable cultural clashes that have become the new norm. Once isolated, minority groups have increasingly lost the protection of distance and have become targets of ambitious development projects. The remote Xinjiang region is home to about eleven million Uighurs, a Turkic ethnic group that is culturally, religiously, linguistically, and physically distinct from the ethnic Han. Currently, about 41 percent of Xinjiang's population of almost twenty-four million is Han due to significant inward migration. Colorful Uighur markets have been razed and replaced with ugly concrete blocks while the glittery signs of progress Han style are evident in gated enclaves separated from the bleaker conditions that prevail. The boomtowns in the oil and gas regions of Xinjiang offer glaring contrasts to prevailing local lifestyles and living standards as locals take a backseat to Han in commerce and government.

Chinese is the language of upward mobility, but even this is a limited option for fluent locals as Han-managed companies entice Han workers to relocate to Xinjiang with higher wages and better benefits. Uighurs are have-nots in their homeland and attribute evident disparities to systematic discrimination. Han get the best jobs, best salaries, and live the relatively good life. As Han enclaves expand and disparities grow more visible and acute, there is a natural sense of relative deprivation while the security forces heighten tensions. Chinese explain their dominating presence in terms of skills and financial resources lacking in western China. They point out that by any measure—health, education, nutrition, living standards—people are far better off now than twenty years ago and can't quite understand why the people are so angry and ungrateful. Chinese officials blame the local people for their own failings, but locals feel that discrimination has prevented them from sharing in the fruits of growth and that their way of life is endangered.

China's rapid economic modernization has increased the urgency of tapping Xinjiang's vast oil and gas potential, but well-qualified locals confide they can never get good jobs as Han-run firms prefer to recruit more expensive talent from outside the region. A young Uighur barber fluent in Chinese who I met with a degree in chemical engineering could not even get an interview in the booming petrochemical sector. Minority policies have done little to nurture interethnic trust or improve interethnic disparities in income, education, and employment favorable to Han. Officially, there is a system of preferences for local minorities, but in practice discrimination is a constant impediment to realizing aspirations. Denigrating and condescending Han stereotypes about Uighurs are suffused with menace that draws on fear.

In the post-9/11 world, Beijing has cracked down on "Islamic extremism" in Xinjiang. National security and the "war on terror" are trumping concerns about religious freedom and human rights, but measures aimed at quelling unrest are proving counterproductive and alienating the majority of the population that has not engaged in violence or advocated separatism. The government invokes the dangers of "the three evil forces of separatism, extremism and terrorism" to justify its escalating crackdown on Uighurs but is radicalizing the local population due to extreme state repression of Islam.

This heavy-handed trampling on religious sensitivities is, like in Tibet, generating a clash of civilizations (see chapter 5). In 2009, for example, violent riots in Urumchi, the capital of Xinjiang, left at least 200 and possibly 800 dead and 1,600 injured, mostly ethnic Han. The police incited the inter-ethnic violence, the worst episode in decades, by targeting a peaceful Uighur student demonstration. The ensuing rioting spread like wildfire. In response, the security forces stepped up draconian measures that feed such grievances and anti-Han sentiments. Subsequently, in the summer of 2013 there was a series of violent incidents authorities attributed to terrorists while the number of Uighurs arrested for "endangering state security" rose sharply that year. Significantly, all over China citizens annually engage in tens of thousands of defiant protests, riots, violence, sabotage, kidnappings, and civil disobedience to draw attention to abuses of power and corruption because it is often the only way for them to draw attention to such problems and hold officials accountable. While the state also cracks down on such "criminal behavior" and "hooliganism," it doesn't adopt a province-wide lockdown, or lockup, as in contemporary Xinjiang.

In January 2014 police detained Ilham Tohti, a prominent Uighur academic economist based in Beijing, and accused him of inciting and organizing Uighur separatism. He was a prominent advocate of policy reform who stressed the need to balance the dictates of national unity with minority autonomy. Apparently he erred in telling the international media that the root cause of problems in Xinjiang is not separatism, arguing that suppression of everyday religious practice is spreading discontent and an upsurge in religious militancy; clearly the truth doesn't always set one free. The roundup of Uighur intellectuals has intensified since 2017 with more than one hundred sent to the indoctrination camps under the pretext of vocational training. The jailing of high-profile scholars, editors, and writers is part of a larger campaign to eradicate Uighurs' ethnic identity and silence those best placed to defend it (Ramzy 2019).

With moderates ending up behind bars it is no wonder that militancy is on the rise, creating a dynamic of escalating violence as state security clamps down even further and more Uighurs give up hope for moderate reforms. Beijing identifies the problem as the extremism of a small group of separatists rather than acknowledging the broader desire for self-rule. Its reliance on harsh methods only radicalizes the situation and makes it a more extensive security problem as militants seek support and inspiration in the near abroad of Central Asia. In this febrile situation both sides are cutting off options as they retreat into a cycle of escalating state and terrorist violence. Under the circumstances, the state's integrationist initiatives face deep levels of distrust and hostility.

Eruptions of violence and terrorist incidents reduce prospects for reforms and increase reliance on dead end repressive measures that perpetuate instability. Although Beijing shrugs off its responsibility by exaggerating the role of tiny terrorist groups such as the East Turkestan Islamic Movement (ETIM), pent-up grievances over government repression and curbs on religious practices are the root causes of such outbreaks.

Islam is a touchstone of Uighur identity, so banning students and government employees from fasting during Ramadan and prohibitions on any religious meetings, prayer gatherings, Quranic instruction, or Islamic ceremonies without the express consent of local authorities antagonizes Uighurs who also resent curbs on Uighur-language education. Fearing the rise of jihadism, the government is also encouraging secularization, threatening in some districts to shut down shops that refuse to sell alcohol or tobacco, forcing merchants to choose between their religious principles and livelihood. In the cultural sphere, authorities have introduced new regulations that further infringe on religious practices and customs central to Uighurs' Islamic identity, such as banning "abnormal" beards, fasting during Ramadan, veils, and other face coverings for women.

In this brave new world in a region shaped over the centuries by Silk Road trade and sustained cultural interactions, the state now arrogates the power to control levels of religious devotion. Successful Uighur businessmen were arrested in 2017 because they had not prayed enough at a funeral while local party chiefs risk demotion for being too observant if they don't smoke or drink alcohol. These efforts to extinguish Uighur culture and identity generate a powerful backlash. Beijing's crackdown justified in terms of a rising Uighur "terrorism" has been a self-fulfilling prophecy and pushes people to embrace a more Islamic identity. Contemporary Xinjiang thus presents a volatile mix of Uighur ethnonationalism and heightened religious mobilization in the face of an uncompromising state.

March 1, 2014, became China's 9/11, the day that Islamic Uighur terrorists slashed their way into the collective consciousness of ethnic Han. A group of militant Uighurs attacked Chinese citizens in Kunming with machetes, killing 29 and wounding 143 people. The desire for state revenge, China's war on terror, reemphasizes the same repressive policies that have not been working in the restive province. The government attributes this savage attack, the worst ever outside Xinjiang, to ETIM, a Uighur secessionist group that supports the establishment of an East Turkestan. This is the name many Uighurs prefer for their homeland that refers to a short-lived state in the 1940s before incorporation by China in 1949. The Kunming attack followed an October 2013 incident in which a car driven by a Uighur family careened into a crowded sidewalk adjacent to Tiananmen Square in Beijing before crashing and bursting into flames. This "attack" was also blamed on ETIM. State authorities believe these incidents signal that Uighur extremists are taking their fight outside their region and organizing terrorist attacks in the Han heartland. Such brazen challenges to state authority and prospects of further such incidents escalate repression that radicalizes more Uighurs while derailing moderate reforms in ethnic policies. China's security forces can certainly contain this threat, but in doing so they are perpetuating it. This drastic approach has produced an inevitable backlash and an intensified crackdown that draws on methods deployed previously in Tibet.

State repression in Xinjiang has intensified since 2017 when old fashioned CPP tyranny and Maoist excess got a high-tech boost. Cutting-edge surveillance and monitoring technology coupled with the introduction of a grid system of checkpoints, police stations, armored vehicles, and frequent patrols raise the visibility and effectiveness of security forces at the expense of privacy and any vestiges of civil liberties. Movements are carefully tracked and racial profiling is unapologetically applied while bags are X-rayed and bodies, irises, phones, and IDs are scanned. Everyone has to carry ID cards that link to a database that includes biometric data and personal information, including DNA collected during medical checkups. Based on this accumulated data, people are classified as "unsafe, "safe," or "normal," a designation that determines access to jobs, housing, travel, malls, auditoriums, museums, and hotels. Purchasing a kitchen knife requires registering the purchaser's identifying data onto the blade. The Orwellian police state features more widespread surveillance such as ubiquitous face recognition CATV, the installation of GPS in all vehicles, spy apps in all mobile devices, and restriction to WeChat communication software because it grants police full access to all calls, texts, and shared content. Going to the market is no longer the casual outing it once was as shoppers have to pass through invasive airport-like security checks and police can randomly demand mobile phones and examine all content. And thus, moderates are radicalized.

By curtailing Uighurs' human rights, Beijing is undoing any goodwill it might gain from raising living standards. The calculated insults to Islamic sensitivities in the name of law and order also carry a considerable reputational cost with Islamic nations, including Silk Road neighbors. Xinjiang is the gateway to the much-touted Belt and Road Initiative aimed at forging links among China, Central Asia, Europe, and the Middle East, and thus the repercussions of the crackdown may have a wider impact. In those nations, policing terrorism doesn't necessitate or justify an assault on religious identity, thus Beijing may find its crackdown counterproductive both in terms of domestic and international blowback. As Uighur specialist James Milward observes, "Nothing shreds soft power abroad like coils of razor wire at home" (Milward 2018). Prospects for ethnic policy reform are limited because longstanding repression has widened the gulf separating the Uighurs and Han. There is little trust.

Beijing's explicit Han ethnonationalism has increased the stakes of identity politics, a politicization that feeds mutual antagonisms. Terrorist incidents targeting ethnic Han further limit the government's room for maneuver. While the Uighurs feel victimized, ethnic Han also feel victimized and have long complained that the state has coddled the minorities and given them unfair advantages and benefits. There is a strong emotional aspect of contemporary Han nationalism that is hyper-sensitive to criticism and considerable cyber-nationalist anger directed at minorities for their ingratitude for all that has been bestowed on them. Moreover, as Yu argues, "It is believed that Tibet and Xinjiang are cards that the U.S. plays in containing the rise of China [and] have never been seen solely as domestic problems but ones intricately linked to foreign forces" (2016). Compromise in this context is unlikely.

Even if Beijing could introduce more appealing integrationist policies and moved toward more genuine political autonomy for Xinjiang, the legacy of violence and distrust imperils such efforts. Beijing often invokes the ethnic problems of the former Soviet Union and Yugoslavia as object lessons for China to avoid. Although there is scant prospect of China being engulfed by ethnic turmoil, Xinjiang is a strategically important region. As a result, while intensified economic exploitation is proceeding, loosening the state's grip is deemed too risky, meaning there is little chance that ethnic tensions will subside.

It is worth emphasizing that Beijing is also tackling the wrong problem by focusing on the chimera of separatism. There is virtually no chance that Xinjiang will separate from China, but preventing this phantom scenario consumes China's security first approach to managing ethnonationalism. This invented menace stokes ethnic polarization and precludes effective policy reforms. Chinese are openly racist toward Uighurs, attitudes that are only reinforced by unrest. If draconian security measures are the answer, Xinjiang should already be pacified. Beijing has tried repression to manage its minority problems over several decades with disappointing results and more recently has emphasized improving living standards, but absent efforts to more fully involve minorities in crafting policies and granting them more autonomy in internal affairs the unstable impasse and cycles of unrest will persist. China's problems in Xinjiang reflect the absence of a strategy for wooing Uighurs. They have no stake in their governance, and under such circumstances, improvement in their status or their relations with the authorities seems unlikely. Beijing has steamrollered over Islamic sensitivities by suppressing religious practices, relying on all stick and no carrots, and is now caging the masses it has alienated and fears.

The expanding number of Uighurs who run afoul of authorities face indefinite imprisonment at reeducation camps. By some estimates nearly 10 percent of the entire population of eleven million Uighurs, roughly one million people, has been incarcerated. Such harsh measures reflect officials' view that the problem of jihadism requires extreme tactics and that half measures will only allow the situation to fester.

INDIAN MUSLIMS

The living standards of India's 177 million Muslims, about 15 percent of the nation's total population, lag the Hindu majority (80 percent) with lower levels of education and employment. Poverty is declining overall in India across all groups due to economic growth, but at a relatively slower pace in the Muslim community. A 2013 World Bank study estimates that 34 percent of Muslims in urban India lived below the poverty line compared to 19 percent of Hindus, and the incidence of poverty among them is declining at a slower rate (Panagariya and Mukim 2013). The 2006 Sachar Report commissioned by the government revealed that Muslims are marginalized with a low share of public sector jobs, formal employment, school and university places, and seats in politics. They earn less, have limited access to banks and finance, are less literate, and are a minuscule presence in the police and military forces. Congress long relied on Muslims at elections, not needing to point out the risks of a Bharatiya Janata Party (BJP)–led government, but this practice of sectional pandering could not save the party from humiliating defeats in 2014 and 2019 at the hands of the BJP, the party that embraces Hindutva (Hindu chauvinism) and its ethnoreligious nationalist agenda (see chapter 2).

As in China, Muslims are a target for discrimination and spasmodic large-scale violence, often involving the complicity of politicians and state security forces. The 1992 razing of the Babri Mosque in Ayodhya by Hindu militants associated with the Rashtriya Swayamsevak Sangh (National Patriotic Organization) and BJP was a watershed in communal relations, sparking periodic rioting and tit-for-tat violence since then. In consequence, there has been a pronounced ghettoization of Muslims in urban areas as they seek protection within their own communities. These segregated areas are typically less well served by social services and lead to less interaction between Hindus and Muslims, accentuating the polarization.

These ghettoes also prove to be handy targets for Hindu militants as occurred in Gujarat in 2002 when marauding rioters went on a rampage terrorizing Muslim enclaves while police looked on. They were seeking revenge for the burning of a train carrying pilgrims from the disputed Babri Mosque site, claiming the lives of fifty-eight Hindus. This religious dispute sparked large-scale riots across the nation and challenges even today the nation's secular identity rooted in tolerance. Various government investigations into the Gujarat pogrom have come to different conclusions about culpability, but international human rights organizations assert there is considerable evidence that state authorities were involved with the sectarian violence and failed to intervene in a timely manner.

The slaughter of some two thousand people in Gujarat, mostly Muslims, and the displacement of ten thousand more over a period of four weeks came on Prime Minister Narendra Modi's watch as chief minister of the state. Some critics accuse him and the BJP of inciting the riots while others wonder why security forces did not intervene sooner to stop the bloodshed. Even so, these allegations have not hampered Mr. Modi's political career and rise to leadership of the BJP.

Ayodhya is a talismanic site of religious tensions and the ground zero of Muslim grievance in modern India, one targeted by Hindu extremists who embrace an excluding and assertive Hindutva. It is sacred space that is claimed by both Muslims and Hindus and has sparked the worst sectarian violence in India since Partition in 1947. In 1992, Hindu fanatics demolished the Babri Mosque situated on the disputed site, enraging Muslims. In 1993 the Congress Party poured fuel on the fire by enacting the Ayodhya Act that preserved the status quo of a demolished mosque and imposed limits on prayer at the site. Rival claimants have taken the case to the courts, but the litigation has not resolved the dispute and the scars of antagonism and distrust linger.

The battle is over a 2.7 acre piece of land in Uttar Pradesh in northern India. The now demolished Babri Mosque stood on the site since the sixteenth century. Hindus claim that the mosque was built over the birthplace of Ram, a Hindu god, and a temple dedicated to him. There is, however, no archaeological evidence for this assertion. In a strange 2010 ruling, the High Court divided the site into three parcels, awarding the most sacred and bitterly contested portion where the mosque once stood to a Hindu group. Anticipating the consequences, prior to publicizing the verdict, security forces were deployed, text messaging was blocked, and a curfew was imposed in Muslim-majority Kashmir.

The BJP catapulted into power in 1998 on the back of the Ayodhya dispute, demonstrating the popular appeal of Hindutva. Voters were energized by the communal violence and the religious identity politics of the BJP. An investigation concluding that senior leaders of the BJP were involved in the demolition of the mosque, arguably enhancing their status among voters. Since Modi's ascent to office, BJP politicians have promised to build a Hindu temple on the disputed grounds, an act that would enrage Muslims and certainly lead to communal violence. They have provoked in other ways as well.

LEGISLATING BIAS

Under Modi, the central government passed legislation in 2017 banning the Islamic practice of talaq whereby a husband may divorce his wife by thrice repeating his intention to do so. This meddling in Muslim marriage practices was touted as an initiative to protect women but stands in contrast to inaction on widespread abuses and discrimination against women in Hindu society. The ban on talaq, and three-year imprisonment for violators, energizes the BJP's Hindutva base. It was a deliberately provocative intrusion that had little to do with women's rights and everything to do with electoral grandstanding and pandering to anti-Muslim prejudice. Communalism is the BJP's calling card, so whether it involves downplaying the fact that Muslims designed and built the magnificent Taj Mahal, cutting haj subsidies for Muslim pilgrims, or marginalizing the cultural and civilizational legacies of Mughal (Islamic) rule in textbooks (see chapter 2), the point is to denigrate Muslims and use the powers of majoritarianism to undermine the principles of tolerance and inclusiveness that are enshrined in India's secular, constitutional democracy. The politics of hate and fearmongering are deliberately divisive. Not wanting to seem "weak" on Muslims, Congress, the main opposition party that once dominated Indian politics, failed to publicly condemn the legislation and its equivocations amounted to complicity.

In early 2019, the BJP amended the previously religion-blind Citizenship Act that had been a foundation of India's secular and inclusive democracy, facilitating acquisition of Indian citizenship for six besieged non-Muslim minority communities (Hindus, Christians, Sikhs, Buddhists, Jains, and Parsis from Afghanistan, Pakistan, and Bangladesh who came to India before December 31, 2014). Hindutva ideologues see this amendment as the logical conclusion of the 1947 Partition: India as Hindu homeland versus Muslim Pakistan/Bangladesh. In addition, ethnic Bengalis are targeted by the 2017 National Register of Citizens (NRC) in Assam, an administrative measure that ostensibly aims at evicting any illegal migrants though in practice, and in the unofficial but quite public politics, it's clearly about evicting "Bangladeshis," the preferred term for Othering local Bengalis (Dutta 2018).

The new discriminatory measure tasks the Bengalis of Assam, most of who were displaced by the 1971 Pakistan civil war, with proving they belong, no mean feat given the circumstances of their arrival. The politics of Assam have traditionally been on linguistic rather than religious lines. Assamese linguistic chauvinism is very strong and led to a separatist movement. In this complex matrix of rival chauvinistic maneuvering, the Citizenship Bill is designed to "rescue" the Bengali Hindus among the four million Bengali residents of Assam facing statelessness as a result of the NRC process aimed at excluding Bengali Muslims. This toxic amendment is politically useful as the BJP can brandish it to mobilize votes in the Hindu heartland on the strength of bragging, "No Muslims please, this is India" (Sharma 2019).

However, as local writer Samrat Choudhury explains, "The fear that drives both the NRC and Citizenship Bill centers on illegal migrants from Bangladesh. It's not only 'no Muslims please,' but more specifically 'no Bangladeshis please.' The fight between the Assamese chauvinists and the Hindu chauvinists is over the definition of Bangladeshi, primarily linguistic and religious respectively" (personal communication, January 2019). Both sets of partisans are banking on the dubious but reliable electoral appeal of discrimination.

KASHMIR

Kashmir is a land of sweeping valleys and pristine lakes in the Himalayan region of northwestern India that is claimed in full by India and Pakistan and ruled in part by both. China also asserts claims there and controls a much smaller portion of Kashmir in the northeastern area of Ladakh called Aksai Chin, a mostly uninhabited high-altitude desert area. The Sino-Indian War in 1962 was related to rival claims in this border region.

A UN Line of Control, ostensibly a temporary boundary awaiting a plebiscite to gauge the popular will, separates Pakistan and India in what has become a heavily militarized zone of occupation. It is the unfinished business of the 1947 Partition, the disastrous British policy that sparked communal violence and lead to the death of some one million amid the uprooting and relocation of Muslim and Hindu communities. The bitter adversaries have frequently skirmished and fought three wars over Kashmir (1947, 1965, and 1999), a territorial dispute that is perhaps the most divisive legacy of British colonial rule in the subcontinent. India stands accused of a heavy-handed occupation in Kashmir, where it has some half million troops stationed; the population in the Kashmir valley is about four million and 95 percent are Muslims. India counters that Pakistan sponsors militant Islamic groups that attack Indian forces in Kashmir and also mounted terrorist attacks in New Delhi and Mumbai.

In 1947 Hari Singh was the reigning maharajah of Kashmir when the British hastened their departure and Partition took its toll in lives and political chaos. At the time, some three-quarters of the population was Islamic. Fearing Pakistani designs on Kashmir, New Delhi convinced the maharajah to accede to Indian rule and dispatched troops to drive out Pakistani paramilitary forces. This precipitated the 1947 war that ended with a UN-negotiated ceasefire in 1948 with the promise of a plebiscite to allow self-determination by Kashmiris. This promise has never been implemented, and since then Kashmir has served as a major source of tension and contestation between the neighbors, again erupting into war in 1965 and 1999. Because of these conflicts and the possession of nuclear weapons by both claimants, Kashmir is considered one of the most dangerous and volatile flashpoints in Asia.

Kashmiri nationalism is viewed as a threat to Indian national unity and a secessionist movement that needs to be squashed. Ramachandra Guha asserts that there are four main factors driving Kashmiri separatism: 1) distance from the Indian cultural and administrative heartland; 2) the appeal of nationalism to young men; 3) legal impunity for Indian security forces committing human rights abuses; and 4) New Delhi's support for corrupt politicians in Kashmir (2012, 19). The excessive use of force to impose central control fans the flames of separatism, creating new martyrs to be avenged by successive generations of Kashmiris because the Armed Forces Special Powers Act shields soldiers from accountability. The escalating secession-repression dynamic creates a basis for ceaseless conflict.

Guha warns against romanticizing India's "little nationalisms" because they can be as ugly as the looming majoritarian nationalism they confront. He suggests reconciling these subnationalisms with the inclusiveness of India by providing meaningful autonomy within the Union. India is, after all, one of the most plural nations in the world, accommodating a large number of religions and ethnicities. But crafting a resolution that accommodates the agendas of both little and large nationalisms seems unlikely because they are antithetical in aims. Certainly, Guha has a point that the leaders of Hurriyat, the Kashmiri secessionist movement, do not seem inspiring candidates to lead Kashmir into a twenty-first-century land of the free, but India's military occupation polarizes the political situation and encourages thuggery and collaboration while preserving the smoldering status quo.

Religion is a critical aspect of the Kashmir deadlock as the harsh occupation by Hindu India produces an Islamic backlash among Kashmiris. The local Sufi Islamic tradition remains resilient, but Indian brutishness has radicalized some to join fundamentalist militant groups, with encouragement from Pakistan. Kashmiri nationalism and separatism are thus intertwined with an increasingly militant Islamic identity. Indian shifts blame to Pakistan for the spread of jihadist Islam but by relying on draconian policies has sowed the seeds of this radicalization. In February 2013 India executed a Kashmiri, Afzal Guru, for allegedly conspiring with Islamic militants who carried out an attack on Parliament in 2001, sparking clashes in the strife-torn region. India holds Pakistan responsible for orchestrating the terrorist attack in New Delhi and the incident almost sparked the fourth war between the nuclear-armed rivals as one million soldiers were mobilized along the border.

Security forces killed the five Muslim militants linked to Pakistan-based Jaish-e-Mohammed who carried out the attacks. Guru was convicted of conspiring with them and offering them shelter, but flaws in the prosecution's evidence and inadequacies of legal representation cast a cloud over the verdict. His abrupt execution before informing relatives and denial of a family funeral aroused further ire in Kashmir. Critics assert that the conviction was based on circumstantial evidence and the execution timed to electoral maneuvering as the Congress Party sought to deflect BJP criticism that it is "soft" on Islamic militancy.

While India castigates Pakistan and Islamic fundamentalists, it is not easy to deny Kashmiris' desire for an end to the Indian occupation. Kashmiris are subject to state-sponsored terrorism as security forces and their accomplices resort systematically to extra-judicial means to combat those who have become radicalized by the occupation. While the specter of Islamic radicalism is invoked to justify repression, this diverts attention from local desire for freedom and overlooks limited support among Kashmiris for a more fundamentalist Islam. But in the post-9/11 world, Islam has become the enemy of convenience, one that justifies extreme actions. Kashmiris are portrayed as the terrorist Other, agents of Pakistan, that must be suppressed by whatever means and deserve what they get.

Kashmir is where Indian and Pakistani nationalisms clash, sidelining Kashmiri aspirations. Given its location and history, Kashmir serves as a lightning rod for India's renascent Hindutva fundamentalism and its Pakistani Islamic counterpart. The territory embodies familiar characteristics of nationalism—historical injustice, threat, border disputes, and fanaticism stoked by religious zealotry. India and Pakistan are implicated in using Kashmir to fuel nationalism and the security services in both actively stoke tensions.

Arundhati Roy, an activist writer, asserts that the excesses in Kashmir are part of a larger Islamophobia played out all over India: "The Indian military occupation of Kashmir makes monsters of us all. It allows Hindu chauvinists to target and victimize Muslims in India by holding them hostage to the freedom struggle waged by Muslims in Kashmir" (Ali 2011, 71). Successive generations of Kashmiris know India for its violence and curbing of civil liberties. In the popular Indian imagination Kashmir looms as an ethereal holiday destination with breathtaking vistas, but the besieged capital of Srinagar tells a different story. Kashmir also is portrayed as a place of Pakistani perfidy, and hotbed of Islamic fundamentalism and terrorism, feeding into the Hindu nationalism that has grown more fervent under Prime Minister Modi and his BJP.

It is hard to measure the toll of clashing aspirations in Kashmir, but over eighty thousand civilians have been killed there during India's occupation and yet, except in times of acute crisis, it slips under the global media radar screen. Indians remain largely unaware of the brutal realities while some rationalize the excesses as a necessary evil. Kashmiris have been traumatized by the faceoff and by the massive Indian security presence, the highest per capita in the world.

Basharat Peer, author of *Curfewed Night* (2008), offers a Kashmiri perspective. He writes: "The line of control did not run through 576 kilometres of militarised mountains. . . . It ran through everything a Kashmiri, an Indian and a Pakistani said, wrote, and did. . . . It ran through the reels of Bollywood coming to life in dark theatres, it ran through conversations in coffee shops and on television screens showing cricket matches, it ran through families and dinner talk, it ran through whispers of lovers. And it ran through our grief, our anger, our tears, and our silence" (Peer 2008, 221).

Peer maintains that the abuses and oppression he graphically and hauntingly describes in his book persist because soldiers are exempted from prosecution for any crimes they commit. Recalling Mao Zedong's dictum about political power flowing from the barrel of a gun, Peer dubs Kashmir a "siege democracy," insisting that in a referendum the people would vote overwhelmingly for independence. For Peer, "Kashmir exposes a blind spot in the self-deluding mainstream liberal consensus about the Idea of India, a monstrous conceit that ignores many realities on the ground" (interview December 2012).

Since we met, the crackdown has intensified, and Kashmir again witnessed massive protests after the killing of twenty-two-year-old militant commander Burhan Wani in July 2016. In response, the Indian troops fired on crowds indiscriminately, killing dozens of civilians, mostly teenagers, and wounding thousands. An estimated 124 people lost their eyesight due to the use of special nonlethal pellets as crowd-control ammunition. Meanwhile, extra-judicial killings, enforced disappearances, torture, illegal detentions, rape, and humiliation have become an unbearable routine in the everyday life of Kashimiris. In early 2019 a suicide bomber killed more than forty of India's security forces, leaving a video about his thirst for vengeance, a sentiment reciprocated by Prime Minister Modi. Following the bombing, in a BBC television interview in New Delhi, a young man said it was unimaginable that such an uncivilized incident could happen in India, although for Kashmiris the uncivilized has become all too familiar.

For Peer, "The status quo in Kashmir is more dangerous and horrifying than any fears of it turning into a 'jihadist hotspot.' And the greatest, most effective advertisement for recruitment for militant groups is the killing, blindings, and the humiliation of young people in Kashmir. I feel the fears cited are highly exaggerated and used as a dubious argument to look away from the harsh reality of Kashmir today. What Kashmir has been living with is worse than any nightmarish scenario people outside Kashmir can come up with" (Peer 2016). Fresh generations are baptized in the legacies of loss and rage, ensuring that the struggle for azad (freedom) continues.

MINDANAO

In 2017, IS militants occupied the city of Marawi on the island of Mindanao, managing to hold off the Philippines military for several months before escaping (IPAC 2017). This brazen attack highlighted the grievances that have sustained a prolonged Islamic insurgency in the region. Mindanao has been a site for regional terrorist operations and training camps for Abu Sayyaf, a homegrown terrorist organization, and the Islamic separatist groups Moro Islamic Liberation Front (MILF) and the Moro National Liberation Front (MNLF) (Abu Bakar 2015). In this southernmost province of the Philippines, remote from Manila, there is a rich history of lawlessness and brigandage. The adjacent Sulu archipelago long served as a hub of piracy and still provides sanctuary for smugglers, terrorists, and traffickers.

The southern insurgency has been one of the world's longest running conflicts as Islamic insurgents have fought for substantial autonomy or independence from the Catholic majority nation. Numerous military and political efforts to resolve the conflict have not produced lasting peace. The fundamental grievance is the mass resettlement of Catholic Filipinos from northern provinces to the island that Muslims view as their homeland. As a result of this huge influx of Christians, Muslims now account for just 20 percent of the island's population. The insurgency began in 1969 when Nur Misuari, a University of Manila professor, established the MNLF, with the goal of creating an independent state of Bangsamoro including Mindanao, Sulu, and the Palawan islands, sparking violent clashes with the military. Mostly due to an escalating communist insurgency on the main island of Luzon, in 1972 President Ferdinand Marcos declared martial law and intensified pacification efforts in Mindanao. In 1975, with Nur Misuari in Libya, Marcos prevailed upon Colonel Muammar Gaddafi, under the auspices of the Organization of the Islamic Conference, to broker what became known as the 1976 Tripoli Agreement granting autonomy in parts of Mindanao and allowing the establishment of a shariah law judiciary and independent security forces in those regions. Marcos, however, unilaterally pared back the territory subject to the accord and thereby ended the ceasefire. This betrayal added to Muslims' sense of grievance and subsequent efforts have focused on regaining the territorial and political concessions made in the Tripoli Agreement.

There have been several efforts to reach a settlement in the post-Marcos era, but none proved lasting. In 1996 the government of President Fidel Ramos reached what it called a Final Peace Agreement establishing the Autonomous Region in Muslim Mindanao (ARMM), but the MNLF splintered. A more militant faction, the MILF, resumed armed conflict and seized a town and numerous hostages in 2000. In response President Joseph Estrada declared all-out war on the militants. The ARMM also proved to be a dysfunctional government, rife with corruption and undermined by various armed groups and clan-based power politics. Misuari, the first governor of ARMM, was jailed between 2001 and 2008 for inciting rebellion, undermining trust and prospects for a sustainable peace. President Gloria Arroyo then tried to reach an accord with the MILF in 2008 but the agreement was declared unconstitutional by the Supreme Court, sparking renewed violence by militants targeting Christian communities. This conflict displaced half a million residents as they fled the war zone in central Mindanao. The peace process regained some momentum in 2010 under President Benigno Aquino, but in 2013 the MNLF resumed armed conflict, killing more than two hundred residents of Zamboanga City and displacing 150,000 others.

In 2014 it seemed that the southern Philippines was on the verge of peace after four decades of a violent insurgency that claimed some 120,000 lives. In the Comprehensive Agreement on Bangsamoro (CAB), the MILF reached an agreement with the central government to grant significant political and financial autonomy to five provinces called Bangsamoro (Islamic homeland) in exchange for the MILF disarming and ending the separatist insurgency. However, as with three previous accords, the end to hostilities proved elusive. The CAB was delayed in 2015 by a botched covert police operation in Mindanao. The police were trying to capture two terrorist bombers with links to Jemaah Islamiyah, the Indonesian-based regional terrorist organization, who were at a camp operated by a MILF splinter group. In the fighting that ensued, forty-four police were killed along with a number of Islamic militants. MILF viewed this as hostile action inconsistent with the CAB while security forces insisted that such an agreement did not preclude antiterrorist operations. The accord collapsed largely due to opposition in the Philippines' Congress to approve the provisions agreed to following the deaths of so many police.

President Rodrigo Duterte, elected in 2016, is the former mayor of Davao, the largest city in Mindanao. He revived the delayed deal as part of his larger plans for devolving power to the regions. There are hopes he can succeed where his predecessors have failed, but the gulf between central government and local perceptions, the polarization of Muslim and Christian communities, and the scars of four decades of conflict and factionalism among militant groups remain formidable obstacles. Successive failed negotiations across the decades reinforce perceptions among some Muslims that fighting is the only way to get what they want. Militant groups embracing radical options tap into this alienation. More moderate organizations that commit to the peace process risk their legitimacy and are subject to fragmentation as frustrated hardliners withdraw. The sporadic peace process undermined law and order along with moderate voices, ceding power not only to Islamic militants but also long-established clan-based warlords who are deeply entrenched and bankroll private armies. Mindanao's problems are not chiefly driven by religious antagonisms but sanctified and exacerbated by them. And these problems are unlikely to fade even if a Bangsamoro is realized because economic and educational backwardness, political dysfunction, and lawlessness are likely to persist and undermine the project.

In 2019 the government held autonomy referenda in Mindanao that won broad support among Muslims for the Bangsamoro Organic Law. There are high expectations for the Bangsamoro Autonomous Region in Muslim Mindanao, an entity that will be granted more institutional and financial capacity through enhanced resource wealth-sharing mechanisms (Asia Foundation 2019). Yet realization of Bangasamoro is unlikely to end hostilities as militant groups other than the MILF such as Abu Sayyaf and the IS-linked Maute militants retain power to derail political agreements while voters on Sulu rejected the plan. Aside from managing regional services for four million residents in central and western Mindanao, the new government faces the challenge of decommissioning tens of thousands of armed militants and providing sustainable alternatives, a risky process that could easily go wrong. The Bangsamoro accord promises Muslims much of what they have been fighting and dying for, but the region is not well prepared for assuming the responsibilities of autonomy, partly due to prolonged conflict that has held back development of the economy and human resources. Development aid and educational initiatives are crucial building blocks during the transition.

For the people of Mindanao, the conflict situation has meant large and sometimes prolonged displacements and an atmosphere of fear. People are free to practice Islam in a majority Christian environment and have now gained greater political authority, but poverty remains a source of grievance that carries the potential for a revival of radicalization.

ABU SAYYAF

Abu Sayyaf (bearer of the sword) is a radical terrorist organization operating under the banner of Islam from the Sulu archipelago and Mindanao that has long engaged in banditry and kidnapping while also demanding a separate state for Filipino Muslims. It split from the MNLF due to its opposition to negotiations and first drew global attention in 1991 with a grenade attack that killed two American evangelists and subsequently mounted a number of bombings in the 1990s. Its founder fought in Afghanistan against the Soviet Union back in the 1980s and allegedly received $6 million from a relative of Osama bin Laden and later drew funds from a Saudi charity that covered operational costs. It was never a very large group, with a maximum of 1,500 fighters, but in the 2000s, its leadership, funding, and membership were decimated by counterterrorist operations. However, it developed links with Jemaah Islamiyah and the MILF and remained active as a hardcore militant group, bombing a ferry in 2004 that killed 116 people, the worst terrorist incident ever in the Philippines. Since then it has been the target of Philippines military counterterrorist operations with support from US special forces as part of the war on terror. Abu Sayyaf and other smaller militant groups opportunistically embrace jihadist ideology but mostly focus on making money through extortion and kidnapping for ransom. Since coming to power in 2016, Duterte has taken a hardline against Abu Sayyaf, intensifying military operations while dangling the possibility of a political settlement through federalism. In 2017, however, Abu Sayyaf experienced a significant setback during a raid on a tourist resort in Bohol in the central Philippines where its leader died in a shootout.

ISLAMIC STATE

Islamic State (IS) has shown an ability to tap into local discontent and attract new recruits, but the eruption of the well-orchestrated Marawi attack in 2017 demonstrated that it has far greater capacity than anticipated. In May, pro-IS jihadists took over Marawi City, the largest Muslim city in the Philippines, and managed to hold off the Philippines military for five months. Abu Sayyaf and another smaller IS-affiliated group Maute clashed with security forces trying to arrest a militant leader. Over the following months of the siege, over 1,000 were killed, including 925 militants and 165 government soldiers while 300,000 were displaced by the pitched urban battles that left the historic city in ruins. In October 2017 troops killed the two leaders of the uprising and declared the devastated city liberated. Paradoxically, this defeat was a publicity coup for the militants, boosting their prestige while revealing a sophisticated capacity and international linkage to IS central in the Mideast unknown to security officials before the attack.

Assumptions that global jihadist ideology has little appeal in Mindanao due to deep cultural barriers have been disproved by Marawi. The government's repeated delays on implementing a political accord and overreliance on military means to contain the problem have discredited moderates in the eyes of militants and frustrated youth. This deadlock has created fertile conditions for recruiting the angry and disaffected to jihadist ideology in which the devout not only have principles but are ready to fight for them. MILF has sheltered Jemaah Islamiyah jihadists whose uncompromising stand offers an appealing contrast to the politics of negotiated compromise. For splinter groups such as the IS-backed Maute and other disaffected members, jihadism offers a powerful allure.

While IS suffered a military defeat in the Philippines, the prolonged standoff carries political implications and raises the specter of more jihadi violence in the Philippines and the region. It could inspire others to engage in extremist acts and adds another grievance for locals to hurl at the central government and for recruiting new members. The decimation of IS forces in Syria and Iraq may not mean the end of its affiliated operations in Southeast Asia. As with jihadists returning from Afghanistan and Iraq, militants who slipped away from Marawi are battle-hardened veterans who can use their experience and skills to train others. Foreigners also played a key role in recruiting fighters internationally and mobilizing funding funneled through a global chain of command. The presence of several Indonesian fighters and a Malaysian planner and coordinator points to a transnational network operating in the maritime borderlands and the weakness of multilateral coordination and cooperation between the three nations' security forces in countering this threat. The attack also underscored the weakness of Philippines intelligence gathering. Malaysia and Indonesia have Islamic majority populations, but both have resolutely cracked down on terror networks, nearly eliminating Jemaah Islamiyah as a terrorist threat and forcing it into a prolonged dormancy. Security forces in those nations suspect that counterparts in Mindanao have mixed loyalties and are enmeshed in local clan-based networks that compromise counterterrorist operations. They are therefore leery of sharing information and skeptical about the benefits of trilateral cooperation.

The IS utopian vision calling for justice, equality, and prosperity may seem divorced from prevailing realities in Mindanao but exerts a strong appeal for the young and disenchanted looking for something to which to commit. Countering that appeal is a major challenge for the central government and security forces because it does not take that many dedicated terrorists to wreak havoc.

PATANI

In the southern provinces of Thailand there is a longstanding separatist struggle by Malay Muslims who view the central government in Bangkok as interlopers (Satha-Anand 2015). In 1909 Great Britain ceded the four northern provinces of its colony in Malaya, previously the Islamic Sultanate of Patani, where the population was culturally and linguistically Malay and predominantly Muslim, to Buddhist majority Siam (Thailand). This diplomatic maneuver sparked Asia's longest separatist movement as the population transferred to Siam's political control never accepted their fate and rallied to the banner of the Patani United Liberation Organization (PULO). For more than a century this campaign has persisted, pitting Muslim insurgents against the security forces of Siam/Thailand. PULO still exists, but as is often the case in such movements there has been a splintering and leadership of the struggle has shifted to the Barisan Revolusi Nasional Melayu Patani (Patani-Malay National Revolutionary Front [BRN]) that commands the most fighters among the separatist organizations. BRN was established in the early 1960s with the goal of gaining independence for Patani from Thai rule. Thai security forces intensified efforts in the 1980s to crush the separatists, forcing reorganization and the creation of a clandestine network to mobilize resources and manpower. From 2004 BRN has become more active, launching hundreds of small-scale attacks a year, mostly against police and military targets (Mark 2018).

The specter of transnational jihadist violence inspired by IS remains hard to dispel despite the decline of IS in Syria and Iraq. IS involvement is suspected in the radical extremist violence in the Philippines and Bangladesh and it is linked with fundamentalist Indonesian groups. There is as yet no evidence, however, to suggest IS involvement with the BRN and it has publicly disavowed jihadism. The struggle for Patani is Islamic but not jihadist and not inspired by Salafism/Wahhabism. BRN is aware that associating with IS or al-Qaeda would have a negative impact, attracting intensified counterterrorist operations on the part of Thailand and a less hospitable cross-border operating environment in Malaysia. Moreover, embracing Salafism would backfire among a population that favors "traditional" Islamic syncretic practices, moderation, and the Shafi'i school of Islamic jurisprudence. The BRN and other local militant groups oppose IS jihadist ideology and castigate IS for being un-Islamic due to its intolerance and brutality. Local identity is complex and interwoven, drawing on religion, ethnicity, culture, and language in addition to the drawbacks of minority status in Thailand (ICG 2016). It is a parochial ethnoreligious-nationalist movement focused on liberating Thailand's four southernmost provinces and there is at present no appetite for joining a wider religious struggle.

But such a possibility is imaginable. Snooky, the protagonist in Timothy Mo's novel *Pure* (2012), is a kathouey ("ladyboy") sex worker from Bangkok turned brutal jihadist who gets ensnared in espionage intrigue and a regional network of terrorists with training camps stretching from southern Thailand to Mindanao. It is a rollicking read that suggests the possibilities. Snooky endures various indignities, including the painful removal of a sexually explicit lower back tattoo, in order to go undercover at an Islamic college where she is supposed to find out about the terrorists' planning and operations. Initially reluctant and coerced into spying, as an operative she gets high on violence and is never more alive than after a disco bombing in Phuket that kills over two hundred patrons, reminiscent of real-world Bali in 2002. In this zany tale of sly ironies and bawdy wit, the author provides an irreverent rendering of fundamentalism and its pretensions while raising the alarm of a resurgent transnational network of religious extremists (Yegar 2002).

In contrast, BRN has not engaged in suicide bombings, mostly targets security forces, ceased beheadings, and generally refrains from terrorist attacks causing mass casualties because it understands that too much violence risks losing local sympathies. The point is to provoke a heavy-handed security response to generate local support while driving the Buddhist population out of the south by sowing fear. The insurgency has claimed over 7,000 lives over the past two decades, peaking in 2007 when 836 people were killed. An estimated 60 percent of all casualties since 2009 have been civilians, the collateral damage of this calibrated insurgency. The number of terrorist incidents has waned from a 2010 peak of 2,061 to 489 in 2017, suggesting the heavy security presence is having an impact. This decline in activity also reflects greater restraint and more careful targeting to minimize civilian casualties.

BRN has mostly left tourist targets alone. Phuket and Koh Samui, favorite beach destinations for global travelers, are close by and represent lucrative sources of income and jobs, thus adopting such a strategy risks a backlash from locals and harsh retaliation by security forces, derailing plans for independence. However, in 2015 BRN did bomb an underground parking lot in the tourist island Koh Samui and in August 2016 carried out several small-scale incendiary attacks on popular seaside tourist towns south of Bangkok. Then in May 2017 the BNR set off two bombs in a crowded shopping mall in the south, with over sixty casualties, suggesting that BNR remains dangerous. It also operates in something of a "Wild West" context of drug and people smuggling, illegal gambling, and the sex trade, meaning that solely looking at the conflict through the lens of religion is misleading.

Following the death of BRN's founding leaders in 2016 and 2017, the group has been in transition, but the subsequent discovery of a bomb factory in Malaysia suggests that it remains committed to a violent strategy. Since the Thai military junta took over in 2014 ongoing peace talks have stalled and the BRN is skeptical about the government's commitment to anything aside from their complete surrender. There are more security checkpoints in the south, increasing the risk of being discovered and making it more difficult for the BNR to move around freely. On the other hand, the heightened security presence and allegations of abuses committed with impunity facilitates recruiting efforts. Although southern Thailand seems inhospitable for IS, al-Qaeda, or other militant jihadist groups, the situation is fluid and could change if locals are radicalized by human rights violations or if the government closes the door on substantive negotiations, thereby undercutting relatively moderate militants.

IMPLICATIONS

This survey of how Muslim minorities are faring in Asia makes it hard to generalize. We see that some Muslim minorities explicitly boast global terrorist links such as in Mindanao in the southern Philippines, while authorities allege such cross-border links for Uighurs in Xinjiang with central Asia and Kashmiris with Pakistan. Southern Thailand is a case in which efforts to establish such links have been resisted by local separatists. In these cases, the usual grievances of minorities are invoked to justify violence and Islam serves to legitimize jihad against nonbelievers. China is the only case in which the government intrudes on freedom of religion and bans specific religious and cultural practices, norms, and gestures. Being a Muslim minority is difficult across the region, and discrimination is common, but as nearly one million Uighurs know all too well, only in China is one's faith itself grounds for incarceration. For Uighurs, like the other minority groups under study, identity is a hybrid layering of ethnic, linguistic, cultural, and religious influences in the context of systematic repression and marginalization. There is little hope in Beijing's policy of treating their search for dignity and religious freedom as an ideological virus to eradicate (HRW 2018).

State-sponsored violence and social prejudice are mutually reinforcing in ways that harden identities among disadvantaged minorities. In such circumstances, moderates are easily portrayed as quislings, while the palpable grievances generate a supply of potential recruits and a demand for action that extremist groups channel in pursuing their agendas. The clashes of ethnoreligious subnationalism with majoritarian repression strengthen Islamic identity, becoming the basis for solidarity in resisting state encroachment and thus the target for security forces, perpetuating cycles of violence.

Chapter Eight

Politicizing Blasphemy

Nadeem Aslam's *The Golden Legend* (2017) transports us to contemporary Pakistan and the tragic trajectories of love in a nation teeming with the angry and inconsolable, a culturally rich society riven with intolerance. We encounter the various ways that the blasphemy laws are abused and wielded to pursue vendettas, silence opponents, and dispose of the unwanted. In the imaginary town of Zamana someone is exposing residents' blasphemous transgressions over the loudspeakers of mosque minarets in the wee hours of the night, inciting vigilantes to wreak vengeance on the exposed. The story initially focuses on a couple, both architects, who pay a steep price for being tolerant and reasonable in a land beset with abiding resentments and unrequited ambitions. The husband's grandfather wrote a massive tome that went missing from the family library about the syncretic interactions of religions and cultures over the centuries that serves as a foil to the paroxysms of fundamentalist intolerance that currently prevail. The grandson finds the missing book on the day he is inadvertently killed by a CIA agent's errant bullet in a shootout with fundamentalists. The treasured book is subsequently torn into pieces by a Pakistani intelligence officer as a warning to the grieving widow if she doesn't publicly forgive the American while Islamic fundamentalists threaten her if she does. She tries to sew it back together, piece by piece, with golden thread, even as her enemies close in around her.

We learn the couple all but adopted a Christian girl whose father is a household servant. Tragically, the girl's father is the lover of a Muslim widow whose father is a local cleric and neighbor. Their secret is revealed over the minaret's sound system during one of their trysts. As a result, the adjacent Christian neighborhood is razed by an enraged mob. Subsequently, the Christian daughter is baselessly accused of blasphemy by a scheming Muslim businessman eager to supplant her in a minor business deal. Rather than languishing in jail as is the fate of suspected blasphemers, she makes her escape with the help of a chance acquaintance, a Kashmiri who dropped out of a terrorist training camp operating in Pakistan. The lovers make their way to an island in a nearby river where the architect couple had built a mosque with four entrances converging on a common prayer room, a symbolic effort to promote reconciliation between rival Islamic sects. They abandoned the project, however, due to a sectarian murder on the island perpetrated by a Wahhabist. Throughout the story this aspect of Arabization is portrayed as an alien, violent, and subversive influence, distorting religious practice, warping Pakistani identity, and accentuating intolerance.

The narrator explains that the accused Christian daughter "was not religious, but she was sympathetic to the idea that religion might offer consolation to those who had been humiliated in life" (Aslam 2017, 51). And for those feeling this humiliation, accusing someone of blasphemy empowers and offers some revenge even if those targeted are blameless and have nothing to do with their frustrations. Misery does love company.

There is no going back. Across Asia, blasphemy charges have become a weapon of choice against minorities, conferring the mantle of sanctity on accusers seeking power, influence, vengeance, or harboring larcenous desires. The rules of the game are one sided in favor of the denouncers as an allegation of sacrilege is tantamount to a guilty verdict in the court of zealots' opinion. The ominous shadow of vigilante justice intimidates and isolates as anyone ready to defend the accused or question the allegation is also risking ostracism, violence, and even a death sentence. Blasphemy is an accelerator on social media, igniting wildfires among the angry devout yearning for enemies to destroy. The Internet has played a powerful role in whipping up outbursts and providing a platform for those eager to gain a following by pandering to primeval passions on the pretext of safeguarding religious precepts. Before the advent of the Internet there were relatively few charges of blasphemy, but now broadband warriors can fire up sanctimonious battalions by using blasphemers as clickbait. And in 2018 Indonesians gained access to a free blasphemy app called "Smart Pakem" that makes it easier to circulate unsubstantiated allegations of impiety. Moderate Muslims who have fought a losing battle against the spread of blasphemy charges now ponder why the government actually requested this app be made available on the Google Pay Store. With the firefighters and arsonists collaborating, blasphemy appears to be a toxic growth sector.

One suspects that blasphemy is simply too handy a hammer to leave unused in the machinations of power politics. There has been a remarkable surge of cases in twenty-first-century Asia that appears linked with Arabization. The spread of Wahhabi and Salafist religious norms and practices in Asia, thanks to the generous patronage of Saudi Arabia, has transformed Islamic communities across the region at the expense of tolerance. Arabization has undermined and transformed longstanding understandings and inter-actions among different groups—religious, ethnic, and political—that have sparked sectarian and communal tensions, often with violent outcomes. These developments are intensifying rifts among different sects of Islam and targeted minorities. This purifying, reformist movement emanating from the Middle East is not only about theological matters. Such issues provide a principled and sacred basis for more prosaic concerns regarding power. They also spark culture wars that ignite identity politics and infuse nationalism, conflating faith and nation in ways that convert diversity into flashpoints of confrontation.

It is not a coincidence that the typhoon of Arabization that is battering Asia has led to sharpened attacks on Shi'a and Ahmadis, minority Muslim sects that are shrilly denounced by hardline Sunni clerics as non-Muslim apostates. This is in line with Saudi Arabia's escalating geopolitical rivalry with Shi'a Iran and desire to project itself as the true voice of Islam. These sectarian antagonisms are not new, but there has been an intensification of campaigns to rally the devout and enlist the state in campaigns of persecu-tion. This is part of the process of melding religion and nationalism, one that shapes and sharpens identities.

The concepts of blasphemy and heresy stem from that primordial need to Other, to define who is and who is not part of the group. All religions establish rules governing what is acceptable behavior and what is not. They also determine what religious practices should be followed and what should be avoided. Well beyond these boundaries, religions identify certain adher-ents and devotees as blasphemers and heretics, apostates who do not conform to mainstream practices and beliefs. They become the target of fanatics who find such people intolerable and persecute them. Perhaps more importantly, they also serve as useful quarry for individuals and institutions involved in gaining, regaining, and asserting power. Apostasy is in the eye of the behold-er (and the believer), constituting a renunciation of core beliefs and practices. To clarify our terms, "heresy" is the act of holding an "opinion contrary to orthodox or accepted doctrine," originating in the Greek word for "choice." "Blasphemy" is to "abuse" or "speak irreverently of something held to be sacred" and its root is the Greek for "evil-speaking." While there are clear differences in the terms, in practice there is considerable overlap. One who blasphemes is considered a heretic and heresy is often based on blasphemous words or actions. Apostasy is the renunciation or abandonment of a religious or political belief and apostates are those who do so.

Within Islam the Sunni are the dominant sect while Shi'a and Ahmadiyya are minorities frequently subject to ostracism, harassment, and violence. Buddhism, Hinduism, and Christianity are also divided within, but without the outbursts of internecine violence that have become more common among Islamic sects in Asia.

LEGAL JEOPARDY

Laws and regulations related to blasphemy and apostasy are on the books in 39 percent of all nations (Pew 2016b). Beyond blasphemy laws there are also other laws, regulations, and ordinances that amount to de facto blasphemy laws that prohibit "harm to religious sentiments" or inciting hatred or otherwise stirring up religious tensions. Religious leaders and followers have legitimate concerns about what is said, written, broadcast, or otherwise disseminated because it is offensive and/or generates misunderstanding about religious beliefs and practices. Problematically, however, such laws are so vague and sweeping that they can be invoked arbitrarily to stifle freedom of expression, pursue vendettas, target minorities, intimidate opponents, and advance political agendas. Wrapped in the sanctifying cloak of religion, certain groups with self-serving agendas can claim a veneer of legitimacy for oppressing others by making accusations of blasphemy.

The British colonial legacy of laws that prohibit wounding religious sentiments is embedded in the contemporary penal codes of former colonies in Asia. In Malaysia, for example, Penal Code Section 298 stipulates that "whoever, with deliberate intention of wounding the religious feelings of any person, utters any word or makes any sound in the hearing of that person, or makes any gesture in the sight of that person, or places any object in the sight of that person, shall be punished with imprisonment for a term which may extend to one year or with fine or with both" (US Library of Congress). Sentences for those deemed to have seditious intentions are harsher. The government forbids non-Sunni Islam, bars Muslims from converting to other religions, and can impose fines, detentions, and canings on Muslims found guilty of contravening shariah. Muslims who deviate from prevailing Sunni principles may be detained and placed in "rehabilitation" centers where they are instructed in government-sanctioned Islamic practice. Proselytization by non-Islamic religious groups and distribution of religious texts is controlled quite strictly. Sedition laws are invoked to prosecute anyone who insults Islam or the government's policies on religion. Critics contend that the conflation of Islam, Malay ethnic identity, and the long dominant United Malay National Organization Party politicized such prosecutions and suppressed dissent under the guise of protecting religious sentiments. Books and media are also subject to religious scrutiny and censored accordingly. In 2008 the Internal Security Ministry barred Christian publications from using Allah to refer to God, arguing the term is specific to Islam, but subsequently relented as long as it was made clear that the publications were intended for non-Muslims. Blasphemy prosecutions focus on Muslims and range from women drinking beer and committing adultery to practicing yoga, while punishment, as in Indonesia, includes canings.

Section 295A of Myanmar's Penal Code states that "anyone who, by spoken or written words or visible representations, insults or attempts to insult the religion or the religious beliefs of persons with the deliberate and malicious intent of outraging the religious feelings of such persons shall be punished with imprisonment and/or a fine." In a 2015 prosecution for blasphemy in Myanmar, a bar manager from New Zealand and two local colleagues were sentenced to two and a half years of imprisonment for posting on Facebook an image of the Buddha wearing headphones (Moe and Ramzy 2015). That same year, a writer was sentenced to two years of imprisonment with hard labor for a speech criticizing religious groups for using religion to promote discrimination. Amnesty International called for overturning this verdict, arguing that "the growing influence of extremist Buddhist nationalists and their hateful rhetoric in Myanmar is deeply troubling. Instead of taking steps against these groups' attempts to incite discrimination and violence, the government seems intent on compounding the problem by imprisoning those speaking out against religious intolerance" (Amnesty International 2015).

Thailand, although never colonized, also bans speech, writings, or gestures that defame Buddhism or monks and criminalizes sowing discord or insulting religious groups. This has caused anxiety among editors as they proceed carefully on stories that implicate monks in conduct inconsistent with religious precepts, although there has been extensive media coverage of some scandalous high-profile corruption and sexual misconduct cases. In addition, Thai law bans masquerading as a monk, novice, or clergyman of any religion.

In the Philippines, Article 133 of the Revised Penal Code provides that "anyone who, in a place devoted to religious worship or during the celebration of any religious ceremony shall perform acts notoriously offensive to the feelings of the faithful" may be subject to imprisonment. In 2013 a man was convicted of this crime for disrupting a religious ceremony by brandishing a placard and voicing his advocacy of birth control. The Catholic Church opposes birth control and was lobbying against the Reproductive Health legislation that was being deliberated at the time. The protestor called on the assembled clergymen to refrain from abusing the power of the pulpit to sway public opinion. Aggrieved Catholics sued him and prevailed as the court ruled that he was in violation of Article 133.

BLASPHEMY AS BLUDGEON

Pakistan

Blasphemers and atheists in Asia have a tough time, although exactly who is guilty of blasphemy depends less on religion than on politics and vigilantism.

Blasphemy charges are used to cut down political figures literally and figura-
tively, pursue personal vendettas, settle disputes, and bludgeon the vulnerable. They also appeal to primordial inclinations and serve to channel and
vent frustrations by targeting minorities.

Pakistan inherited its blasphemy law from British India from which it was
partitioned in 1947. In the 1980s, Pakistan's president General Muhammad
Zia-ul Haq introduced the death penalty for any blasphemy against the
Prophet Muhammad. Zia was a military dictator who seized power in a coup
d'état and declared martial law in 1977. He sought to gain domestic credibility by becoming a staunch proponent of a more fundamentalist Islam at odds
with the more mystical and syncretic practices of Sufism that prevailed. He
also extensively revised the school curriculum to inculcate "proper" Islamic
values.

As the writer Kamila Shamsie argues, under Zia," All political parties
were banned, their leaders imprisoned if they weren't in exile, except for the
right-wing religious party, the Jamaat-e-Islami; advancement in the army and
government became tied to a willingness to espouse Zia's Islam; school
curriculums were 'Islamised'—which meant science fell out of favour, religious instruction was raised above all other subjects and the heroes of Pakistan's history were men who killed (usually Hindus and Sikhs) in the name
of religion" (2011, 15). The rise of Pakistani fundamentalism was thus a
state-directed project benefitting from Saudi largesse. The Saudis sponsored
the building of madrasah and mosques, offering scholarships to promising
students to study in the Islamic homeland. This Arabization spread intolerance and the politicization of blasphemy to eliminate or intimidate those who
opposed or got in the way of this tectonic shift.

Shamsie adds, "By the mid-80s an extremist version of Islam had not only
been codified in law but had made its way into daily life. Moreover, the
Soviet invasion of Afghanistan and India's acts of brutality against the largely Muslim population of the Kashmir Valley provided seemingly endless
opportunities for pro-jihad propaganda. And then, of course, there was Saudi
Arabia, delighted with the Wahhabism of Pakistan's new head of state and
only too happy to spend its petrodollars funding Wahhabi mosques and ma-
drassas in Zia's beleaguered nation" (Shamsie 2011, 16).

These developments contextualize Zia's attempts to narrowly define national identity by widening "the scope of the blasphemy laws. . . . In an
entirely skin-crawling manner, the newly fanged laws made perfect sense for
Zia's rule—if you're going to claim that your authority stems from your role
as champion of Islam, then you have to show yourself zealous in finding and
punishing those who offend Islam, both at home and abroad" (Shamsie 2011,
16).

Shamsie finds "Kafkaesque" an eerily apt concept

designed for the blasphemy laws: if one person had said something blasphemous, their words could not be repeated, not even to a policeman or in a court of law, because voicing the blasphemous words would itself be an act of blasphemy, and so the accuser would become the accused. Those charged under the blasphemy law were immediately imprisoned and placed in solitary confinement, awaiting trial, for their own protection; failure by the police to do so, the logic went, left open the possibility that the accused would be killed either by their neighbours (if they weren't imprisoned) or by other inmates (if they were imprisoned) because passions run so high over blasphemy charges. (Shamsie 2011, 18)

The situation is not improving. Pakistani journalist Annie Zaman reports, "In present day Pakistan, to accuse someone of committing blasphemy, is not only an instant vigilante death sentence, it is also one of the most frequently used tools used to clamp down on dissent and free speech in online and offline spaces" (Zaman 2018). She adds, "The country has witnessed a clamp down on free speech and political activism under the all-encompassing blanket of fighting cyber-crimes and blasphemy. There are many cases of young Pakistanis who are intimidated, harassed and forced to compromise their political views due to the fear of being accused of blasphemy. Social media has made it easier for authorities to trap and book someone under blasphemy law in Pakistan." Apparently just liking a Facebook posting can be grounds for blasphemy. Judges are afraid to preside over such cases due to threats, while lawyers who defend those accused of blasphemy risk the wrath of fundamentalists who equate an accusation with guilt. One such lawyer said that taking on such cases is like "walking into the jaws of death" and tragically was murdered soon thereafter.

The law currently makes the death penalty mandatory for all those found guilty as the life imprisonment option was eliminated in 1991 by a Federal Shariah Court judgment. Blasphemy is now an unpardonable offense in contemporary Pakistan so there is no leeway to plead for mercy and no lenience shown to those who apologize; blasphemers can't repent, they can only die. However, nobody has been executed due to the revised blasphemy law. In 2008 the judiciary issued a stay on the death penalty and the Supreme Court has not ratified any lower court conviction for blasphemy (Julius 2016). Nonetheless, many languish on death row or are serving life sentences based on lower court convictions and there have been numerous extra-judicial killings (at least sixty-five since 1990) targeting those accused of blasphemy. Moreover, it can take several years to reach a verdict on blasphemy cases during which time the defendant is jailed based purely on the suspicion of guilt.

Mazhar (2015b) notes, "In the collective imagination of mainstream Pakistan, blasphemy is not a pardonable offense and anyone who believes otherwise is also committing blasphemy and must similarly pay with their life."

But this consensus is inconsistent with the Hanafi school of thought that is the predominant theological orientation of Pakistani Sunnis. Associated commentaries and interpretations (hadiths) elaborate on questions of Islamic law and practice by the four schools of thought recognized in Sunni Islam. Hanafi is one of these schools and has the largest following in the world.

Abu Hanifa, founder of the Hanafi school of thought, ruled that, "blasphemers who ask for a pardon would be spared the death penalty," and this position has been affirmed by Hanafi scholars for centuries ever since. Apparently, the current misinterpretation of the Hanafi stance on blasphemy is based on the opinion of a fourteenth-century Hanafi scholar named Bazzazzi that was debunked by one of the most eminent South Asian Islamic scholars, Imam Ibn Abidin. The author of Pakistan's current blasphemy law mistakenly attributed Bazzazzi's misinterpretation of Hanafi to his debunker, Imam Ibn Abidin, invoking the latter's respected name to justify the "unpardonable offense" interpretation of blasphemy that in fact he had actually refuted as a complete misinterpretation of the Hanafi position (Mazhar 2015c). Nonetheless, the author of Pakistan's blasphemy law and his supporters baselessly claim there was an *ijma* (consensus of scholars) that blasphemy carries a *hudd* (divinely ordained) punishment of death, with no possibility of pardon. Thus, the mandatory death sentence for those found guilty of committing blasphemy in Pakistan rests on a demonstrably false foundation of shoddy reasoning. The true Hanafi position allows for pardon, but that is cold comfort to those being sentenced to death and languishing on death row in addition to those subject to extra-judicial killing based on this false interpretation.

Mazhar (2014) has also looked into how nonbelievers (Christians, Jews, Hindus, etc.) are treated regarding blasphemy, again finding a much more forgiving and lenient stance based on the hadiths than what is practiced in Pakistan today. He asserts that the intolerant view is Wahhabist in origin and that Hanafi hadith explicitly warned against it, instead issuing a fatwa that a non-Muslim blasphemer cannot be killed unless he/she is a habitual offender. This fatwa was signed by hundreds of imam around the Islamic world declaring that non-Muslims cannot be killed for a single offense of blasphemy and issuing a pardon in such cases is acceptable.

Punjab governor Salman Taseer was assassinated in 2011 by Mumtaz Qadri, a policeman assigned to protect him, due to the governor requesting a pardon for Asia Bibi, a Christian woman accused of blasphemy. Mazhar writes, "Mumtaz Qadri, who is a devout Barelvi, would be surprised, I am sure, to learn that the founder and most respected figure of his sect had endorsed pardon for non-Muslim blasphemers, and the view that non-Muslims cannot be killed for a single offense of blasphemy" (Mazhar 2014). This view is also shared by Maulana Maududi, founder of Jamaat-e-Islami, one of the main religious political parties in Pakistan.

In his defense, the police bodyguard claimed that killing Taseer was justified because he was guilty of blasphemy for having questioned the legality of Pakistan's blasphemy law. Taseer had called it a "black law," lamenting that it was being abused to harass minorities and subjecting politicians to a litmus test based on the preferences of unelected religious leaders, thus drawing the ire of many clerics. So-called black laws are legal instruments that allow the state to engage in inhumane acts against its own citizens, with full impunity.

In court, the killer's defense counsel argued that the Holy Prophet Muhammed had sent men to punish blasphemers and that it was justifiable for individuals to act unilaterally against them. The judge said that any cases of blasphemy should be dealt with according to the law and that nobody has the right to take matters into their own hands. Prime Minister Imran Khan, elected in 2018, endorsed the controversial blasphemy law while campaigning, signaling that it still enjoys official sanction.

In October 2018, however, the Supreme Court made a remarkable and rare ruling in overturning Asia Bibi's conviction for blasphemy. She had been in jail since 2009 despite dubious evidence and spent eight years on death row. Two senior officials who spoke out in her defense were assassinated and she became the focus of an international campaign to overturn the blasphemy law. Although the Supreme Court declared her innocent and ordered her immediate release in October 2018, she remained in protective custody. Following the ruling, extremist groups called for her death, threatened the judges who declared her innocent, and secured government agreement to block her exit from the country in exchange for calling off massive street rallies. A final petition to review the verdict was rejected in January 2019, removing the last legal hurdle for her departure to Canada where she now resides.

The current hardline on blasphemy making no distinction between single and repeat offenders or between Muslims and nonbelievers defies the consensus of religious scholars of the Hanafi school that is the ostensible basis of Islamic jurisprudence in Pakistan. Why doesn't that matter?

Mazhar argues that blasphemy has become a tool for persecuting minorities and public figures in politics, media, and academia who don't conform to the views of religious hardliners. It is also used to settle personal vendettas and property disputes. The blasphemy law is invoked far more than before with an especially sharp surge since 2010. Prior to the enactment of a stricter blasphemy law in 1987, there were only seven accusations from 1927 to 1986, while between 1987 and 2014 there were 1,335 cases (Mazhar 2014). In 2014 alone there were more than ninety cases. There has been a similar increase in extra-judicial killings related to blasphemy; from just two between 1946 and 1987 to fifty-seven from 1987 to 2014. Allegations of blasphemy and the nasty consequences constitute a systematic method of persecuting religious minorities. Of the total 1,335 accusations of blasphemy between 1987 and 2014, 494 involved Ahmadis, 187 Christians, and 21 Hindus, for a total of 702 cases, or 52 percent of all cases during this era; these minorities constitute just 4 percent of Pakistan's population. Religious actors have thus weaponized the law to promote their political agenda of religious intolerance and conformity (Mazhar 2015b). Significantly, contemporary religious scholars have shifted their interpretations based on contemporary sentiments, shedding previous positions that became politically awkward and dangerous in favor of hardline positions. Mazhar asserts that clerics know that their stand on blasphemy being unpardonable contradicts shariah and overturns 1,200 years of Hanafi jurisprudence but refuse to acknowledge this publicly because they think doing so would not only undermine their authority but also put them at risk of violent retribution.

Despite these severe political headwinds, in 2003 the Grand Mufti Rafi Usmani, considered the most authoritative *faqih* (Islamic Jurist) in Pakistan, provided a step-by-step procedure for obtaining pardon for blasphemy (Mazhar 2015b). Perhaps he felt safe because the 1991 court ruling on which the mandatory death sentence is based doesn't provide strong backing as four of the seven ulema consulted by the court ruled that blasphemy is a *pardonable offense*. The plot thickens. There was a petition to overturn the final ruling in favor of mandatory death sentences for blasphemers, but the architect of the law prevailed upon Prime Minister Nawaz Sharif to intervene and convince the court to reject the petition. Thus, political pusillanimity overturned the majority ruling by the ulema against a mandatory death sentence for blasphemy and allowed the harsher minority view to prevail.

Although religious authorities know that their unforgiving interpretation of blasphemy is wrong, according to Mazhar they rationalize it in terms of the public good (*maslihat*), fearing that acknowledging they are wrong will help promote the agenda of secularists. Apparently "the idea being promoted is that Islam is in a fragile state and under attack, both externally from the West, and internally through growing secular voices. Thus, reverting to the authentic Hanafi position, which resonates with the 'secular' demand for clemency and lenience in blasphemy, is tantamount to collusion with this 'repugnant' force" (Mazhar 2015b). He adds, "The mission then becomes to claim and retain ownership of this religio-political power play, even if it is at the expense of intellectual integrity and human lives" (Mazhar 2015b). Dispelling such myths, however, runs the risk of running afoul of those who have no compunction against wielding the law as a weapon against opponents.

No stone goes unturned as religious watchdogs in Pakistan monitor online social media to ensure that bloggers don't transgress and make an example of those who do. For example, in 2017 two Christian relatives were arrested, interrogated, and tortured by police based on allegations they posted blasphemous content online and agitation by hardline religious activists. One jumped from the fourth-floor window of the police station after being abused by officers who demanded that he sexually assault his cousin. Subsequently, after the story gained media attention, the police were forced to withdraw a charge of attempted suicide filed against the victim. Alas, the blatant politicization of Pakistan's blasphemy law against minorities and opponents serves as a model for other nations (Gregory 2012).

Indonesia

Populism in Indonesia is expressed in the radical Islamic movement and targets moderates, ethnic Chinese, and religious minorities. Indonesia's Islamist activists mobilize support through manufacturing political controversy and manipulating populist emotions. The Islamic Defenders Front (IDF, or Front Pembela Islam in Indonesian) is a mass populist organization that is dismissed by some as a thuggish vigilante group that targets vice and also serves as a cat's paw for political interest groups (see chapter 4).

The politicization of blasphemy is manifest in Indonesia where the once popular ethnic Chinese Christian candidate running for governor of Jakarta was defeated and subsequently jailed in May 2017 due to his comments that allegedly insulted Islam. Basuki Tjahaja Purnama, popularly known as Ahok, actually won the first round of voting but was defeated in the second round because his campaign was derailed by the IDF, which organized mass street demonstrations, drawing as many as five hundred thousand protesting his alleged insult of Islam.

At one of these rallies, President Jokowi appeared and prayed onstage, lessening tensions but also granting legitimacy of a sort to the massive street protests and emboldening hardliners. Jokowi also called for a rapid investigation of the blasphemy charges, not wanting to appear as if he was protecting his protégé or draw criticism of his Islamic credentials. This "blasphemy election" and the court proceedings provided a barometer of religious tolerance and free speech in Indonesia and showed the strength of religious hardliners.

Ahok boasted an approval rating of 76 percent going into the gubernatorial campaign and was considered a shoo-in, but accusations of blasphemy sapped his support. At a campaign rally in 2016, Ahok remarked that the Quranic verse al-Maidah 51, warning Muslims against taking Jews or Christians as allies, was being misused by some clerics to argue that Muslims must not vote for a Christian. Several days later, a deceptively edited video of his remarks went viral on the Internet. The quasi-government Indonesian Ulema Council (MUI) then issued a fatwa accusing Ahok of blasphemy, and the radical IDF, known for attacking Muslim minorities, churches, and nightclubs, organized demonstrations demanding that he be tried and imprisoned.

Ahok was subsequently arrested and put on trial for blasphemy. He continued to campaign but lost by 58 to 42 percent. Subsequently the court found him guilty of blasphemy and sentenced him to two years in jail, an unexpectedly harsh sentence given prosecutors had recommended two years of probation on lesser charges. In the febrile atmosphere of fundamentalist Islamic politics in contemporary Indonesia, with anti-Ahok protestors demonstrating angrily outside the courtroom, the judiciary bowed to public pressure.

The Supreme Court turned down Ahok's appeal despite evidence submitted by his lawyer that proved the tape at the heart of the controversy had been tampered with. This tape omitted key words to alter the meaning of what Ahok actually said, making it appear that he was criticizing the Quran when his actual comments were aimed at how hardliners were misleading people about a specific verse by insisting that Muslims are banned from voting for non-Muslims. The verse in question, al-Maidah 51, is actually ambiguous and subject to different interpretations as to what it means and whether it has any implications regarding voting behavior. Nonetheless, the edited version of Ahok's speech posted online suggesting he was criticizing the Quranic verse rather than the Islamic leaders interpreting it, proving decisive in his defeat, a case of how influential fake news can be. His efforts to challenge hardliners' propaganda and politicization of blasphemy eventually landed him in jail, sending a chill throughout the polity. In January 2019 he was granted an early release from detention after serving twenty-one months in prison.

The IDF tapped into longstanding anti-Chinese sentiments, warning that Ahok, an ethnic Chinese Christian, was helping Beijing gain influence in Indonesia and helping them win large-scale infrastructure contracts that would undermine national interests. This prejudice was also evident in the case of Meliana, an ethnic Chinese Buddhist woman in north Sumatra who was convicted of blasphemy for requesting that the mosque across the street turn down the deafening volume of the loudspeakers used in the adhan (call to prayer) (Suryadinata 2019). In July 2016 her request sparked rioting, arson attacks, and looting that lead to the destruction of fourteen local temples and monasteries, egged on by social media. At the end of the year, locals filed a police report demanding an investigation of her on blasphemy charges that ended with her being found guilty and sentenced to eighteen months' imprisonment in August 2018. Moderate religious leaders and even the vice president weighed in, arguing that Meliana should not be subject to criminal prosecution, but a range of hardline clerics and organizations supported the prosecution. The charges occurred against the backdrop of local interethnic tensions related to widespread poverty among the Islamic majority, the relative wealth of local ethnic Chinese, and anger about a Buddhist statue they erected. Unfortunately for Meliana, her case also coincided with the Islamic hardliner agitation against Ahok in Jakarta, generating a favorable climate for making an example of her. Emboldened by the politicization of the Ahok case in the name of religion, hardliners in north Sumatra trumped up charges to transform a disgruntled housewife and angry neighbor into a useful target and unlikely symbol of anti-Islamic subversion. The Supreme Court upheld the blasphemy verdict and her eighteen-month sentence in March 2019, making her the first person in Indonesia to be jailed for complaining about the volume of a mosque's loudspeakers.

The attacks on Ahok were also proxy battles against President Joko Widodo who is his political mentor. Ahok was Jokowi's vice governor and running mate in 2012, and when Jokowi became president in 2014, he handed the baton to Ahok. So the rallies against Ahok also targeted Jokowi and were an attempt to bait him into defending his protégé and run the risk of being tarnished by the blasphemy charges, or staying on the sidelines, effectively conceding the political space to the IDF. Before the blasphemy charges, Ahok was expected to waltz to victory so his defeat by a weak candidate, and subsequent imprisonment, threatened Jokowi.

Worried about where this might lead, President Jokowi issued a decree in 2017 allowing the government to disband organizations that advocate an agenda at odds with Panca Sila (the nation's founding secular principles) as enshrined in the Constitution. He then moved swiftly to disband Hizb ut-Tahrir, an ultraconservative Islamic political movement that rejects secularism, democracy, and religious tolerance in defiance of Panca Sila. It calls for establishing a Pan-Islamic state and advocates violence to achieve its goal. By moving against this group, Jokowi forcefully moved to preserve secularism and served notice to his Islamic hardliner opponents. Following Jokowi's decree on mass organizations, these opponents accused the president of de-Islamicizing Indonesia and undermining democratic freedoms. This helps explain why Jokowi chose the head of MUI to be his vice presidential running mate for the 2019 elections, the man responsible for issuing the fatwa against Ahok. Even so, secularism remains vulnerable to the whims of empowered clerics, blasphemy allegations, and court decisions.

The implications of the new law for the IDF are serious because it advocates adoption of shariah law nationwide and thus violates the principles of Indonesia's secular constitutional democracy. However, its sympathizers have penetrated Islamic political parties, moderate Muslim social organizations, schools, and universities, and it is adept at using social media to push its hardline message and hound those who dissent or oppose its fundamentalist agenda. The IDF has been quite successful in mainstreaming its fundamentalist message and shifting public discourse in favor of its program. Once dismissed as being in the business of "crowds for hire" or a gang of extortionists and muscle working for rival patrons, it gained considerable stature by taking down Ahok. This had much to do with his Chinese ethnicity but by trumping up charges of blasphemy the IDF provided religious cover for widespread prejudice. Certainly, it is biddable and engages in thuggery, but it is also enormously influential and makes things happen, or not as it sees fit. It managed, for example, to get a 2012 Lady Gaga concert canceled by suggesting violent consequences if she was allowed to perform. Whether religious mafia or true believers, it is undeniable that the IDF has clout, but it now must tread carefully due to Jokowi's edict.

Jokowi also reached out to Muhammadiyah and Nahdlatul Ulama to make common cause against fundamentalism and secure their support for maintaining the nation's founding principles of tolerance for diversity. Even so, the radical Islamic message taps into deep-seated grievances fed by glaring income disparities, widespread poverty, and a sense of marginalization among villagers and the urban poor. Social, political, and economic trends generate ongoing opportunities for radical Islamic populists despite the government's efforts to boost village development funding and expand job opportunities by attracting foreign investment. The growing economic influence of China over Indonesia leaves the government vulnerable to charges it is selling the nation out to the ancestral homeland of the wealthy elite that dominate the Indonesian economy.

In terms of identity politics, the IDF sows fear and polarizes, in December 2017 threatening to target any business that required Muslim employees to wear Santa Claus outfits or other Christmas garb. This declaration aimed to enforce a 2016 fatwa issued by the quasi-government MUI. Nothing came of the threat, but for some who resent the encroachment of Christian culture in a Muslim majority nation, this belligerence plays well even if most shrug it off and enjoy the festive atmosphere. It has also been behind police raids on gay sex establishments. Indonesia has long been tolerant of gay culture and few people lost sleep over what others were doing in bed, but this tolerance of diversity runs counter to the zealotry of Islamic fundamentalists. This bigotry is unleashed in campaigns against businesses catering to such tastes and civil society organizations that provide support for the LGBT community.

In contemporary Indonesia, Islamists and groups such as the IDF exercise significant political influence because democracy generates competition for votes. Candidates are judged on many issues, but their stance on Islam and willingness to support an Islamic agenda has become a litmus test for cultivating religious leaders who offer spiritual and political advice to their followers. These leaders have stature and credibility in their local communities and can sway voting behavior. Under the authoritarian Suharto government (1967–1998), religion as a political force and Islamist leaders were kept in check, but democratization has opened space for a greater role of Islam in politics. In national polls Islamic parties have not done well in post–New Order Indonesia, but candidates need to walk a tightrope between the nation's secular ideals and the noisy hardline Islamic minority that seeks an expanded role for religion in the polity (Vatikiotis 2018). And at the local level, candidates are far more beholden to such charismatic leaders and more inclined to embrace their agenda. The spread of local ordinances that invoke aspects of shariah regarding personal behavior, and vigilante patrols enforcing them, illustrates the grassroots appeal and power of religion. Highly motivated hardline leaders thus have an outsize impact because of their ability to mobilize supporters by staking out strong, distinctive positions that appeal to voters who think the political system is unresponsive to their needs.

The activism of hardliners generates intimidation. In this tense atmosphere, judges and courts are under strong public pressure to find defendants guilty when accused of blasphemy and to mete out harsh sentences. There is a temptation to appease the loud rabble-rousing protestors outside the courts and fear about angering them. There are stark implications for a democracy that is increasingly hostage to unelected hardline Islamists who astutely and assiduously work social media and dominate street politics to push their conservative agenda and harass politicians and the institutions of government into heeding their bidding.

In 2011, for example, Islamic hardliners went on a rampage to protest what they viewed as an overly lenient sentence given to a Christian for blaspheming Islam. He was sentenced to five years in prison, the maximum term, for distributing books and pamphlets deemed to foment hatred toward Islam. The protestors torched two churches in venting their anger that the defendant was not sentenced to death even though the penal code does not provide for the death penalty in cases of blasphemy. In 2012 a civil servant from Sumatra was sentenced to two and a half years in prison just for declaring himself an atheist on Facebook. That same year Tajul Muluk, a Shi'a Muslim religious leader from East Java, was sentenced to two years' imprisonment for blasphemy, increased to four years on appeal. This was in the context of an anti-Shi'a rampage targeting his village and the local place of worship, forcing the entire community of three hundred to evacuate. The MUI issued a fatwa accusing him of deviant teachings, resulting in the police arresting him on blasphemy charges merely for practicing a variant of Islam that does not conform to the majority Sunni belief system. These religious opinions (fatwas) serve as guidance for Indonesian Muslims to practice their religious beliefs but are not legally binding in the Indonesian criminal justice system.

Amnesty International (2014) asserts that "blasphemy laws such as those above are fundamentally incompatible with Indonesia's obligations under international human rights law and, specifically, violate legally binding provisions on freedom of expression, thought, conscience and religion, equality before the law and freedom from discrimination. Civil society, human rights groups and academic institutions in Indonesia raise the issue frequently." The blasphemy law also impinges on the second amendment of the 1945 Constitution, enacted in 2000, that guarantees freedom of expression, thought, conscience, and religion.

Azis Anwar Fachruddin, an Islamic Indonesian graduate student, laments that "Muslims seem to be easily offended recently. It is not rare nowadays for Islamic groups to claim religious defamation" (Fachruddin 2016). He went on to note, "The definition of religious defamation is unclear and vague, and as such is prone to being unjustly used to criminalize people who do not deserve it. The result of all of this, besides the abuse of the law, is that people may be afraid to exercise their rights to be critical of Muslims who use religion to justify inexcusable actions." Blasphemy law, he asserts, is thus being deployed to insulate religious leaders from scrutiny or accountability and deprive people of freedom of expression and religion. The law is also used to prosecute and imprison religious minorities and practitioners of traditional religions.

Indonesia's blasphemy law dates from 1965, but there were few prosecutions until the presidency of Susilo Bambang Yudhoyono (known as SBY), totaling eighty-nine from 2004 to 2014 with no acquittals, during his two terms in office. The MUI gained strong support from President Yudohoyono, who invited it to weigh in on shaping government policy regarding religious affairs during his tenure. This top-level political backing for relying on fatwas as a basis for shaping government policy enhanced the influence of the MUI (Amnesty International 2014). Between 2014 and 2018 under Jokowi, there have been over two dozen blasphemy prosecutions and fifteen people have been found guilty with no acquittals. While Jokowi has cultivated an image of promoting freedom of expression and human rights, the situation remains grave. Human Rights Watch laments that "he is content to allow abusive blasphemy prosecutions to continue unchecked" (Harsono 2017). And his running mate in 2019 was formerly the head of the MUI and implicated in fatwas of intolerance and the anti-Ahok campaign. Clearly Jokowi felt he needed protection from similar agitation.

Beyond the law, Harsono adds, "there is a new and equally sinister form of abuse of the right of freedom of expression linked to the same strain of intolerance fueling the recent spate of blasphemy prosecutions: vigilante-style persecution by militant Islamists of individuals who publicly express support for Ahok or concern about the blasphemy law" (Harsono 2017). Since 2016, militant Islamists have targeted dozens of people with online threats, verbal harassment, and physical intimidation. This harassment can lead to legal troubles. For example, a 2016 Facebook posting by a Muslim living in Kalimantan questioned why fellow residents of Balikpapan were traveling to distant Jakarta to join an anti-Ahok rally organized by militant Islamists. This sparked a campaign of harassment and accusations of blasphemy targeting the poster. Subsequently, the MUI issued an edict that the poster was guilty of blasphemy, his employer transferred him to a remote location in reprisal, and his son was bullied in school. Police then arrested him and in 2017 he was sentenced to two years in prison for spreading hatred against Muslims. Clearly this pandering to the prejudices of militant Islamists threatens tolerance and diversity in Indonesia (Harsono 2017).

Indonesian rights groups have long campaigned for the blasphemy law to be revoked and have twice applied for judicial review. In 2010 and again in 2013, however, Indonesia's Constitutional Court upheld the blasphemy law, ruling that it did not infringe on religious freedom and that it was essential to maintaining religious harmony. Indonesia's blasphemy law was promulgated in a presidential decree issued by President Sukarno in 1965, a gesture toward Muslim groups by this secular playboy who alienated many by maintaining close relations with communists. Suharto, his successor, prevailed on Parliament to transform the decree into law in 1969 and an antiblasphemy clause was added to the penal code. Under the authoritarian rule of Suharto (1967–1998), only ten people were prosecuted under the 1965 blasphemy law while from 2002 to 2016 106 people were prosecuted and convicted of blasphemy (Amnesty International 2014). Rafiqa Qurrata A'yun, a law professor at the University of Indonesia, argues that "the recent spike in blasphemy cases in Indonesia occurred as political Islam found space in an increasingly democratised system following the end of Suharto's authoritarian rule in 1998" (A'yun 2016). Since then, blasphemy provisions have been added to various laws, such as the Electronic Information and Transaction Law and the Child Protection Law. She adds, "The strengthening of blasphemy laws have resulted in religious minorities being criminalised and discriminated against. Groups such as Ahmadiyya and Shiites have been subject to these laws for publicly practicing their faiths." In her view the law is being used to suppress other religions, especially non-Sunni Muslims. She raises the specter of Pakistan where thousands of people have been prosecuted and convicted of blasphemy, often under pressure from Islamic hardline vigilante groups, and many others subject to extra-judicial killings. She concludes that "the interests of religious majorities always loom over blasphemy investigations. That means blasphemy cases are easily politicised," adding, "political actors may be tempted to influence blasphemy investigations to curry favour with religious majorities for their own political benefit."

Several indicators over recent years point to rising religious intolerance in the world's largest Muslim majority nation, including growing discrimination and attacks against religious minorities, and a recent wave of vitriol against the LGBT community. Under the Yudhoyono administration, hardline Islamic groups were tolerated and deployed. The defeat and incarceration of Ahok has given such pressure groups a taste of power and confidence, raising questions about Indonesia's democratic progress, the prospects for unity and diversity, and the fate of ethnic and religious minorities subject to the onslaught of Arabization.

Bangladesh

Prosecutions for blasphemy crimes are carried out under provisions of the penal code that criminalize deliberate or malicious intent to "hurt religious sentiments" and allow the government to ban publications that risk "provoking an uprising or anything that creates enmity and hatred among the citizens or denigrates religious beliefs" (Hoque 2018). In 2013 Islamist groups agitated in mass rallies demanding the government take legal action against dozens of bloggers they felt were violating these provisions. These rallies occurred in the context of major confrontations over the government's decision to prosecute leaders of Islamic religious parties that were deemed guilty of collaborating with Pakistan in the civil war that culminated in Bangladesh's independence in 1971. This settling of scores with those viewed by many as traitors enjoyed widespread popular support in what is called the "Shahbag movement" demanding justice and accountability, but this 2013 surge of vengeful secularist sentiments sparked a strong backlash from hardline Islamic groups that protested a witch hunt targeting Islamic party elders four decades after the events. This was also a time when extremists took matters into their own hands and hunted down secularist bloggers and hacked their heads off with machetes (see chapter 4). Prime Minister Sheik Hassina brushed off demands for a blasphemy law, pointing out that existing penal code provisions serve the same purpose. But just to make sure, later in 2013 by presidential decree revisions to the Information and Communications Act established a de facto blasphemy law (Hoque 2018). Under this sweeping amendment, any statement published or transmitted by anyone that causes offense or might hurt religious beliefs is subject to prosecution. Such a vague provision is open to abuse by those pursuing vendettas or seeking to sideline political opponents and puts religious minorities and secularists on notice.

Four of the atheist bloggers who were not beheaded were prosecuted on grounds virtually identical to blasphemy so the absence of such a law doesn't impede efforts to go after heretics or apostates, while a prominent advocate of LGBT rights discovered the rule of law doesn't really matter in a dysfunctional polity when machete-wielding fundamentalists remain on the loose. Those who beheaded him in front of his mother remain unidentified and free. Proponents of secularism and critics of religious fundamentalism are also at risk. One of the atheist bloggers who survived his machete attack, getting a reprieve from the grim reaper, was subsequently arrested on charges of "offending Islam and its Prophet."

Secularists also face significant dangers in a society subject to intensified Arabization. Tolerance has receded rapidly, and one principal of a college was arrested because the school library had a copy of Taslima Nasrin's book *Shame (Lajja)*, a publication banned in 1993 about a Hindu family persecuted in Bangladesh. The torments and indignities inflicted on them by the Muslim majority were often petty but relentless. However, when Hindus tore down the Babri Mosque in India, this act of desecration reverberated across the subcontinent, inciting deadly reprisals against Hindu minorities that engulfed the family. The author remains in exile abroad, unable to return home due to death threats and the risk of being prosecuted on grounds of blasphemy due to her frank sexuality and criticisms of Islam.

Heavy metal groups are also not exempt from the pious. In 2017 Brazilian heavy metal bands Krisiun and NervoChaos were detained on arrival at Dhaka airport, forcing cancellation of the sold-out concert. They were accused of being "Satanic," no doubt contributing to their popular appeal, and thus unacceptable to the gatekeepers of piety.

Ahmadiyya

The Ahmadiyya Islamic faithful in Asia have paid a high price for their belief that Muhammed was not the last prophet. Despite acting, eating, fasting, and praying like Muslims, worshipping in mosques, and hewing to Islamic rites and rituals, they are not accepted as Muslims by Sunni majorities in nations in which they reside. Worldwide there are currently an estimated ten to twenty million Ahmadis. They do not believe that Muhammed was the final prophet, instead following the teachings of Mirza Ghulam Ahmad, a nineteenth-century religious leader who established his reformist sect in what is now India's Punjab region. Ahmad claimed he was the Messiah promised in Islamic holy texts, but mainstream Muslims regard this as heresy and have periodically attacked Ahmadi mosques and seek to ban the sect. Ahmad claimed that his role was to defend and propagate Islam peacefully and to establish world harmony by reviving the neglected Islamic values of peace, forgiveness, and sympathy for everyone. Ahmadis combine a messianic tradition with efforts to purify Islam of foreign accretions and see themselves as reformers promoting a renaissance of Islam by returning to the original precepts as practiced by Muhammad. Their missionary tradition and zeal for conversions provokes a strong backlash among other Muslims who insist that Ahmadis are not Muslims. Ahmadi Muslims assert that military jihad is not justified because Islam, as a religion, is not being attacked militarily but rather via media and cultural onslaught and thus Muslims should respond accordingly. Ahmadiyya categorically rejects acts of terrorism or violence, an awkward stance for hardline clerics who preach jihad and extoll the purifying value of violence.

Ahmadis are subject to persecution in most Asian countries where they exist. Indian law, however, regards them as Muslims, there are no legal restrictions on their activities, and the judiciary has ruled that other Muslims cannot declare them apostates because they acknowledge that there is no God but Allah and that Muhammed was his messenger. This does not mean that they escape the violence and discrimination that all Muslims are subject to in India, and they also suffer prejudice from other Muslims and are excluded from their councils and institutions. This includes the state's recognized body of Islamic legal scholars. But they are not subject to the extremes of blasphemy laws as in neighboring Pakistan or Bangladesh or singled out for mob violence and mayhem.

In 1980 the MUI issued a fatwa declaring that the Ahmadis are heretics and not practicing a legitimate form of Islam. Persecution of Indonesia's Ahmadis, numbering nearly 500,000 in a nation of nearly 270 million, has increased in recent years and violent attacks against them go unpunished. Indeed, there seems to be a degree of collusion between security forces and local vigilante mobs as police are often reluctant to get involved while attacks are being perpetrated. Despite this state-sanctioned persecution, Ahmadis have remained resilient and defiant, nurturing a solidarity drawing on shared oppression (Connley 2016).

So why has there been a surge of anti-Ahmadi agitation in twenty-first-century Indonesia? The recent increase in blasphemy cases targets Ahmadis and is attributed to vendettas, political machinations, the dynamics of power networks, and the spread of a less tolerant Salafist orthodoxy. Anti-Ahmadi activism in Indonesia is related to attempts by certain groups and institutions to regain or enhance their political and religious authority. The demise of Suharto's New Order in 1998 did not abruptly rupture the networks of power that the regime had nurtured to enhance its power, but close association with the Suharto regime undermined their credibility and weakened their standing in a new political landscape with multiple new contenders for power and influence. Democratization heightened competition, enabling individual ulama to bypass political authorities to strengthen their individual power bases. In this situation, heresy accusations are a useful tool to gain attention and attract a following in the sound bite world of social media.

The MUI was established by Suharto to manage Islam and harness its social, political, and economic power in support of the state, but it had awkward relations with the initial post-Suharto presidents and struggled to find a role. It offered guidance and opinions in accordance with government positions and policies and thus was more of a state bureaucratic entity than a fountain of spiritual insights and guidance enjoying grassroots support. It was viewed more as an extension of the state than as a protector of Islam and the ummah (community of believers). The dilemma facing the MUI was how to navigate the cross-currents of democratization and widespread repudiation of New Order legacies. The state was fearful of an untethered Islamic extremism and the MUI was in search of a new role. Having confronted competition and hostility in the initial era of reformasi, the MUI found a lifeline in issuing high-profile fatwa on blasphemy. Ahmadis proved a useful target because they were unloved and unpowerful with little social capital. Arousing anger against them helped certain groups gain a high profile and follow-ing. As a social media–friendly issue that is simple and powerfully emotive, the MUI found blasphemy in general and the Ahmadis in particular useful to regain relevance as the officially sanctioned arbiter of religious affairs.

President Susilo Bambang Yudhoyono played a critical role in reviving the MUI in an attempt to reign in more unruly elements, but in this he did not succeed. As one op-ed lamented,

> President Susilo Bambang Yudhoyono has shown disappointing timidity in the matter. As in Pakistan, support for religious political parties is not high but radical Muslim groups wield a disproportionate amount of street influence—and in this way succeed in shaping the responses of politicians and govern-ment officials. After all, in Pakistan it was Zulfikar Ali Bhutto, a "progressive" leader, who brought in a constitutional amendment to declare the Ahmadis non-Muslim to appease religious lobbies. It is to be hoped that Indonesia, which has moved ahead politically and economically with much speed after getting rid of Suharto, will tackle the intolerance with the same determination it has shown in dealing with the Islamist terror group Jemaah Islamiyah. (Hin-du 2011)

This did not happen. Jacqueline Hicks argues, "Ahmadiyah's case seems to be a theological 'zero-sum game' in which their beliefs cannot co-exist with those of other Muslims" (2014, 322). She identifies two discourses on blasphemy: "religious essentialism" and "political instrumentalism." The in-strumentalist interpretation highlights the role of opportunistic elites manipu-lating the masses behind the banner of blasphemy while religious essential-ism focuses on theological affronts with reference to particular passages of holy texts that could be interpreted as mandating action. She notes, "it is remarkable how the issue of heresy generally, and Ahmadiyyah in particular, has served the interests of all of these bodies, conferring them with new levels of authority and substantially raising their profile" (322).

Paradoxically, from 2005 onward, the MUI regained its role of maintain-ing "social cohesion" by stirring up religious anger about alleged instances of blasphemy that sparked sectarianism. In *Riots, Pogroms, Jihad: Religious Violence in Indonesia* (2006) John Sidel highlights the fragmenting pressures associated with Indonesia's democratic transition. Religious authority in In-donesian Islam is very widely dispersed, creating an intensely contested space in which various actors and institutions are vying to accumulate sym-bolic capital and enhance their legitimacy. This situation plays to the strength of radicals who stake out extreme positions to gain attention, thereby shifting the terms of debate and pressuring others to respond as a way of shoring up their religious credentials. Blasphemy is an easily understood concept, vis-cerally emotive, and thus suited to the snappy sensationalism of social media. Grandstanding on heresy is an effective means to enhance status and challenge established hierarchies because it is so hard to challenge. Blasphemy charges are bulletproof in that anyone who questions them can then be accused. In the Indonesian context of divergent Islamic traditions and the modernist-traditional divide, mainstream leaders can find common ground in anti-Ahmadi agitation.

So why was SBY unwilling to act decisively against intolerance? He relied on support from Islamic parties in Parliament and was eager to resolve the separatist issue in Aceh, a province in Sumatra where there has been a long history of a more devout Islam. So for reasons unrelated to religion SBY was willing to pursue an expedient policy, but it is not clear he could have had much impact at the grassroots level even if he wanted to. Suryana (2018) notes a case in which SBY intervened to help a displaced Shi'a community without success because local officials, police, and religious leaders pushed back, arguing that allowing them to return to their homes would undermine social harmony. He argues that the diminution of presidential powers in post–New Order Indonesia limits their ability to intervene and protect minority rights. These curbs on executive power were imposed in response to the authoritarian excesses of Suharto and a desire to nurture checks and balances consistent with a vibrant democracy. Thus, institutional factors have hindered presidents' ability to respond even if they were inclined to do so. Given that the blasphemy law enjoys broad public support and confers powers on influential individual and institutional actors, prospects for reform appear remote especially in a climate of intensified political competition in which candidates are all eager to burnish their religious credentials and leery of opening themselves to attack on grounds of offering comfort to blasphemers.

The central government also prioritizes preserving the mainstream social order in ways that leave minorities vulnerable. Maintaining overall harmony and order is served by scapegoating minorities who act as sanctioned targets for social discontent. From this perspective there is little incentive for preventing communal violence and much to gain from repressing designated "heretics" like the Ahmadi and Shi'a communities. There is thus a degree of complicity between the state and clerics in identifying and persecuting "rogue" religions deemed guilty of insulting Islam and thereby posing a threat to social order.

Following his controversial impeachment in 2001 that removed him from the presidency, Abdurrahman Wahid sought to repeal the blasphemy law. Gus Dur, as he was popularly known, headed the Nahdlatul Ulama, the nation's largest Muslim organization with more than forty million members that promotes a tolerant form of Islam. Due to widespread violence against Ahmadis, the former president joined human rights groups in petitioning the Constitutional Court in 2009 to review the law, arguing that it violated the human rights of nonmainstream faiths by criminalizing them. The Constitutional Court rejected the petition, arguing that the law was necessary to protect public order.

SBY's cabinet weighed in decisively against the Ahmadis by banning a broad range of their practices (but not the sect itself) in a 2008 Ministerial Joint Decree. This government decree followed a series of attacks on sect members and their places of worship by the IDF. The government called on sect members to renounce their religious principles and abandon propagation of their faith rather than protect them from mob violence. Two provincial governments, East and West Java, passed decrees banning all activities of the Ahmadi community, including use of electronic media, and barred them from displaying mosque and school signs. Another fourteen provinces and regencies have issued anti-Ahmadi decrees since 2006.

The central government's 2008 decree was partly in response to demonstrations by vigilante mobs in Jakarta demanding a ban on Ahmadis, threatening violence if the state failed to act. With an eye to the 2009 elections, SBY ordered Ahmadiyya leaders and members to cease activities but stopped short of banning the organization. This compromise made matters worse, inciting a cascade of attacks that police not only failed to stop but actually watched and, allegedly, participated in. SBY thus in trying to appease hardliners actually emboldened them and created an atmosphere of impunity. SBY's Religious Affairs Minister Suryadharma Ali even advocated a total ban on the Ahmadiyya, suggesting Indonesia follow the "Pakistan road" of banning and criminalizing their activities.

President Joko Widodo campaigned on promoting pluralism and tolerance but since taking office in 2014 has also confronted the limits on executive power and the power of street politics where hardliners have preached intolerance and gained a massive following. In 2016 he intervened to help a beleaguered minority faith in West Kalimantan called Gafatar, but local residents and officials proceeded with the forcible eviction of faith members. Yet again locals defied the president's wishes. However, in a rare victory for minority faiths, in 2017 the Constitutional Court ruled that followers of native faiths like Gafatar could list their religion on their national identity cards. Previously, citizens had to list one of the six officially sanctioned religions that are essential to access a range of services and obtain required documents. Those whose faith was not one of the official six had to leave the space on religious affiliation blank and thereby risk being identified as an atheist, a blasphemous offense, or masquerade as an adherent of one of the approved religions and leave themselves vulnerable to accusations of falsifying their identity. The court ruling benefits some four hundred thousand native faith adherents but provides no succor to Ahmadis or Shi'a who in some cases are required to renounce their faith to obtain a national identity card with refusal meaning denial of state services other citizens enjoy. The national and local governments are thus complicit in undermining minorities' basic constitutional rights and encouraging attacks against them in defiance of the International Covenant on Civil and Political Rights that Indonesia signed in 2006.

In Pakistan, the nation with the world's largest community of Ahmadis, numbering some two to five million, the situation is similar. Their freedom of religion has been impeded by various ordinances, acts, and constitutional amendments. Based on a 1974 law, the state declared them to be non-Muslims. A decade later General Zi-ul-Haq, the nation's military ruler at that time, issued an ordinance that forbids Ahmadis to call themselves Muslim or act like Muslims, meaning they are banned from expressing the Islamic creed or calling their places of worship mosques. They are also banned from using the traditional Islamic greeting, worshipping in Sunni mosques or public prayer rooms, performing the Muslim call to prayer, preaching, seeking converts, disseminating religious materials, or publicly quoting from the Quran. In short, they are legally forbidden to practice their faith in public. Violations are subject to three years' imprisonment. To obtain a national identity card or passport, all applicants must sign an oath declaring Mirza Ghulam Ahmad to be a false prophet and all Ahmadis to be non-Muslims. In this atmosphere of state-sanctioned discrimination, Ahmadis are subject to extensive harassment, exclusion, and violence. Religious teachers reinforce official sanctions by encouraging intolerance toward them in their network of schools nationwide.

As Pakistani novelist Mohammed Hanif observes, "This country has a poor record of protecting its religious minorities, but we outdo ourselves when it comes to Ahmadis. Members of the sect insist on calling themselves Muslims, and we mainstream Muslims insist on treating them like the worst kind of heretics" (Hanif 2017). They have been subject to "sustained acts of brutality" and yet the state has done nothing to protect them. Given the dangers of being identified as an Ahmadi it is hard to gauge the actual numbers as many live under the radar and refuse to take part in the census or publicly declare their identity. Judges sentence them to death for blasphemy just for practicing their faith, while some never live to see their day in court due to "mob justice." The only Pakistani scientist to win a Nobel Prize is an Ahmadi, explaining why efforts to commemorate him are subject to denunciations. Hanif notes the sad irony that "Pakistan was essentially created to protect the religious and economic rights of Muslims who were a minority before India's partition in 1947. But since the country's inception, we have created new minorities and keep finding new ways to torment them."

In 2010, Islamic extremists entered two Ahmadi mosques in Lahore during Friday prayer services and opened fire before blowing themselves up, killing eighty-six and injuring more than a hundred more. Reacting to this particularly gruesome attack, the Calcutta *Telegraph* fumed about the origins and horrors of identity politics and sectarian violence: "Unfortunately, the experience of brutality is not new to any of the minority communities. Torn between conflicting notions of community and nationhood, Pakistan has come to define citizenship entirely on the basis of religion, but here too confusion has led it to accord primacy to the majority community of Sunnis and to certain set notions of what constitutes Islam" (Telegraph 2010).

SHI'A AT RISK

Shi'a is a minority sect of Islam practiced in several Asian nations. Shi'a and Sunnis share the basic fundamental creeds of Islam, believe there is no God but Allah, fast during Ramadan, pray five times a day, have the same dietary restrictions, and perform the haj to Mecca in which entry is restricted to Muslims. The essential differences hinge on the interpretations of Islam's early history and the issue of succession after the Prophet Muhammad died.

Like Ahmadis, Shi'a face considerable discrimination by the Sunni majority, and this has intensified with the wave of Arabization in the twenty-first century and the deepening rift between Saudi Arabia (the home of Sunni Islam) and Iran (the home of Shi'a Islam). Historically, Shiism has had a significant impact on Islamic thought and practice around the region and the legacy of this syncretism remains evident despite efforts by some Sunni reformists to purge practice and ritual of these and other accretions (Formichi and Feener 2015).

The 1979 Iranian Revolution that swept clerics into power and established a theocracy motivated the faithful around the world but also raised red flags for authorities. This Islamic cultural revival sparked interest in Islam in general and the Shi'a sect in particular. Across Southeast Asia there are three main groups of Shi'a: those who descended from Arab traders with long-standing roots, those who studied Islam in post-1979 Iran due to intensified interactions between Shi'a ulama around the region with their Iranian counterparts, and Indonesian students who were inspired by the revolution at a time when the New Order (1967–1998) was acting to depoliticize Islam (Zulfiki 2013).

Zulfiki argues that in Indonesia there is a process of undeclared stealth conversion. This spiritual metamorphosis happens through preaching, education, dissemination of publications, friendships, and kinship bonds, but is not made explicit due to the dangers involved. Zulfiki argues, "For Shi'is living in a hostile Sunni environment, another unique aspect of their teachings is *taqiyya*, which is the doctrinal basis for stigmatised Shi'is to implement strategies of dissimulating personal and social identity in their interaction with the Sunni majority" (2013, 272). By engaging in certain rituals, gestures, and ceremonies, they work to blend in. Shi'is are required to engage in missionary activity and proselytize but in general do so without explicitly invoking their sect's name, instead emphasizing their goal of establishing an

Islamic society. However, there are a number of institutions, foundations, publishing houses, and educational programs that openly affirm their Shi'a character in books, gatherings, curriculum, and daily life. Shi'is navigate a hostile environment by relying on a combination of indirect and direct strategies. Among moderate Sunnis there has been a degree of recognition and acceptance of Shi'is, but this is not the case in the wider public.

While Arabization has spread intolerance, moderate Islam remains resilient in Indonesia. The Nahdlatul Ulama and Muhammadiyah, massive religious organizations engaged in a variety of social welfare endeavors with tens of millions of members, have been largely neutral toward Shi'ism, or at least not actively hostile. Moderate Muslim public intellectuals have also adopted conciliatory stances. In addition, Shi'is gained official state recognition in Indonesia through their national organization, the Indonesian Council of Ahli Bait Associations. This happened under President Abdurahman Wahid, a sympathetic moderate Muslim and leader of Nahdlatul Ulama who openly advocated pluralism.

The MUI that issues fatwas on religious matters has not been especially antagonistic toward Shiites, although in 1984 it ruled that Sunnis should be protected from Shiite teachings. More problematically vigilante groups egged on by radical clerics have attacked Shiites and their mosques and schools, killing and intimidating. Shiites thus remain a stigmatized minority and continue to rely on obscuring their identities, drawing on Sunni texts and sources in their proselytizing and otherwise adjust to the norms and rules of the Sunni majority.

It may seem far fetched given the small numbers of Shi'a in Indonesia, but that doesn't prevent some clerics from whipping up concerns about a global Shi'a-led armed revolution targeting Indonesia. Out of the nation's approximately 225 million Muslims, only about two million are Shi'a, so hyping fears of a violent takeover represents the type of manufactured threat that helps rally the faithful.

Sectarian violence and discrimination is not new to Indonesia but seems to be intensifying with the rise of fundamentalist zealotry and the temptation to play the religious card. The precarious position of the Shiites was underscored by a 2013 case petitioning the Indonesian Constitutional Court to rescind the blasphemy law. This petition was filed by several Shi'a, some of whom had been convicted for blaspheming Sunni Islamic teachings, amid a surge in religious intolerance and violence targeting their community. Just as in 2009, the court ruled that the law was constitutional and crucial to maintaining social harmony.

The situation facing Shiites in Pakistan is far graver as hundreds are killed every year by zealots from Sunni militant groups that have declared them infidels and one-half of all Muslims there think they are non-Muslims (Julius 2016). Muhammad Ali Jinnah, the nation's founding father, was raised in a

Shiite family, although he apparently converted to Sunni Islam later in life. General Zia made notable concessions to the Shiite community on school curriculum and exempted them from paying the state's zakat tax so they could directly distribute alms to the needy, but state complicity in sectarian violence against them intensified on his watch.

It is hard to estimate the Shiite population of Pakistan because of the incentives to disguise one's affiliation and dangers of not doing so. Estimates range from sixteen to thirty million while a 2009 Pew poll found that 10 to 15 percent in the survey identified as Shi'a (Pew 2009). Sunni extremists believe that eliminating Shi'a is part of their divine responsibility to rid Pakistan of heretics. Although Shi'a are a small minority in Pakistan's population of nearly 205 million, they account for some 70 percent of all blasphemy cases brought against Muslims.

In Quetta, a major city in western Pakistan in the province of Balochistan, the ethnic Hazari Shi'a community has been subject to extensive targeted killings. In Quetta there are more than half a million Hazari Shiites who live in two encampments that are walled off with barbed wire from the rest of the city. Paramilitary groups man checkpoints that control traffic in and out of the ghettoes and are suspected of complicity in the spate of killings. Since 2013 more than five hundred Hazaris have been killed and over six hundred injured in these attacks, but state security forces have done little to respond. Hazaris are especially vulnerable in that they have distinctive facial features that make it easy to identify them compared to other Pakistani Shi'a who can blend in.

Julius asserts that "one of the fundamental causes of the rise in the number of blasphemy cases in the decades from 1991 to 2012 has been the harsher penalties for blasphemy added in 1991. The increasing number of cases clearly indicates that the blasphemy laws have become an easy tool to use and that they have been used prolifically" (2016, 101). In a Freedom House report that highlights the nonreligious aspect of blasphemy prosecutions, Prudhomme concludes that "Pakistan's blasphemy laws are routinely used to exact revenge, apply pressure in business or land disputes, and for other matters entirely unrelated to blasphemy" (2010, 74).

IMPLICATIONS

Where there are blasphemy allegations there is political purpose and an attempt to undermine tolerance for diversity by infusing national identity with majoritarian malevolence. Surveying the situation in Asia, it is clear that blasphemy laws are a powerful weapon for undermining secular democracy and asserting an illiberal agenda. These laws leverage piety and conjure up transgressions in ways that have less to do with protecting religion than imposing intolerance and mainstreaming it. Democratic competition creates space for this escalating attack on diversity. The mere threat of denunciation is often enough to ensure compliance while making examples of easy targets—religious and ethnic minorities—spreads a chilling message that empowers the hatemongers and mobocracy. The toxic social media–hyped Othering in service of nationalism nurtures majoritarian solidarity while provoking confrontational identity politics and sectarian tensions that are as "useful" as they are corrosive.

Chapter Nine

Contesting Sexuality

The confluence of sexuality and religion is profoundly revealing in terms of national identity. Sexuality may not define national or religious identity, but misogyny and oppression of diversity do. A nation's identity is evident in how a society treats its minorities and vulnerable populations, how it handles matters of gender and sexuality, and by what is tolerated and not. Because sexuality is also crucial to individual's well-being, his or her identity, and the politicized culture wars that have erupted across Asia, it serves as a barometer of how contemporary Asia is evolving, and not.

Religions weigh in on sex and sexual identity by establishing norms of proper conduct, reassuring ritual, and clarifying what is sacred and sacrilegious. Religious rules and values proscribe and sanctify certain types of behavior related to sex such as birth, menstruation, masturbation, monogamy, polygamy, divorce, incest, celibacy, birth control, interaction between the sexes, and seclusion. Religion is invoked to sanctify marriage, and in some cases divorce, and plays a key role in ceremonial functions related to birth, circumcision, and coming of age. It bans sex before marriage, only condones heterosexual relations within a marriage, and requires monogamy in Buddhism, Hinduism, and Christianity, while Islam permits polygamy. Homosexuality is not accepted by any world religion and heavily stigmatized, reinforcing the sense of isolation felt by many gays and denying them the spiritual solace that belonging confers.

In this chapter we explore various dimensions of sex and sexuality in Asia, but this is such a massive topic with such significant variations and evolving contexts that we can only focus on a few themes. Here we examine the notion of "love jihad" and prevailing conditions regarding sexual violence, homophobia, and LGBT in the context of religion and identity. Given that people's sexuality is an essential aspect of their identity and well-being, it is important to scrutinize how it is influenced by state laws, religious practice, and vigilantism especially given the ruinous impact of the "weaponized" Internet on chosen targets.

Sex and sexuality confront a vexing variety of social taboos. Interactions between the sexes are carefully monitored, especially when they involve those of different faiths, a situation rendered more complex in India due to the caste system. In India, caste adds a layer of deeply rooted taboos that render crossing the lines hazardous for those involved, as Arundhati Roy explores with devastating clarity in her *God of Small Things* (1997). One's religion is a powerful marker of suitability and unsuitability for a potential partner, meaning that interfaith marriage is fraught with tension and not only between those getting married. Relatives and communities are often deeply offended by marriage outside the fold of fellow believers. Often the debate over conversion is framed in patriarchal terms of who is taking whose women in which men arrogate to themselves the right to make decisions for women and reject their choices as a male prerogative. Typically, families insist, and customs dictate, that the female partner converts to the husband's faith, but there are exceptions and in some cases the couple may fend off such demands by declaring agnosticism or atheism.

Courtship is a sensitive issue because it is a prelude to marriage, a process of determining compatibility between families, communities, and individuals that is heavily influenced by religion. Courtship involves men wooing young women, almost everywhere a timeless and perennial pursuit that is usually conducted according to prevailing social norms and religious traditions. Transgressions elicit a range of responses from family and community. Letting lovers choose as they wish is not the norm in traditional societies in which compatibility between families is often deemed at least as important as between the prospective couple. Of course, there is always the option to elope, but that usually comes at a steep cost ranging from family estrangement to violence.

LOVE JIHAD

The literal meaning of jihad is "effort" but refers to "holy war" or a fight against the enemies of Islam. Pairing this term with love suggests that deep affection is a passion harnessed to some larger struggle against religious enemies. In common parlance, love jihad is a concept that is used to arouse passions against Muslims seducing girls from other religions, an accusation made in emotive language aimed at inciting resistance to the alleged onslaught. It is a term only the enemies of Islam invoke.

In contemporary India, much is made of alleged love jihad by Muslim men seducing young Hindu women in order to marry and convert them. The

Rashtriya Swayamsevak Sangh (RSS) and BJP support "Romeo patrols" to intervene and disrupt such liaisons. It doesn't matter that a far greater problem for Hindu women is the prevalent practice of what is euphemistically referred to as "Eve teasing," meaning sexual harassment of women in public places by men that ranges from lewd comments and gestures to groping. The scourge of rape that afflicts India, with more than one hundred reported a day, mostly involving Hindus raping Hindus, is clearly a far greater threat to women, but just as rape is not really about sex, preventing love jihad is not really about protecting women; in both the key is men exerting power over women. What matters most to the Romeo patrols is the imagined stealing of "our" women by "them" and the gross injustice that "their" converts diminish Hindu numbers. Less important, apparently, for these defenders of women's honor are surveys that find half of Indian women report being sexually harassed, endemic sexual abuse of children, and a high prevalence of rape. Defending women from the largely imagined Muslim menace, however, trumps safeguarding them from these far greater actual threats.

Self-appointed guardians of women's virtue prowl the streets of northern India on the lookout for improper conduct that extends from uncovering illicit cow slaughter to interfaith dating. If Uttar Pradesh, now under BJP control, was an independent nation, it would be the world's fifth most populous with more than two hundred million residents, including forty million Muslims. Periodic riots and anti-Muslim hostility have sparked greater piety and solidarity among Muslims who find solace in their faith and support from their community, further fanning Hindu anxieties. Hindutva has thus played a significant role in promoting greater devotion among Hindus and Muslims that undermines trust and intensifies antagonisms.

In Uttar Pradesh, the BJP has been implicated in inciting riots, calling on the faithful to revenge insults and protect Hinduism from its enemies. Its leaders argue that love jihad represents an existential threat to India, conjuring up the imaginary threat of becoming a Muslim majority nation; currently Muslims constitute about 15 percent of India's population. Yogi Adityanath, the chief minister of Uttar Pradesh, is a Hindu monk famous for his private militia, the Hindu Yuva Vahini (Hindu Youth Force). Battling the phantom enemy of love jihad and his proven ability to arouse Hindu mobs against Muslims propelled him into the chief minister's office in 2016. His credentials are suggestive about the nature of Modi's India, impugned as the age of cretinism by Pratap Bhanu Mehta (Mehta 2018b).

Vigilantes, acting their part in this orchestrated drama, share information on social media about alleged Muslim machinations, including lists of dubious authenticity that detail how much money will be paid "jihadis" for seducing Hindu women. The alleged bounties are highest for upper-caste Brahmins (nearly $9,000) and lowest for Buddhist girls ($2,200). For the hardcore Hindu activists these alleged offers of lavish cash rewards are a call to arms and a license to intimidate and harass girls they judge to be involved in risky behavior. They claim that their goal is to save these women from sexually depraved Muslims on the prowl, although these efforts appear to be more of an assertion of patriarchal control and prejudice.

These Islamic lotharios are depicted as resourceful, deceptive, and relentless: "Most Muslim love jihadis, Chauhan insisted, disguise themselves as Hindus. A pamphlet doing the rounds in Saharanpur offers an insight into their methods: when girls go to recharge the talk time on their mobile phones, some stores pass on their numbers to love jihadis who seduce them via text messages. If that doesn't work, the jihadis pose as electricians, car mechanics and vegetable vendors to gain access to middle-class Hindu homes and seduce their daughters" (Sethi 2015).

In 2017 there was a notorious court case in Kerala regarding a young woman who converted to Islam and married a Muslim man against her parents' wishes at the end of 2016 (Bhatia 2017). Her father petitioned the court to annul the marriage, alleging without producing any proof that the husband had links to some local affiliate of IS, the Islamic terrorist organization, and that he was on a mission to bring his daughter to Syria where she would become a sex slave for jihadis or a suicide bomber. In May 2017 the Kerala High Court annulled the marriage in a curious decision hinging on the daughter's alleged gullibility and the judge's view that it was abnormal for a girl to convert, especially one with "moderate intellectual" capacity. Following the verdict, Hadiya, the twenty-four-year-old daughter, was put in the care of her family. Her parents opposed the match and wanted to reconvert her, a family drama that attracted breathless reporting nationwide, generating exactly the type of spectacle that inspires the RSS faithful. Over the summer, video clips of the family drama went viral, prompting feverish media coverage of the "terrorist" bride, a sign of how conversion and love jihad had become hot button issues in India's escalating culture wars. The Kerala police actually investigated over seven thousand cases of conversion between 2011 and 2016 and found not a single case of forced conversion, but this is explained away as indicating how crafty the jihadis can be. Hadiya, however, proved to be awkwardly articulate and showed no signs of being brainwashed, merely demanding her fundamental rights. An appeal to the Supreme Court ruled in her favor, restoring her marriage, and she was allowed to resume school and make her own decisions.

The popular obsession with love jihad plays on prejudices that draw on longstanding stereotypes about depraved, sex-crazed Muslims. These clichés about Islamic Casanovas stoke patriarchal anxieties about religious warfare in which the enemy is abducting and ravishing "our" women. This imagined defilement has been a staple in popular literature, but social media and Internet portals have intensified the moral panic and disseminated it more widely and vividly in the twenty-first century. Moreover, this has become a highly politicized meme subject to artful manipulation by BJP politicians and their followers. Ironically, while frenzied mobs run rampant and cause considerable mayhem and vigilantes kill people for butchering cows or consuming beef, the government and judiciary give more attention to conversions and alleged seductions.

This RSS-backed campaign has intensified in Uttar Pradesh under the leadership of Hindu hardliner Chief Minister Yogi Adiranath. While individuals are traumatized by Romeo patrols' heavy-handed interventions, the implications for any interactions between Muslims and Hindus are stark, generating risks of nasty consequences for those who aren't careful. Politicizing dating and subjecting anyone who fraternizes across religions to harassment and salacious rumor mongering is bound to polarize already divided communities. When a Hindu wife demands that her husband be examined to ensure his foreskin is intact because he had a Muslim lover, the situation has truly deteriorated. The inflammatory speeches and incitements to violence spark riots that sharpen antagonisms, stoke religiosity, and also encourage relocation to communal enclaves, a circling of the wagons, that diminishes everyday interactions and facilitates Othering.

Hindus however are not taking the love jihad sitting down and have mounted counteroffensives. In Agra, Uttar Pradesh, the Hindu Jagran Manch (HJM), an affiliate of the RSS, launched a "reverse love jihad" in 2017, setting a target of 2,100 Muslim brides for Hindu boys in the next six months. HJM doesn't advocate forcibly converting Muslim women but welcomes them to do so and offers security to protect against any backlash. HJM also distributed pamphlets outside schools offering "tips" on how to identify Muslim boys masquerading as Hindus, the point being that no Hindu girl would knowingly marry a Muslim. In West Bengal Hindu activists rallied on Valentine's Day in 2017 to urge Hindu boys to be friendly to women of both faiths and mount a courtship counteroffensive to fend off Muslim predators. They also warned women about the deceptions that Muslims resort to.

These concerns of Hindus in India are shared by Buddhists in neighboring Sri Lanka and Myanmar (see chapter 5). The Ma Ba Tha Islamophobic campaign and marriage laws enacted in 2015 address these same concerns about the imagined and feared rampant sexuality of Myanmar's Muslims whose practice of polygamy grants them a potentially significant fertility edge. These concerns about a snowballing Muslim population are also propagated by the BBS in Sri Lanka. The image of predatory Muslims preying on defenseless maidens resonates powerfully in these societies and plays a key role in majoritarian mobilization that draws on nationalist sentiments and shapes national identity. The war for wombs is hotly contested as non-Muslims fear demographic extinction and rally support by stoking bigotry to prevent this improbable scenario.

The imagined threat of demographic extinction at the hands of fast-breeding, evangelizing Muslims is central to majoritarian mobilization in India, Sri Lanka, and Myanmar (Kesavan 2018). Several Indian provinces and Myanmar have passed laws that strictly regulate religious conversion. Their goal is to prevent conversion to Islam or Christianity; conversion to Hinduism, on the other hand, is welcome and referred to as *ghar wapsi*, or "homecoming." In the discourse of Hindu majoritarianism, all Muslims and Christians are imagined to be ancestrally Hindu.

EROTIC HINDUISM?

Free speech and a free press have been essential to the concept of India and a functioning democracy. These freedoms are at risk from the Hindu chauvinists Modi represents. They take exception to criticism and anyone who strays from their orthodox interpretations of Hinduism. The "Doniger affair" reflects a right-wing ascendance in Indian politics and society that is gathering momentum. It is a sign of the times that in 2014 an Indian publishing house bowed to intimidation and the prospects of losing a lawsuit by withdrawing and promising to pulp all copies of *The Hindus: An Alternative History*. This "alternative" by Wendy Doniger, a University of Chicago professor, angered Hindu nationalists and the self-appointed guardians of religious orthodoxy. Colonial-era laws that are still valid in the contemporary penal code make it a crime to outrage the religious feeling of Indians, a sweepingly vague concept that has facilitated criminal and civil lawsuits that overwhelmingly favor the plaintiff. This law undermines the freedom of speech and expression guaranteed in the 1949 Constitution and puts all writers on notice. Hindus and Muslims have invoked this law to ban books they deem offensive. The Indian government amended the Constitution in 1951 granting it the power to curb free expression and ban books, while libel laws are a further source of intimidation and means for powerful interests to suppress what are deemed undesirable books and articles. In the end, no copies of Doniger's book were pulped because they sold out as Indian's reacted to the scandalous accusations by rushing out to buy the book and in any event have access to Kindle versions. Thus, the book-banning campaign backfired spectacularly, underscoring that there is widespread tolerance and belief that people should get to decide what they read rather than have ill-informed vigilantes invoke colonial laws in order to impose their blinkered views.

The Doniger affair focused on her "heretical" interpretations of eroticism and sexuality in Hindu traditions and the norms that right-wing Hindu groups seek to enforce. Doniger pointed out that accusations in the lawsuit that her book is "filthy and dirty" represent false advertising because her scholarly exegesis of Hindi scriptures is anything but smutty (Doniger 2014a). She chides contemporary Hindu chauvinists for making common cause with Victorian Christians, who early on sought to repress and expunge the sexual aspects of these scriptures. Ironically, Doniger writes, "In my defense, I can tell you there is a lot of sex in Hinduism and therefore a lot of puritanism in Hindutva; where there are lions there are jackals" (Doniger 2014a). Her mistake lay in trying to resurrect the vital traditions of earthy mythology and spirited mockery of the gods, emphasizing the way that Hinduism was practiced and celebrated before it was hijacked and purified by an upper-caste male elite eager to "rescue" Hinduism from its popular manifestations (Doniger 2014b).

Anyone who visits the Khajuraho complex of temples can see there is a healthy regard for the erotic in detailed sculptures depicting voluptuous sirens (apsaras) engaged in various sex acts that call to mind the sensuality of the Kama Sutra, an ancient Hindu text. This cluster of Hindu-Jain temples is a World Heritage site built in the tenth and eleventh centuries and is dubbed the "sexiest temple" in India, although guides can direct visitors to similar sculptures tucked away in many other temples around the subcontinent. While only 10 percent of the sculptures there are explicitly erotic and only 20 percent of the Kama Sutra is about sexual positions and techniques, both suggest that there is a sensual tradition in Hinduism that backs up Doniger's interpretations and undermines the more prudish views of her contemporary critics.

SEXUAL VIOLENCE

Rape is not about sex but does suggest much about rapists' sexuality. It is a sexuality based on violence, coercion, intimidation, and fear. While men and boys are also at risk, it is predominantly a scourge inflicted on women and girls. Rape is about misogyny, patriarchy, and power. Sexual violence happens everywhere, sometimes as a weapon of war aimed at degrading and demoralizing the enemy, but mostly it is just a common and particularly cruel way of exerting dominance and/or exacting revenge.

State security forces mostly commit such crimes with impunity whether in war or during occupations or antiterrorist operations. Often these soldiers enjoy the protection of laws that shield them against prosecution or liability, but even if they don't, accountability is extremely rare. The suffering and indignities imposed on women in war are usually borne in silence and, compounding the crime, often stigmatized.

The veneer of civilization is quickly stripped away during war where so much that is taken for granted suddenly evaporates. Pakistan, for example, used rape as a weapon during the 1971 civil war that saw East Pakistan prevail and gain independence as Bangladesh. Pakistan set up rape camps where perhaps half a million women were subjected to this grave indignity, with at least twenty-five thousand, and probably far more, becoming impregnated. Bangladesh calls them Birangonas (war heroines) to honor their sacrifice in the struggle for independence. Many were Hindu, but most were Muslims and their rapists were also Muslims, meaning that this barbarity was less about religion than inflicting pain and shame on the defenseless. Due to the stigma of rape many victimized women committed suicide or had abortions. Survivors were often shunned by their families and a patriarchal society that did not want to deal with their trauma. In patriarchal revenge, women who had collaborated with the Pakistan army suffered a similar fate at the hands of Bangladeshi men.

It has taken decades to exhume the tragedies of violence against women in war, most notably Japan's comfort women system of sexual slavery that extended across the region. The comfort stations were also rape camps and enslaved women from every territory Japan invaded and "liberated" during its Pan Asian rampage from 1931 to 1945. The perpetrators felt they were acting in the name of the emperor in a holy war and thus any and all actions were justified because he was considered a deity, the chief priest of state Shinto, the animistic religion that became the basis for emperor worship from the late nineteenth century. Tokyo's inadequate efforts to address this issue since it was "exhumed" in the early 1990s have ensured that this horror casts a long shadow over the twenty-first century and divides Japan from the neighbors that suffered most. In Sri Lanka too, rape was used as a weapon of degradation and subjugation by the state security forces targeting the Tamil population during a protracted civil war and Kashmiris living under the sizeable boot of the Indian Army know this abasement all too well.

Rape is a scourge in Asia with the highest rates reported in Papua New Guinea. In terms of crime statistics, data on rapes are only rough indicators because it is everywhere an underreported crime and is defined differently across nations. A 2013 *Lancet* study found that about 11 percent of men in the Asian countries surveyed (Bangladesh, China, Indonesia, Cambodia, Papua New Guinea, and Sri Lanka) admitted to nonpartner rape (Lancet 2013). This ranged from a high of 41 percent in Papua New Guinea to 13 percent in Indonesia, 8 percent in China and Cambodia, 6 percent in Sri Lanka, and 4.3 percent in Bangladesh. Reports of male rape of men are less common, with 3 percent of respondents across the region reporting having done so, but as with the entire study it is important to bear in mind that the data are based on self-reporting and therefore should be interpreted with caution.

Based on international data, India does not appear to be a high-risk country for rape, about 1.8 per 100,000, the lowest in South Asia and significantly lower than in the United States (27.3) and United Kingdom (17). In Asia, India also compares favorably to Pakistan (28), South Korea (13.8), the Philippines (6.3), and Thailand (6.7), while Japan (1) is lowest in Asia (among nations for which data are available). What these statistics signify is hard to tell because Sweden, one of the most gender-sensitive nations in the world, has an astounding rate of 63.5, suggesting that definitions of rape and reporting vary widely. India records some 40,000 rapes a year, somewhat higher than China's 32,000 and less than half the United Kingdom's 85,000 cases in a country with 65 million people versus India's 1.3 billion. It is important to emphasize that rape is underreported everywhere, but this may not be equally so and depends greatly on the institutional support for rape victims.

Such reassuring comparisons do not refute the fact that India has a severe rape problem as media reports of horrific sex crimes appear with stunning and numbing regularity. Amartya Sen, the Nobel Prize–winning Indian economist, argues, "High frequency of rape may not be the real issue in India, but all the evidence suggests that India has a huge problem in seriously monitoring rape and taking steps to reduce it. The failure of the police to help rape victims and to ensure the safety of women is particularly lamentable" (Sen 2013). He also draws attention to huge regional differences as New Delhi has a rape rate nine times higher than in Calcutta, a gap that he doesn't attribute to greater efficiency in data collection.

India's domestic media has brought into sharper focus the nation's rape problem after a particularly grisly rape on a New Delhi bus in 2012. Since then society has taken notice and registered moral outrage at something that was not new or uncommon. Sen notes how class and caste influenced the public reaction to this woman's rape: "It was easier for the Indian middle classes, including the educated middle classes, to take an immediate interest in the predicament of a young medical student than it would have been in the case of a rape of a poor and socially distant Dalit woman" (Sen 2013).

The veil of silence fell quickly, and what had long been tolerated or quietly endured was seen to be barbaric and out of touch with contemporary norms. Politicians, prosecutors, and police scrambled to adapt to the new climate of intolerance toward rape and the insensitivity toward victims that had prevailed. Globally too, the media took notice, tarnishing India's image and heightening safety concerns about travel there. Apparently even nuns are at risk as the Vatican acknowledged in 2019 that local Catholic priests had been sexually abusing them, a betrayal of their vows, the sisters, and parishioners.

Pakistani Raza Habib Raja draws attention to the "culture of rape" in South Asia that is based on patriarchal misogyny (Raja 2014). He asserts that rape is especially stigmatized in South Asia "due to linkage of women's chastity with family honor. The linkage in turn promotes silence from the victim and her family as rape if it becomes known would bring 'dishonor' to the family." As a result, "The tendency to remain silent actually encourages rapists as it removes fear of any retribution." He also argues that there is a tendency to blame the victim, to insinuate that the victim had been careless or provocative and in some way is responsible for inciting the rape. This blame the victim attitude is certainly not confined to South Asia, but the author thinks that this recasting of victims into culprits is especially intense there and reinforces patriarchal assumptions that influence the work of the police and the judiciary.

Sen has examined crime statistics and gender birth ratios, finding a striking correlation between incidence of rape and areas in India where "boy preference" sexual selection by parents has created an excess of males (Sen 2013). Where rape rates are highest—the northern and western states—so too is selective abortion of female fetuses while lower rates for both are common in the south and east of India. What explains this significant geographical correlation? Sen provides no answer about causality, but it is interesting that the northern and western states also have the greatest incidence of communal violence and overlap the BJP's "homeland" of Hindu chauvinism.

Is the high incidence of rape due to the gender imbalance, that is, less women, more rape? The logic here is that sex-selective termination of pregnancies means that there are too few women, meaning that desperate men resort to rape to satisfy their urges. But China has an even worse sex ratio and there is no evidence of the ghastly sex crimes reported with such frequency as in India. The "excess" number of men in China is thirty-four million while in India it is thirty-seven million. In both countries the shortage of brides threatens the traditional masculine role in terms of maintaining the family bloodline and the failure to get married is socially marginalizing (Denyer and Gowen 2018). Aside from igniting a crisis of masculinity, there is concern that the shortage of women could lead some men to embrace socially regressive behavior including rape to "prove" their manhood, while others sink into depression and loneliness due to the stigma and social ridicule. This situation can lead desperate families to engage in sex trafficking, abduction. and child marriages in which the brides' interests are a low priority.

A Chinese informant cautions against drawing conclusions from available data, questioning the accuracy of reporting. She also thinks rapid urbanization is making a big difference because "cities in China are incredibly safer compared to many other cities in the world. This is due to: 1. larger police presence on the street 2. tighter security control. e.g. no guns, all subways requiring security check etc. Rape cases happen in rural areas but of course they rarely make it into national news." She explains that "young people born in rural areas mostly go to urban cities to look for employment opportunities. I am not just talking about Beijing or Shanghai but about provincial capitals in each and every province. They are developing incredibly fast with all the security controls as seen in Beijing. Given that the majority of aimless young males leave, I imagine rape cases in rural areas probably would not be as much. Of course, the 'leftover' male might still resort to rape, but this is rarely reported." She adds, "I personally do not think censorship plays a huge role. Rape incidents, as long as they are isolated, are not a concern for the state as long as no one digs out the systematic reasons behind (such pathologies). The state fears collective action the most, individual cases, no matter how brutal, are manageable unfortunately" (personal communication January 2018).

Perhaps India has reached a turning point as outrage has translated into harsher penalties. But then again, maybe not. Brand India has been indelibly sullied by reports that 40 percent of the over forty thousand rapes a year involve girls less than seventeen years of age, probably representing the tip of the iceberg given the stigmatization, threats, and violence faced by anyone filing a police complaint. Because only 3 percent of prosecuted rape cases end up with a conviction, there is little fear among rapists that they will be punished for their actions. The gruesome gang rape, torture, and murder of a student on a bus in New Delhi in 2012 galvanized public opinion in support of stronger state action to quell the plague by dealing with rapists more harshly and expeditiously, but this has had little impact on the number of sex crimes in India. The collective handwringing and judicial reforms have proven ineffective in stemming sexual violence. The relatively high percentage of young men in India is a contributing factor and involuntary celibacy among them may indeed be a factor, but caste and patriarchy contribute to a deeply misogynistic and conflicted culture that venerates goddesses and mothers while desecrating their daughters. In rural areas, landlords have long acted with impunity and view local women from the purview of their seigniorial rights. Those below are there to serve those above and resistance or efforts to hold the powerful accountable are seen through the prism of caste entitlement. Local police are often complicit, siding with the powerful against their victims, ignoring crimes, destroying evidence, and otherwise perverting the course of justice.

In traditional societies across Asia, empowerment of women has generated a backlash by men threatened by challenges to the patriarchal order. Rape is about imposing, controlling, and submission. It is also a weapon in India's culture wars between traditional norms and a modern emancipated India and also between Hindutva zealots and religious minorities. Rape often involves the powerful preying on the weak, knowing the system is tilted in their favor. In the context of the Hindu caste system, perpetrators from the top echelons enjoy considerable impunity while those from lower castes are more vulnerable to vigilante justice as the slow wheels of justice test the patience of the entitled who seek retribution as a means to regain dignity. In some cases, rape can involve the abject lording it over the wretched, as those with little vent their frustrations on those with less who are weaker and seen as competitors.

An Indian friend posted this on her Facebook page in April 2018: "A child was raped. In a temple. She was out grazing her horse. They denied her broken body a burial. In a graveyard. Because the bodies of dead Muslims encroach the land of Hindus. Turn out the lights. Shut down the press. Stay home in this unfathomable darkness and mourn the India we have lost forever." She was reacting to the gruesome gang raping of eight-year-old Asifa Bano in the state of Jammu Kashmir in January 2018. She was found with broken legs, a smashed skull, and signs of torture. The accused rapists were a retired government official, four police officers, one of their juvenile relatives, and the temple custodian. BJP politicians intervened to protest the arrest of the rapists while lawyers tried to prevent a filing of charges. Asifa belongs to a nomadic Muslim herding community that local Hindus resent for grazing in their area. There is speculation that the Hindu villagers sought to intimidate the nomads into leaving by raping and murdering the child. After luring her away from grazing the horses they confined her in a temple for several days and drugged her during the tawdry ordeal until they strangled her to death and smashed her skull with a stone, all within the confines of a sacred religious space. Lawyers for the defendants argued that "they are encroaching our forests and water resources" as if that justified the rape and murder of a child. And the agony was compounded by Hindu right-wing activists who prevented the family from burying the girl in a local cemetery plot owned by the nomads, threatening them with violence if they persisted.

In the state of Jammu Kashmir where Indian troops have slaughtered more than seventy thousand Kashmiri Muslims during their longstanding occupation, raping many of them first and torturing countless more, fear of violence and reprisals runs high. In this context of military death squads and indignities, any conflict between Hindus and Muslims in the state, especially such a barbaric crime against a child, stirs communal tensions. Mainstream Indian reporting about Kashmir is also usually tentative as government concerns about "national security" often trump awkward truths and cases like this involve the sensitive issue of religious honor. The tragedy of Asifa's rape and murder, however, became more than a religious flashpoint, evolving into a national political battle over identity between Hindutva fanatics outraged that "victimized" Hindus were being held accountable for crimes against "people who don't matter" versus India's liberal elite and middle classes.

In the end, the family carried her mangled body seven miles to another village to bury her. This sordid saga held a mirror up to relatively privileged Indians and they did not like what they saw, something all too familiar, a scourge of rapes in which perpetrators don't fear accountability if they are more powerful and better connected than the victims. This thuggery intruded on the more uplifting images of a rising India powered by the recrudescent nationalism embraced by the BJP that never misses a chance to blame Congress and its latte-sipping "libtards," "sickularists," and "chattering classes" for all of India's ills. The media and protestors vented anger against the BJP and the shame of a government that has been overly tolerant of Hindu vigilantism and derelict in protecting minorities and the underprivileged, but the BJPs base remains loyal.

In Modi's India, communal tensions have escalated and vigilantes feel emboldened by a government that averts its eye from the savagery of its core supporters. Pratap Bhanu Mehta, a respected academic and columnist, lamented that "India's moral compass has been completely obliterated, carpet-bombed out of existence by the very custodians of law, morality and virtue who give daily sermons on national pride" (Mehta 2018a). He also condemned "the instrumental use of brutal violence against children to terrorise communities, and to turn perpetrators into victims." Dr. Visvanathan, a Delhi-based social scientist, lamented to the BBC, "Everyone is complicit—we the people, media, politicians. There's no concept of human rights anymore. There are Hindu rights and Muslim rights. Our loyalties are now to religion, caste, groups and clubs" (Biswas 2018). In Modi's India, such violence incites outrage, indignation, and "whataboutery" that flares and then fades until the next outrage. Dr. Visvanathan explains, "Our reactions veer from silence to indifference to hysteria. Then we go back to sleep and wake up again to react to the latest incident of outrage." Sadly, as Pratap Bhanu Mehta writes, "Like so much expression of outrage in India, it will be more about satiating our conscience than about staring the enormity of evil in the face. It is an evil that, whether we like it or not, we have authorised and let pass" (Mehta 2018a).

In commenting on the rape and murder of Asifa, Bangladeshi author Taslima Nasrin blogged that focusing on religion is misleading: "Had the girl been a Hindu and not a Muslim, perhaps those men would have captured, imprisoned, raped, and finally killed her in exactly the same way. Both the poor and the rich know that killing the poor usually reduces the chances of trouble. I don't believe that those men would have allowed the girl to walk on unscathed in the jungle had she been a Hindu. A rape takes place in India every 14 minutes. Hindu men rape Hindu women every day. They don't spare anyone, from old women to one-year-old children. Muslim men rape in the same way. They don't spare any women of any age." She adds, "Those who rape are usually not interested in the name, address and religion of those they are raping. They're only concerned with the body. The more tender it is, the more delicious" (Nasrin 2018). In her view, rape is not about religion, class, or caste but rather a crime of opportunity rooted in misogynistic norms and macho values. She writes, "Rape is muscle power, male power, penis power. The bottomline: the act of putting a crown on, or flying the flag of victory from, the bald head of the male organ is also known as rape." Referring to the rape of an eighteen-year-old Dalit by an BJP Rajput politician in

Uttar Pradesh, Taslima argues, "it is not caste but hatred for women, the notion that women are of a lower class."

Vulnerability + patriarchy + misogyny + impunity are thus the roots of India's rape crisis, meaning that tougher sentencing is unlikely to make much of a dent in the rape every fourteen minutes status quo. Reading a May 2018 article about a foreign tourist who was drugged, raped, and beheaded in Kerala, I came across references to a cluster of other horrors including a sixteen-year-old girl who committed suicide after being gang raped by eight men in the northern state of Haryana and a nineteen-year-old woman in the same state who was raped by five men, including the driver of the autorickshaw she hailed. And then there was the case of two men who were arrested for murdering a sixteen-year-old by burning her alive and beating her parents. This was in retaliation for her reporting a rape that involved the two men to the local village elders' council. These councils have no legal powers but are often involved in settling local disputes to bypass the slow-moving and costly judicial process. The men were sentenced to a regime of pushups and ordered to pay about $750 in compensation. Enraged that she sought to hold them accountable, the men exacted deadly revenge. A few days later in the same eastern state of Jharkhand another teenager was raped and set on fire, with burns covering 95 percent of her body. In this case, the perpetrator said the girl spurned his offer of marriage, saying she wasn't ready, so he later attacked her when she was alone.

This string of violent sexual assaults came less than a month after the cabinet issued an executive order approving the death penalty for the rape of girls younger than twelve in response to the brutal rape and murder of eight-year-old Asifa and the doubling of reported rapes of children in the past five years, numbering some five thousand. In addition, the minimum prison term for other female rapes has been lengthened from seven to ten years, with provision for life imprisonment. Registered cases of sexual violence have also been steadily rising since the fatal gang rape on a bus in New Delhi in 2012, perhaps because women feel the public climate is somewhat more supportive of rape victims, bolstered by media coverage and street protests. Less charitably, the BJP bears some responsibility for the rape surge due to a climate that is more supportive of zealots railing against the decline of traditional values and norms that seeks to put women and castes back into their "proper" places. Similar passions endanger other vulnerable groups.

ASIA'S HOMOPHOBIA

A 2013 Pew survey on sexual attitudes reveals a relatively high level of intolerance toward same-sex relations in Asia. In North America, Europe, and much of Latin America there is a broad acceptance of homosexuality, while this is not the case in Africa or in predominantly Muslim nations. South Korea is the sole Asian nation where Pew found a significant increase in tolerance of homosexuality over the past decade. Overall, Pew correlates the degree of religiosity and wealth with attitudes toward homosexuality with richer and more secular being more tolerant. It finds that "there is far less acceptance of homosexuality in countries where religion is central to people's lives—measured by whether they consider religion to be very important, whether they believe it is necessary to believe in God in order to be moral, and whether they pray at least once a day" (Pew 2013a).

In Asia, views of homosexuality vary as a majority think it is acceptable in the Philippines (73 percent) and Japan (54 percent) while in South Korea (39 percent) and China (21 percent) there is considerably less support. Given the high level of religiosity in the Philippines, strong acceptance of homosexuality marks it apart from other nations where religion is central to people's lives. Overall, women tend to be more tolerant than men and the young more than their elders. In Japan, 83 percent of those younger than thirty say homosexuality should be accepted, compared with just 39 percent of those fifty and older. Similarly, 71 percent of younger South Koreans accept homosexuality but just 16 percent of those fifty or older do so. For those aged eighteen to twenty-nine, Pakistan (2 percent), Indonesia (4 percent), and Malaysia (7 percent), all Muslim majority nations, rank lowest in tolerance toward homosexuality among the Asian nations surveyed. In the same nations, the over fifty-year-old cohort is even less tolerant.

Clearly, the LGBT community confronts inhospitable attitudes in Asia due to religious sentiments. In the 2013 survey on Muslims, the Pew Foundation (2013b) found that clear majorities in Muslim majority nations believe that certain behavior like drinking alcohol, homosexuality, prostitution, suicide, or having sex outside of marriage are unacceptable and immoral. In Southeast Asia, 95 percent believe that homosexuality is morally wrong, and 94 percent condemn sex outside marriage as immoral while the corresponding figures in South Asia are 79 percent and 87 percent. Western popular culture is seen as a threat by 51 percent in Southeast Asia versus 59 percent in South Asia. In South Asia (61 percent) there is considerably more concern about the compatibility of modern society and leading a religiously devout life as a Muslim than in Southeast Asia (36 percent).

A more recent International Lesbian, Gay, Bisexual, Trans, and Intersex Association (ILGA) survey found that 32 percent of regional respondents saw a conflict between their religious beliefs and same-sex desire (ILGA 2016). The survey report concludes that "no matter how insistently the voices representing organized religions condemn same sex relationships, huge swathes of the populations see no conflict between those religious beliefs and same sex desire. This suggests that anti-LGBT rationales based on religious dogmas are often given disproportionate focus." The national tallies are in-

structive about the need to refrain from sweeping generalizations about Asia
as conflict between religious beliefs and same-sex desire ranged from 9
percent in Japan, 12 percent in China, 20 percent in Vietnam, and 25 percent
in India to 41 percent in Malaysia, 43 percent in the Philippines, 44 percent
in Pakistan, and 51 percent in Indonesia.

Asked if human rights protections should apply to everyone equally regardless of sexual identity, combining the strongly agree with the somewhat
agree versus the somewhat disagree and strongly disagree the 2016 ILGA
survey yields the results shown in table 9.1.

Table 9.1.   Human Rights Protections Apply to Everyone?

Nation	Yes	No
Malaysia	55%	21%
Japan	59%	17%
India	69%	15%
Indonesia	57%	26%
Vietnam	72%	14%
Pakistan	69%	17%
Philippines	72%	13%
China	53%	15%

Source: ILGA 2016 Survey.

These results suggest that concern about protecting the human rights of the
LGBT community is well entrenched across the region. It is also indicative
that those who strongly agree that being LGBT should be a crime constitute a
minority in Asia: 5 percent in Japan, 11 percent in Vietnam, 12 percent in
China, 13 percent in the Philippines, 21 percent in India, 24 percent in Malaysia, 27 percent in Indonesia, and 41 percent in Pakistan. These findings
indicate that homophobia in Asia is not especially virulent and that support
for criminalizing the LGBT community is weak despite religious sentiments.
Although the ILGA survey provides some encouragement, the more negative
assessment in the Pew poll barometer of attitudes about the LGBT community in contemporary Asia suggests that discrimination remains deeply entrenched while tolerance appears to be ebbing.

FADING TOLERANCE?

Hostility toward sexual minorities is not new to Asia, but the decline in
tolerance toward them is. The LGBT movement has become a threat to
traditional, conservative lifestyles based on patriarchy and is often portrayed
as a Trojan horse sent by the West to undermine ostensibly longstanding

norms and values. Asia, however, has a rich tradition of homosexuality and exceptional tolerance of what is now deemed by some as deviant sexuality. The colonial encounter and imperialism certainly had an impact on stigmatizing such sexuality with the British criminalizing in 1861 "acts against the order of nature" that encompassed oral and anal sex, rendering nonvaginal sex illegal. The target was homosexuality, setting a precedent allowing the state to intervene in sexual relations, a legacy that yet lingers in the penal code of the former colonies and has become embedded in what are portrayed as "traditional" values and norms.

INDONESIA

In 1984 I arrived in Jakarta as a Fulbright Fellow to conduct fieldwork and archival research on Indonesia's colonial history. While living in Pasar Blora in central Jakarta I met a number of my young male neighbors who were sex workers in a nearby notorious park. "Waria" is the term used to refer to transsexuals, cross-dressers, and transgenders in Indonesia and they were not usually closeted and mostly lived flamboyantly, seeming to enjoy a degree of tolerance and acceptance. Often they teasingly called each other banci (tranny), but I never heard anyone expressing homophobic views and I was told that in Indonesia people understood that men and women have spirits that sometimes go one way or the other, but this natural state was not subject to condemnation. In my neighborhood I would see the waria transform themselves from their stubble with kretek cigarette hanging out morning look to glamorous streetwalker persona as they prepared for work. They tended to stand out from the other streetwalkers due to their height and beauty and were in high demand, apparently even during Ramadan, the month of fasting for Muslims when they typically refrain from sex. But in those days Indonesian Islam was more relaxed while piety was left to individual choice and discretion. Aging waria who no longer could make ends meet from trysts often joined in wandering minstrel bands that would busk along alleys busy with open air eateries, often paid to leave diners in peace. Even in late 1990s post–New Order Malang, a provincial town in eastern Java, the waria were quite public and numerous and being gay didn't seem all that stigmatized. Thus, I was taken aback by poll results that 90 percent of Indonesians now believe that LGBT represents a threat and that same-sex relations were not permitted according to their religion. In twenty-first-century Indonesia, Islamic hardliners have shifted public discourse on LGBT issues toward intolerance and managed to stigmatize what had previously been widely tolerated. Even gay emojis and stickers were banned in 2016 on messaging apps like LINE, Whatsapp, Facebook, and Twitter because the government believes that depictions of same-sex couples holding hands and the rainbow flag transgress social norms and religious values.

In 2014 the Indonesia Ulama Council (MUI) issued a fatwa banning LGBT in Indonesia and proclaimed it was a crime punishable by death (although capital punishment is not sanctioned by the government). This fatwa has increased the discrimination and risks that the LGBT community faces because it is a religious edict issued by a government-authorized council and is therefore taken to be the official mainstream view even if it violates the civil and human rights of Indonesia's LGBT people. A respected Islamic scholar Khaled M. Abou El-Fadl opposes this trend, arguing for a "version of Islam, which is progressive, and respecting of the human rights of marginalized groups . . . rather than a bigoted version of Islam which diminishes and admonishes the basic human rights of LGBT individuals in the name of religion" (Sa'dan 2016, 30). Khaled, known for his criticism of Arabization and puritanical Wahhabi influences, argues that promoting human rights is a way to save Islam from "dishonor." He maintains that the ostensible gap between shariah and human rights is more about politics than religion and emphasizes the common ground of "parallel basic principles of freedom, justice, and equality" (35). In doing so he seeks to expose how Islam has been appropriated as a "tool for dogma" and stresses the need for breaking down the "thick wall that separates humans because of their different sexualities," arguing that the fatwa has "created a gulf that separates God from his creation" (37). This argument doesn't appear to have swayed hardline clerics in search of targets.

In recent years the media has reported about the IDF in Indonesia taking matters into its own hands, smashing up bars and nightclubs and imposing a more puritan morality. The influence is evident in bans on alcohol sales, the closure of red-light districts, police raids on gay saunas, attacks against LGBT activists and waria, and even public canings of homosexuals in conservative Aceh. It is the only province in Indonesia allowed to enact shariah bylaws, including one hundred lashes of the cane for those found guilty of homosexuality. In 2018 a dozen waria beauticians were arrested by police in Aceh and publicly humiliated as police cut off their hair, stripped, and beat them, forced them to change into men's clothing, and then subjected them to improvised gender reeducation by making them do calisthenics and speak in low voices.

Hate speech targeting the LGBT community has proliferated and social media spreads messages about cleansing society of gays, lesbians, and waria, sending a chilling message to sexual minorities and those who try to defend their human rights. These human rights defenders working for civil society organizations are often subject to vilification on the social media postings of Islamic groups that go viral, subjecting them to online intimidation and defamation that has led to physical abuse and violence (Frontline Defenders

2017). They and those they defend are a vulnerable target for religious zealots emboldened by the 2015 fatwa condemning homosexuality and cheerleading by government officials and politicians, some of whom are reluctant to stand up for LGBT people for fear of a public backlash. The IDF and likeminded groups committed to eradicate LGBT connect on social media and gather after Friday prayers at mosques, clearly enjoying the imprimatur of clerics. They engage in violent raids of LGBT gatherings and subject community leaders and their families to frequent threats of violence. The police are complicit in this harassment. In 2017 there were over three hundred arrests for deviant sexuality and in a notorious 2017 Jakarta raid the police forced prisoners arrested at a sauna to parade naked, videotaped them, and then surreptitiously posted it online. The police then arrested some of those in the video on pornography charges.

In a November 2017 article titled "Don't Punish Love," *Tempo* magazine took a stand against intolerance and the clerics who promote it. They cited recent cases of vigilante justice when locals in one case dragged an unmarried couple out of their rooms, stripped and paraded them in public, and forced them to admit their crimes. The vigilantes videotaped the incident and then posted it online. It speaks volumes about the climate of fear that prevails in contemporary Indonesia that *Tempo* endorsing the rule of law counts as bold, but the wrath of the mob incited by religious clerics has intimidated citizens and emboldened vigilantes to take matters into their own hands while trampling on laws and constitutional rights. These clerics promote "the concept of 'the law prevailing in the community' as the determinant of whether someone can be charged with a crime. This phrase of 'the law prevailing in the community' is inconsistent with the universal basis of the law that all regulations on crime must be available in written form. No one ought to be convicted of a crime purely on the basis of 'habitual' law. Such a regulation would actually foster vigilantism" (Tempo 2017).

At the end of 2017, following lengthy hearings that began in 2016, the Constitutional Court narrowly ruled 5–4 against an amendment to the Indonesian Criminal Code to revise Article 284 on adultery, currently restricted to a married man or women engaging in sexual relations with a person who is not his or her spouse. The MUI and other religious advocates sought to extend the scope of the law to criminalize all sexual relations that occur outside of marriage. The National Commission on Violence against Women and other human rights activists argued that doing so would make it more difficult for rape victims to press charges, would penalize sexually active teenagers, put religious minorities at risk, and outlaw all LGBT sexual relations. Opponents of the revision invoked scientific arguments and civil liberties, citing the notorious 2010 case of a woman gang raped by eight men in Aceh who was then publicly caned for committing adultery.

The Constitutional Court ruled that amending the law was a matter for Parliament. Jokowi has appointed moderates to the court during his term ensuring that it is a voice for tolerance in a nation where religious zealots have promoted intolerance toward sexual and religious minorities. Nonetheless, the LGBT community remains vulnerable to prosecution under the nation's pornography law, which has been used to criminalize same-sex relations. And they are subject to homophobia whipped up by clerics leveraging social media in their campaign of persecution.

These proponents of persecution and intolerance did as the court suggested and in 2018 managed to get new legislation passed in the Parliament that criminalizes same-sex relations, bans extramarital sex, stipulates harsher penalties for blasphemy, and criminalizes criticism of the president and parliamentarians. They took advantage of impending local and national elections to pressure lawmakers to enact the legislation, making it difficult for anyone to oppose lest they suffer at the ballot box. As Jun Honna at Ritsumeikan University in Kyoto explains, "The war on blasphemy, the war on LGBT and the war on drugs are now the cheapest political tools to mobilize votes in democratic elections in Indonesia" (personal communication August 2018). This crackdown on the LGBT community is ironic given that the national motto is "Unity in Diversity." The 2018 legislation is a victory for these forces of intolerance and vigilantism that is certain to end up on the Constitutional Court's docket. This backsliding on civil liberties and democratic freedoms in the context of election politics is a troubling barometer for Indonesia and forces reconsideration of its democratic identity. Enforcing the ban would overwhelm Indonesia's already overcrowded prisons, one of the results of Jokowi's crack down on drugs.

MALAYSIA

The situation facing the LGBT community in Malaysia is also hostile. Former prime minister Najib Razak reiterated time and again that Malaysia would not defend LGBT rights and in 2018 he compared the gay community to IS, calling both a threat to Islam. Homosexuality is illegal as the former British colony has retained the colonial-era Section 377 in the penal code. This means that same-sex sexual activity and other "deviant" sexual behaviors "against the order of nature" are subject to prosecution, with guilty verdicts carrying a sentence of whipping and a maximum prison term of twenty years.

The most infamous Section 377 case involved the "sodomy trials" of Malaysian opposition leader Anwar Ibrahim. He had a falling out with his former mentor Prime Minister Dr. Mohammed Mahathir in 1998 when he was finance minister and deputy prime minister. He went from being groomed as a successor to imprisonment and being banned from politics over allegations of having sex with a male aide. Having exhausted all avenues of appeal, Ibrahim began serving a five-year prison sentence in 2015. He argued that he was the victim of a political witch hunt and that the charges were trumped up to sideline him. Given the slim evidence and dubious testimony, many Malaysians agreed and in 2018, in one of the most dramatic upheavals in postindependence Malaysia, the ruling Barisan Nasional Front coalition headed by Razak was unexpectedly ousted by a political coalition led by Dr. Mahathir, a then spry ninety-two year old who pledged to secure a royal pardon for Ibrahim and eventually hand him the reins of power. From mentor to persecutor to handmaiden, Mahathir has made amends, inadequate as they may seem. After all, Anwar paid a very high price in terms of his freedom, family life, and public humiliation.

For Malaysia's LGBT community, bullying in schools, discrimination in the workplace, exposure to violence, and limited access to health care are some of the many remaining challenges. A 2014 Human Rights Watch report described the many abuses trans women face, including "arbitrary arrest, physical and sexual assault, imprisonment, discriminatory denial of health care and employment" (HRW 2014). The rising tide of Arabization has created a more dangerous environment of intolerance in a nation where "cross-dressing" laws remain in force and are actively used to target transgender people.

SINGAPORE

In April 2013 the Singapore High Court rejected a petition to repeal a colonial-era British law criminalizing sex between men; although never enforced, acts of "gross indecency"—what a phrase—can be punished by up to two years in prison. Every June, there is a Pink Dot event held in the usually buttoned-down city-state to promote gay rights that once attracted as many as twenty thousand people. Though Singapore has tried to loosen up over the past decade or so, managing to shed its puritan image with some success, gays want more. The city-state, however, wants less and now limits access to the Pink Dot celebrations to those who hold the island's national identity card, thus barring tourists from attending.

THAILAND

Thailand perhaps has the most welcoming image for the LGBT community as kathoey (ladyboy) bars are abundant and there doesn't seem to be significant official prejudice. It markets itself as a pink destination catering to the queer market. Although there is no overt persecution of the LGBT community, the social stigma of homosexuality is considerable, especially within the family. Buddhist temples run programs to "cure" teenagers of their "affliction" and make them more "manly," reflecting paternal concerns that their children will be treated like freaks of nature. A Kon Thai Foundation survey found that 50 percent of Thais believe that homosexuality is wrong, and gays tend to be marginalized. In the absence of legal protection, they are subject to discrimination. It's a curious situation that gays can live openly but find little social acceptance. In 2015, however, a Gender Equality Act was enacted that prohibits discrimination against someone "of a different appearance from his/her own sex by birth." This is the first Southeast Asian government that prohibits discrimination on the grounds of gender expression. The challenge will be to translate this pioneering law into changed attitudes and social norms in schools, the workplace, and at home. One-third of LGBT high school students suffer physical abuse by other students compared to 17 percent in the United States, while many also report verbal abuse by family members.

According to a UNDP, USAID report, "The history of homosexuality and transgender behaviours in Thailand has led to a complex and contradictory situation with the outward appearance of acceptance, and higher visibility of transgender people than in most countries, but with hostility and prejudice towards LGBT people, as well as institutionalized discrimination, still prevalent" (2014a). Moreover, LGBT people live within a society with strong pressure to be a good citizen and be filial to one's family. This is compounded with the notion that one's sexuality or gender must not go against accepted norms and should not bring shame to one's self and family. Sodomy was decriminalized in 1956, however, and the government no longer considers homosexuality a mental illness. Transgenders are not allowed to do military service as biological males are required to do, but since 2011 they are barred based on Gender Identity Disorder instead of Permanent Mental Disorder, a change that LGBT groups lobbied for.

Most Thais are Theravada Buddhists, a religion with "negative views of sexual orientation and gender identity that does not conform to social norms, viewing it either as a punishment for sins in past lives, or as a lack of ability to control sexual impulses and tendencies" (UNDP, USAID 2014a). This survey found that transgender people suffer significant employment discrimination and are relegated to working in hospitality, entertainment, or the sex work industry. Furthermore, lack of relationship recognition also leads to same-sex couples having unequal status to heterosexual couples in areas such as the ability to access social services, spousal insurance and benefits, and joint bank loans. Thai media generally portrays LGBT people in a negative way or as stock characters of comic relief on television shows. The study concludes that "while there is some appearance of acceptance for LGBT persons in Thai society, many face discrimination from family, education, media, legal, government, economic and religious structures, institutions and establishments."

MYANMAR

In 2013 Aung San Suu Kyi, as the opposition leader in Myanmar, advocated in favor of legalizing homosexuality, arguing that institutionalized discrimination was depriving many of necessary health care and thus worsening the HIV/AIDs epidemic. True but somewhat misleading. In arguing for greater compassion, she invoked a sexually transmitted disease, perhaps useful in terms of persuading a conservative society that discrimination is counterproductive, but such scaremongering also reinforces negative stereotypes about gays. Shared needles by drug users and rampant unprotected sex in the burgeoning sex industry are more important factors in Myanmar's HIV/AIDs crisis. Decriminalizing homosexuality is difficult in a conservative society in which many frown on open discussion of sex or promoting sex education. It is a Buddhist society in which sexual orientation is seen as karmic fate. For those who commit adultery, being reborn as LGBT is seen by some Buddhists as an appropriate karmic "punishment" because they are the object of lifelong mockery and discrimination. Alas, the police often subject LGBT people to extortion, abuses, and violence. As a former British colony, the notorious Section 377 is in the penal code, giving the police license to harass. There is social space for LGBT in Burmese tradition as nat kadaw (spirit mediums), but the signs are mixed and advocacy organizations like Color Rainbow report limited progress in gaining acceptance and legal protections. But as Myanmar transitions toward democracy, LGBT activists have leveraged a more vibrant human rights discourse into a spirited LGBT rights movement. This has empowered queer Burmese to advocate for reforms and inclusion while also promoting greater self-acceptance (Chua 2018). Perhaps the first ever rainbow-splashed pride boat parade in 2019, part of Yangon's fifth LGBT festival, is a harbinger of change.

PHILIPPINES

Although 80 percent of Filipinos are Roman Catholic, and the Church's conservative stand on social issues is influential, the Philippines might be the most tolerant Southeast Asian nation toward the LGBT community. Yet it also has the worst record in the region for violence targeting the trans community; 41 transgender people were murdered in the Philippines between 2008 and 2016, more than anywhere else in Southeast Asia. Bear in mind it also has the highest overall murder rate in the region by far.

As the 2013 Pew survey notes, over 70 percent of Filipinos are okay with homosexuality, but this high level of tolerance doesn't translate into acceptance. Gays are all too familiar with discrimination, abuse, and violence and suffer discrimination in the job market, education, health care, and housing. Too often they are also shunned by their families. Back in 2009, however, the Philippines lifted a ban that had prevented openly gay and bisexual men and women from serving in the military. Despite his Dirty Harry tough guy image, President Rodrigo Duterte is sympathetic to same-sex marriage, yet another issue on which he is at odds with the Church.

There are no laws criminalizing homosexuality and in 2017 lawmakers in the House of Representatives unanimously passed a law that prohibits bias on the basis of sexual orientation, gender identity, or expression. It also adopted a civil partnership bill that grants gay and transgender couples the same legal rights as heterosexual married couples. However, the bill stalled in the Senate due to the maneuverings of evangelical Christian lawmakers and the lack of strong leadership in support of the legislation. Although there are local ordinances that ban bias based on gender identity, almost all of them lack the force of law.

Many pious Filipino Catholics ignore the Church's conservative stand on birth control and most support Duterte's war on drugs that relies on extra-judicial killings despite strong Church opposition, so people are accustomed to living with contradictions between religious mores, lifestyles, and private choices. Pope Francis has given Catholic LGBT people around the world a sense of acceptance even if it is not explicit. Yet the Church's stand against same-sex marriage impedes legal reform, meaning that gay partners lack the basic rights accorded to heterosexual couples including inheritance, pensions, and medical and burial decisions in addition to hospital and prison visitations. They also cannot adopt children. The mainstream media contributes to LGBT marginalization through sensational coverage of LGBT events, stereotyping gay men, virtually ignoring lesbians and transgender people, and implicitly promoting transphobia and homophobia. Overcoming this situation will remain difficult until the Church abandons its opposition and that seems unlikely.

NORTHEAST ASIA

Taiwan

Taiwan is one of the most LGBT-friendly societies in Asia, with an active gay community and possibly the largest annual gay pride parade in the region, attracting tens of thousands of sashaying revelers in colorful and wild outfits. Many are tourists from around the region who enjoy the taste of freedom denied at home. In 2019 Taiwan finally became the first Asian nation to legalize same-sex marriage, a much-anticipated outcome due to the 2016 election of Tsai Ing-wen as president, the island's first female leader who heads the Democratic Progressive Party. During her election campaign she stopped short of making promises about same-sex marriage but her reformist zeal in contrast to the traditionalist Kuomintang raised expectations of sweeping changes that appeal to younger voters. Perhaps too much so as she and her party got bogged down in fighting simultaneous battles on labor and judicial and pension reforms, in addition to transitional justice initiatives. In December 2016, polls showed Taiwan to be almost evenly divided over same-sex marriage. Even though Christians represent less than 5 percent of the population, they are a cohesive political force that spearheaded opposition, staging mass rallies, and mounting a nationwide campaign that resonated with older voters across the political divide to thwart the LGBT agenda.

Jennifer Lu at Taiwan Tongzhi Hotline Association, an advocacy group for LGBT rights, argues, "marriage equality is not just a matter for gay and lesbian people, but also an important reflection of Taiwan's democratic values and of a society that respects diversity" (interview December 2016). According to Professor Rwei-ren Wu from Academia Sinica in Taipei, this is not only an issue that divides generations but also represents "Taiwan's first culture war" (interview December 2016). In his opinion, Taiwan is a "pariah state," increasingly isolated due to the pervasive "one China" policy that leaves it in global purgatory. It is therefore important, he argues, that Taiwan embraces a progressive liberal agenda to build bridges and win friends with liberal democracies. Thus, mainstream support for LGBT rights is much more than a battle for justice and equality at home: It is an effort to project a modern, cosmopolitan image that sharpens the distinction with China and positions Taiwan as an appealing exemplar of the liberal values, norms, and trends in advanced societies around the world. While almost all of Taiwan's residents have been able to register same-sex partnerships with local governments, these do not provide the same legal rights as marriage. In May 2017 Taiwan's Constitutional Court ruled current laws defining unions as between a man and a woman are invalid and that barring gay couples from marrying violated "the people's freedom of marriage" and "the people's right to equality." The court gave Parliament until May 2019 to revise or enact laws regarding same-sex unions, and thereafter gay couples are automatically allowed to register under the existing legal framework. Taiwan thus reinforced its identity as a beacon for liberalism and human rights, projecting an image that offers a stark contrast to China and much of the rest of Asia where homophobic inclinations remain resilient in public discourse. However, in November 2018 a series of referenda in Taiwan offered a stinging rebuke to this agenda. Voters rejected same-sex marriage and LGBT-inclusive education proposals. The referenda results were not legally binding but certainly cast a shadow over legislative initiatives regarding the 2017 court decision endorsing same-sex unions. Just meeting the court deadline, in May 2019 the legislature passed a same-sex marriage law that grants various legal protections similar to those enjoyed by heterosexual couples but disappointed many in the LGBT community who sought a revision of the civil code. While allowing same-sex couples the right to register their marriages, it limits adoption rights to biological children of a partner and doesn't address issues specific to transnational couples. Even so, the bill represents a significant step forward and victory for the LGBT community.

South Korea

Homosexuality is not illegal, but there are strong filial pressures as elsewhere in East Asia to continue the family bloodline by having children in a heterosexual marriage. Gays and lesbians are also subject to hate crimes and face mockery and discrimination. South Korean lawmakers introduced antidiscrimination laws to protect gay rights in 2007, 2010, and 2013, but retreated in the face of pressure from conservative Christian legislators and their influential constituents who adamantly oppose recognition; Christians make up about one-third of the population.

In 2014 the local Seoul assembly, facing fierce opposition from Christian groups, decided to pull the plug on the city's human rights charter that included a sexual orientation nondiscrimination clause. These groups also promoted a new sex education curriculum that makes no mention of homosexuality, while in 2017 the military ran a sting operation to root out gays in the military. Discriminatory comments about LGBT people by relatively liberal President Moon Jae-in, elected in 2017, indicate how polarizing the issue is in a deeply conservative nation where politicians fear the wrath of Christian voters. No South Korean political party endorses same-sex marriage or the promotion of LGBT rights despite global trends. Public support for LGBT rights remains low and anti-LGBT rallies are consistently larger than pro-LGBT events. But South Korea's eighteenth Korea Queer Culture Festival held in 2017 included officials from the Jogye Order of Korean Buddhism that lent the event establishment influence and prestige in support of social equality and acceptance of sexual minorities. "[The] Buddha has taught us [that] everyone, regardless of his or her sexual orientation, can attain perfect enlightenment. Sexual minorities must not be discriminated against," said Hyo Rok, a senior nun and professor at Seoul University of Buddhism (Agence France-Presse 2017).

There are other signs of change. In 2017 the Supreme Court ordered the government to allow Beyond the Rainbow, an LGBT rights foundation, to register as a charity, endorsing lower court rulings against the Ministry of Justice. Previously the foundation was getting the bureaucratic runaround as agencies kept passing the buck, stating that the charity's activities did not come under their jurisdiction. Denying registration for the foundation prevented the group from accepting tax-deductible donations, and now it can do so and expand the scope of its advocacy and support programs.

The Asan Institute for Policy Studies found a sharp increase in the percentage of respondents claiming to have no reservations about LGBT, 23.7 percent in 2014 compared to 15.8 percent in 2010 (Asan 2015). It reported a similar trend in support of same-sex marriage, increasing from 17 percent in 2010 to 29 percent in 2014 with more than 60 percent in favor among those in their twenties. Thus, time seems to be on the side of LGBT rights in South Korea, but the political sensitivity of the issue and the lack of public empathy or awareness suggests progress will be far slower than advocates hope.

Japan

In late nineteenth-century Japan, Victorian visitors were aghast at mixed public bathing and the ubiquity of carved stone phalluses, and when Japan's modernizing elite became aware of these censorious views it was cause for national embarrassment. A nation trying to modernize and impress discovered that what was considered normal was frowned upon as morally suspect. The rectification campaign did not eliminate mixed public bathing but did start a trend, while most phalluses were removed from public view. It is somewhat ironic now that the city of Kawasaki holds an annual ceremony in which locals parade giant phalluses around town in front of hordes of foreign tourists appreciating this exuberant tradition while licking penis-shaped lollypops, popsicles, and ice cream cones and scooping up keychains and other themed memorabilia.

Japanese society may not actively discriminate against the LGBT community, but it is not very supportive either, embracing the equivalent of a "don't ask, don't tell approach" that concedes social space as long as nobody ostentatiously occupies it. On television, gays are fetishized to reinforce stereotypes, allowed leeway as entertainers but rarely portrayed in a serious manner. Acceptable as long as they amuse.

Tokyo Disneyworld is an odd place to make a political statement, but the theme park now hosts same-sex wedding ceremonies. When a lesbian couple tied the knot there at a commitment ceremony in its Cinderella Castle in 2012, dubbed Japan's first gay wedding, Mickey and Minnie attended as celebrants, all decked out in wedding finery. At first Disneyworld had balked over what is always a critical issue: What to wear? The couple was asked if one of them could wear a dress and the other a tuxedo—but in the end they both got to wear dresses. Given its family-friendly reputation based on predictable banality and mainstream entertainment, Disneyworld's edgy venture into the business of gay weddings is a symbolic victory of sorts even though the government doesn't recognize such unions. Japan may enjoy a vibrant tradition of homosexuality, but polite Japanese society tends to avoid the subject rather than celebrate it.

In recent years, there have been some encouraging signs that Japan is belatedly beginning to embrace diversity—at least when it comes to sexual identity—but so far only small steps have been made. Tokyo's Shibuya Ward in recognizing same-sex partnerships and Disneyworld's catering to such marriages are steps in the right direction, but the conservative national government has provided no leadership on ending discrimination. Small civil society organizations are pitching in, for example, by preparing emergency disaster manuals for non-Japanese in the LGBT community and lobbying government officials and politicians. But as Japan gets ready to host the 2020 Olympics, there is much work to be done to raise awareness and establish programs that meet the needs of Japan's LGBT community—and to ensure that Japan provides a proper and inclusive welcome for tourists.

Ironically, Japan's rich artistic tradition reveals a culture that once reveled in sexual diversity. Where did that disappear to? Well, some of it made its way to Toronto's Royal Ontario Museum. A 2016 show curated by Asato Ikeda, "A Third Gender: Beautiful Youths in Japanese Prints," displayed ukiyo-e woodblock prints focused on bawdy representations of sexuality from the Edo Period (1603–1868), an era before Victorian values, and Christian guilt, began to cast a shadow over Japan.

While older men coveted and fought over their young and effeminate male lovers, known as *wakashu* (the "third gender"), we see that older women were also drawn to their virile charms. The show informs us that, in principle, wakashu were active agents in heterosexual sex, but that older women were often initiators due to their seniority. And who knew that a nun wrote a guide in the seventeenth century on the practice and etiquette of female masturbation for ladies-in-waiting who apparently got tired of waiting and availed themselves of strap-on and double-headed dildos? We also encounter androgynous *onnagata* (men—usually wakashu—who played female roles) in kabuki, who embodied an idealized femininity. All this, and more.

This art depicting the sexual diversity and fluid sexual norms that characterized Edo culture reveals a world far removed from the taboos that later emerged—a world that is today kept under wraps by establishment morality. In 2015 there was a hit exhibition of *shunga* (erotic woodblock prints) in London that was turned down by several leading Tokyo museums before finding a home at the small and remote Eisei Bunko Museum in Tokyo's Mejiro neighborhood. It turned out to be enormously popular—local crowds seemed to revel in explicit depictions of their country's more decadent traditions. Why curators are reluctant to display this vibrant art remains uncertain, but one suspects that the extravagantly tumescent genitalia might be a factor in a society that values discreet understatement.

Gay marriage is part of a broader debate in Japan about the changing nature of the modern family and human rights that confronts a national identity that is in denial about such diversity. This identity is shaped more by the intolerant views of the ruling conservative elite than the evident degree of public tolerance. The Constitution guarantees equal treatment and bans discrimination, but for Japan's LGBT community, this remains an unrealized dream. Gay couples are denied equal rights ranging from income tax treatment to joint mortgages, inheritance, and pensions. Advocates argue that this constitutes discrimination and imposes financial penalties on gay couples that violate their constitutional rights.

Public opinion is not an obstacle to gay marriage in Japan. But openly gay politicians are rare and political parties don't actively court this constituency. A major barrier to legalizing gay marriage is the ruling Liberal Democratic Party (LDP). In the 2012 election campaign that brought the ultraconservative Shinzo Abe back to power, the LDP expressed its opinion that no additional measures are required to protect the rights of gays and lesbians. It also dashed hopes for equal social security and inheritance treatment, asserting that these are intended for heterosexual couples. Controversially, right-wing firebrand Sugita Mio, an LDP Diet member, in July 2018 denounced gays as unproductive and pilloried government spending on programs to support same-sex couples because they don't bear children. She warned that the spread of same-sex couples will lead to greater unhappiness in society, commenting, "A society deprived of 'common sense' and 'normalcy' is destined to lose 'order' and eventually collapse." She denied that LGBT face discrimination although a government survey found that 49 percent of the public believes they do (Osaki 2018). Prime Minister Abe dismissed calls for her dismissal, incongruously citing her youth as a compelling reason for not doing so; she was fifty-one at the time, young only by the standards of the LDP's gerontocracy.

China

Like in Japan, same-sex relations were once celebrated in China and older men vied for the favors of younger men; this carried no social stigma. But in this "golden age" of promiscuous homosexuality, gay was not an identity but more of an acceptable recreation for married men with families. After 1949 the Chinese Communist Party promoted puritanical values, outlawed prostitution, homosexuality was stigmatized, and gays were subject to imprisonment. Subsequently, China decriminalized homosexuality in 1997 and as of 2001 it is no longer officially termed a mental illness.

Things have relaxed considerably in the twenty-first century as the LGBT community has carved out space in cities around the nation and being gay is no longer quite like being an alien subject to hate crimes or righteous denunciation. There are gay bars, support groups, and pride parades, the police don't abuse them, and in 2009 the *China Daily* featured a picture of an embracing gay couple who had just conducted a symbolic ceremony near Tiananmen Square. But progress in terms of wider social acceptance confronts a deep-seated value of filial piety and the family duty of having children. Coming out to one's own family or employer remains rare even as surveys show that acceptance of LGBT people is increasing, at least in principle. Indifference is perhaps the most common attitude toward gays. Experts believe that a majority of China's estimated sixty-plus million gays enter into heterosexual marriages in order to fend off questions and pressures while discreetly maintaining a gay lifestyle. The media also reports more gay men and women having marriages of convenience.

But the Party has deep misgivings about this trend. Weibo, the largest online social media platform in China, banned gay content for a few days in 2018 but later retracted this order after widespread condemnation. A Chinese employee of Weibo told me, "A lot of my friends in NGOs wrote letters to my company's CEO to ask them to change the policy. I don't know exactly what is going on behind the sudden retraction, but I speculate it might be the higher authority experiencing a change of mind." This employee adds, "At the very beginning, I think it is a directive from the top that imposes the ban rather than an autonomous decision by Weibo since more posting on Weibo is always a good thing for the company. But after the strong reaction from the public, the authoritative body felt the policy was not worth the price" (interview August 2018). But why ban the hashtag #IAmGay in the first place and send a message to users that they had shared "illegal content"? It's hard to imagine this hashtag represents a threat to the government or social order. The government incited global denunciations and reversed itself, an acknowledgment that it made a mistake in trying to block a sea change in cultural values favoring tolerance. Issuing this gag order to stifle LGBT voices, however, is part of a larger campaign.

In June 2017 China issued a directive banning displays of homosexuality in audiovisual content on the Internet. The same directive lists nine taboo categories of content including "abnormal" sexual relations such as incest, homosexuality, and sexual abuse, "unhealthy" views on marriage such as extramarital affairs, sexual freedom, and wife swapping, as well as prostitution, rape, masturbation, or anything that is "highly sexually stimulating." These new regulations draw criticism from LGBT activists because their lifestyle is linked with perversion, abuse, and sex work, officially marginalizing and condemning them and their advocates. There seems to have been little progress since 1979 when a crackdown on homosexuality was conducted based on an antihooliganism law. Weibo also banned a commentator in 2017 who posted an essay critical of the new regulations.

In the name of socialist values regulators are also cracking down on gay fiction (danmei) because homosexuality is deemed unacceptably vulgar. In 2017 the government introduced an evaluation system for online literature websites that demands fictional works "reflect core socialist values and abide by moral norms." This Orwellian initiative also triggered an online backlash as youthful audiences vented frustrations. Now online literary platforms will be assessed annually on a one-hundred-point scale, with thirty points assessed based on "value guidance and style of thought." Websites will also be judged on whether they include enough literature reflecting socialist values—twenty points—with deductions for works that undermine "moral norms" or "reflect distorted values or ethics." Works on Party and military history are mandatory, but any novel that distorts or desecrates that history can incur a five-point penalty. And if authorities judge any work guilty of a serious political error, they can fail the website. The minimum passing grade is sixty points and websites with low scores are subject to public criticism and managers are "invited" in for a "chat" with regulators. Authors of gay fiction are adjusting accordingly, nicknaming sex "the indescribable act below the neck" and urging readers to use their imagination to fantasize what can't be written explicitly or to access sex scenes on uncensored overseas websites. Interestingly, danmei represent a twenty-first-century cultural import from Japan, and just as there, China's readership is mostly female as are the authors. Coincidentally, in 2017 Hong Kong courts ruled that same-sex partners of government employees are entitled to the same benefits as heterosexual partners and that same-sex partners of expatriates have the right to live in the territory as dependents, but the Beijing beholden Hong Kong government has appealed both rulings.

SOUTH ASIA

Sexual orientation is embedded in the region's ongoing cultural wars. The homophobic legacy of British colonialism remains embedded in the penal codes of the former colonies of Pakistan, Bangladesh, India, and Sri Lanka. The notorious Section 377 reads:

> Unnatural offences.—Whoever voluntarily has carnal intercourse against the order of nature with any man, woman or animal, shall be punished with 1 [imprisonment for life], or with imprisonment of either description for a term which may extend to ten years, and shall also be liable to fine. Explanation.— Penetration is sufficient to constitute the carnal intercourse necessary to the offence described in this section.

In 2013 the Indian Supreme Court overturned a lower court decision in 2009 ruling that Section 377 is unconstitutional, thereby reinstating the law that criminalizes homosexuality. This was a stunning reversal, sending a chilling message to the gay and lesbian community. This ruling seems absurd considering that a few months later in 2014 the Supreme Court moved to recognize transgender people as a third gender with legal rights to the full range of government social services and welfare programs that help marginalized groups overcome the disadvantages of entrenched discrimination. Now hijra can identify themselves on official documents as transgender and claim the same civil rights as men and women. "The spirit of the [Indian] constitution is to provide equal opportunity to every citizen to grow and attain their potential, irrespective of caste, religion or gender," the court said in its order. The 2014 national election was the first in which all voter registration forms allowed a third gender choice ("other") and a total of 28,000 voters out of some 815 million declared as such. The ruling affects nearly five million hijra nationwide, many of whom work irregularly and precariously in entertainment and prostitution.

That took care of the T in LGBT, but gays, bisexuals, and lesbians envied the rights that they lost in 2013 when a different bench of the Supreme Court upheld Section 377 that criminalizes "sex against the order of nature," a provision that apparently applies exclusively to consensual gay sex while overlooking paid sex with hijra. Overall, transgender tend to be poor while homosexuals are regarded as having middle- and upper-class backgrounds. The latter thus represent more of a threat to mainstream Hindu family values and are targeted accordingly. Hijra, in contrast, occupy a sacred space of sorts in Hinduism and are typically invited to births and weddings because of their imagined magical powers. The Hindu epic *Mahabarata* features a transgender presence in which the male Shikhandi (who was born a female) plays a heroic role in martial victory. Hijra also figure prominently in Arundhati Roy's novel *The Ministry of Utmost Happiness* (2017) that probes issues of gender politics, sexual identity, and social injustice against the backdrop of authoritarian nationalism. She walks readers through India's house of horrors that beset the collective conscience. It is a powerful book about the betrayals that are daily fare for India's minorities and marginalized and their intensified suffering in the dystopia of Hindutva tyranny and rampant human rights abuses.

In recent years the LGBT community has become increasingly visible in India and widely accepted despite the contradictory judicial rulings. In some ways this is an accurate barometer of changing Indian values and norms in transition, a period when some cling to old established ways as others adjust to new realities regarding identity, sexuality, dignity, and freedom. In urban areas, attitudes are more tolerant but there are frequent reports of beatings, honor killings, and discrimination that ensure many remain closeted if only to spare their families the social shaming that would ensue. Being openly gay or transgender remains heavily stigmatized and as in other Asian societies elicits social slights, prejudice, and violence. Efforts to repeal the law commenced in 1991 but it was not until 2017 that the Supreme Court unanimously ruled that the right to individual privacy is a fundamental right under the Indian Constitution and that a person's sexual orientation is a privacy issue.

Then in a stunning victory for common sense, human rights, and the LGBT community, the Supreme Court's Constitutional Bench issued a landmark ruling in 2018 decriminalizing homosexuality and lifting the ban on gay sex. It is indicative of shifting public attitudes that none of the political parties lobbied publicly in support of intolerance. The only opposition to decriminalization came from small Christian groups while the BJP, the voice of conservative moral values, did not deploy its immense institutional powers to whip up mob sentiments against decriminalization. Perhaps sensing that the momentum for tolerance was irreversible, it avoided a battle already lost, playing it careful in the run up to the 2019 national elections. But there are looming battles over gay marriage and civil unions while eradicating social stigma remains crucial but difficult.

The court held that Section 377 violates the constitutional rights of the LGBT community to "equal citizenship and equal protection of laws" and asserted that choice of partner is inherent to the fundamental right to privacy. The judges also invoked human rights and dignity to strike down the colonial-era statute. The chief justice, Dipak Misra, called the ban on gay sex "irrational, indefensible and manifestly arbitrary" (Gettlemen et al. 2018). Taking on the BJP's mobocracy and drift toward illiberalism, he added, "majoritarian views and popular morality cannot dictate constitutional rights." Another justice wrote that being gay should be understood as a "variation," not an "aberration," of human nature (Wire 2018). The ruling provides some relief from the climate of fear and persecution endured by the LGBT community, expanding the space for personal freedom by rejecting state-sponsored homophobia and discrimination, but a lot remains to be done. Justice Indu Malhotra, the only woman justice, reached out to the rainbow spectrum, asking forgiveness by declaring that "history owes an apology" (Gettlemen et al. 2018). Under Prime Minister Modi, however, there are few signs of contrition.

Nepal

Neighboring Nepal, a Hindu majority nation, is lauded as a global beacon on LGBT rights. The LGBT community, until recently vilified as "social pollutants," has won significant legal victories in Nepal's courts over the past decade that confer social and political rights including legal recognition of a third gender. The landmark 2007 Supreme Court decision not only legally recognized the third gender category and endorsed "self-feeling" as the basis for this identity but also called on the government to audit all laws for bias against LGBT people and revise them. As in India, there is a rich tradition of hijras and this was probably a factor in the favorable judicial ruling. In 2010 the third gender category was on election ballots and in 2011 Nepal became the world's first nation to include a third gender category in its national census, while in 2015 passports were first issued that recognized a third gender. That year the government supported legalization of same-sex marriage and Nepal became the tenth country in the world to explicitly protect the rights of LGBT people in its constitution. In many respects, however, society is racing to catch up with these legal revisions as government officials still harass LGBT groups, stigma lingers, and acceptance in families, schools, and the workplace remains problematic. Unlike, India, Pakistan, and Bangladesh, Nepal was never colonized and so doesn't have the Section 377 legacy, but an "unnatural sex" clause was introduced in the penal code in the 1960s. The first time this was used to target LGBT activism in 2004, the court ruled that homosexuality is not a crime and dismissed the case. Nonetheless, as civil war violence intensified in the 2000s, abuses targeting LGBT people escalated. Thanks to the large UN field office established at that time, there was a degree of protection and support for advocacy. This encouraged many LGBT people to enter the mainstream of politics and government, running for office and landing jobs that raised their profile and wider consciousness about their concerns, giving them positions that enabled them to influence discourse and policy making. In a traumatized society in which so many felt vulnerable, there were possibilities for forging alliances and gaining local sympathy while the large international presence provided support for enacting global norms related to human rights and sexual orientation. Yet despite legal victories, social acceptance and realizing these rights remain elusive goals (interviews with civil society activists April 2019).

Bangladesh

In Bangladesh being openly gay is literally risking your neck as two gay blogger activists were hacked to death with a machete in front of one of their mothers by a group of Islamic fundamentalists in 2016. One of them worked at the American embassy in Dhaka for the US Agency for International Development while also editing *Roopbaan*, Bangladesh's first LGBT magazine. Al-Qaeda took responsibility for this killing, one of a cluster that targeting secular bloggers and public intellectuals that year. Due to the climate of fear and the ineffectual response of police, many gays went into hiding and many bloggers stopped blogging.

Bangladesh also retains the British-era Section 377 that criminalizes homosexuality, contributing to a climate of homophobia that threatens the LGBT community. Referring to this law, the interior minister suggested that the two bloggers brought the attack on themselves. Unlike in India or Nepal,

Bangladesh has not moved to extend any legal or constitutional protections to LGBT people. Indeed, security forces are openly hostile as the Rapid Action Battalion, the nation's crack commando unit, arrested twenty-eight people at a community center for holding a "homosexual party." Because the arresting officers witnessed no actual sex act, "unnatural" or otherwise, they could not be detained under Section 377. Instead they were arrested for illegal narcotics possession, in this case a cache of sexual stimulants. Prospects for decriminalizing homosexuality are not very good as the ruling Awami League has made numerous concessions in recent years to mollify conservative Islamic groups and does not want to antagonize clerics or give them an issue to exploit politically.

IMPLICATIONS

To the extent that national identity and religion is conflated, sexuality becomes a handy target for political opportunists and conservatives with axes to grind. State meddling in what happens in bedrooms, in families, and between consenting adults, riding a wave of religiously inspired conservatism that has bolstered intolerance and patriarchal prerogatives, aims to dictate and circumscribe private matters. As discussed earlier, the shifting landscape of sexuality in Asia provides a degree of encouragement in that lifestyles deemed totally inappropriate are now far more public, if not common, than two short decades ago. This is due not only to advocacy and agitation but also to the mainstreaming of diversity in popular culture, making continued efforts to reinforce and impose sex role stereotypes appear antediluvian. The trend toward greater social acceptance of diverse sexualities and incremental erosion of patriarchal assumptions is precisely why culture wars have escalated, generating opportunities for conservative religious authorities to regain influence and politicians to grandstand on "family values."

These reactionary voices are gaining ground. In Asia's Islamic communities, Arabization has spawned greater intolerance across age groups as appeals to piety have convinced most that their religious beliefs are incompatible with same-sex relations. Youth in other parts of Asia are more open to same-sex relations but institutional barriers, low awareness, and limited empathy impede legal reforms and protection of LGBT civil and human rights. Overall, despite some significant progress and encouraging signs, hostility toward the LGBT community also remains robust among Hindus, Buddhists, and Christians. There has also been little progress on curbing the rampant problem in all religious communities of sexual violence due to patriarchal attitudes, misogyny, and impunity.

The riptide of religion, sexuality, and identity plays out in fiercely contested culture wars that infringe on human rights and diversity while indelibly influencing nation branding on the global stage. A reactionary political backlash has flared, feeding off the threat posed by liberal trends associated with globalization. The patriarchal values embedded in nationalism gain impetus from threats, whether they be forces of globalization, terrorism, or disputes over territory. Nationalism is always in search of a target and seeks to impose obedience, conformity, and a strong state that coexists uncomfortably with civil liberties, diversity, and nonconformity. Traditionalists find solace and strength in amped-up nationalism and religious piety, mobilizing the institutions of politics and faith in support of their intolerant agenda. Across Asia, in different ways, this program is contested with varying degrees of success. In authoritarian China, where resistance of any sort elicits a powerful state response, monitoring is intense and penalties can be high, but there is a certain degree of leeway so that some of those labeled "deviants" have carved out vibrant niches of diversity. In states where the wave of Arabization has gained momentum, the state has been coopted in the imposition of conservative values and in tolerating intolerance, including vigilantism. Hinduism in Nepal has not been an impediment to state-sanctioned tolerance, but despite a cultural tradition of tolerance Hindutva in India has slowed progress until recent Supreme Court decisions prioritized privacy and dignity. As in most of Asia, including Buddhist and Christian societies, social acceptance and family approval remain elusive. Although the LGBT community has made significant progress in Taiwan in gaining social and judicial support, conservatives have been effective in mobilizing opposition to same-sex marriage and slowing the pace of reform.

It appears that the Internet is a double-edged sword, propagating liberal values on sexuality, diversity, tolerance, and minority rights but also endowing opponents the means to mobilize opposition, stoke intolerance, coopt politicians, and intimidate nonconformists. In Asia's culture wars, the Internet is an accelerator of polarization, a highly contested process that has propelled reforms supportive of women's and LGBT rights while expanding the range of acceptable sexual identities.

Chapter Ten

Conclusion

In writing about the *politics* of religion, nationalism, and identity, I analyze how the mutually reinforcing dynamic between religion and nationalism carries powerful implications for how people view their world and act in it. The politicization of religion confers sacral legitimacy on the bond of people with nation and on those who manipulate such bonds for political gain. Conflating national identity with religion in the diverse societies of Asia breeds majoritarian intolerance that marginalizes ethnic, linguistic, religious, and sexual minorities, subjecting them to various indignities and violence, both by state security forces and by vigilantes empowered by a sense of mission and impunity.

Asia's religious, ethnic, and sexual minorities are marginalized and at risk from malevolent majoritarian impulses that in some cases spark a violent backlash. In the case of China, after decades of a failed carrot-and-stick approach to assimilation and violent outbursts in protest, it's now all stick as Xinjiang is subject to authoritarian repression on an unprecedented scale. To be a Uighur Muslim is grounds for imprisonment in what the authorities euphemistically describe as "vocational" training centers, a new addition to the impressive lexicon of repression in contemporary China, where "troublemakers" are neutralized by being "touristed," "tax evaded," or in extreme cases "suicided" (Zha 2018). Islamic minorities in the Philippines and Thailand have also been radicalized by discriminatory policies, while India's large Muslim community has endured prejudice and violence and yet remains relatively quiescent and unradicalized under the shadow of state vigilance and Hindutva intimidation. In Myanmar, overall relations between Muslims and Buddhists are tense, in recent years punctuated by eruptions of violence and rioting. In the western state of Rakhine, some 730,000 Muslim Rohingya were driven into neighboring Bangladesh, not the military's first ethnic clearance operation targeting them. Prospects for repatriation appear unpromising given the hostility directed at the Rohingya and fear of reprisals should they return. Ma Ba Tha, the ultranationalist Buddhist organization, did not orchestrate this exodus, but the hatemongering by Wirathu, its most prominent voice, has incited wider anti-Muslim sentiments and stoked fears about an Islamic demographic time bomb. This same fear animates the Islamophobic hatemongering of Gnanasara, a Sri Lankan militant monk who leads BBS and advocates a Sinhalese Buddhist national identity. These extremist Sinhalese and Burmese monks pine for Buddhist-only nations much like Hindutva activists yearn for a purified Hindu homeland and Islamic hardliners fantasize about regional caliphates where the secular boundary between religion and government is eliminated. Such identity dreams contend with the reality of ethnic, religious, and linguistic diversity.

These diversity deniers also impose a stifling morality on Asia's sexual minorities, seeking to dictate what happens in private and public between consenting adults. Religions are averse to the modern array of sexual lifestyles that have become the de facto norm in Asia. For many people, there is a disconnect among their lifestyles, prevailing patriarchal norms, and the traditional family model embraced by organized religion. To some extent these "dissidents" have carved out and expanded niches of acceptance, but the LGBT community continues to face a stigma that enjoys religious blessing and legal sanction. Tolerance is not in the vocabulary or mindset of ethnoreligious zealots, and sexual minorities suffer from their bigotry and sometimes violent impulses. Gay activists in Bangladesh were beheaded, while elsewhere gays are jailed and even caned for their preferences. Courts in India and Taiwan have shown a greater empathy and nudged governments to advance the human rights and dignity of the LGBT community, often in defiance of religious puritans. Although touting conservative family values, some religious leaders also sexually abuse the vulnerable and weak, as with Catholic priests in India, who treated nuns like sex slaves, part of a global problem confronting the Vatican.

The nexus of politics, religion, and nationalism in Asia paints a disturbing picture of societies riven by violence and menace. The sanctified extremism on display is at odds with the dignified piety commonly associated with religion. Opportunists stoke the flames of sanctimonious passions and tap into anger and resentments looking for an outlet, often invoking religion to justify agendas that have little to do with the philosophical or humanistic tenets of their faiths. They provoke culture wars to manipulate the theater of politics, gaining attention and an aura of power from staging grand spectacles and grisly incidents as in the Bangladesh bakery attack in 2016 and the 2019 suicide bombings at churches and hotels carried out in Sri Lanka. Invented or exaggerated threats or insults to religion are a common pretext for deeds that are less about spirituality than enforcing conformity, neutralizing opponents, or exacting revenge. Taking umbrage has become the default response for those looking for an excuse.

Accusations of blasphemy have proliferated with the advent of social media, spreading allegations and unproven accusations that have the effect of guilty verdicts on the accused. Recent high-profile blasphemy cases of Christians, such as Bibi, a farm worker in Pakistan, and Ahok, the ousted governor of Jakarta, draw international attention, but even more Ahmadiyya and Shi'a Muslims are targeted by the Sunni majority. This is a virulent Othering that is state sanctioned where laws are used selectively as cudgels and vigilantes take justice into their own hands.

There are even apps for reporting transgressions, and social media is a hothouse for whipping up righteous indignation. This apparent plague of blasphemy is not due to a surge of impiety but rather the onslaught of globalization and perceived or hyped threats to cherished traditions, values, culture, and identity. Under such circumstances, lines delineating acceptable/unacceptable are drawn more conspicuously and defended more tenaciously. Religious and spiritual leaders are also engaged in an intensified competition to attract followers and mobilize them, using social media to disseminate and inflame. In the crowded space for online clerics, nothing equals the pulling power of blasphemy charges, so what used to be overlooked, tolerated, or dealt with quietly is now packaged for mass consumption, the ultimate clickbait for the devoted. In a world in which religion is no longer the default option, one full of impious distractions, social media also generates solidarity and enforces conformity, enabling clerics to amplify and assert their authority.

Across Asia the Internet is the accelerant of religious fanaticism, endowing keyboard trolls with a powerful voice in virtual communities where sensationalism rules in an echo chamber of spiraling indignation and resentments. Globalization propagates gilded lifestyles of reproach, providing constant reminders of relative deprivation that are the breeding ground of rancor and envy. The twenty-first-century "age of anger" limned in these pages conveys a sense of the unhappiness, rage, and fury that find expression and a semblance of dignity in religious identities. Religion provides the seething and vexed with the vocabulary, moral purpose, and righteous calling to challenge and denounce the unwelcome and marginalized targets. The Internet is their force multiplier, creating virtual communities of the unhappy and enraged that enable engagement and mobilization based on shared values, traumas, and collective outrage. Whether targeting an imagined "love jihad" by Muslim lotharios in India or Myanmar, interfaith dating and marriage, allegedly licentious lifestyles, or income disparities, mobile phone networks are the infrastructure and connective tissue of mobocracy. Across Asia we see unelected religious leaders whipping mobs into a frenzy while pressuring governments into making concessions, coopting politicians, or derailing election campaigns. Religious groups like the RSS in India, IDF in Indonesia, BBS in Sri Lanka, Ma Ba Tha in Myanmar, and Hezafat in Bangladesh wield considerable political influence to push agendas that are only partly about religion.

It does not take much to ignite the dry kindling of discontent in Asian societies, generating opportunities and vulnerabilities to exploit in the name of faith and creed. Rigid dogmas of intolerance are proliferating that are roiling once tolerant diverse societies, amplified by hatemongering and vilification. The hawkers of dogma fan fears and threats to create a siege mentality that is also a call to arms. Militant monks in Sri Lanka and Myanmar have embraced such insidious tactics, leading Islamophobic campaigns that stir an irrational malevolence and paranoia that nurtures a remarkably baseless, self-pitying sense of victimization. They find their counterparts among Hindutva activists and Islamic clerics who also recklessly and purposefully unleash orgies of violence.

Hindutva, the angry face of Hinduism, swirls menacingly through the subcontinent, spreading vigilantism and bloodshed based on a hyped Islamic threat. Under Prime Minister Modi, it has become a state-sanctioned assault on India's secular norms and vast Muslim population. Islamophobia is something of an industry, whipped up among the willing to achieve political goals and to "saffronize" history, heritage, education, and identity. The sorrows of inequality, poverty, and caste provide willing foot soldiers deployed in the name of an imagined Mother India, a purified Hindu homeland, where non-Hindus are the enemy to be reconverted or eliminated. Activists and leaders are shrewdly adept at the theater of politics, brandishing potent religious symbols, the collective trauma of Partition, and contested sacred sites to create a simulacrum of solidarity in a nation marked by deep divisions. They rend the fabric of a secular, diverse nation with their ethnoreligious grandstanding in pursuit of an unobtainable monoculture in a polychromatic society. In such circumstances, religion becomes the wellspring of prejudice and mayhem, igniting a ferocity among the devoted unleavened by compassion. As Indian intellectual Pratap Bhanu Mehta remarked in March 2019, "Religion, that very thing that behooves us to transcend our identity, is being reduced to the identity that marks you, for which you will be targeted" (Donthi 2019).

Globalization is generally associated with the West, but Arabization is a competing contagion in Asia that emanates from Saudi Arabia. Through lavish Saudi funding of mosque building and educational programs, the haj and migrant labor, a puritan Salafist Islam has transformed the religious landscape of Asia, promoting intolerance and extremism. Moderate Sufi Islam has come under attack, as have adherents of Shi'a and Ahmadiyya in societies in which tolerance once prevailed. Zealotry has become mainstreamed and religion politicized as Arabization takes global Saudi Arabia's overall geostrategic ambitions and rivalry with Shiite Iran. Projecting a Sau-di-based Salafist orthodoxy enhances Riyadh's soft power in Islamic soci-eties. The Internet connects Saudi-based clerics with regional counterparts who seek and enforce their opinions, both gaining authority and legitimacy through these exchanges that position Saudi Arabia as the Islamic homeland. While some governments like Bangladesh, Pakistan, and Indonesia welcome Saudi largesse, there is a disconnect between the inflexibly strict tenets of Salafism and the disparate and diverse cultures and societies in South and Southeast Asia. Many governments, however, can't afford to be picky about proffered funding, but this situation renders them vulnerable, in this case to the insidious influence of Arabization that undermines secularism and em-powers fundamentalist groups associated with extremism and terrorism.

As much as Western influences may be alien, so too is the sociocultural baggage of contemporary Arabization. The spread of Islam in Asia has been a longstanding, evolutionary process of evolving fusions over several centu-ries that draws on successive waves of interaction from commerce, pilgrim-ages, and war. Contemporary orthodox zealots may want to cleanse local religious practices of syncretic "pollutants," but these are deeply rooted, ensuring puritanical Salafism confronts cultural resistance and tempered ac-commodation. Interactions that were once intermittent and episodic, howev-er, are now sustained and intensified by the Internet, eliminating borders and distances that are also eroded by improved transport. These developments help accelerate and deepen the processes of "purification" and reform. More-over, outrages can be shared instantaneously that nurture imagined commu-nities of the traumatized and outraged, generating solidarity among the faith-ful and opportunities for fanatics. It took the Internet to turbocharge dakwah (preaching) and bring preachers into every laptop and mobile phone, a high-tech immanence that is certainly not only about what is sacred and holy.

Christians in Asia are mostly minorities and across the region have been the target of majoritarian brutalities, with horrific consequences when suicide bombers attacked packed churches in Sri Lanka on Easter Sunday in 2019 as mass was being celebrated, killing over 250 and maiming hundreds more. Liberation theology has been salient in Timor Leste and the Philippines where the Church, especially its local leaders, have played a key role in anti-authoritarian movements. Christianity has also played a decisive role in Ko-rean anticolonialism and subsequently in mobilizing dissent in modern South Korea. Yet the big story is the explosive popularity of evangelical Christian-ity, especially Pentecostalism, that is taking Asia by storm. In China, one of the most inhospitable nations in the world for religion, Pentecostalism has thrived. But it has done so at the sufferance of authorities and operates in the gray zone of official forbearance. This fragility has motivated pastors to embrace patriotism with biblical fervor as a way to mollify the government and thereby safeguard converts from the authoritarian excesses inflicted on dissidents and renegades. In South Korea, success has been predicated on flamboyant celebrations and embracing shamanistic traditions, while in Indonesia and India, targeted and disadvantaged minorities have found solace and safety. Everywhere the gospel of prosperity has been a key drawing card, while the grid of rules and codes of behavior have appealed to many caught in the deracinating transformations of a rising Asia and the receding bonds of community in mobile, urbanizing societies.

Religion is eminently useful for those who have political agendas because it confers virtue and ignites passion. Combining religion with ethnonationalism taps into primordial fervor and unleashes fanaticism in the name of god and nation, transforming ignoble misdeeds into sacred duty. Whether it's the BJP's Hindutva in India, Ma Ba Tha in Myanmar, or the BBS in Sri Lanka, the conflation of religion and national identity is a formula for a glowering majoritarianism threatening to minorities. Proponents of ethnonationalism wrapped in the robes of religion target the evident diversity in their societies and agitate against it. This cloak of faith promotes impunity for these perpetrators, some of who cheerlead others into gross violations of human rights.

The essence of religion is peaceful, otherworldly, and enlightening, a way of living to abide by that inspires thoughtful, charitable, and altruistic engagement, except when it doesn't. The gap between precepts and practice does not impugn the former but rather highlights how the tenets are elusive aspirations. In sum, where there is power there are scoundrels and opportunists who are adept at enlisting the ardor of religion and nationalism for political purposes. In doing so, they seek to bolster their moral authority and legitimacy, but as we found there are no shortage of examples of them unleashing destructive torrents and inflicting traumas that scar and precipitate retribution, repression, and cycles of violence. Alas, all too often such powerful manipulators sin with impunity. But why is this politics of ethnoreligious nationalism escalating?

My view is that humans cling to nonrational orientations. A wholly secular, rational and logical world doesn't satisfy a spiritual/psychic need, and thus people respond to emotional-spiritual-mythic gestures, symbols, and rhetoric. The global surge in politicized religion and religious politics is driven by the radical disruptions of intensified globalization that threaten traditional verities and established norms. There is rampant disappointment and sagging confidence in secular nationalism because it seems so inadequate a defense against this relentless assault and doesn't provide a compelling assertion of values or articulate the basis for a moral community. In contrast, religious austerity and extremist violence respond to the yearning for renewal and purification in corrupt and flawed polities, offering an uplifting vision for a moral order and reassertion of proper values in society. This revivalism, calling for sinners to repent and a vanquishing of evil, appeals to the disappointed and disillusioned. Grandiose spectacles and the contagion effect of the crowd transport people to a less mundane space where grim realities can be eclipsed by gilded glimmerings of hope and redemption swathed in spirituality and nationalist scapegoating. Decisive actions and agendas offer relief from governments wallowing in destructive and interminable bickering. Tough leaders who speak their minds, embrace bold plans, and challenge political pieties, in contrast to dull, consultant-trimmed wonks, appeal to the primordial and tribalist inclinations of human beings. Problematically, the secular nationalism of colonial independence movements has mostly fizzled out (South Korea being a notable exception) or been appropriated by uninspiring politicians, while the populist craving for grandeur, moral certainties, and vengeance remains resilient.

In assessing this angry and alarmed Asia, it is also important to consider the large youth cohorts in South and Southeast Asia facing uncertain job prospects in a rapidly changing world that is also displacing their elders, leaving them both feeling powerless. Globalization subverts established norms and the social order, shredding reassuring certainties and undermining dignity and self-respect. This amorphous process unleashed by distant global forces beyond national control ramps up a desire for greater control and certainty that responds to the siren songs and hyped promises of ethnoreligious nationalism. These ominous songs reverberate with greater impact in Asia's heterogeneous societies in which diversity spurs enmities and rivalries that stoke an intensified longing for solidarity to ward off threats imagined and real. Moreover, the bonds of social cohesion have loosened and frayed as globalization is propelling intensified and sustained interactions in a cyber-charged encounter with forces of modernization that is transforming internal dynamics and aspirations and heightening competition across the board, creating more "losers" and accentuating divisive disparities. There has also been an upsurge of rights-driven movements spurred on by international norms and institutions that threaten the privileges and prejudices of the entrenched. In addition, migration creates diaspora communities that gain the wherewithal to meddle back in their homelands, while temporary overseas employment exposes workers to new influences and norms that they spread on their return. It is thus a multipronged maelstrom sweeping Asian societies as they navigate the rapids of modernization toward becoming the fulcrum of the world economy. In such a situation the passengers are looking for a strong helmsperson who projects confidence about steering clear of the hazards and belief that better times are coming.

The dysfunctions of government, however, coupled with the staleness and predictability of secular messaging provide an uninspiring spectacle. This creates opportunities in the theater of politics for those who can provide inspiration and rekindle hope among those who have lost it. Even in China where the government is not subject to the people's will, Xi Xinping has worked hard to cultivate a cult of personality and unabashedly invokes pre–Chinese Communist Party civilizational tropes to do so. He is famous as the leader who promotes the Chinese Dream (attempting to dictate even that), recalls China's greatness, and strides boldly on the international stage, no longer sticking to the script of self-effacing, colorless leaders like his post-Mao predecessors. He may be mocked as a Winnie the Pooh meme on social media, but he amps up Han nationalism and has presided over a sustained assault on civil liberties in the name of nationalist glory, the minatory new religion of China.

Asian political spaces are no longer just about mainstream parties and election campaigns, as social media has taken the keys away from the gate-keepers and given a voice to bloggers, clerics, monks, priests, outsiders, and anyone else with a mobile phone, enabling direct connections with the multi-tudes. This cyber-recasting of the political landscape has vast implications that mainstream politicians and parties ignore at the risk of irrelevance.

Just as the proliferation of earbuds for consumers of online digital music has transformed the aesthetics of music production in a space where loud sonic peaks now prevail, the political arena demands the equivalent. In this denuded soundscape in which the dynamic range of recordings is compressed and engineered at incessantly maximum loudness levels (not to be confused with volume), the subtle and diverse audio ecosystems of the vinyl album have all but disappeared (Milner 2019). So too the politics of loudness that reduces the dynamic range of political discourse and subtleties of policy debates by incentivizing inflammatory rhetoric and snappy soundbites. Pre-cisely because mobilizing the committed base is key, politicians and influ-encers crank up the loudness of provocations and fireworks with disregard for the repercussions.

The genie is out of the bottle and, with the exception of China, there is no going back to the circumscribed political arenas of the past that were much easier to control. This brave new world for Asia promises to be one in which the solace of religion retains a buoyant appeal for those threatened by esca-lating globalization and ethnonationalistic assaults on the bonds of cohesion and tolerance. While the rising tide of ethnonationalism is destabilizing and gaining momentum from the perceived threats of globalization, religion serves as both an oasis of order and a useful weapon amid intensified culture wars about identity. In the aftermath of ethnoreligious conflict lingering en-mities and prejudices are the sanctified embers of violence that can flare abruptly, leaving more scars to be avenged. This is not an issue for relatively homogenous nations like Japan and South Korea, but in the ethnically heterogenous nations that predominate in Asia, where charlatans and zealots stoke and manipulate vengeful forces, significant risks remain.

The momentum of majoritarianism in Asia has unleashed the nightmares of ethnoreligious nationalism and provoked a hardening of identities, reduc-ing the scope for accommodation. This phenomenon has also triggered a backlash of subnationalisms contesting majoritarian chauvinism. The secular state is undermined by these developments and as we noted this has led to democratic backsliding, concessions to religious hardliners, and resorting to repressive tactics that undermine secular principles. The postcolonial leaders were the champions of those secular precepts, but in vastly different circumstances, twenty-first-century leaders' commitment to these principles is ceding ground to the survival instinct as they do what it takes to retain power and fend off challengers, by fair means and foul. It has long been an article of faith that the ends don't justify the means, but this precept is fading in Asian democracies where retaining power is depicted as an existential imperative because the opponents can't be trusted. Citing Bangladesh, some argue that the government has a point because the main political opposition and affiliated groups champion antithetical views regarding national identity and have a violent track record in support thereof (Ahmed 2019). Yet if such a zero-sum calculus prevails, then what is the purpose and meaning of democracy and secular ideals? Illiberal democracy may be better than no democracy at all, but it remains fool's gold, appearance without substance, eroding the foundations of the state in the name of preserving it. Denying a voice in mainstream politics to the angry and alienated is not a sustainable solution to maintain that system or the integrity of the political process. The risk to inclusiveness and radicalizing the excluded are undeniable, while the consequences are unpredictable and could well come back to haunt both the venal and well-intentioned.

Glossary

Abangan—Indonesian term for relatively less devout Javanese Muslims who practice a syncretic version of Islam.

Adivasi—Indigenous people of South Asia, with 104 million in India alone.

Ahimsa—Buddhist term for nonviolence; virtue of causing no harm to others.

Ahmadiyya—Muslim movement whose adherents believe that its founder Mirza Gulam Ahmad (1839–1908) was the Mahdi or promised messiah.

al-Qaeda—Radical Sunni Muslim terrorist organization dedicated to the elimination of a Western presence in Arab countries and militantly opposed to Western foreign policy. Founded by Osama bin Laden in 1988.

Allah—Arabic origin name for God worshipped by Muslims.

AQIS (al-Qaeda Indian Subcontinent)—South Asian branch of al-Qaeda.

Arabization—The spread of Arabic culture and puritanical Islam to non-Arab populations, especially the contemporary promotion of Saudi Arabian influence in Islamic societies.

ARSA (Arakan Rohingya Salvation Army)—Small Islamic militant group of Rohingya in western Myanmar.

Awami League—Center/left ruling party in Bangladesh associated with preserving secularism.

Ayodhya—Controversial sacred site in northern India believed to be the birthplace of the Hindu god Rama that is contested by Hindus and Muslims.

Babri Mosque—Sixteenth-century Islamic place of worship at Ayodhya that was demolished by Hindu zealots in 1992.

Bamar (Burmese)—Majority ethnic group in Myanmar.

BBS (Bodu Bala Sena [Buddhist Power Force])—Ultranationalist Buddhist organization in Sri Lanka promoting Islamophobia and Sinhalese majoritarianism.

BJP (Bharatiya Janata Party)—India's ruling conservative national party associated with Hindu extremism.

BNP (Bangladesh Nationalist Party)—Center/right opposition political party in Bangladesh that played a key role in restoring democracy in 1990 and is now associated with Islamist groups.

Brahmins—The highest-ranking caste among Hindus. They serve as priests and guardians of sacred knowledge and practices who make a living from a range of occupations, especially farming. In contemporary society, they constitute about 5 percent of the entire Hindu population.

British Raj—British colonial government.

Congress—The dominant liberal political party in India during the twentieth century under the leadership of the Gandhi dynasty that has lost popularity and ceded power to the conservative BJP.

dakwah—Preaching and outreach activities aimed at proselytizing Islam.

Dalit—Indian term used for untouchables; the people classified as below the four Hindu castes who have been subject to extensive discrimination. They constitute about 16 percent of India's Hindu population, about 200 million people.

ETIM (East Turkestan Islamic Movement)—Movement of militant Muslim Uighur separatists seeking freedom from Chinese dominance. Designated a terrorist group by the United States in 2002, it is believed to serve as an umbrella organization for various splinter groups, but much is not known about its international links, size, and to what extent it represents the aspirations of Xinjiang's Uighurs. The threat to China appears hyped to justify repressive policies in the region.

fatwa—Ruling on an Islamic religious issue or point of law by Islamic cleric.

Gestapu—The 30th of September Movement or G30S that is shorthand for the mass killings of hundreds of thousands of people in 1965–1966 by paramilitary groups and military forces targeting alleged communists. During the New Order, the Suharto government tried to shift blame onto the communists, but this narrative has been debunked.

ghar wapsi (homecoming)—Religious conversion of non-Hindus to Hinduism.

Ghorkaland—The proposed state for those living in the hilly tracts near Darjeeling in northeast India who wish to be governed separately from the state of West Bengal due to ethnolinguistic differences that have sparked a series of strikes and political agitation.

Hadiths—Interpretative theological commentaries in Sunni Islam on the Quran and words and views of the Prophet Muhammad that provide legal analysis and moral guidance. There are four main schools of jurisprudence followed by Muslims around the world.

haj—Pilgrimage to Mecca, the holiest city for Muslims, located in Saudi Arabia. All Muslims are expected to make this religious journey at least once in their lifetimes if at all possible.

Han—China's majority ethnic group.

Hefazat-e-Islam (Guardians of Islam)—Islamist group in Bangladesh that seeks to influence state policies by mobilizing street demonstrations in favor of stricter observance of Islam.

Hinduism—The main religion in India and Nepal.

Hindutva—Hindu chauvinism or nationalism that promotes a majoritarian political and social agenda that confronts India's considerable diversity. Often associated with political violence, extremism, and intimidation targeting non-Hindus.

ijtihad—Independent reasoning by a qualified Islamic scholar to find a solution to some legal question.

Islamists—Those who focus on promoting the political role of Islam and are often associated with fundamentalism and Arabization.

Jamaat-e-Islami (JI)—Banned Islamic radical party in Bangladesh that collaborated with Pakistan in opposing the war of liberation in 1971.

Jamaat-ul-Mujahideen (Assembly of Islamic Warriors)—Banned Islamic terrorist organization operating in Bangladesh.

Jemaah Islamiyah (JI)—Islamic terrorist group in Southeast Asia.

jihad (holy war)—Religiously sanctioned armed struggle against nonbelievers to defend Islam, a legitimizing concept appropriated by terrorist groups.

kalar—Vulgar slur used in Myanmar referring to South Asians and Muslims.

Komeito—Political party in Japan linked to the Buddhist Soka Gakkai organization.

Laskar Jihad (Warriors of God)—An Islamist, anti-Christian paramilitary organization that burned churches and killed and maimed thousands of Christians in Ambon and the Maluku Islands in 2000 and enjoyed some support from Indonesian security forces. It has disbanded.

license raj—Indian term for elaborate system of regulations and red tape that is at the core of the systemic bureaucratic corruption associated with obtaining official permissions. Seen to inhibit economic growth and is a legacy of Nehru's planned economy from the 1950s.

Lord Shiva—One of the principle deities in Hinduism.

madrasas (Islamic schools)—Students receive a religious education including memorization and interpretation of the Quran.

Mughal—Sixteenth-century Muslim empire in the Indian subcontinent that bequeathed a rich Islamic cultural and socioeconomic legacy.

Muhammad (570 CE–630 CE)—Prophet and founder of Islam.

Muhammadiyah—Second largest Islamic nongovernmental organization in Indonesia with about thirty million members that was founded in 1912 and is associated with reformist practices, provision of education, and other social services in addition to promoting religious tolerance.

Nahdlatul Islam (NU)—Largest nongovernmental organization in Indonesia with more than forty million members that was founded in 1926 and is associated with orthodox and traditional doctrines and opposes Muhammidiyah's modernist agenda. In addition to running schools and hospitals, it also has a political party and is an advocate of religious tolerance and campaigns against extremism.

New Order (*Orde Baru*)—Term coined by Indonesian President Suharto (1966–1998) to differentiate the regime he launched in 1966 with that of Sukarno, his popular predecessor. This was an authoritarian military-dominated regime that made significant headway on economic development and population control but is remembered for the massacres of hundreds of thousands during Gestapu in 1965–1966 and is associated with endemic corruption, nepotism, and cronyism.

NLD (National League for Democracy)—Aung San Suu Kyi's political party based on social-democratic principles founded in 1988 that was central to the pro-democracy struggle in Burma, renamed Myanmar. It rose to power in the 2015 general elections in which the people repudiated the military regime but has faced significant challenges in mitigating the various negative legacies of military misrule.

NPA (New People's Army)—Outlawed Communist guerilla group founded in 1969 in the Philippines that is now designated a terrorist group and still active.

OBC (Other Backward Class)—Collective term in India that refers to disadvantaged castes that constitute some 40 percent of the nation's population. They are entitled to politically controversial reserved places in higher education and public sector employment designed to improve their welfare.

Partition—Refers to the traumatic division of the Indian subcontinent into the sovereign states of India and Pakistan in 1947 by the British government that ended colonial rule and sparked widespread sectarian violence. This poorly planned exit caused the deaths of one million people and displaced fourteen million more as Hindu and Muslim populations migrated along religious lines across the newly drawn borders. This collective trauma left a legacy of ill will between the two nations and is invoked in contemporary identity politics.

Pentecostalism—A Protestant Christian renewal movement that espouses vigorous evangelism and places emphasis on followers' direct and personal experiences with God and spiritualism as the basis for empowerment. There are many different Pentecostalist denominations, but they all believe in becoming "born again" as devout believers. Congregations in Asia have grown very rapidly.

Pesantren—Islamic boarding schools in Indonesia where local religious leaders imbue students with basic values and religious learning.

Quran—The central religious text of Islam that is sometimes romanized as Koran.

RSS (Rashtriya Swayamsevak Sangh [National Patriotic Organization])—Indian right-wing nationalist group founded in 1925 that advocates Hindutva and promotes intolerance. It is the parent organization of the BJP and central to the Sangh Parivar group.

Rohingya—Muslim inhabitants of Rakhine, the western Myanmar state, that have long been subjected to discrimination, persecution, and forced relocations. In 2017–2018 more than seven hundred thousand were driven from their homes into Bangladesh, an ethnic clearance operation conducted by Myanmar's military under the guise of antiterrorist operations.

Saffronization—The majoritarian agenda of right-wing Hindu nationalist organizations named after the saffron robes of Hindu ascetics that glorifies ancient Hindu cultural history and inter alia seeks to rewrite textbooks accordingly.

Saffron Revolution—Demonstrations by monks and citizens in Myanmar from August to October 2007 protesting sharp and sudden fuel price hikes that focused criticism on the military government, leading to a brutal crackdown that sparked international condemnation and gave momentum to the pro-democracy movement led by Aung San Suu Kyi.

Salafism—A reform movement in Sunni Islam rejecting religious innovation and promoting adoption of shariah (Islamic law) that is associated with puritanical practices, literal readings of sacred texts, and jihadism. A fundamentalist movement linked with Wahhabism that has spread through Arabization.

Sangh Parivar—Umbrella organization of dozens of Hindu nationalist groups affiliated with or inspired by RSS.

sangha—Buddhist community of monks, nuns, novices, and laity.

santri—Designation used in Indonesia to identify those Muslims who are more orthodox and devout in their religious observance.

shariah—Islamic law.

Shia—The smaller of the two main branches of Islam, about 10 to 15 percent of all Muslims, that follows religious practices similar to Sunni but embraces different doctrines. Shia Muslims are often subject to persecution by Sunni Muslims.

Shinto—Animist Japanese religion that was hijacked by the state in the late nineteenth century to provide ideological support for the emperor system.

shuddhi (reconversion)—A social-political movement by Hindus in India that aims to reduce or reverse conversions of Hindus to other religions.

Sinhalese—Majority Buddhist ethnic group in Sri Lanka.

Soka Gakkai (value creation society)—A lay Buddhist religious organization in Japan involved in politics through the Komeito party.

Sufism—Sunni Muslims who engage in mystical and syncretic practices rejected by more puritanical Muslims despite their commitment to intensification of faith.

Sunnah—Literature central to Islamic theology that examines the traditional customs and practices of the Islamic community.

Sunni—The largest branch of Islam constituting nearly 90 percent of all Muslims that differs with Shia over succession to Muhammed and theological matters. It is the world's largest religious denomination.

taingyintha—Burmese; refers to one of the officially recognized national races in Myanmar.

talaq—The Islamic practice of initiating divorce.

theyyam—A popular ritual form of worship in Kerala in southern India performed at temples that involves dancing, drumming, trance, and transformation of lower-caste performers into deities.

Uighur—Turkic ethnic group of Muslims in central Asia that are being persecuted in China's western province of Xinjiang.

ummah—Islamic community of believers.

Wahhabism—Puritanical, fundamentalist Sunni Islamic movement named after an eighteenth-century preacher who sought to purge religious practice of syncretic accretions. It is the form of Islam embraced by the Saudi Arabian monarchy and is a central component of Arabization. It is often used interchangeably with Salafism despite some theological differences.

Suggested Further Reading

Anderson, B. 2001. "Western Nationalism and Eastern Nationalism." *New Left Review*, May–June.

Anderson, B. 2006. *Imagined Communities: Reflections on the Origin and Spread of Nationalism*. Third edition. London: Verso.

Appiah, Kwame Anthony. 2018. *The Lies that Bind: Rethinking Identity*. London: Profile Books.

Armstrong, J. 1982. *Nations Before Nationalism*. Chapel Hill: University of North Carolina Press.

Asad, Talal. 1983. "Anthropological Conceptions of Religion: Reflections on Geertz." *Man, New Series*, 18, no. 2 (June): 237–59.

Asad, Talal. 2003. *Formations of the Secular: Christianity, Islam, Modernity*. Stanford, CA: Stanford University Press.

Brass, P. R. 2003. "The Partition of India and Retributive Genocide in the Punjab, 1946–47: Means, Methods, and Purposes." *Journal of Genocide Research* 5: 71–101.

Breuilly, J. 1993. *Nationalism and the State*. Manchester: Manchester University Press.

Breuilly, J. 2001. "The State and Nationalism." In *Understanding Nationalism*, 32–52. Polity, Cambridge.

Brubaker, R. 2004. *Ethnicity Without Groups*. Cambridge: Harvard University Press.

Calhoun, C. 1997. *Nationalism*. Buckingham: Open University Press.

Calhoun, C. 2007. *Nations Matter: Culture, History and the Cosmopolitan Dream*. London: Routledge.

Casanova, José. 2011. "The Secular, Secularizations, Secularism." In *Rethinking Secularism*, edited by Craig Calhoun, Mark Jurgensmeyer, and Jonathan Van Antwerpen, 54–75. New York: Oxford University Press.

Chatterjee, P. 1986. *Nationalist Thought and the Colonial World: A Derivative Discourse?* New Jersey: Zed Books.

Connor, W. 1990. "When Is a Nation?" *Ethnic and Racial Studies* 13: 92–103.

Connor, W. 1994. *Ethnonationalism: The Quest for Understanding*. Princeton, NJ: Princeton University Press.

Eisenstadt, Shmuel Noah. 2000. "Multiple Modernities." *Daedalus* 129, no. 1: 1–29.

Geary, P. J. 2002. *The Construction of Nationhood: Ethnicity, Religion and Nationalism*. Princeton, NJ: Princeton University Press.

Geertz, C. 1973. *The Interpretation of Cultures: Selected Essays*. New York: Basic Books.

Gellner, E. 1983. *Nations and Nationalism*. Ithaca, NY: Cornell University Press.

Gellner, E. 1996. "The Coming of Nationalism and Its Interpretations: Myths of Nation and Class." In *Mapping the Nation*, edited by G. Balakrishnan, 98–145. London: Verso.

Gottowik, Volker, ed. 2014. *Dynamics of Religion in Southeast Asia: Magic and Modernity*. Amsterdam: Amsterdam University Press.

Greenfeld, L. 1992. *Nationalism: F ive Roads to Modernity*. Cambridge, MA: Harvard University Press.

Greenfeld, L. 2003. *The Spirit of Capitalism Nationalism and Economic Growth*. Cambridge, MA: Harvard University Press.

Guibernau, M. 2004. "Anthony D. Smith on Nations and National Identity: A Critical Assessment." *Nations and Nationalism* 10: 125–41.

Gurevitch, M., S. Coleman, and J. Blumer. 2009. "Political Communication: Old and New Media Relationships." In *Media Power in Politics*, edited by D. Graber, 45–56. Washington DC: CQ Press.

Hastings, A. 1997. *The Construction of Nationhood: Ethnicity, Religion and Nationalism*. Cambridge: Cambridge University Press.

Hobsbawm, E., and T. Ranger. 1983. *The Invention of Tradition*. Cambridge: Cambridge University Press.

Huntington, S. 1996. *The Clash of Civilizations and the Remaking of World Order*. New York: Simon and Schuster.

Juergensmeyer, Mark. 1993. *The New Cold War? Religious Nationalism Confronts the Secular State*. Berkeley: University of California Press.

Juergensmeyer, Mark. 2006. "Nationalism and Religion." In *The Sage Handbook of Nations and Nationalism*, edited by Gerard Delanty and Krishan Kumar, 182–91. London: Sage Publications.

Juergensmeyer, Mark. 2008. *Global Rebellion: Religious Challenges to the Secular State*. Berkeley: University of California Press.

Juergensmeyer, Mark. 2010. "The Global Rise of Religious Nationalism." *Australian Journal of International Affairs* 64, no. 3: 262–73.

Juergensmeyer, Mark, Margo Kitts, and Michael Jerryson. 2013. *The Oxford Handbook of Religion and Violence*. Oxford: Oxford University Press.

Kaldor, M. 2004. "Nationalism and Globalization." *Nations and Nationalism* 10: 161–77.

March, L. 2012. "Nationalism for Export? The Domestic and Foreign-Policy Implications of the New 'Russian Idea.'" *Europe-Asia Studies* 64: 401–25.

Muller, Z. Jerry. 2008. "Us and Them: The Enduring Power of Ethnic Nationalism." *Foreign Affairs Magazine*, March–April.

O'Leary, B. 1997. "On the Nature of Nationalism: An Appraisal of Ernest Gellner's Writings on Nationalism." *British Journal of Political Science* 27: 191–222.

Oxford Dictionary of English. 2010. Third edition. Oxford: Oxford University Press.

Ozkirimli, U. 2010. *Theories of Nationalism: A Critical Introduction*. Second edition. Basingstoke: Palgrave Macmillan.

Renan, E. 1994. "Qu'est-ce qu'une Nation?" In *Nationalism*, edited by J. Hutchinson and A. D. Smith, 17–18. Oxford: Oxford University Press.

Said, Edward. 1978. *Orientalism*. New York: Vintage.

Said, Edward. 2001. "The Clash of Ignorance." *The Nation*, October 4.

Saunders, R. A. 2008. "The Ummah as Nation: A Reappraisal in the Wake of the Cartoons Affair." *Nations and Nationalism* 14, no. 2: 303–21.

Smith, A. D. 1991a. *National Identity*. London: Penguin Group.

Smith, A. D. 1991b. "The Nation: Invented, Imagined, Reconstructed? *Millennium—Journal of International Studies* 20: 353–68.

Smith, A. D. 1995. *Nations and Nationalism in a Global Era*. Cambridge: Polity.

Smith, A. D. 1998. *Nationalism and Modernism*. London: Routledge.

Smith, A. D. 2000a. *The Nation in History: Historiographical Debates about Ethnicity and Nationalism*. Cambridge: Polity Press.

Smith, A. D. 2000b. "Theories of Nationalism Alternative Models of Nation Formation." In *Asian Nationalism*, edited by M. Leifer, 1–20. London: Routledge.

Smith, A. D. 2002. "When Is a Nation?" *Geopolitics* 7: 5–32.

Smith, A. D. 2008. *The Cultural Foundations of Nations: Hierarchy, Covenant and Republic*. Oxford: Blackwell.

Van Den Berghe, P. 1978. "Race and Ethnicity: A Sociobiological Perspective." *Ethnic and Racial Studies* 1: 401–11.

Van Den Berghe, P. 1981. *The Ethnic Phenomenon*. New York: Elsevier.

Van Den Berghe, P. 1994. "A Socio-Biological Perspective." In *Nationalism*, edited by J. Hutchinson and A. D. Smith, 96–102. Oxford: Oxford University Press.

Van Den Berghe, P. 2001. "Sociobiological Theory of Nationalism." In *Encyclopaedia of Nationalism*, edited by A. S. Leoussi, 273–79. New Brunswick: Transaction Publishers.

van der Veer, Peter. 2012. "Religion, Secularism and National Development in India and China." *Third World Quarterly* 33, no. 4: 721–34.

van der Veer, Peter. 2013. "Nationalism and Religion." In *The Oxford Handbook of the History of Nationalism*, edited by John Breuilly, 655–71. Oxford: Oxford University Press.

Bibliography

Abu Bakar, Carmen. 2015. "Globalization: Issues, Challenges and Responses Among the Moros of the Southern Philippines." In *Southeast Asian Muslims in the Era of Globalization*, edited by Ken Michi and Omar Farouk, 106–26. New York: Palgrave-McMillan.

Agence France-Presse. 2017. "Gay Rights Supporters Parade Amid Rain, Protests in Seoul." *The Nation*. July 15. http://www.nationmultimedia.com/detail/breakingnews/30320860.

Ahmed, Kazi Anis. 2019. "Bangladesh's Unfinished Revolution." South Asia Program, Hudson Institute. February 15. http://www.southasiaathudson.org/blog/2019/2/15/bangladeshs-unfinished-revolution?fbclid=IwAR3R-RI2Y53jY30Kk5fTU7Jccs4JT-We59J4MKs5Ow7z4IDJAz3lJ-t_pK4.

Ali, Tariq. 2011. *Kashmir: The Case for Freedom*. London: Verso.

Al Maenna, Tariq A. 2013. "Neo-Fascism on the Rise in Sri Lanka." *Gulf News*. February 23. https://gulfnews.com/opinion/op-eds/neo-fascism-on-the-rise-in-sri-lanka-1.1150052.

Amnesty International. 2014. "Prosecuting Beliefs: Indonesia's Blasphemy Laws." London: Amnesty International.

Amnesty International. 2015. "Myanmar: Guilty Verdict for 'Insulting Religion' Must Be Overturned Immediately." London: Amnesty International.

Anam, Tahmima. 2011. *The Good Muslim*. London: Harper Collins.

Anderson, Benedict. 1983. *Imagined Communities: Reflections on the Origin and Spread of Nationalism*. London: Verso.

Anderson, Benedict. 2001. "Western Nationalism and Eastern Nationalism." *New Left Review*, May–June.

Anderson, Paul. 2017. "Challenges, Theories and Methods in Studying Chinese Pentecostalism." In *Global Chinese Pentecostal and Charismatic Christianity*, edited by Feggang Yang, Joy K. C. Tong, and Allen H. Anderson, 345–54. Amsterdam: Brill.

Anderson, Perry. 2012. *The Indian Ideology*. London: Verso

Annan, Kofi. 2017. "Towards a Peaceful, Fair and Prosperous Future for the People of Rakhine." *Advisory Commission on Rakhine State*. http://www.rakhinecommission.org/the-final-report/.

Appiah, Kwame Anthony. 2018. *The Lies that Bind: Rethinking Identity*. London: Profile Books.

Archer, R. 1995. "The Catholic Church in East Timor." In *East Timor at the Crossroads: The Forging of a Nation*, edited by P. Carey and C. Bently, 120–36. Honolulu: University of Hawaii Press, 1995.

Armstrong, J. 1982. *Nations before Nationalism*. Chapel Hill: University of North Carolina Press.

Asad, Talal. 1983. "Anthropological Conceptions of Religion: Reflections on Geertz." *Man, New Series* 18, no. 2 (June): 237–59.

Asad, Talal. 2003. *Formations of the Secular: Christianity, Islam, Modernity*. Stanford, CA: Stanford University Press.

Asan. 2015. "Over the Rainbow: Public Attitude toward LGBT in South Korea." *The Asan Institute for Policy Studies*, April 17. http://en.asaninst.org/contents/over-the-rainbow-public-attitude-toward-lgbt-in-south-korea/.

Ashiwa, Yoshiko, and David L. Wank. 2009. *Making Religion, Making the State*. Stanford, CA: Stanford University Press.

Asia Foundation. 2019. "A Momentous Moment for Mindanao." *The Asia Foundation*, January 16. https://asiafoundation.org/2019/01/16/a-momentous-moment-for-mindanao/.

Aslam, Nadeem. 2017. *The Golden Legend*. New York: Knopf.

Aung San Suu Kyi. 2013. "Suu Kyi Calls on Citizenship Law to Be Revised." https://arakandiary.blogspot.com/2013/04/suu-kyi-calls-on-citizenship-law-to-be.html.

A'yun, Rafiqa Qurrata. 2016. "Politics Complicate Blasphemy Investigations in Indonesia and Around the World." *The Conversation*, November 22. http://theconversation.com/politics-complicate-blasphemy-investigations-in-indonesia-and-around-the-world-68817.

A'yun, Rafiqa Qurrata. 2018. "Behind the Rise of Blasphemy Cases in Indonesia." *The Conversation*, May 14. https://theconversation.com/behind-the-rise-of-blasphemy-cases-in-indonesia-95214.

Banerjie, Monideepa. 2017. "BJP Says I Eat Beef, None of Their Business, Says Mamata Banerjee." *NDTV*, April 21. https://www.ndtv.com/kolkata-news/bjp-cant-decide-who-is-big-hindu-or-small-hindu-says-mamata-banerjee-1684403.

Bass, Gary. 2013. *Blood Telegram: India's Secret War in East Pakistan*. New York: Random House.

Bays, Daniel H. 2003. "Chinese Protestant Christianity Today." *The China Quarterly* 174: 488–504.

Bays, Daniel H. 2012. *A New History of Christianity in China*. Malden: Wiley-Blackwell.

Bhatia, Rahul. 2017. "The Year of Love Jihad." *The New Yorker*, December 31.

Biswas, Soutik. 2018. "Why Did India Wake Up So Late to a Child Rape and Murder?" *BBC*, April 18.

Bradshaw, Peter. 2017. "The Venerable W Review: The Poisonous Monk behind Myanmar's Anti-Muslim Vendetta." *The Guardian*, October 10.

Brass, Paul. 2003a. "The Partition of India and Retributive Genocide in the Punjab, 1946–47: Means, Methods, and Purposes." *Journal of Genocide Research* 5: 71–101.

Brass, Paul. 2003b. *The Production of Hindu-Muslim Violence in Contemporary India*. Seattle: University of Washington Press.

Breuilly, J. 1993. *Nationalism and the State*. Manchester: Manchester University Press.

Breuilly, J. 2001. "The State and Nationalism." In *Understanding Nationalism*, 32–52. Cambridge: Polity.

Brubaker, R. 2004. *Ethnicity without Groups*. Cambridge, MA: Harvard University Press.

Brubaker, R. 2012. "Religion and Nationalism: Four Approaches." *Nations and Nationalism* 18, no. 1 (January): 2–20.

Buchanan, Francis. 1799. "A Comparative Vocabulary of Some of the Languages Spoken in the Burma Empire." *Asiatic Researches* 5: 219–40.

Butterfield, F. 1986. " Nuns and Priests Working with Communists Divide Church." *New York Times*, March 2. https://www.nytimes.com/1986/03/02/world/nuns-and-priests-working-with-communists-divide-church.html.

Calamur, Krishnadev. 2017. "The Misunderstood Roots of Burma's Rohingya Crisis." *The Atlantic*, September 25.

Calhoun, C. 1997. *Nationalism*. Buckingham: Open University Press.

Calhoun, C. 2007. *Nations Matter: Culture, History and the Cosmopolitan Dream*. London: Routledge.

Cao, Nanlai. 2012. "Elite Christianity and Spiritual Nationalism." *Chinese Sociological Review* 45, no. 2: 27–47.

Carey, P. 1999. "The Catholic Church, Religious Revival, and the Nationalist Movement in East Timor, 1975–98." *Indonesia and the Malay World* 27, no. 78: 77–95.

Casanova, José. 2011. "The Secular, Secularizations, Secularism." In *Rethinking Secularism*, edited Craig Calhoun, Mark Juergensmeyer, and Jonathan Van Antwerpen, 54–75. New York: Oxford University Press.

Chan, Aye. 2005. "The Development of a Muslim Enclave in Arakan (Rakhine) State of Burma (Myanmar)." *SOAS Bulletin of Burma Research* 3, no. 2 (Autumn): 396–420.

Chatterjee, P. 1986. *Nationalist Thought and the Colonial World: A Derivative Discourse?* London: Zed Books.

Cheesman, Nick. 2017. "How in Myanmar 'National Races' Came to Surpass Citizenship and Exclude Rohingya." *Journal of Contemporary Asia* 47 (2017): 1–20.

Cheesman, Nick, and Nicholas Farelly, eds. 2016. *Conflict in Myanmar: War, Politics, Religion.* Singapore: Iseas-Yusof Ishak Institute.

Chega! The Report of the Commission for Reception, Truth and Reconciliation in Timor-Leste (CAVR), Executive Summary. CAVR: Dili, 2005.

Chibber, Pradeep K., and Sandeep Shashtri. 2014. *Religious Practice and Democracy in India.* Cambridge: Cambridge University Press.

Chong, Terence. 2018. "Introduction." In *Pentecostal Megachurches in Southeast Asia: Negotiating Class, Consumption and the Nation*, edited by Terence Chong, 1–17. Singapore: ISEAS-Yusof Ishak Institute.

Chua, Lynette. 2018. *The Politics of Love in Myanmar.* Stanford: Stanford University Press.

Connley, Aleah. 2016. "Understanding the Oppressed: A Study of the Ahmadiyah and Their Strategies for Overcoming Adversity in Contemporary Indonesia." *Journal of Current Southeast Asian Affairs* 35, no. 1: 29–58.

Connor, W. 1990. "When Is a Nation?" *Ethnic and Racial Studies* 13: 92–103.

Connor, W. 1994. *Ethnonationalism: The Quest for Understanding.* Princeton: Princeton University Press.

Crouch, Melissa. 2014. *Law and Religion in Indonesia.* London: Routledge

Crouch, Melissa, ed. 2016. *Islam and the State in Myanmar: Muslim-Buddhist Relations and the Politics of Belonging.* Oxford: Oxford University Press.

Dalrymple, William. 2005. "India: The War over History." *New York Review of Books* 52, no. 6 (April 7): 62–65.

Dalrymple, William. 2010. *Nine Lives: In Search of the Sacred in Modern India.* London: Bloomsbury.

Das, Madhuparna. 2014. "RSS Leader Mohan Bhagwat Justifies 'Ghar Waspi,' Says Will Bring Back Our Brothers Who Have Lost Their Way." *Indian Express*, December 21. https://indianexpress.com/article/india/politics/bhagwat-dares-oppn-says-if-dont-like-conversion-bring-law-against-it/.

Deb, Siddartha. 2004. *The Point of No Return.* New York: Harper Perennial.

Deb, Siddartha. 2016. "Unmasking Modi." *New Republic*, May 3.

Denyer, Simon, and Annie Gowen. 2018. "Too Many Men: China and India Battle with the Consequences of Gender Imbalance." *Washington Post Magazine*, April 24.

Desai, Radhika. 2004. *Slouching Towards Ayodhya: From Congress to Hindutva in Indian Politics.* Second revised edition. New Delhi: Three Essays.

Devji, Faisal. 2013. *Muslim Zion: Pakistan as a Political Idea.* Cambridge, MA: Harvard University Press.

Devji, Faisal. 2018. "Will Saudi Arabia Cease to be the Center of Islam?" *New York Times*, September 7. https://www.nytimes.com/2018/09/07/opinion/saudi-arabia-islam-mbs.html.

Doniger, Wendy. 2009. *The Hindus: An Alternative History.* New York: Penguin.

Doniger, Wendy. 2014a. "Banned in Bangalore." *International New York Times*, March 7, 8.

Doniger, Wendy. 2014b. "Censorship by the Batra Brigades." *New York Review of Books* 61, no. 8 (May 8): 51.

Donthi, P. 2019. "The Liberals Who Loved Modi," *Caravan*, May 16, 2019. https://caravanmagazine.in/politics/the-liberals-who-loved-modi.

Dube, Siddarth. 2018. *An Indefinite Sentence: A Personal History of Outlawed Love and Sex.* New York: Atria Books.

Dutta, Binayak. 2018. "The Illusive Indian." *East Wind—The Northeast Journal.* http://eastwindjournal.com/2018/12/11/the-illusive-indian/.

Eisenstadt, Shmuel Noah. 2000. "Multiple Modernities." *Daedalus* 129, no. 1: 1–29.

Ellis-Petersen, Hannah. 2018. "Myanmar government is rogue and evil says Bangladesh minister" March 8, *The Guardian.* https://www.theguardian.com/world/2018/mar/08/myanmar-government-rogue-evil-bangladesh-minister-rohingya-refugees.

Embree, Ainslie T. 1990. *Utopias in Conflict: Religion and Nationalism in Modern India.* Berkeley: University of California Press.

Fachruddin, Azis Anwar. 2016. "Persisting Problems from the al-Maidah Debate." *Jakarta Post,* October 18. https://www.thejakartapost.com/academia/2016/10/18/persisting-problems-from-the-al-maidah-51-debate.html.

Farhadian, Charles E. 2005. *Christianity, Islam and Nationalism in Indonesia.* London: Routledge.

Fisker-Nielsen, Anne Mette. 2012. *Religion and Politics in Contemporary Japan: Soka Gakkai Youth and Komeito.* London and New York: Routledge.

Formichi, Chiara, and R. Michael Feener, eds. 2015. *Shi'ism in Southeast Asia: 'Alid Piety and Sectarian Constructions.* Oxford: Oxford University Press.

Frontline Defenders. 2017. "Attacks on LGBT Rights Defenders Escalating in Indonesia."https://www.frontlinedefenders.org/en/statement-report/report-attacks-lgbt-rights-defenders-escalating-indonesia.

Frykenberg, Eric. 2008. *Christianity in India: From the Beginnings to the Present.* Oxford: Oxford University Press.

Gao, Jenny. 2014. "A Talk on Bodu Bala Sena, Sri Lanka's Militant Buddhists." *The Phoenix,* November 3. https://swarthmorephoenix.com/2014/11/03/a-talk-on-bodu-bala-sena-sri-lankas-militant-buddhists/.

Geary, P. J. 2002. *The Construction of Nationhood: Ethnicity, Religion and Nationalism.* Princeton: Princeton University Press.

Geertz, Clifford. 1960. *Religion of Java.* Glencoe, IL: The Free Press.

Geertz, Clifford. 1973. *The Interpretation of Cultures: Selected Essays.* New York: Basic Books.

Gellner, E. 1983. *Nations and Nationalism.* Ithaca, NY: Cornell University Press.

Gellner, E. 1996. "The Coming of Nationalism and Its Interpretations: Myths of Nation and Class." In *Mapping the Nation,* edited by G. Balakrishnan, 98–145. London: Verso.

Gettlemen, J., K. Schultz, S. Raj, and H. Kumar. 2018. "India Gay Sex Ban Is Struck Down. 'Indefensible,' Court Says." *New York Times,* September 6. https://www.nytimes.com/2018/09/06/world/asia/india-gay-sex-377.html.

Gettlemen, J., K. Schultz, S. Raj, and H. Kumar. 2019. "Under Modi, a Hindu Nationalist Surge Has Further Divided India." *New York Times,* April 11. https://www.nytimes.com/2019/04/11/world/asia/modi-india-elections.html.

Ghosh, Palash. 2012. "Hindu Nationalist's Historical Links to Nazism and Fascism." *International Business Times,* March 6. https://www.ibtimes.com/hindu-nationalists-historical-links-nazism-fascism-214222.

Global Village Space. 2017. "Gujarat Law Minister: 'Anyone Who Doesn't Spare Cow, the Government Will Not Spare Him.'" March 31. https://www.globalvillagespace.com/gujarat-law-minister-anyone-doesnt-spare-cow-government-will-not-spare/.

Gottowik, Volker, ed. 2014. *Dynamics of Religion in Southeast Asia: Magic and Modernity.* Amsterdam: Amsterdam University Press, 2014.

Gowen, Annie. 2018. "'We Don't Have Any Fear': India's Angry Young Men and Its Lynch Mob Crisis." *Washington Post,* August 27. https://www.washingtonpost.com/world/asia_pacific/we-dont-have-any-fear-indias-angry-young-men-and-its-lynch-mob-crisis/2018/08/26/9a0a247a-a0aa-11e8-a3dd-2a1991f075d5_story.html?noredirect=on&utm_term=.39f8ffeec1ae.

Greenfeld, L. 1992. *Nationalism: Five Roads to Modernity.* Cambridge, MA: Harvard University Press.

Greenfeld, L. 2003. *The Spirit of Capitalism Nationalism and Economic Growth.* Cambridge, MA: Harvard University Press.

Gregory, Shaun. 2012. "Under the Shadow of Islam: The Plight of the Christian Minority in Pakistan." *Contemporary South Asia* 20, no. 2: 195–212.

Gries, Peter Hays. 2004. *China's New Nationalism: Pride, Politics, and Diplomacy.* Berkeley: University of California Press.

Gries, Peter Hays. 2007. "Narratives to Live By: The Century of Humiliation and Chinese National Identity Today." In *China's Transformations*, edited by Lionel M. Jensen and Timothy B. Weston, 112–128. Lanham, MD: Rowman & Littlefield.

Guha, Ramachandra. 2012. *Patriots and Partisans.* New Delhi: Allen Lane.

Guibernau, M. 2004. "Anthony D. Smith on Nations and National Identity: A Critical Assessment." *Nations and Nationalism* 10: 125–41.

Gupta, Shubhra. 2018. "Padmaavat Movie Review: A Magnificently-Mounted Paean to Rajput 'Aan Baan Shaan.'" *Indian Express*, January 26. https://indianexpress.com/article/entertainment/movie-review/padmavati-movie-review-star-rating-5036330/.

Gurevitch, M., S. Coleman, and J. Blumer. 2009. "Political Communication: Old and New Media Relationships." In *Media Power in Politics*, edited by D. Graber, 45–56. Washington, DC: CQ Press.

Guterres, J. 2008. "Timor-Leste: A Year of Democratic Elections." *Southeast Asian Affairs*, 359–73.

Hadiz, Vedi. 2018. "Islamic Populism in Indonesia." In *Routledge Handbook of Contemporary Indonesia*, edited by Robert Hefner, 296–306. London: Routledge.

Hajari, Nisid. 2015. *Midnight Furies: The Deadly Legacy of India's Partition.* New York: Houghton Mifflin Harcourt.

Hamid. Mohsin. 2007. *The Reluctant Fundamentalist.* New York: Harcourt.

Hanif, Mohammed. 2017. "Pakistan, Land of the Intolerant." *New York Times*, October 19. https://www.nytimes.com/2017/10/19/opinion/pakistan-muslims-ahmadis.html.

Haniffa, Farzana. 2016. "Who Gave These Fellows the Strength? Muslims and the Bodu Bala Sena in Post-War Sri Lanka." In *Sri Lanka: The Struggle for Peace in the Aftermath of War*, edited by Amarnath Amarasingam and Daniel Bass, 109–27. London: Hurst Publishers.

Haniffa Farzana. 2017. "Merit Economies in Neoliberal Times: Halal Troubles in Contemporary Sri Lanka." In *Religion and the Morality of the Market*, edited by D. Rudnyckyi and F. Osella, 116–37. Cambridge: Cambridge University Press.

Hardacre, Helen. 2017. *Shinto: A History.* Oxford: Oxford University Press.

Harsono, Andreas. 2017. "The Toxic Impact of Indonesia's Abusive Blasphemy Law." *Human Rights Watch.* https://www.hrw.org/news/2017/08/07/toxic-impact-indonesias-abusive-blasphemy-law/.

Hasan, Mubashar. 2011. "Historical Developments of Political Islam with Reference to Bangladesh." *Journal of Asian and African Studies* 47, no. 2: 155–67.

Hasan, Mubashar. 2016. "Religious Freedom with an Islamic Twist: How the Medina Charter Is Used to Frame Secularism in Bangladesh." *South Asia@LSE.* London: London School of Economics, June 13. http://blogs.lse.ac.uk/southasia/2016/06/13/religious-freedom-with-an-islamic-twist-how-the-medina-charter-is-used-to-frame-secularism-in-bangladesh/.

Hasan, Noorhaidi. 2018. "Salafism in Indonesia." In *Routledge Handbook of Contemporary Indonesia*, edited by Robert Hefner, 246–56. London: Routledge.

Hastings, A. 1997. *The Construction of Nationhood: Ethnicity, Religion and Nationalism.* Cambridge: Cambridge University Press.

Hazzan, Dave. 2016. "Why the World's Largest Church Still Worships Its Embezzling Former Leader." *Vice*, May 30. https://www.vice.com/en_us/article/zn8be8/why-the-worlds-largest-church-still-worships-its-embezzling-former-leader.

Henn, Alexander. 2014. *Hindu-Catholic Encounters in Goa: Religion, Colonialism, and Modernity.* Bloomington: Indiana University Press.

Hicks, Jaqueline. 2014. "Heresy and Authority: Understanding the Turn against Ahmadiyah in Indonesia." *Southeast Asia Research, SOAS*, September 1.

Hindu. 2011. "Creeping Intolerance." *The Hindu*, February 8. https://www.thehindu.com/opinion/editorial/Creeping-intolerance/article15377401.ece.

Hobsbawm, E., and T. Ranger. 1983. *The Invention of Tradition.* Cambridge: Cambridge University Press.

Holt, John, ed. 2011. *The Sri Lanka Reader*. Durham, NC: Duke University Press.
Holt, John, ed. 2016. *Buddhist Extremists and Muslim Minorities: Religious Conflict in Contemporary Sri Lanka*. Oxford: Oxford University Press.
Hoon, Chang-Yau. 2013. "Between Evangelism and Multiculturalism: The Dynamics of Protestant Christianity in Indonesia." *Social Compass* 60, no. 4: 457–70.
Hoon, Chang-Yau. 2016. "Mapping Chineseness on the Landscape of Christian Churches in Indonesia." *Asian Ethnicity* 17, no. 2: 228–47.
Hoque, Md. Sazzadul. 2018. "Blasphemy Law in Bangladesh." *Center for Inquiry*, September 27. https://centerforinquiry.org/blog/blasphemy-law-in-bangladesh/.
HRW. 2014. Human Rights Watch. "I'm Scared to Be a Woman: Human Rights Abuses against Transgender People in Malaysia." *Human Rights Watch*, September 25. https://features.hrw.org/features/HRW_reports_2014/Im_Scared_to_Be_a_Woman/index.html?_ga=2.254731727.656653231.1496826391-230355381.1496826391.
HRW. 2018. "Eradicating Ideological Viruses: China's Campaign of Oppression against Xinjiang's Muslims." *Human Rights Watch*, Sept 9. https://www.hrw.org/report/2018/09/09/eradicating-ideological-viruses/chinas-campaign-repression-against-xinjiangs.
Huntington, S. 1996. *The Clash of Civilizations and the Remaking of World Order*. New York: Simon and Schuster.
Ibrahim, Azeem. 2017. *The Rohingyas: Inside Myanmar's Hidden Genocide*. Second edition. London: Hurst.
ICC. 2001. *The Untold Tragedies of Maluku*. Washington, DC: International Christian Concern.
ICG. 2016. "Southern Thailand's Peace Dialogue: No Traction." *International Crisis Group*, Briefing no. 148, September 21. https://www.crisisgroup.org/asia/south-east-asia/thailand/southern-thailand-s-peace-dialogue-no-traction.
ICG. 2017. "Buddhism and State Power in Mynamar." *International Crisis Group*, Sept 5. https://www.crisisgroup.org/asia/south-east-asia/myanmar/290-buddhism-and-state-power-myanmar.
ICG. 2018. "The Long Road Ahead for Myanmar's Rohingya Refugee Crisis." *International Crisis Group*. https://www.crisisgroup.org/asia/south-east-asia/myanmar/296-long-haul-ahead-myanmars-rohingya-refugee-crisis.
ILGA. 2016. "The Personal and the Political: Attitudes to LGBTI People around the World." *International Lesbian, Gay, Bisexual and Trans and Intersex Association (ILGA)*. https://ilga.org/downloads/Ilga_Riwi_Attitudes_LGBTI_survey_Logo_personal_political.pdf.
Indian Express. 2018. "Mobocracy Can't be the New Normal, Get a Law to Punish Lynching: SC to Govt." July 18.
IPAC. 2017. "Post-Marawi Lessons from Detained Extremists in the Philippines." *Institute for Policy Analysis of Conflict*, IPAC Report No. 41, November 27. http://www.understandingconflict.org/en/conflict/read/66/POST-MARAWI-LESSONS-FROM-PHILIPPINE-DETAINEES.
Jaffrelot, Christophe. 1996. *The Hindu Nationalist Movement in India*. New York: Columbia University Press.
Jaffrelot, Christophe, ed. 2007. *Hindu Nationalism: A Reader*. Princeton: Princeton University Press.
Jain, Rupam, and Tom Lasseter. 2018. "Indian Prime Minister Leads Nationalist Charge to Rewrite History Books." *Reuters*, March 6.
Jerryson, Michael. 2018. *If You Meet the Buddha on the Road: Buddhism, Politics and Violence*. Oxford: Oxford University Press.
Jeyaraj, D. B. S. 2013. "Defence Secretary Gotabhaya Rajapaksa Openly Supportive of 'Ethno Religious Fascist' Organization Bodhu Bala Sena." *dbsjeyaraj.com*. March 10. http://dbsjeyaraj.com/dbsj/archives/17939.
Jha, Dwijendra Narayan. 2002. *Myth of the Holy Cow*. London: Verso.
Johnson, I. 2017. *The Souls of China: The Return of Religion after Mao*. New York: Pantheon.
Jolliffe, J. 1978. *East Timor: Nationalism and Colonialism*. Brisbane: University of Queensland Press.

Juergensmeyer, Mark. 1993. *The New Cold War? Religious Nationalism Confronts the Secular State*. Berkeley: University of California Press.

Juergensmeyer, Mark. 2006. "Nationalism and Religion." In *The Sage Handbook of Nations and Nationalism*, edited by Gerard Delanty and Krishan Kumar, 182–91. London: Sage Publications.

Juergensmeyer, Mark. 2008. *Global Rebellion: Religious Challenges to the Secular State*. Berkeley: University of California Press.

Juergensmeyer, Mark. 2010. "The Global Rise of Religious Nationalism." *Australian Journal of International Affairs* 64, no. 3: 262–73.

Juergensmeyer, Mark. 2014. "Religious Terrorism as Performance Violence." In *Oxford Handbook of Religion and Violence*, edited by M. Juergensmeyer, M. Kitts, and M. Jerryson, 281–91. Oxford: Oxford University Press.

Juergensmeyer, Mark. 2015. "Myanmar's Buddhist Terrorist." *Religion and Social Change in a Global World Blog*, March 10. http://juergensmeyer.org/ myanmars-buddhist-terrorist/.

Julius, Qaiser. 2016. "The Experience of Minorities Under Pakistan's Blasphemy Laws." *Islam and Christian–Muslim Relations* 27, no. 1: 95–115.

Kaldor, M. 2004. "Nationalism and Globalization." *Nations and Nationalism* 10: 161–77.

Kazi, Seema. 2014. "Kashmir, Gender and Militarization." *Oxford Islamic Studies.* http://www.oxfordislamicstudies.com/article/opr/t343/e0165?_hi=0&_pos=1.

Kesavan, Mukul. 2018. "Murderous Majorities." *New York Review of Books*, January 18. https://www.nybooks.com/articles/2018/01/18/rohingya-murderous-majorities/.

Khan, Shahab Enam. 2017. "Bangladesh: The Changing Dynamics of Violent Extremism and the Response of the State." *Small Wars & Insurgencies* 28, no. 1: 191–217.

Khan, Yasmin. 2007. *The Great Partition: The Making of India and Pakistan*. New Haven: Yale University Press.

Khilnani, Sunil. 1997. *The Idea of India*. New York: Penguin.

Kingston, Jeff. 2006a. "Balancing Justice and Reconciliation in East Timor." *Critical Asian Studies* 38, no. 3: 271–302.

Kingston, Jeff. 2006b. "East Timor's Search for Justice and Reconciliation." *Asia Pacific Journal* 4, no. 1 (January 4). https://apjjf.org/-Jeff-Kingston/1706/article.html.

Kingston, Jeff. 2008. "Burma's Despair." *Critical Asian Studies* 40, no. 1: 3–43.

Koesel, Karrie J. 2013. "The Rise of a Chinese House Church: The Organizational Weapon." *The China Quarterly* 215: 572–89.

Koesel, Karrie J. 2014. *Religion and Authoritarianism: Cooperation, Conflict, and the Consequences*. Cambridge: Cambridge University Press.

Koesel, Karrie J. 2017. "Chinese Patriotic Pentecostals." In *Global Chinese Pentecostal and Charismatic Christianity*, edited by F. Yang, J. K. C. Tong, and A. Anderson, 240–63. Leiden: Brill.

Kuo, Cheng-tian. 2011. "Chinese Religious Reforms." *Asian Survey* 51, no. 6: 1042–64.

Lancet. 2013. "Prevalence of and Factors Associated with Non-Partner Rape Perpetration: Findings from the UN Multi-Country Cross-Sectional Study on Men and Violence in Asia and the Pacific." *The Lancet* 1 (October): 208–18.

Langlois, Jill. 2013. "Indonesia Radicals Rally for 'Myanmar Jihad' After Jakarta Bomb Plot Foiled." *Agence France-Presse*, May 3. https://www.pri.org/stories/2013-05-03/indonesia-radicals-rally-myanmar-jihad-after-jakarta-bomb-plot-foiled-photos.

Leider, Jacques. 2013. "Rohingya: The Name, the Movement and the Quest for Identity." In *Nation Building in Myanmar*, 204–55. Yangon: Myanmar EGRESS/Myanmar Peace Centre.

Leider, Jacques. 2018. "Rohingya: The History of a Muslim Identity in Myanmar." In *Oxford Research Encyclopedias*. Oxford: Oxford University Press.

Lintner, Bertil. 2002. "Religious Extremism and Nationalism in Bangladesh." Religion and Security in South Asia—An International Workshop Asia Pacific Center for Security Studies, Honolulu, Hawaii, August 19–22.

Lintner, Bertil. 2017. "The Truth behind Myanmar's Rohingya Insurgency." *Asia Times*, September 20. http://www.atimes.com/article/truth-behind-myanmars-rohingya-insurgency/.

Lloyd-Parry, Richard. 2005. *In the Time of Madness: Indonesia on the Edge of Chaos*. New York: Grove Press.

Luce, G. H. 1985. *Phases of Pre-Pagan Burma: Languages and History*. Oxford: Oxford University Press.

Madsen, Richard. 1998. *China's Catholics: Tragedy and Hope in an Emerging Civil Society*. Berkeley: University of California Press.

Madsen, Richard. 2004. "Catholic Conflict and Cooperation in the People's Republic of China." In *God and Caesar in China*, edited by Jason Kindopp and Carol Lee Hamrin, 93–106. Washington, DC: Brookings Institution Press.

Madsen, Richard. 2007. *Democracy's Dharma: Religious Renaissance and Political Development in Taiwan*. Berkeley: University of California Press.

Madsen, Richard. 2011. "Religious Renaissance in China Today." *Journal of Current Chinese Affairs* 40, no. 2: 17–42.

Mahmud, Tarek. 2017. "Mongol Shobhajatra Calls to Denounce Militancy." *Dhaka Tribune*, April 14. https://www.dhakatribune.com/bangladesh/2017/04/14/mongol-shobhajatra-calls-denouncing-militancy/?fb_comment_id=1408884542544255_1408960209203355.

Mark, Eugene. 2018. "Insurgents in Southern Thailand Aren't Jihadists." *East Asia Forum*, June 6.

Mazhar, Arafat. 2014. "The Untold Story of Pakistan's Blasphemy Law." *Dawn*, December 9https://www.dawn.com/news/1149558.

Mazhar, Arafat. 2015a. "The Fatwas that Can Change Pakistan's Blasphemy Narrative." *Dawn*, January 4. https://www.dawn.com/news/1154856/the-fatwas-that-can-change-pakistans-blasphemy-narrative.

Mazhar, Arafat. 2015b. "Why Blasphemy Remains Unpardonable in Pakistan." *Dawn*, February 19. https://www.dawn.com/news/1163596/why-blasphemy-remains-unpardonable-in-pakistan.

Mazhar, Arafat. 2015c. "Blasphemy and the Death Penalty." *Dawn*, November 2. https://www.dawn.com/news/1215304/blasphemy-and-the-death-penalty-misconceptions-explained.

McGregor, A., L. Skeaff, and M. Bevan. 2012. "Overcoming Secularism? Catholic Development Geographies in Timor-Leste." *Third World Quarterly* 33, no. 6: 1129–46.

McLaughlin, Levi. 2015. "Komeito's Soka Gakkai Protesters and Supporters: Religious Motivations for Political Activism in Contemporary Japan." *The Asia-Pacific Journal* 13, no. 41 (October 12).

McLaughlin, Levi. 2018. *Soka Gakkai's Human Revolution: The Rise of a Mimetic Nation in Japan*. Honolulu: University of Hawaii Press.

Mehta, Pratap Bhanu. 2018a. "Kathua, Unnao: Shame on Us." *Indian Express*, April 13.

Mehta, Pratap Bhanu. 2018b. "The Age of Cretinism—Case Study on Modi's India." *Sri Lanka Guardian*, August 14. https://www.slguardian.org/the-age-of-cretinism-case-study-on-modis-india/.

Meitzner, Marcus. 2018. "Fighting Illiberalism with Illiberalism: Islamist Populism and Democratic Deconsolidation in Indonesia." *Pacific Affairs* 91, no. 2 (June): 261–81.

Menchik, Jeremy, and Katrina Trost. 2018. "A 'Tolerant' Indonesia? Indonesian Muslims in Comparative Perspective." In *Routledge Handbook of Contemporary Indonesia*, edited by Robert Hefner, 390–405. London: Routledge.

Milner, Greg. 2019. "They Really Don't Make Music Like They Used to." *New York Times*, January 9–10. https://www.nytimes.com/2019/02/07/opinion/what-these-grammy-songs-tell-us-about-the-loudness-wars.html.

Milward, James. 2018 "What It's Like to Live in a Surveillance State." *New York Times*, February 3. https://www.nytimes.com/2018/02/03/opinion/Sunday/china-surveillance-state-uighurs.html.

Milward, James. 2019. "Reeducating Xinjiang's Muslims." *New York Review of Books*, February 7. https://www.nybooks.com/articles/2019/02/07/reeducating-xinjiangs-muslims/.

Mishra, Pankaj. 2002. "One Man's Beef." *The Guardian*, July 13.

Mishra, Pankaj. 2014. "Modi's Idea of India." *International New York Times*, October 24.

Mishra, Pankaj. 2017. *The Age of Anger*.

Mishra, Pankaj. 2019. "How Narendra Modi Seduced India with Envy and Hate." *New York Times*, May 23. https://www.nytimes.com/2019/05/23/opinion/modi-india-election.html.

Mo, Timothy. 2012. *Pure*. London: Turnaround Books.

Moe, Wai, and Austin Ramzy. 2015. "Myanmar Sentences 3 to Prison for Depicting Buddha Wearing Headphones." *New York Times*, March 17. https://www.nytimes.com/2015/03/18/world/asia/myanmar-sentences-3-to-prison-for-defaming-buddhism.html.

MSF. 2017. "Rohingya Crisis—A Survey of Six Pooled Surveys." *Medecins sans Frontieres*. https://www.msf.org/myanmarbangladesh-rohingya-crisis-summary-findings-six-pooled-surveys.

Muller, Z. Jerry. 2008. "Us and Them: The Enduring Power of Ethnic Nationalism." *Foreign Affairs Magazine*, March–April.

Mullins, Mark. 1998. *Christianity Made in Japan: A Study of Indigenous Movements*. Honolulu: University of Hawaii Press.

Mullins, Mark. 2017. "Becoming a Multicultural Church in the Context of Neo-Nationalism: The New Challenges Facing Catholics in Japan." In *Scattered and Gathered: Catholics in Diaspora*, edited by Michael Budde, 112–30. Eugene, OR: Cascade Books.

Naipaul, V. S. 1990. *India: A Million Mutinies*. New York: Viking.

Nandy, Ashish. 1991. "Hinduism versus Hindutva: The Inevitability of a Confrontation." *Times of India*, February 18. https://www.sscnet.ucla.edu/southasia/Socissues/hindutva.html.

Nasrin, Taslima. 2018. "The Rapes at Kathua and Unnao." *Free Though Blogs*, April 13. https://freethoughtblogs.com/taslima/.

NHK. 2017. "New Democratic Party in Myanmar Poised to Challenge Aung San Suu Kyi." October 18. https://www3.nhk.or.jp/nhkworld/en/news/editors/1/newdemocraticpartyinmyanmar/.

Nemoto, Kei. 1991. "The Rohingya Issue: A Thorny Obstacle between Burma (Myanmar) and Bangladesh." *Burma Library*. http://www.burmalibrary.org/docs14/Kei_Nemoto-Rohingya.pdf.

Nemoto, Kei. 2016. "Burma's (Myanmar's) Exclusive Nationalism." In *Asian Nationalisms Reconsidered*, edited by Jeff Kingston, 218–29. Abingdon, UK: Routledge.

Nevins, Joseph. 2005. *A Not-So-Distant Horror: Mass Violence in East Timor*. Ithaca, NY: Cornell University Press.

Nussbaum, Martha. 2008. *The Clash Within: Democracy, Religious Violence, and India's Future*. Cambridge, MA: Harvard University Press.

Oblau, Gotthard. 2005. "Pentecostal by Default? Contemporary Christianity in China." In *Asian and Pentecostal: The Charismatic Face of Christianity in Asia*, edited by Allan Anderson and Edmond Tang, 411–36. London: Regnum Books International.

O'Leary, B. 1997. "On the Nature of Nationalism: An Appraisal of Ernest Gellner's Writings on Nationalism." *British Journal of Political Science* 27: 191–222.

Osaki, Tomohiro. 2018. "LDP Lawmaker Mio Sugita Faces Backlash after Describing LGBT People as 'Unproductive.'" *Japan Times*, July 24. https://www.japantimes.co.jp/news/2018/07/24/national/politics-diplomacy/ldp-lawmaker-mio-sugita-faces-backlash-describing-lgbt-people-unproductive/.

Ozkirimli, U. 2010. *Theories of Nationalism: A Critical Introduction*. Second edition. Basingstoke: Palgrave Macmillan.

Panagariya, Arvind, and Megha Mukim. 2013. "A Comprehensive Analysis of Poverty in India." *Policy Research Working Paper 6714*. Washington, DC: World Bank.

Pedersen, Morten B. 2008. *Promoting Human Rights in Burma: A Critique of Western Sanctions Policy*. Lanham, MD: Rowman & Littlefield.

Peer, Basharat. 2008. *Curfewed Night*. New York: Simon and Schuster.

Peer, Basharat. 2016. "Kashmir and the Inheritance of Loss." *New York Times*, July 25. https://www.nytimes.com/2016/07/25/opinion/kashmir-and-the-inheritance-of-loss.html.

Petrie, Charles. 2007. "Statement of the UN Country Team in Myanmar." October 24. http://yangon.unic.org/index.php?option=com_content&task=view&id=.

Pew. 2007. *Spirit and Power: A 10-Country Survey of Pentecostals*. Washington, DC: The Pew Forum on Religion and Public Life.

Pew. 2009. "Mapping the Global Muslim Population." *Pew Research Center*. https://www.pewforum.org/2009/10/07/mapping-the-global-muslim-population/.

Pew. 2013a. "The Global Divide on Homosexuality: Greater Acceptance in More Secular and Affluent Countries." *Pew Research Center.* http://www.pewglobal.org/2013/06/04/the-global-divide-on-homosexuality/.

Pew. 2013b. "The World's Muslims: Religion, Politics and Society." Washington, DC: Pew Research Center. http://www.pewforum.org/2013/04/30/the-worlds-muslims-religion-politics-society-beliefs-about-sharia/.

Pew. 2014. "6 Facts about South Korea's Growing Christian Population." *Pew Research Center*, August 12. http://www.pewresearch.org/fact-tank/2014/08/12/6-facts-about-christianity-in-south-korea/.

Pew. 2015a. "The Future of World Religions: Population Growth Projections, 2010–2050." *Pew Research Center*, April 2. http://www.pewforum.org/2015/04/02/religious-projections-2010-2050/.

Pew. 2015b. "Indians Adore Modi." *Pew Research Center*, September 17. http://www.pewresearch.org/fact-tank/2015/09/17/indians-adore-modi/.

Pew. 2016a. "Trends in Global Restrictions on Religion." *Pew Research Center*, June 23. http://www.pewforum.org/2016/06/23/trends-in-global-restrictions-on-religion/.

Pew. 2016b. "Which Countries Still Outlaw Apostasy and Blasphemy?" *Pew Research Center.* https://www.pewresearch.org/fact-tank/2016/07/29/which-countries-still-outlaw-apostasy-and-blasphemy/.

Pew. 2017. "The Changing Global Religious Landscape." *Pew Research Center*, April 5. http://www.pewforum.org/2017/04/05/the-changing-global-religious-landscape/.

Pilgrim, Sophie. 2015. "Buddhist Monk Calls UN Expert 'Whore' over Muslim Support." *France24*, January 21. https://www.france24.com/en/20150121-burma-buddhist-monk-un-expert-whore-anti-muslim-wirathu.

Pinheiro, Paulo Sergio. 2007. Special Rapporteur, UN Human Rights Council. "Human Rights in Myanmar." UN Human Rights Council, December 7. https://www2.ohchr.org/english/bodies/hrcouncil/docs/6session/A.HRC.6.14new.pdf.

Prudhomme, J. 2010. *The Impact of Blasphemy Laws on Human Rights.* New York: Freedom House. https://freedomhouse.org/sites/default/files/Policing_Belief_Full.pdf.

Raja, Raza Habib. 2014. "The Culture of Rape in South Asia." *Huffington Post*, August 23.

Ramsay, Zara. 2016. "Religion, Politics and the Meaning of Self-Sacrifice for Tibet." *Contemporary South Asia* 24, no. 1 March: 75–93.

Ramzy, Austin. 2019. "China Targets Prominent Uighur Intellectuals to Erase an Ethnic Identity." *New York Times*, January 5. https://www.nytimes.com/2019/01/05/world/asia/china-xinjiang-uighur-intellectuals.html.

Rao, Anupama. 2009. *The Caste Question: Dalits and the Politics of Modern India* Berkeley: University of California Press.

Ratzinger, J. 1984. "Instruction on Certain Aspects of the Theology of Liberation." *The Vatican.* http://www.vatican.va/roman_curia/congregations/cfaith/documents/rc_con_cfaith_doc_19840806_theology-liberation_en.html.

Renan, E. 1994. "Qu'est-ce qu'une Nation?" In *Nationalism*, edited by J. Hutchinson and A. D. Smith, 17–18. Oxford: Oxford University Press.

Reporters without Borders. 2018. *World Press Freedom Index.* https://rsf.org/en/india.

Reuters. 2017. "One in Five Indonesian Students Support Islamic Caliphate: Survey." November 2. https://www.reuters.com/article/us-indonesia-islam-radicalism/one-in-five-indonesian-students-support-islamic-caliphate-survey-idUSKBN1D20KW.

Ricklefs, M. C. 2012. *Islamisation and Its Opponents in Java: A Political, Social, Cultural and Religious History, c.1930–Present.* Honolulu: University of Hawaii Press.

Roy, Arundhati. 1997. *God of Small Things.* New York: Random House.

Roy, Arundhati. 2017. *The Ministry of Utmost Happiness.* New York: Knopf.

Sa'dan, Masthuriyah. 2016. "LGBT, Religion and Human Rights: A Study of the Thought of Khaled M. Abou El-Fadl." *Indonesian Feminist Journal* 4, no. 1 (March): 30–37.

Sahoo, Sarbeswar. 2018. *Pentecostalism and Politics of Conversion in India.* Cambridge: Cambridge University Press.

Said, Edward. 1978. *Orientalism.* New York: Vintage.

Said, Edward. 2001. "The Clash of Ignorance." *The Nation*, October 4.

Saito, Ayako. 2014. "The Formation of the Concept of Myanmar Muslims as Indigenous Citizens: Their History and Current Situation." *The Journal of Sophia Asian Studies* 32, Institute of Asian Cultures, Sophia University, Tokyo.

Saltz, R. 2018. "Padmaavat and All that Useless Beauty." *New York Times*, January 26. https://www.nytimes.com/2018/01/26/movies/padmaavat-review.html.

Sarvakar, Veer. 1923. *Hindutva: Who Is a Hindu?* Bombay: Bhave. https://archive.org/details/hindutva-vinayak-damodar-savarkar-pdf.

Satha-Anand, Chaiwat. 2015. "Red Mosques: Mitigating Violence against Sacred Spaces in Thailand and Beyond." In *Southeast Asian Muslims in the Era of Globalization*, edited by Ken Michi and Omar Farouk, 197–220. New York: Palgrave-McMillan.

Saunders, R. A. 2008. "The Ummah as Nation: A Reappraisal in the Wake of the Cartoons Affair." *Nations and Nationalism* 14, no. 2: 303–21.

Schonthal, Benjamin. 2015. "Making the 'Muslim Other' in Myanmar and Sri Lanka." In *Islam, State and Society in Myanmar*, edited by Melissa Crouch, 234–67. New Delhi: Oxford University Press.

Schonthal, Benjamin. 2016. "Environments of Law: Islam, Buddhism, and the State in Contemporary Sri Lanka." *The Journal of Asian Studies* 75, no. 1 (February): 137–56.

Schonthal, Benjamin, and Matthew J. Walton. 2016. "The (New) Buddhist Nationalisms? Symmetries and Specificities in Sri Lanka and Myanmar." *Contemporary Buddhism* 17, no. 1: 1–35.

Schroter, Susanne, ed. 2010. *Christianity in Indonesia-Perspective of Power*. Berlin: LIT Verlag.

Sen, Amartya. 2013. "Indian Women: The Mixed Truth." *The New York Review of Books*, October 10. http://www.nybooks.com/articles/2013/10/10/indias-women-mixed-truth/.

Senaratne, Rajitha. 2019. "Dr. Rajitha Senaratne Alleges That Several Groups Such As the National Thowheed Jamath and Bodu Bala Sena Were Initially Funded by a 'Defence Ministry Secret Fund' When Gotabaya Rajapaksa Was Defence Secretary." *dbsjeyaraj.com*, April 30. http://dbsjeyaraj.com/dbsj/archives/63833.

Seth, Andrew. 2003. *Burma's Muslims: Terrorists or Terrorised?* Canberra: Australian National University, Strategic and Defence Studies Centre.

Sethi, Aman. 2015. "Love Jihad in India and One Man's Quest to Prevent It." *The Guardian*, January 29. https://www.theguardian.com/world/2015/jan/29/love-jihad-india-one-man-quest-prevent-it.

Shamsie, Kamila. 2011. "Speak No Evil." *Index on Censorship* 40, no. 1 (March): 14–20.

Sharma, Mihir. 2019. "India Risks Becoming a Hindu Pakistan." *Japan Times*, January 14. https://www.japantimes.co.jp/opinion/2019/01/14/commentary/world-commentary/india-risks-becoming-hindu-pakistan/.

Shortt, Rupert. 2012. *Christianophobia: A Faith under Attack*. London: Rider.

Sidel, John. 2006. *Riots, Pogroms, Jihad: Religious Violence in Indonesia*. Singapore: NUS.

Singh, Shivan Shankar. 2018. "These Are Modi's Biggest Failures" *The Print*, June 17. https://theprint.in/opinion/these-are-modis-biggest-failures-a-data-analyst-on-why-he-is-quitting-bjp/71533/.

Smith, A. D. 1991a. *National Identity*. London: Penguin Group.

Smith, A. D. 1991b. "The Nation: Invented, Imagined, Reconstructed?" *Millennium—Journal of International Studies* 20: 353–68.

Smith, A. D. 1995. *Nations and Nationalism in a Global Era*. Cambridge: Polity.

Smith, A. D. 1998. *Nationalism and Modernism*. London: Routledge.

Smith, A. D. 2000a. *The Nation in History: Historiographical Debates About Ethnicity and Nationalism*. Cambridge: Polity Press.

Smith, A. D. 2000b. "Theories of Nationalism Alternative Models of Nation Formation." In *Asian Nationalism*, edited by M. Leifer, 1–20. London: Routledge.

Smith, A. D. 2002. "When Is a Nation?" *Geopolitics* 7: 5–32.

Smith, A. D. 2003. *Chosen Peoples: Sacred Sources of National Identity*. Oxford: Oxford University Press.

Smith, A. D. 2008. *The Cultural Foundations of Nations: Hierarchy, Covenant and Republic*. Oxford: Blackwell.

Soans, N. 2018. "Padmaavat Movie Review." *Times of India*, February 2. https://timesofindia. indiatimes.com/entertainment/hindi/movie-reviews/padmaavat/movie-review/62622503. cms.

Soumya, Elizabeth. 2014. "Sacred Cows and the Politics of Beef in India." *Al-Jazeera*, April 20.   https://www.aljazeera.com/indepth/features/2014/04/india-bjp-piggybacks-cow-milk-votes-2014417142154567121.html.

South, Ashley. 2008. *Ethnic Politics in Burma: States of Conflict*. London: Routledge.

Sri Lanka Mirror. 2016. "Thowheed Jamath, BBS Both Funded by Single Secret Account." December   5.   https://webcache.googleusercontent.com/search?q= cache:zmDJfsSmbU4J:https://srilankamirror.com/news/796-thowheed-jamath-bbs-both-funded-by-single-secret-account+&cd=1&hl=en&ct=clnk&gl=jp&client=gmail.

Stewart, James John. 2014. "Muslim-Buddhist Conflict in Contemporary Sri Lanka." *South Asia Research* 34: 241–46.

Subramanian, Samanth. 2015. *This Divided Island*. London: Atlantic.

Suryadinata, Leo. 2019. "Identity Politics in Indonesia: The Meliana Case." *Yusok Ishak Institute, Institute for Southeast Asian Studies*, no. 4 (January 23).

Suryana, A'an. 2018. "Indonesian Presidents and Communal Violence against Non-Mainstream Faiths." *Southeast Asia Research, SOAS, University of London*, 1–14.

Tagore, Rabindranath. 1917. *Nationalism*. San Francisco: Book Club of California.

Taylor, Robert H. 2009. *The State in Myanmar*. London: Hurst.

Telegraph. 2010. "Target Practice." *The Telegraph*, May 31. https://www.telegraphindia.com/ opinion/target-practice/cid/523556.

Tempo. 2017. Commentary. "Don't Punish Love." *Tempo*, November 23. https://en.tempo.co/ read/913499/dont-punish-love.

Tin Win Akbar. 2013. "Recent Religious Riots in Myanmar: The Current Situation of Burmese Muslims." *Asia Peace Building Initiatives*. http://peacebuilding.asia/recent-religious-riots-in-myanmar-the-current-situation-of-burmese-muslims/.

TNN. 2018. "No Evidence for 'Love Jihad' in Kerala: Home Ministry." *Times of India*, January 3.

UN. 2018. "Myanmar: Senior UN Human Rights Official Decries Continued Ethnic Cleansing in Rakhine State." United Nations Human Rights, Office of the High Commissioner, March 6.   https://www.ohchr.org/EN/NewsEvents/Pages/DisplayNews.aspx?NewsID=22761& LangID=E.

UNDP, USAID. 2014a. *Being LGBT in Asia: Thailand Country Report*. Bangkok.

UNDP, USAID. 2014b. *Being LGBT in Asia: The Philippines Country Report*. Bangkok.

UNHRC. 2018. "Report of the Independent International Fact-Finding Mission on Myanmar." *United Nations Human Rights Council*, A/HRC/39/64, August 27. https://www.ohchr.org/ EN/HRBodies/HRC/MyanmarFFM/Pages/ReportoftheMyanmarFFM.aspx.

US Library of Congress. "Blasphemy and Related Laws." https://www.loc.gov/law/help/ blasphemy/index.php#Malaysia.

Vajpeyi, Ananya. 2012. *Righteous Republic: The Political Foundations of Modern India*. Cambridge, MA: Harvard University Press.

Vajpeyi, Ananya. 2014. "The Triumph of the Hindu Right." *Foreign Affairs*, September/ October: 150–57.

van Bruinessen, Martin. 2002. "Genealogies of Islamic Radicalism in Post-Suharto Indonesia." *South East Asia Research* 10, no. 2: 117–54.

van Bruinessen, Martin. 2015. "Ghazwul Fikri or Arabization? Indonesian Muslim Responses to Globalization." In *Southeast Asian Muslims in the Era of Globalization*, edited by Ken Michi and Omar Farouk, 61–85. New York: Palgrave-McMillan.

Van Den Berghe, P. 1978. "Race and Ethnicity: A Sociobiological Perspective." *Ethnic and Racial Studies* 1: 401–11.

Van Den Berghe, P. 1981. *The Ethnic Phenomenon*. New York: Elsevier.

Van Den Berghe, P. 1994. "A Socio-Biological Perspective." In *Nationalism*, edited by J. Hutchinson and A. D. Smith, 96–102. Oxford: Oxford University Press.

Van Den Berghe, P. 2001. "Sociobiological Theory of Nationalism." In *Encyclopaedia of Nationalism*, edited by A. S. Leoussi, 273–79. New Brunswick: Transaction Publishers.

van der Veer, Peter. 2012. "Religion, Secularism and National Development in India and China." *Third World Quarterly* 33, no. 4: 721–34.

van der Veer, Peter. 2013. "Nationalism and Religion." In *The Oxford Handbook of the History of Nationalism*, edited by John Breuilly, 655–71. Oxford: Oxford University Press.

Varshney, Ashutosh. 2002. *Ethnic Conflict and Civic Life: Hindus and Muslims in India.* New Haven: Yale University Press.

Varshney, Ashutosh. 2014. "The 2015 Question." *Indian Express*, December 30.

Vatikiotis, Michael. 2018. *Blood and Silk: Power and Conflict in Modern Southeast Asia.* London: Weidenfeld and Nicolson

Vejayavardhana, D. C. 1953. *The Revolt in the Temple: Composed to Commemorate 2,500 Years of the Land, the Race, and the Faith.* Colombo: Sinha.

Vivekanda, Swami. 1947. *The Complete Works of Swami Vivekananda.* 9 volumes. Hollywood, CA: Vedanta Press and Bookshop.

Von der Mehden, Fred R. 1963. *Religion and Nationalism in Southeast Asia.* Madison: University of Wisconsin Press.

Wade, Francis. 2017. *Myanmar's Enemy Within: Buddhist Violence and the Making of a Muslim "Other."* London: Zed Books.

Walton, Matthew. 2015. "The Post-Election Future of Buddhist Nationalism in Myanmar." *East Asia Forum*, November 19. http://www.eastasiaforum.org/2015/11/19/the-post-election-future-of-buddhist-nationalism-in-myanmar/.

Walton, Matthew. 2016. "What Are Myanmar's Buddhist Sunday Schools Teaching?" *East Asia Forum*, December 16. http://www.eastasiaforum.org/2014/12/16/what-are-myanmars-buddhist-sunday-schools-teaching/.

Walton, Matthew. 2017. B*uddhism, Politics, and Political Thought in Myanmar.* Cambridge: Cambridge University Press.

Weiss, Stanley. 2017. "Saudi Arabia's Influence on Growing Islamic Extremism in Indonesia." *Huffington Post*, September 1.

Wikileaks. 2009. "Terrorist Finance: Action Request for Senior Level Engagement on Terrorism Finance." December 30. https://wikileaks.org/plusd/cables/09STATE131801_a.html.

Wilson, Chris. 2008. *Ethno-Religious Violence in Indonesia: From Soil to God.* Abingdon, UK: Routledge.

Wirathu, U. 2017. "Daw Aung San Suu Kyi a Threat to National Religion and Identity." *Irrawaddy*, December 7. https://www.irrawaddy.com/in-person/u-wirathu-daw-aung-san-suu-kyi-threat-national-religion-identity.html.

Wire. 2018. The Wire Staff. "Supreme Court Scraps Section 377; 'Majoritarian Views Cannot Dictate Rights,' Says CJI." September 7. https://thewire.in/law/supreme-court-scraps-section-377-majoritarian-views-cannot-dictate-rights-says-cji.

Wong, Edward. 2018. "US Weighs Sanctions Against Chinese Officials over Muslim Detention Camps." *New York Times*, September 9. https://www.nytimes.com/2018/09/10/world/asia/us-china-sanctions-muslim-camps.html.

Yegar, Moshe. 1972. *The Muslims of Burma.* Wiesbaden, Germany: Harassowitz.

Yegar, Moshe. 2002. *Between Integration and Secession: The Muslim Communities of the Southern Philippines, Southern Thailand and Western Burma/Myanmar.* Lanham/Oxford, UK: Lexington Books.

Yu, Jing. 2016. "Tibet, Xinjiang, and China's Strong State Complex." *The Diplomat*, July 28. https://thediplomat.com/2016/07/tibet-xinjiang-and-chinas-strong-state-complex/.

Zaman, Annie. 2018. "In the Name of God." *Daily Times*, March 4. https://dailytimes.com.pk/writer/annie-zaman/.

Zha, Jianying. 2018. "China's Bizarre Program to Keep Activists in Check." *The New Yorker*, December 24 and 31. https://www.newyorker.com/magazine/2018/12/24/chinas-bizarre-program-to-keep-activists-in-check.

Zhao, Suisheng. 2004. *A Nation-State by Construction: Dynamics of Modern Chinese Nationalism.* Stanford, CA: Stanford University Press.

Zulfiki. 2013. *The Struggle of the Shi'is in Indonesia.* Canberra: ANU Press.

Index

254–255
Gnanasara Thero, Galagoda Atte: as
    militant monk, 126–127, 128, 129–131,
    132–133, 134, 250; Wirathu and, 126,
    132–133, 134
God of Small Things (Roy), 214
The Golden Legend (Aslam), 185–186
The Good Muslim (Anam), 95
Guardians of Islam (Hefazat-e-Islam), 101,
    102
Guha, Ramachandra, 174
Gujarat, 22, 31, 33, 38, 40, 170–171
Guru, Afzal, 175
Gusmao, Martinho, 53, 54
Gusmao, Xanana, 50, 53

Habibie, B. J., 52, 82
Hajari, Nisid, 19
haj pilgrimage, 21, 35, 78, 85, 108
halal labeling, 131
Hambali, 91
Hamid, Mohsin, 79
Hanafi school of thought, 192, 193, 194
Hanif, Mohammed, 208
Haniffa, Farzana, 127, 132
Harsono, Andreas, 200
Hasan, Noorhaidi, 87
Hasina, Sheikh: in Bangladesh, 94, 96, 97,
    99, 100–101, 104, 105, 107, 108, 158,
    202; Rohingya and, 158
Hazzan, Dave, 62–63
healing, miracle, 62, 62–63, 66
heavy metal bands, 203
Hefazat-e-Islam (Guardians of Islam), 101,
    102
Henan, 68–69
Henn, Alexander, 65
heresy, 187
Hicks, Jacqueline, 205
Hinduism: in Bangladesh, 202–203; cows
    in, 15–16, 19–20, 29–31, 35, 65; in
    culture wars, 21–23, 33, 40; in India,
    15–16, 19–20, 21–23, 29–31, 33, 35,
    40, 65, 213–214, 214–219, 220–222,
    223–226, 228, 243–245, 245, 247; in
    Indonesia, 55; Pohela Boishakh and,
    101; sexuality and, 213–214, 214–219,
    220–222, 223–226, 228, 243–245, 245,
    247; in Sri Lanka, 127

Hindutva: Ayodhya and, 21, 35, 36, 170,
    171–172; BJP and, 15–16, 17, 18, 20,
    21, 22, 23, 24, 26, 27, 28, 30, 31,
    32–34, 35–40, 41, 63–64, 66, 161, 170,
    171, 172, 173, 175, 215, 217, 222, 224,
    224–225, 226, 245, 254; Bollywood
    and, 40–41; Christianity and, 63–65,
    66; Congress Party and, 15, 17, 28, 33,
    37, 38, 171, 175; defined, 15;
    democracy and, 18, 32, 34–39;
    extremism of, 20–29; fundamentalism
    of, 27, 30, 38, 175; identity and, 16, 18,
    19, 21, 26, 27–28, 29, 30, 34, 36, 38,
    39, 41, 66; implications of, 41;
    majoritarianism and, 15, 20, 36, 41; of
    Modi, 15–16, 21–22, 218, 225, 252;
    nationalism and, 15–16, 17, 18, 20,
    21–22, 23, 27, 33, 34–35, 37, 38, 39,
    63, 64, 66; overview of, 9, 15–17,
    249–250, 252, 254; of RSS, 15–17, 20,
    21, 22–23, 24, 27, 28, 29, 31, 170, 215,
    216–217; saffronization of, 24, 28–29,
    29, 32, 35–36, 39–41, 64; Sangh
    Parivar, 20, 21, 64; sexuality and, 215,
    219, 222, 223, 224, 244, 247; social
    media and, 32, 39; subnationalisms
    defying, 23–27
Hitler, Adolf, 16, 17
Hobsbawm, E., 5
Holocaust, 16, 17, 147
Holy Artisan Bakery, 93–94, 100, 102
homophobia: colonialism and, 229, 232;
    against LGBT community, 213,
    226–229, 232, 236, 238, 243, 245, 246
Horta, Jose Ramos, 52, 53, 54
Hossen, Mohammed Anwar, 99
Huntington, Samuel, 7
Hurriyat, 174

Ibrahim, Anwar, 232
ICMI. *See* Association of Muslim
    Intellectuals
The Idea of India (Khilnani), 30
identity: as key concept, 4, 7–8; overview
    of, 1–2, 3, 4, 7–8, 9, 10, 249, 250, 251,
    252, 254, 256. *See also specific topics*
identity politics: Arabization and, 83, 85,
    86, 87, 89, 99, 108; blasphemy and,
    187, 198, 208, 211; monks and, 134;

About the Author

Jeff Kingston is professor of history and the director of Asian studies at Temple University Japan, where he has taught since 1987. He was a Fulbright fellow in 1984–1985 in Indonesia, earned his PhD in history at Columbia University, and graduated with a BS in foreign service from Georgetown University. He is the author and editor of a dozen books on Asia and has published widely in academic journals and in the mass media where he is frequently interviewed.

www.ingramcontent.com/pod-product-compliance
Lightning Source LLC
Chambersburg PA
CBHW021810270326
41932CB00007B/123